THE FIRST WOMEN LAWYERS

This comparative study explores the lives of some of the women who first initiated challenges to male exclusivity in the legal professions in the late nineteenth and early twentieth centuries. Their challenges took place at a time of considerable optimism about progressive societal change, including new and expanding opportunities for women, as well as a variety of proposals for reforming law, legal education, and standards of legal professionalism. By situating women's claims for admission to the bar within this reformist context in different jurisdictions, the study examines the intersection of historical ideas about gender and about legal professionalism at the turn of the twentieth century. In exploring these systemic issues, the study also provides detailed examinations of the lives of some of the first women lawyers in six jurisdictions: the United States, Canada, Britain, New Zealand and Australia, India, and western Europe. In exploring how individual women adopted different legal arguments in litigated cases, or devised particular strategies to overcome barriers to professional work, the study assesses how shifting and contested ideas about gender and about legal professionalism shaped women's opportunities and choices, as well as both support for and opposition to their claims. As a comparative study of the first women lawyers in several different jurisdictions, the book reveals how a number of quite different women engaged with ideas of gender and legal professionalism at the turn of the twentieth century.

For Mary Estelle
and for
Donna, Stella and Emma

The First Women Lawyers

A Comparative Study of Gender, Law and the Legal Professions

Mary Jane Mossman

·HART·
PUBLISHING

OXFORD AND PORTLAND, OREGON
2006

Published in North America (US and Canada) by
Hart Publishing
c/o International Specialized Book Services
920 NE 58th Avenue, Suite 300
Portland, OR 97213-3786
USA
Tel: +1-503-287-3093 or toll-free: +1-800-944-6190
Fax: +1-503-280-8832
Email: orders@isbs.com
Website: www.isbs.com

© Mary Jane Mossman 2006

Hart Publishing, Salter's Boatyard, Folly Bridge, Abingdon Rd, Oxford, OX1 4LB
Telephone: +44 (o)1865 245533 Fax: +44 (o)1865 794882
Email: mail@hartpub.co.uk
Website: http//:www.hartpub.co.uk

British Library Cataloguing in Publication Data

Data Available

ISBN-13: 978-1-84113-590-8 (paperback)
ISBN-10: 1-84113-590-9 (paperback)

Typeset by Forewords, Oxford
Printed and bound in Great Britain by
TJ International, Padstow, Cornwall

Acknowledgements

This comparative study of the first women lawyers evolved over several years of research and reflection about issues of gender, law and the legal professions. I am grateful to the Osgoode Society for Legal History for its support and encouragement at an early stage of my historical research. The comparative research was greatly assisted by funding from the Social Science and Humanities Research Council of Canada, and I am especially grateful to anonymous peer reviewers who affirmed their confidence in this project. Osgoode Hall Law School of York University provided me with a Research Fellowship for six months at an important point, and the law school has also been generous with funding for summer research assistants. I am also grateful to York University for the Walter Gordon Fellowship in 2004–05, which enabled me to complete this manuscript in a timely fashion; and to the University of Ottawa's Gordon Henderson Chair in Human Rights at the beginning of the project.

The research for this study could not have been undertaken without the enthusiastic support of the library staff at Osgoode Hall Law School: Professor Balfour Halévy, Special Collections Librarian Judy Ginsberg, Reference Librarians Marianne Rogers and Louise Tsang, the Inter-Library Loan assistant, Maureen Boyce, and other members of the staff of the Law Library; I also received special help with European materials from Julianna Drexler at Collège Glendon. I also thank the staff at a number of archives: the Oriental and India Office at the British Library in London, the Section des Manuscrits de la Bibliothèque Royale in Brussels, the archives at Lincoln's Inn, and university archives at Dalhousie, the University of British Columbia, and the Law Library at McGill University.

In addition, many colleagues and friends have been generous with their time, their willingness to listen, and their suggestions: Beverley Baines, Jane Banfield, Paula Bartley, David Bell, Carl Berger, Naomi Black, Tony Blackshield, Daniel Boyer, Bettina Bradbury, Marianne Brandis, Joan Brockman, Ine Corstjens, Brettel Dawson, Maeve Doggett, Jonathan Dudley, Caroline Forder, Ursula Franklin, Linda Gehrke, Jerry Ginsburg, Philip Girard, Cameron Harvey, Douglas Hay, Leslie Howsam, Mary Kinnear, Angie MacDonald, Laurel Sefton MacDowell, Denis Magnusson, Jeanette Neeson, Michael Robertson, Lynda Tanaka, Nadine Taub, Joanna Tie Ten Quee, Margaret Thornton, Ann Wilton, Carol Wilton and Lois Yorke. I also acknowledge with special thanks the assistance of Hazel Pollack at Osgoode in fine-tuning the manuscript; and the warm encouragement of Noli Swatman, the late Greg Jacobs, and other staff in York University's Office of Research Administration.

This project has also benefitted from the work of a number of dedicated and hard-working student research assistants: Cindy L Baldassi did an outstanding job during the most critical period of this project, tracking down elusive books, articles, and citations. At Osgoode, Ami Atal, Tamara Barclay, Leanna Bayliss, Wendy Greyling, Courtney Harris, Gail Henderson, Christine Jenkins, Linda Knol, Emma Rhodes, and Christine Vanderschoot provided enthusiastic assistance, as did Victoria Mainprize at Dalhousie and Anila Srivastava at the University of British Columbia. Professor Karen Pearlston and Reference Librarian Louise Tsang also undertook follow-up research at the British Library and at Lincoln's Inn in London, which was much appreciated. I am also grateful to Richard Hart and others at Hart Publishing for support and assistance in the publication process.

In addition, I am pleased to acknowledge the *Canadian Journal of Women and the Law/Revue Femmes et Droit*, whose editors kindly agreed to permit me to reproduce parts of the Introduction and of chapter 5 which were earlier published in the *Journal/Revue*.

Beyond the research challenges, I thank Brian Bucknall for patient and insightful words about writing and the creative imagination, several family members who very kindly read parts of this manuscript, and especially Mary Estelle Mossman for weekly words of encouragement until the task was finished. The book is dedicated to her memory, and to three other women in my family who always supported my aspirations.

Contents

Portraits of Women Lawyers

PORTIAS OF TODAY

The Illustrated London News, 13 November 1897.

MDLLE. LYDIA POËT,
Italy.

MRS. C. WAUGH MAC-CULLOCH,
U.S.A.

MADAME ANNA AKESSON,
Finland.

MRS. LUTES,
U.S.A.

MRS. L.-J. ROBINSON-SAWTELL,
U.S.A.

MDLLE. JEANNE CHAUVIN,
France.

MRS. MYRA BRADWELL,
U.S.A.

MDLLE. KATRINE DAHL,
Norway.

MRS. BELVA LOCKWOOD,
U.S.A.

MDLLE. ELSA ESCHELSSON,
Sweden.

MDLLE. NANNA BERG,
Denmark.

MDLLE. SARMISA BILCESCO,
Roumania.

MDLLE. MARIE POPELIN,
Belgium.

MADAME SIGNÉ SILEN,
Finland.

MISS CLARA BRETT MARTIN,
Canada.

MISS LETITIA WALKINGTON,
Ireland.

MISS FLORENCE CRONISE,
U.S.A.

MADAME E. KEMPIN-SPYRI,
Switzerland.

MRS. ELLENA KNOWLESS HASKELL,
U.S.A.

FRÄULEIN ANITA AUGSPURG,
Germany.

MRS. SHORTRIDGE FOLTZ,
U.S.A.

MISS CORNELIA SORABJI,
India.

MISS MARY GREENE,
U.S.A.

Introduction

The First Women Lawyers

PROLOGUE: CONTEMPORARY QUESTIONS ABOUT WOMEN AS LAWYERS

[What] difference does it make that Clara Brett Martin succeeded in becoming a lawyer in 1897, and what difference should it make that the legal profession increasingly includes large numbers of women as well as men? Beyond the ... careers of individual women lawyers, what impact will the advent of a significant number of women in the legal profession have on the practice of law, on legal rules and concepts, on the roles lawyers play in our society? Most importantly, will women who become lawyers be just like men who are lawyers, or will they bring a new dimension to lawyering?[1]

THIS BOOK HAD its beginnings in these questions, first posed in May 1986 in the historic surroundings of Osgoode Hall in Toronto. The occasion was the Law Society's first ever continuing education programme on 'Women in the Legal Profession,'[2] and the audience included a large number of women lawyers, many of them newly-admitted members of the profession. Passing through the old winding corridors of Osgoode Hall, the heart of the Ontario legal profession for nearly two hundred years, the participants gathered expectantly in the large lecture hall. Even before the programme started, the sight of so many *women*, all of whom were also *lawyers*, confirmed an unprecedented transformation in the demography of the Canadian legal profession. For, although a few women had chosen to become lawyers in earlier decades, the highly accelerated rate of women's entry to the legal profession after 1970 was

---

[1] MJ Mossman, 'Portia's Progress: Women as Lawyers – Reflections on Past and Future' (1988) 8 *Windsor Yearbook of Access to Justice* 252 at 266. See also Law Society of Upper Canada, *Crossing the Bar: A Century of Women's Experience 'Upon the Rough and Troubled Seas of Legal Practice' in Ontario* (Toronto, Law Society of Upper Canada Archives, 1993) at 41; and RL Abel, 'Comparative Sociology of Legal Professions: An Exploratory Essay' (1985) 1 *American Bar Foundation Research Journal* 5 at 40.

[2] CLE Programme 'Women in the Legal Profession' (Toronto, Law Society of Upper Canada, 13 May 1986). Similar programmes were later offered by law societies and bar associations across Canada, as well as by the National Association of Women and the Law in Winnipeg in February 1987.

'nothing short of revolutionary.'[3] Indeed, even taking account of significant expansion in the legal profession between the early 1960s and the 1980s, the rate of expansion for women lawyers was still disproportionately large: while the number of male law students across Canada doubled between 1962–63 and 1980–81, the number of female law students increased twenty four times in the same period.[4] Reflecting an optimistic future for this 'revolution in numbers' of women in law, Justice Rosalie Abella predicted in her keynote speech that '... with any luck, 15 years from now if someone tries to organise a conference on Women in the Legal Profession, we will wonder what they're talking about.'[5]

Such optimism, however, has been increasingly tempered by a sense of paradox: while individual women have achieved significant success in law, there is continuing evidence of systemic gender barriers. Certainly, there have been some notable achievements, including the fact that nearly equal numbers of men and women are now law students in most Canadian provinces, with even higher proportions of women students in civil law programmes in Québec.[6] Women have been appointed judges of provincial and federal courts, including Chief Justice of the Supreme Court of Canada;[7] partners and even managing partners of major law firms; tribunal chairs and CEOs; and deans and professors of law schools.[8] A woman lawyer was briefly Prime Minister of Canada, and two women

---

[3] RL Abel, 'United States: The Contradictions of Professionalism' in R Abel and P Lewis (eds), *Lawyers in Society: the Common Law World,* vol I (Berkeley, University of California Press, 1988) 186 at 202.

[4] RL Abel, above, n 1 at 23 and Table 3. See also Canadian Bar Association, *Touchstones for Change: Equality, Diversity and Accountability – the Report on Gender Equality in the Legal Profession* (Ottawa, Canadian Bar Association, 1993) at 25; DAA Stager with HW Arthurs, *Lawyers in Canada* (Toronto, University of Toronto Press, 1990) at 159–60; Cameron Harvey, 'Women in Law in Canada' (1970–71) 4 *Manitoba Law Journal* 9; and L Silver Dranoff, 'Women as Lawyers in Toronto' (1972) 10 *Osgoode Hall Law Journal* 177.

[5] R Silberman Abella, 'Women in the Legal Profession' in CLE Programme, above, n 2 at 21. See also Cynthia Fuchs Epstein, 'Women in Law: Old Dilemmas, New Dilemmas,' above, n 2 at 16–18.

[6] Current statistics reveal that women law students constitute 50% or more of most common law programmes at Canadian universities: see 'Key Facts about Canadian Common-Law Schools' in *LSAT Registration and Information Book (Canadian),* 2003–2004 (Newtown, PA, Law School Admission Council, Inc, 2003) at 60. See also BM Mazer, 'An Analysis of Gender in Admission to the Canadian Common Law Schools from 1985–86 to 1994–95' (1997) 20 *Dalhousie Law Journal* 135.

[7] See *Touchstones for Change,* above, n 4 at 50–51. Justice Bertha Wilson was appointed to the Supreme Court of Canada in 1982; Justice Claire L'Heureux-Dubé was appointed in 1987 and Justice Beverley McLachlin in 1989. Justice Wilson retired in 1991. Justice McLachlin became Chief Justice of the Supreme Court of Canada in 2000, the same year in which Justice Louise Arbour became a member of the Court. Justice L'Heureux-Dubé retired in 2002 and Justice Marie Deschamps was appointed to the Court. In 2004, Justice Arbour resigned, and Justices Rosalie Abella and Louise Charron were appointed to two existing vacancies; thus, for the first time in 2004, four of nine members of the Supreme Court of Canada were women. See also RM Salokar and ML Volcansek (eds), *Women in Law: A Bio-Biographical Sourcebook* (Westport, CT, Greenwood Press, 1996).

[8] See *Touchstones for Change,* above, n 4 at chapters 5–9.

lawyers have been appointed federal Minister of Justice.[9] Beginning in the
1970s, Canadian law schools began to offer courses about women and the
law,[10] and women lawyers established a national policy organisation and a
national law journal.[11] In recent years, moreover, many women lawyers
have successfully participated in test case litigation and legislative lobbying
on issues about gender equality, particularly in relation to equality guarantees in the *Canadian Charter of Rights and Freedoms*.[12] Indeed, as a
special American report published in 1999 concluded, women lawyers
were 'the story of the [twentieth] century':

> They've gone from being exiled from the corridors of political and corporate
> power to treading them en masse. Once banished from the nation's law schools
> (and from Harvard Law School until as recently as 1950) they now make up
> nearly half of this year's entering class. Women lawyers have forced the most
> exclusive law firms to open their doors. Just as importantly, they've forced the
> most entrenched male partners to open their minds. (Well, most of them.)[13]

Paradoxically, however, a stream of academic research, professional inquiries, and judicial task force reports in several jurisdictions has revealed
how issues of gender equality in the law and the legal professions continue
to present contemporary challenges. A number of academic studies suggest
that women lawyers generally remain, in Margaret Thornton's telling
phrase, mere 'fringe-dwellers of the jurisprudential community.'[14] For
example, in their study of men and women lawyers in large firms in
Toronto in the early 1990s, John Hagan and Fiona Kay concluded that
women lawyers did not succeed as well as their male colleagues, even
when women invested in their careers to the same extent as men; the

---

12 Hon Kim Campbell was Prime Minister of Canada (1993), having previously served as the
first woman Minister of Justice (1990–1993). Hon Anne McLellan was also Minister of Justice
(1997–2002).

10 According to a survey of course offerings on 'Women and the Law' in Canadian law schools
for 1977–80, conducted by Professor Jane Banfield of York University (survey on file), eight law
schools were providing such a course; for example, see B Baines, 'Women and the Law: Course
Materials' (Kingston, Queen's University Faculty of Law, 1974). See also MJ Mossman,
' "Otherness" and the Law School: A Comment on Teaching Gender Equality' (1985) 1
Canadian Journal of Women and the Law 213.

11 Female lawyers and law students organised the first national conference of Women and the
Law in Windsor, Ontario in 1974; the conference resulted in the creation of the National
Association of Women and the Law: see LS Dranoff, *Women in Canadian Law* (Toronto,
Fitzhenry and Whiteside, 1977) at 87. The first issue of the *Canadian Journal of Women and the
Law/ Revue Femmes et Droit* was published in 1985.

12 See S Razack, *Canadian Feminism and the Law: The Women's Legal Education and Action
Fund and the Pursuit of Equality* (Toronto, Second Story Press, 1991); and M J Mossman, 'The
Paradox of Feminist Engagement with Law' in Nancy Mandell (ed), *Feminist Issues: Race, Class
and Sexuality*, 2nd edn (Scarborough, Prentice Hall Allyn and Bacon Canada, 1998) 180.

13 'The Story of the Century,' *The American Lawyer*, March 1999, at 49.

14 M Thornton, *Dissonance and Distrust: Women in the Legal Profession* (Melbourne,
Oxford University Press, 1996) at 3–4. See also M Thornton, 'Feminist Jurisprudence: Illusion
or Reality' (1986) 3 *Australian Journal of Law and Society* 5.

authors identified a 'glass ceiling' for women lawyers in many of these firms.[15] The Canadian Bar Association's report in 1993 confirmed this academic research, but also warned that the 'glass ceiling' was often experienced by minority women as a 'steel door,'[16] pointing out how gender intersects with women's race, class, sexual orientation, language, dis/ability, religion, marital and/or parental status, age, and educational background to create additional barriers. Similarly, in her more recent study of men and women lawyers in British Columbia, Joan Brockman found persistent discriminatory attitudes towards women lawyers, not just among older lawyers who were members of the 'old boys' club' and thus 'relics of the past,' but also among the 'baby dinosaurs,' younger male lawyers who were growing up to replace them.[17] Studies in the United Kingdom,[18] in the civil law jurisdictions of Europe,[19] and in the United States[20] have reached similar conclusions. Thus, as Judith Resnick gloomily reported about the work of American judicial task forces on gender bias, 'a decade of academic and court-based documentation of deep-seated and endemic unfairness has not undermined the resiliency of legal culture;' although judicial task forces may 'authorize inquiry, ask forbidden questions, [and] obtain information, ... [professional cultures] still remain impenetrable to profound change.'[21]

[15] J Hagan and F Kay, *Gender in Practice: A Study of Lawyers' Lives* (Oxford, Oxford University Press, 1995) at 182. See also K Hull and R Nelson, 'Gender Inequality in Law: Problems of Structure and Agency in Recent Studies of Gender in Anglo-American Legal Professions' (1998) 23 *Law and Social Inquiry* 681; and S O'Donovan-Polten, *The Scales of Success* (Toronto, University of Toronto Press, 2001).

[16] *Touchstones for Change*, above, n 4 at 11 and 60–61.

[17] J Brockman, *Gender in the Legal Profession: Fitting in or Breaking the Mould* (Vancouver, University of British Columbia Press, 2001) at 200.

[18] See C McGlynn, *The Woman Lawyer: Making the Difference* (London, Butterworths, 1998); H Sommerlad and P Sanderson, *Gender, Choice and Commitment: Women Solicitors in England and Wales and the Struggle for Equal Status* (Aldershot, Ashgate/Dartmouth, 1998); and S Fredman, *Women and the Law* (Oxford, Clarendon Press, 1997).

[19] See U Schultz and G Shaw (eds), *Women in the World's Legal Professions* (Oxford, Hart Publishing, 2002). See also C Menkel-Meadow, '"Feminization" of the Legal Profession: The Comparative Sociology of Women Lawyers' in R Abel and P Lewis (eds), *Lawyers in Society: Comparative Perspectives*, vol III (Berkeley, University of California Press, 1989) at 196; and C Menkel-Meadow, 'The Comparative Sociology of Women Lawyers: The "Feminization" of the Legal Profession' (1987) 24 *Osgoode Hall Law Journal* 897.

[20] See M Harrington, *Women Lawyers: Rewriting the Rules* (New York, Plume Books, 1995); D Rhode, *Justice and Gender: Sex Discrimination and the Law* (Cambridge, MA, Harvard University Press, 1989); K Berger Morello, *The Invisible Bar: The Woman Lawyer in America 1638 to the Present* (New York, Random House, 1986); and C Menkel-Meadow, 'Exploring a Research Agenda of the Feminization of the Legal Profession: Theories of Gender and Social Change' (1989) 14 *Law and Social Inquiry* 289. See also C Fuchs Epstein, *Women in Law* (New York, Basic Books, 1981) and 2nd edn (Chicago, University of Illinois Press, 1993); R Moss Kanter, 'Reflections on Women and the Legal Profession: A Sociological Perspective' (1978) 1 *Harvard Women's Law Journal* 1; and A Sachs and J Hoff Wilson, *Sexism and the Law: A Study of Male Beliefs and Legal Bias in Britain and the United States* (New York, The Free Press, 1978).

[21] J Resnik, 'Ambivalence: The Resiliency of Legal Culture in the United States' (1993) 45 *Stanford Law Review* 1525 at 1535. See also B Lentz and D Laband, *Sex Discrimination in the Legal Profession* (Westport, CT, Quorum Books, 1995); and M Thornton, above, n 14.

Such conclusions pose significant challenges: they confirm that even with an unprecedented number of women becoming lawyers, the admission of women to the bar has not engendered the law or the legal professions. Instead, gender remains deeply embedded within traditional legal norms and professional cultures; and as Thornton pointed out, 'neither an increase in the number of women nor the passing of time can provide an automatic remedy.'[22] Moreover, as Carrie Menkel-Meadow suggested, the 'success' of individual women in the legal profession may be inversely related to the extent of their commitment to gender issues. As she reflected, 'Are ... women, who act like men, allowed to penetrate the restricted boundaries [of judicial appointment, law firm promotion, and academic success], while those who act more like women are kept out?....'[23] Such questions reveal how Virginia Woolf's claim, that women could enter the professions and 'use them to have a mind of [their] own and a will of [their] own,' remains profoundly contested.[24]

RETHINKING THE FIRST WOMEN LAWYERS: THEMES OF GENDER, PROFESSIONALISM AND WOMEN'S LIVES

The professional and personal challenges that confront women lawyers today did not have their origins in the 1960s, as many have suggested. Rather, they reach back ... to the pioneer generation of women lawyers who were the first to articulate and grapple with the challenges facing women in the legal profession.[25]

As Virginia Drachman argued in her study of women's efforts to gain admission to the bar in the United States in the last decades of the nineteenth century, the history of the first women lawyers is relevant to an understanding of contemporary issues of gender and professionalism. In describing how nineteenth century women lawyers struggled to balance their gender and professional identities,[26] for example, Drachman explained

22 M Thornton, above, n 14 at 291; according to Thornton, 'clubs, corporeality, and corporatism' represent ongoing sites of contestation for women lawyers.
23 C Menkel-Meadow, above, n 19 (*OHLJ*) at 899–900: according to Menkel-Meadow, such questions confront the issue of 'whether women will be changed by the profession, or whether the legal profession will be changed by the increased presence of women.' See also *Touchstones for Change*, above, n 4 at 11.
24 V Woolf, *Three Guineas* (London, Hogarth Press, 1977) lst pub 1938, at 151. See also JC Foster, 'Antigones at the Bar: Women Lawyers as Reluctant Adversaries' (1986) 10:3 *Legal Studies Forum* 287; C Smart, 'Feminism and Law: Some Problems of Analysis and Strategy' (1986) 14 *International Journal of the Sociology of Law* 109; and M Thornton, 'Feminism and the Contradictions of Law Reform' (1991) 19 *International Journal of the Sociology of Law* 453.
25 VG Drachman, *Women Lawyers and the Origins of Professional Identity in America: The Letters of the Equity Club 1887 to 1890* (Ann Arbor, University of Michigan Press, 1993) at vii.
26 VG Drachman, *Sisters in Law: Women Lawyers in Modern American History*

how they adopted clothing styles for legal work which 'mirrored the suits of men lawyers and revealed women lawyers' professional identification with their male colleagues;' by contrast, in social gatherings with other women, more than one of them appeared a 'butterfly of fashion.'[27] However, conflicts between their identities as women and as lawyers were not so easily reconciled when they appeared in court:

> Here was the burden for the nineteenth-century woman lawyer. As a proper lady of her day, social etiquette required that she wear a hat in public. But as a lawyer, professional etiquette demanded that she remove her hat when she entered the courtroom. As a result, the question of the hat once again confronted women lawyers with the enduring challenge of reconciling their traditional role as *women* with their new professional identity as *lawyers*.[28]

Clearly, wearing a hat in public is no longer an issue for women lawyers. However, Drachman concluded that *how* the first women lawyers resolved such issues was important because it revealed their responses to the intersection of gender and legal professionalism, responses that have continuing implications for women in law.[29]

In addition to Drachman's focus on the complexity of women lawyers' identities, other scholars have examined the ideal of nineteenth century legal culture: the 'gentleman's profession.' As Gidney and Millar bluntly stated in their study of professionals in nineteenth century Ontario, for example, maleness was a defining feature of the idea of a profession: an occupation could not be called a profession 'if it was filled with women.'[30] As they concluded, the nineteenth century concept of a 'professional gentleman' was profoundly gendered, demarcating a sphere of public life reserved exclusively for men, and cemented by the professional and social contacts that surrounded practices such as circuit courts.[31] In other Canadian provinces too, there are records of vociferous opposition on the

(Cambridge, MA, Harvard University Press, 1998) at 8. See also D Kelly Weisberg, 'Barred from the Bar: Women and Legal Education in the United States 1870–1890' in DK Weisberg (ed), *Women and the Law*, vol II (Cambridge, MA, Shenkman, 1982).

27 VG Drachman, above, n 26 at 94: Drachman reported that Belva Lockwood (the first woman admitted to the Supreme Court of the United States) attended a meeting of the International Council of Women in 'a pink satin dress adorned with black lace and pearls.' According to Madeleine Stern, Lockwood was 'no bloomer girl': see MB Stern, *We the Women: Career Firsts of Nineteenth-Century America* (Lincoln and London, University of Nebraska Press, 1962) at 209.

28 VG Drachman, above, n 26 at 95 (emphasis added). See also 'Flotsam and Jetsam' (1896) 32 *Canada Law Journal* 84; and *The Bulletin* (Australia), October 1903 at 12.

29 VG Drachman concluded, above, n 26 at 8 and 249, that 'women never completely overcame the sexual discrimination that was so pervasive in the legal profession.... By the mid-twentieth century, women lawyers were far from reaching their goal of equality.'

30 See RD Gidney and WPJ Millar, *Professional Gentlemen: The Professions in Nineteenth-Century Ontario* (Toronto, University of Toronto Press, 1994) at 239.

31 RD Gidney and WPJ Millar, above, n 30 at 141–4.

part of male lawyers to any recognition of a 'Blackstone in petticoats.'[32] Similarly, Michael Grossberg argued that it was masculine values which fundamentally defined 'the place of the lawyer in American society' in the nineteenth century.[33] Describing traditions such as the practice of circuit riding, in which teams of lawyers and judges travelled to each county seat to hold court, Grossberg suggested that these shared experiences cemented values of professionalism that were substantially based on male camaraderie.[34] In such a context, Grossberg concluded that although *women* eventually succeeded in becoming lawyers in the late nineteenth century, they never effectively challenged the *gender* premises of the law and the legal professions: 'women attorneys became – in the useful language of Antonio Gramsci – a "contradictory consciousness" in the legal community, but they did not develop a "counter-hegemony".'[35]

In the context of these scholarly conclusions, my research questions about women lawyers increasingly focused on the history of claims presented by the first women who challenged male exclusivity in the legal professions: to what extent did *women* become lawyers without challenging the *gender* premises of the law and the legal professions? In exploring these issues, moreover, the scope of my inquiry expanded beyond the experiences of early women lawyers in Canada and the United States, particularly as I (re)discovered the stories of women who sought to become legal professionals in other jurisdictions in the late nineteenth and early twentieth centuries. It seems that the turn of the twentieth century was a time of considerable optimism about progressive societal change, including both expanding opportunities for women as well as new proposals for reform of the law and the legal professions. Thus, as women seeking entry to a gentleman's profession, the first women lawyers were confronting contested ideas about women's roles and about legal professionalism. In this context, there seemed to be a number of important questions: how did legal professions respond to women's challenges to the male exclusivity of a 'gentleman's profession'? How did women charac-

---

[32] Oscar Bass, secretary of the Law Society of British Columbia, in a letter about the admission of women to the bar of British Columbia: see WW Pue, *Law School: The Story of Legal Education in British Columbia* (Vancouver, Faculty of Law of the University of British Columbia, 1995) at 223. In addition, a petition to the Nova Scotia legislature in 1917 on behalf of forty barristers and solicitors prayed that 'women be not enabled to practise law in the province': see C Cleverdon, *The Woman Suffrage Movement in Canada* (Toronto, University of Toronto Press, 1950) at 173.

[33] M Grossberg, 'Institutionalizing Masculinity: The Law as a Masculine Profession' in MC Carnes and C Griffen (eds), *Meanings for Manhood: Constructions of Masculinity in Victorian America* (Chicago, University of Chicago Press, 1990) 133 at 150. See also EA Rotundo, *American Manhood: Transformations in Masculinity from the Revolution to the Modern Era* (New York, Basic Books, 1993) at 169–74.

[34] M Grossberg, above, n 33 at 136–7.

[35] M Grossberg, above, n 33 at 148; as he also noted, at 149, 'the first women to appear in law offices did not come to practice law; they came to type and take shorthand.'

terise their right to gain admission to legal professions and their interest in pursuing legal work? And why were some women's gender challenges successful, while other women's claims to become lawyers were resisted, deflected or assimilated by courts and legislatures?

Contemporary records about the first women lawyers reveal that opinions about women as lawyers were both fluid and contested; as well, there were some very divergent views about the significance of women's admission to the bar. For example, newspaper articles tended to report enthusiastically about individual women who succeeded in becoming lawyers: a British journal in the 1890s compared the appearance of Madame Tel Sono, a woman lawyer in Japan in the late nineteenth century, to the wonders of new scientific inventions:

> Every day as she went into the court crowds used to gather and gaze upon her, as together with the telegraph, steam carriages, electric light, and photography, which had only that year been introduced into Japan, she was considered one of the marvels of the age, and her name became known throughout the country.[36]

By contrast, some members of the legal profession disparaged the importance of women's admission to the bar. In an assessment of the impact of women lawyers in Ontario, for example, Justice William Riddell bluntly asserted in 1918 that 'the admission of women to the practice of law [had no] appreciable effect on the Bar, the practice of law, the Bench, or the people.' As he concluded, women's admission to the legal profession was a matter of complete indifference to everyone except 'those immediately concerned.'[37] Indeed, even among women lawyers, there is some evidence that the achievements of the first women who became lawyers were not well recognised; many of them were all too soon hidden from history.[38] The story about a woman lawyers' event in a Toronto restaurant in 1919, at which Clara Brett Martin sat alone and unrecognised by other women at the dinner, suggests that her efforts to gain admission to the Ontario bar two decades earlier – and her status as Canada's first woman lawyer – were not well-known to her women colleagues.[39]

---

36 M Griffith, 'A Japanese Lady Lawyer and Reformer in England' (1893) 10 *Great Thoughts* 91.

37 WR Riddell, 'Women as Practitioners of Law' (1918) 18 *Journal of the Society of Comparative Legislation* 200 at 206.

38 N Cott, 'On Men's History and Women's History' in MC Carnes and C Griffen (eds), above, n 33 at 205. See also B Boutilier and A Prentice (eds), *Creating Historical Memory: English-Canadian Women and the Work of History* (Vancouver, UBC Press, 1997); and R Roach Pierson, 'Experience, Difference, Dominance and Voice in the Writing of Canadian Women's History' in K Offen, R Roach Pierson and J Rendall (eds), *Writing Women's History: International Perspectives* (Bloomington, Indiana University Press, 1991) 79.

39 See C Backhouse, '"To Open the Way for Others of my Sex:" Clara Brett Martin's Career as Canada's First Woman Lawyer' (1985) 1 *Canadian Journal of Women and the Law* 1 at 39. This meeting probably was a forerunner to the establishment of the Women's Law Association of Ontario in 1923: see C Harvey, above, n 4 at 28; and *Crossing the Bar*, above, n 1 at 18.

In this context, this comparative study explores how some women initiated gender challenges to the legal professions in a number of different jurisdictions in the late nineteenth and early twentieth centuries. As *women* who were becoming *lawyers*, their challenges took place in the context of new ideas about women's equality rights and in relation to emerging concepts of legal professionalism at the turn of the twentieth century. Interestingly, there have been few scholarly efforts to connect these two historical developments until quite recently – that is, to see women lawyers as significant to the history of women's rights and also to the history of legal professionalism. As two American historians asserted in the early 1980s, for example, most historical assessments of the professions have failed to incorporate 'a crucial element [about their] modern evolution...: the entry of middle class women into the professional milieu....'[40] Moreover, although both the timing and content of the movements for women's rights and for professionalisation often differed from one jurisdiction to another, a comparative exploration of the experiences of the first women lawyers offers an opportunity to assess how gender intersected with legal professionalism, and how these ideas shaped, or were shaped by, the experiences of some of the first women lawyers.

As a comparative study, this book adopts a wide-ranging definition of the term 'lawyer' to encompass not only those women who gained formal admission to the legal professions, but also others who were engaged in legal work without achieving the status of formal admission. This approach means that it is possible to examine some women's strategies for undertaking work as legal professionals, even when women were not eligible for admission to the legal professions; the experiences of women who worked in law without formal admission reveal how the boundaries of legal professionalism sometimes shifted, and how gender was sometimes accommodated without ever being formally acknowledged. Even among those who were formally admitted as members of legal professions, of course, their status and the nature of their work frequently differed, depending on local situations; in addition, since the roles of lawyers often differed substantially within common law and civil law jurisdictions, comparisons of the experiences of the first women lawyers in these two legal systems provide some interesting insights about the nature of legal practice in different contexts.[41] In adopting a broad definition of legal professionalism, therefore, this study explores a wide range of strategies and experiences among the first women lawyers.

[40] J Jacobs Brumberg and N Tomes, 'Women in the Professions: A Research Agenda for American Historians' (1982) 10 *Reviews in American History* at 275.
[41] See TC Halliday and L Karpik, 'Politics Matter: A Comparative Theory of Lawyers in the Making of Political Liberalism' in TC Halliday and L Karpik (eds), *Lawyers and the Rise of Western Political Liberalism* (Oxford, Clarendon Press, 1997) 15 at 18; and Richard L Abel, 'Comparative Sociology of Legal Professions' in R Abel and P Lewis (eds), above, n 19 at 81.

In addition, this study focuses on gender as *one* factor that shaped the opportunities and choices of the first women lawyers. Clearly, in seeking access to the 'gentleman's profession' of law, women were challenging gendered exclusivity in the legal professions. Thus, this study examines how societal ideas about sexual difference affected women's aspirations and experiences,[42] and how women fashioned legal arguments to challenge and contest these prevailing ideas. Yet, at the same time that gendered realities defined the overall context in which women first challenged male exclusivity in the legal professions, the specific circumstances of individual women clearly shaped the opportunities and strategies available to them. As Glazer and Slater suggested in their study of early women professionals in the United States, women's strategies varied in response to their circumstances, and individual responses reveal 'the texture, the range, and *the limits of the possible* in these women's lives.'[43] Thus, this study attempts to situate aspiring women lawyers within the broader context of legal professionalism and gender, but also to examine the individual lives of women who first presented claims for admission to the legal professions.

The late nineteenth century witnessed a range of new ideas about legal professionalism: important developments in the nature and organisation of legal work, efforts to create or strengthen professional organisations, and significant reforms in legal education.[44] Recent historical and sociological research in a number of jurisdictions has focused on professionalisation projects in the nineteenth century, identifying factors that contributed to the creation or maintenance of occupational groups, including law, as professions. For example, Gidney and Millar traced changes in the idea of a 'professional gentleman,' defined almost exclusively by birth in the early nineteenth century, but determined more often on the basis of merit and competitive examinations by the end of the century.[45] Others have examined the rise of capitalism, the need to achieve market control, and changing roles of the state as theoretical explanations for the process of professionalisation.[46] Yet, to the extent that women's access to the legal

---

[42] See J Wallach Scott, 'Women's History' in P Burke (ed), *New Perspectives on Historical Writing* (Pennsylvania, Pennsylvania State University Press, 2001) 2nd ed, 43 at 63–4; and R Collier, '"Nutty Professors," "Men in Suits" and "New Entrepreneurs": Corporeality, Subjectivity and Change in the Law School and Legal Practice' (1998) 7 *Social and Legal Studies* 27 at 43–5.

[43] PM Glazer and M Slater, *Unequal Colleagues: The Entrance of Women into Professions, 1890–1940* (New Brunswick and London, Rutgers University Press, 1987) at 14 (emphasis added). See also J Parr, *The Gender of Breadwinners: Women, Men, and Change in Two Industrial Towns 1880–1950* (Toronto, University of Toronto Press, 1990) at 9–11; and H Sommerlad, 'The Myth of Feminisation: Women and Cultural Change in the Legal Profession' (1994) 1 *International Journal of the Legal Profession* 31.

[44] See RD Gidney and WPJ Millar, above, n 30; C Wilton (ed), *Inside the Law: Canadian Law Firms in Historical Perspective* (Toronto, The Osgoode Society, 1996); BJ Bledstein, *The Culture of Professionalism: The Middle Class and the Development of Higher Education in America* (New York, W W Norton & Co, 1976); and A Sachs and J Hoff Wilson, above, n 20.

[45] RD Gidney and WPJ Millar, above, n 30 at 205–7.

[46] See M Sarfatti Larson, *The Rise of Professionalism: A Sociological Analysis* (Berkeley,

professions has been addressed in relation to these theories, it has not been examined in detail. For example, it appears that the availability of programmes of university legal education may have fostered women's access to the legal profession, at least in some jurisdictions. For example, women's claims for admission to the bar in some Canadian provinces appear to have coincided with the establishment of university programmes in law; by contrast, Drachman argued that women gained access to state bars some decades earlier in the United States by apprenticing with fathers or brothers who were lawyers, while women's access to university law programmes in Europe was never, by itself, sufficient to obtain admission to the bar.[47] Yet, although different arrangements for legal education at the end of the nineteenth century have attracted considerable scholarly attention, connections between these arrangements and the admission of the first women lawyers remain more obscure. By contrast with women medical students, for example, women law students were not usually educated separately from men, an arrangement which arguably promoted gender equality, but which may also have reinforced professional identities for the first women lawyers, subtly undermining their sense of connection to the goals of the women's movements.

In the past two decades, however, some scholars have begun to consider historical relationships between gender and professionalism. For example, Carrie Menkel-Meadow contributed an important chapter to the international comparative project about legal professions in common law and civil law jurisdictions in the 1980s, identifying some of the factors that influenced the history of women in law; unfortunately, because so few of the individual country reports for the project contained detailed information about women lawyers, her analysis focused substantially on American developments.[48] Thornton's study about women lawyers included both historical and contemporary data, articulating how homosociability and corporatism within legal culture effectively excluded women lawyers, both past and present; although her study was primarily confined to one jurisdiction, Australia, her insights provided considerable inspiration for this comparative study of the history of women in law.[49] Similarly, some studies of the history of women in medicine offer useful theoretical approaches. For example, in her analysis of women's entry to the medical profession in Britain, Anne Witz suggested that male power was often masked within organisational struggles; as she argued, gender

University of California Press, 1979); RL Abel, above, n 41; TC Halliday and L Karpik, above, n 41; and works cited in D Sugarman and WW Pue, 'Introduction: Towards a Cultural History of Lawyers' in WW Pue and D Sugarman (eds), *Lawyers and Vampires: Cultural Histories of the Legal Professions* (Oxford, Hart Publishing, 2003).

[47] VG Drachman, above, n 26 at 40.
[48] C Menkel-Meadow, above, n 19.
[49] M Thornton, above, n 14.

issues were inextricably tied to professional structures and competition for control: 'the twists and turns of the women's struggle, their hollow victories and resounding defeats in the face of the remarkable resilience of the medical profession to the women's claims to practise medicine, reveal just how male power and privilege were sustained within the orbit of professional control.'[50] Such conclusions point to a need to examine how professional structures and organisation may have constrained women's access to professional roles.

Moreover, as Drachman argued, women lawyers were unique among nineteenth-century women professionals because 'their profession made and interpreted the laws that denied women access to the rights of citizenship, including the practice of law.' As a result, women who tried to gain admission to the practice of law were required to change the law itself: 'women had to persuade male judges and legislatures to reinterpret the male-constructed jurisprudence that made their entry into the legal profession *not only unthinkable, but illegal.*'[51] And, although judges may have stressed that they were not expressing their own opinions 'as to the advisability of extending the right [to practise law] to women,' but simply stating 'the law of the country as we now find it,'[52] their decisions confirmed that women were not eligible *as a matter of law* for admission to the bar. Moreover, setbacks experienced by the first women lawyers in the courts had consequences not only for individual claimants, but also for other women who were seeking access to the professions and to public life, including suffrage: negative judicial decisions reinforced traditional legal principles that defined a narrow scope for women in public life and confirmed women's inequality in law.[53] Thus, as Witz argued in relation to women in medicine, the history of professionalism necessitates an exploration of relationships between gender, power and professionalisation.[54]

More recently, interdisciplinary scholarship has begun to focus on the cultural history of lawyers, a project that reflects a diversity of questions, concerns and approaches to 'raise more problematic and wide-ranging understandings of legal professions, their various iterations, and social roles.' To date, these cultural histories have not fully addressed issues about women in law, although David Sugarman and Wesley Pue clearly identified a need to examine 'the gendered character of the profession, ... investigating the role of gentlemanlyness, respectability and masculinity.'[55] Similarly, other scholars of the legal professions have identified questions

---

[50] A Witz, *Professions and Patriarchy* (London and New York, Routledge, 1992) at 102.

[51] VG Drachman, above, n 26 at 2 (emphasis added).

[52] In re *French* (1905) 37 New Brunswick Reports 363, *per* Hanington, J.

[53] See Joan Hoff, *Law, Gender and Injustice: A Legal History of US Women* (New York, New York University Press, 1991), especially at chapter 5.

[54] A Witz, above, n 50 at 102; Witz argued that it is necessary to '[move] the sociology of professions onto a less androcentric terrain' and '[gender] the agents of professional projects.'

[55] WW Pue and D Sugarman (eds), above, n 46 at 15–16 and 22.

about gender inequalities as important factors in understanding professionalisation, suggesting that 'the impact of "feminization" on the ideologies and strategies of the professions ... merits further investigation.'[56] Such questions reveal a need to link the history of professionalism to issues of gender, and to explore the culture of legal professions in relation to women's challenges to male exclusivity.

For example, it is clear that women who were seeking to become lawyers in the late nineteenth century were presenting their claims to courts and legislatures in the midst of expanding opportunities for women, including access to higher education and to paid work. In addition, nineteenth-century family law reforms in many jurisdictions had removed some traditional constraints on women's activities outside the home; and suffrage campaigns in many countries were actively identifying goals for women as citizens, fully entitled to participate in the public sphere. The organised women's movements, with growing connections across international boundaries, emphasised these changes in women's opportunities for education, paid work, and participation in public life as part of a broad and progressive reform agenda designed to achieve full equality for women. In such a context, the admission of women to the bar appears to be part of the history of gender equality movements, including the struggle to achieve women's suffrage.[57] Indeed, there is some evidence that the timing of women's achievement of the franchise often coincided with the enactment of legislation to permit women to become lawyers, connections which reinforce the argument that access to professional work was one goal of the organised women's movements.

Yet, connections between the history of women lawyers and this larger history of women's legal and social emancipation remain ambiguous. Clearly, the first women lawyers shared aspirations for economic independence and participation in public life with other women who began to engage in paid work in the second half of the nineteenth century. In addition to such aspirations, however, some women needed to work because of declining opportunities to achieve economic support through marriage.[58] Yet, when women began to seek entry to male professions, it

[56] M Burrage, K Jarausch and H Siegrist, 'An Actor-Based Framework for the Study of the Professions' in M Burrage and R Torstendahl (eds), *Professions in Theory and History: Rethinking the Study of the Professions* (London, Sage, 1990) 203 at 223.

[57] See C Bolt, *The Women's Movements in the United States and Britain from the 1790s to the 1920s* (Amherst, University of Massachusetts Press, 1993); LJ Rupp, *Worlds of Women: The Making of an International Women's Movement* (Princeton, Princeton University Press, 1997); O Banks, *Faces of Feminism: A Study of Feminism as a Social Movement* (New York, St Martin's Press, 1981); M Vicinus (ed), *A Widening Sphere: Changing Roles of Victorian Women* (Bloomington and London, Indiana University Press, 1977); L Kealey (ed), *A Not Unreasonable Claim: Women and Reform in Canada 1880s–1920s* (Toronto, Women's Educational Press, 1979); and S Burt, L Code and L Dorney (eds), *Changing Patterns: Women in Canada* (Toronto, McClelland and Stewart, 1988).

[58] See L Holcombe, *Victorian Ladies at Work: Middle-Class Working Women in England and Wales 1850–1914* (Hamden, CT, Archon Books, 1973).

appears that they initially focused on access to medicine, not law; and women generally succeeded in gaining access to medical faculties in universities in most jurisdictions before women began to seek admission to the bar. According to Barbara Harris, the earlier successes of women doctors occurred because they were more easily accepted in nineteenth-century societies than women lawyers: women doctors could claim that their careers were natural extensions of women's nurturing and healing roles in the home, and also that they were protecting feminine modesty by treating women patients. Thus, the role of women doctors could be explained as an extension of women's roles in the 'private' sphere; by contrast, women lawyers were clearly 'intruding on the public domain explicitly reserved to men.'[59] Interestingly, in a number of jurisdictions, some of the first women doctors were active in movements for women's equality, both in their own countries and internationally; by contrast, women lawyers' relationships to the organised women's movements often appear more tenuous.[60] In this context, it seems that there were differing conceptions of new roles for women, and that they shaped different kinds of opportunities, including different professional opportunities, for women lawyers.

Indeed, efforts to define more precisely why women finally succeeded in gaining access to the legal professions at the end of the nineteenth century have presented challenges for historians. In a detailed review of the timing of women's admission to the legal professions in Europe, for example, James Albisetti concluded that a precise definition of factors that promoted women's access to the legal professions remained elusive. As he concluded, 'what is most striking is the relative simultaneity of the process in countries with widely different economic, social, political, religious and professional traditions.'[61] Indeed, after identifying a variety of possible factors to explain the opening of the legal professions to women, including levels of modernisation, the degree of institutionalisation of the bar, differences between Protestant and Catholic countries, different patterns and systems for legal education, and general concerns about overcrowding in the legal professions, Albisetti concluded that there was no consistent explanation for the timing of women's admission to European legal professions. As Albisetti noted, in relation to the legislation enacted in France in

---

[59] BJ Harris, *Beyond Her Sphere: Women and the Professions in American History* (Westport CT, Greenwood Press, 1978) at 110–12. See also JC Albisetti, 'Portia Ante Portas: Women and the Legal Profession in Europe, ca 1870–1925' (2000) 33 *Journal of Social History* 825 at 825–6; and V Drachman, *Hospital with a Heart: Women Doctors and the Paradox of Separatism at the New England Hospital, 1862–1969* (Ithaca, Cornell University Press, 1984).

[60] See PM Glazer and M Slater, above, n 43. Citing Jerold Auerbach, *Unequal Justice: Lawyers and Social Change in Modern America* (New York, Oxford University Press, 1976), PM Glazer and M Slater explained how criteria of merit and objectivity were used to exclude women, Jews and Blacks from the legal professions in the United States; they also suggested, at 241–3, that many of the first women professionals did not identify with the organised women's movements.

[61] JC Albisetti, above, n 59 at 847.

1900 after Jeanne Chauvin's unsuccessful application for admission to the Paris bar, 'the best explanation for the law opening the French bar to women was that it served the interests of one person, Jeanne Chauvin.'[62]

In spite of this apparently reluctant conclusion, Albisetti's assertion points to the necessity of examining not only systemic factors in the history of gender and of professionalism, but also the individual circumstances and aspirations of the first women lawyers. That is, while societal changes with respect to gender roles and ideas about legal professionalism may have defined the overall contexts in which women first attempted to challenge male exclusivity in the legal professions, the circumstances of individual women shaped their specific opportunities and strategies as they sought to achieve their personal goals; as Joy Parr argued, there is a need to take account of issues such as class, race and ethnicity, for example, to understand how 'social identities ... are forged in particular spatial and temporal settings.'[63] At the same time, as Ruth Roach Pierson warned, any account of a woman's life is always constructed within a gendered historical context, so that *both* individual experiences and the overall social context are important: 'a conception of experience lies at the intersection of theory and practice in women's history writing.'[64]

Yet, an attempt to explore the individual circumstances of the first women lawyers and the historical context in which their claims were presented is challenging; as feminist scholars have pointed out, the lives of professional women often reveal contradictions and ambiguities.[65] In relation to Clara Foltz, the first woman lawyer in California, for example, Barbara Allen Babcock explained that:

> Disjunction – between what she said and did, what she aspired to and achieved, and even between what she most fervently proclaimed at one point and another – is typical of Foltz's life.... Because of her ambivalence about what women should do and be, and because she tried so many things professionally and personally, her life and thought have a fractured, sometimes even frantic, quality....'[66]

Similarly, in assessing the life of Myra Bradwell, the subject of the first

---

62 JC Albisetti, above, n 59 at 846.

63 J Parr, above, n 43 at 9.

64 R Roach Pierson, above, n 38 at 91.

65 F Iacovetta and M Valverde (eds), *Gender Conflicts: New Essays in Women's History* (Toronto, University of Toronto Press, 1992) at *xvii*. See also J Parr and M Rosenfeld (eds), *Gender and History in Canada* (Toronto, Copp Clark Ltd, 1996); and G Lerner, *The Majority Finds its Past: Placing Women in History* (New York, Oxford University Press, 1979).

66 B Allen Babcock, 'Reconstructing the Person: The Case of Clara Shortridge Foltz' in S Groag Bell and M Yalom (eds), *Revealing Lives: Autobiography, Biography and Gender* (Albany, State University of New York Press, 1990) 131 at 139. See also L Wagner-Martin, *Telling Women's Lives: The New Biography* (New Brunswick, NJ, Rutgers University Press, 1994); and FG Halpenny, 'Expectations of Biography' in R B Fleming (ed), *Boswell's Children: The Art of the Biographer* (Toronto, Dundurn Press, 1992) 3.

case in the United States Supreme Court about women's right to practise law, Carol Sanger noted that Bradwell engaged in 'often underhanded tactics in the name of women's rights.'[67] In addition, Sanger identified Bradwell's life-long opposition to Jewish lawyers, a stance that reflected Bradwell's acceptance of dominant ideas within the legal profession at a time when it was in the process of 'professionalizing itself through hierarchies of religion and race.' Sanger argued that we need to know whether Bradwell 'ever reconciled (or even worried about reconciling) her egalitarian views on women with her exclusionary attitudes toward others,' and that we must read the stories of the first women lawyers to know 'who [they] were and what choices, constraints, and opportunities were like for them.'[68] In this way, the history of the first women lawyers seems to require attention not only to the intersection of gender and legal professionalism but also to the circumstances of their individual lives. As Joan Wallach Scott argued, women's access to the professions requires attention to new questions:

> How are those who cross the threshold received? If they belong to a group different from the group already 'inside,' what are the terms of their incorporation? How do the new arrivals understand their relationship to the place they have entered? What are the terms of identity they establish?[69]

In this study, such questions about individual lives and choices are interwoven with historical contexts concerning gender and legal professionalism; as Gerda Lerner suggested, we need to understand women's 'functioning in [a] male-defined world *on their own terms*.'[70]

TOWARD A COMPARATIVE HISTORY: INTRODUCING THE FIRST WOMEN LAWYERS

> In trying to sort out the reasons for professional women's successes or failures, it is far too facile to say that there were prejudices against women that they had to overcome. The ways in which the prejudice manifested itself were extremely complex and insidious.... As determined, aspiring professionals, women were not easily deterred. They found a variety of ways to respond to the discrimination they faced....[71]

---

67 C Sanger, 'Review Essay: Curriculum Vitae (Feminae): Biography and Early American Women Lawyers' (1994) 46 *Stanford Law Review* 1245 at 1261.

68 C Sanger, above, n 67 at 1261 and 1272.

69 J Wallach Scott, 'American Women Historians, 1884–1984' in JW Scott (ed), *Gender and the Politics of History* (New York, Columbia University Press, 1999) 179. See also N Zemon Davis, 'Women's History as Women's Education' in N Zemon Davis and J Wallach Scott (eds), *Women's History as Women's Education* (Northampton, MA, Smith College Archives, 1985) at 16.

70 G Lerner, above, n 65 at 148–9.

71 PM Glazer and M Slater, above, n 43 at 12.

This study explores the history of the first women lawyers in six jurisdictions in the late nineteenth and early twentieth centuries, assessing the barriers they faced and the strategies they adopted. It begins by examining the efforts of American women, who first claimed admission to state bars in the late 1860s and 1870s, and who were sufficiently numerous by the late 1880s to establish the 'Equity Club,' an organisation that provided information and support to women lawyers all over the United States for a few brief years.[72] By the turn of the century, there were about three hundred women lawyers in the United States; as the *Illustrated London News* wittily exclaimed in 1897, 'the lady lawyer [in the United States] meets us here, there, and everywhere ....'[73] The study then examines women's claims for admission to the bar in Canada, where in spite of geographical proximity to the United States, only one woman had gained admission to a provincial bar by the end of the nineteenth century. However, a number of women's claims for admission to the bar in Canada were litigated in the first two decades of the twentieth century, and courts in Canada frequently relied on American precedents about women's (lack of) eligibility to become lawyers. Although some North American jurisdictions enacted statutes to permit women to become lawyers in the absence of litigated claims, a frequent pattern was an unsuccessful court challenge, followed by intensive lobbying to obtain an enabling statute enacted by state or provincial legislatures. Interestingly, not only leaders in women's equality movements but also male members of provincial and state bars supported some of the claims presented by the first women lawyers. Moreover, variations in the experiences of women who wanted to become lawyers reveal how different ideas about the roles of courts and legislatures influenced decisions in states and provinces on both sides of the border, differences that may reflect the nuances of local politics, social culture and/or legal personalities.

By contrast with these examples in the United States and Canada, many of which involved litigated cases about women's admission to the legal professions, the study then explores the experiences of women in three other common law jurisdictions, all of whom began to engage in legal work without initiating litigation challenges. In Britain, for example, Eliza Orme established an independent law office in London in the mid-1870s, successfully engaging in conveyancing and patent work for several decades; although other women in Britain initiated litigation about their exclusion from the legal professions, Orme 'practised law' without ever seeking admission as a barrister or solicitor. In New Zealand, one of the first jurisdictions to grant women's suffrage in its 1893 legislation, Parliament enacted a statute a few years later to permit women to enter

---

[72] VG Drachman, above, n 25.
[73] 'Portias of Today,' *The Illustrated London News*, 13 November 1897 at 696. See above pp ix–xi.

the legal profession too; thus, when Ethel Benjamin graduated from the LLB programme in Dunedin, she was admitted to the bar in 1897 without much controversy and, significantly, without any need for litigation. And, in the absence of any legislation at all, a judge in India exercised judicial discretion to permit Cornelia Sorabji to plead in a British court in Poona in 1896; although she had successfully completed examinations for the BCL degree at Oxford, her appearance for the defence in a murder case occurred more than two decades before she was formally admitted as a *vakil* and then as a barrister after World War I. These three examples reflect different kinds of strategies to achieve women's goal of engaging in legal work. Indeed, they suggest how the permeability of professional boundaries, changing fortunes in relation to women's political equality in some jurisdictions, or the impact of greater judicial discretion may have permitted fissures in the tradition of male exclusivity in the legal professions.

Finally, this study examines the pattern of litigated challenges which occurred in a number of civil law jurisdictions in Europe in the late nineteenth century: litigation challenges were presented in Italy and Belgium in the 1880s and in France in the 1890s. Although efforts to obtain a legislative amendment succeeded prior to World War I only in France, these three litigation challenges reveal how some women in Europe also aspired to become lawyers. Significantly, however, the arguments presented in these European cases were not substantially different from those adopted in common law jurisdictions, in spite of their quite different origins within the civil law tradition. Indeed, similarities in these legal arguments tend to confirm the widespread acceptance of ideas about 'professional gentlemen' in law at the turn of the last century. In addition, however, this focus on Europe provides an opportunity to explore in some detail how individual male lawyers were often supportive of women's aspirations for admission to the bar, in spite of formal opposition from bar associations, the judiciary and legislators. In this way, the history of women lawyers reveals important connections to the complex politics of legal professions, courts and legislative activity in the late nineteenth and early twentieth centuries.

Overall, although the study does not represent a comprehensive history of the first women lawyers all over the world, it offers some important insights about the contexts in which women in a number of different jurisdictions actively sought to become lawyers at the turn of the twentieth century, and some reflections on their strategies and experiences as the first women in law. To some extent, the selection of jurisdictions in which women sought admission to the bar was defined for this study by the availability of individual personal records concerning women's quests to become lawyers. As will be apparent, the study relies on a number of recent academic theses and dissertations, contemporary news reports, and archival sources of letters and diaries. In relation to archival sources in particular, this study benefited greatly from access to the papers of the Belgian lawyer, Louis Frank (the *Papiers Frank* in the Bibliothèque Royale, Brussels) who corresponded with women lawyers around the world in the late 1890s; the responses from women lawyers in the United States, Canada, New Zealand, and several European jurisdictions provided some important 'voices' for the first women in law.

Moreover, the experiences of these first women lawyers offer some interesting comparisons. For example, it is clear that American women began to seek admission to the bar almost three decades before women in other common law jurisdictions, including neighbouring Canada, a factor that is usually attributed to the impact of political aspirations for equality and citizenship rights following the American Civil War and the period of Reconstruction in the 1870s.[74] However, the timing of women's claims in the United States may have special significance for women lawyers, since their initial efforts to gain access to the legal professions occurred at a time when the goals of women's equality movements were still broadly based and included the right to engage in professional work; by contrast, by the end of the nineteenth century, when women in other common law jurisdictions were first seeking admission to the bar, women's equality movements had become more narrowly focused on suffrage, and they were substantially controlled by middle-class women who had little understanding of women who aspired to professional work and economic self-sufficiency.[75] In this way, differences in the timing of women's first entry to the legal professions may offer insights about different kinds of links between gender and professionalism in the experiences of the first women lawyers.

In addition, it appears significant that colonial legislatures enacted statutes to permit women to practise law in parts of Canada, New Zealand and Australia two decades before the British Parliament did so after World War I; and a British court in Poona exercised judicial discretion to permit Cornelia Sorabji to provide legal representation in British India as early as 1896. In this context, it is clear that colonial legislatures and courts were not always deferential to the metropolitan centre, even though British law was arguably a fundamental aspect of imperial culture transplanted to the colonies.[76] In part, the independence of colonial courts and legislatures may have resulted from the challenges of establishing effective imperial

[74] See A Kraditor, *The Ideas of the Woman Suffrage Movement 1890–1920* (New York, Columbia University Press, 1967), who argued that suffrage goals changed from justice to expediency.

[75] See S Bashevkin, 'Independence versus Partisanship: Dilemmas in the Political History of Women in English Canada' in V Strong-Boag and AC Fellman (eds), *Rethinking Canada: The Promise of Women's History* (Toronto, Copp Clark Pitman Ltd, 1896) 246.

[76] See P Fitzpatrick, *The Mythology of Modern Law* (London and New York, Routledge, 1992) at 107; and D Sugarman, '"A Hatred of Disorder": Legal Science, Liberalism and Imperialism' in P Fitzpatrick (ed), *Dangerous Supplements: Resistance and Renewal in Jurisprudence* (London, Pluto Press, 1991) 34 at 56.

control over the vast territories of the British Empire. Thus, as Bruce Kercher argued, even when colonists formally transplanted English law to settled colonies, Blackstone's principle that 'those who travelled to settled colonies took the law of England with them as a birthright' was never self-enacting; whether because of ignorance or intent, or because most of life is lived beyond the reach of the law, 'what passed for law in the colony often differed sharply from English law.'[77] In this way, the history of women's admission to the legal professions may provide insights about differences in the culture of gender and legal professionalism in Britain and its colonies at the end of the nineteenth century.

At the same time, it seems that many of the first women lawyers were 'lone *voyageurs*,'[78] the *only* women in law in their respective jurisdictions. Although some women lawyers in the United States corresponded with one another as part of the Equity Club in the late 1880s,[79] many of them remained relatively isolated in the practice of law. Nonetheless, there were a number of professional connections. For example, the New Zealand bar referred to an Ontario precedent in establishing its rules for women's dress for court appearances in the 1890s.[80] In addition, the admission of Clara Brett Martin in Ontario in 1897 was cited in the brief accompanying Jeanne Chauvin's claim for admission as an *avocat* in Paris;[81] and the French statute enacted in 1900 to permit women to become *avocats* was later cited in the litigation about women's admission to the bar of Québec.[82] The legal press in Britain and in Canada both commented on Cornelia Sorabji's appearance in a British court in India in 1896,[83] and Ethel Benjamin acknowledged the earlier achievements of both Martin and Sorabji.[84] Moreover, when judges and lawyers were invited to participate in the Congress on Jurisprudence and Law Reform in conjunction with the World's Columbian Exposition in Chicago in 1893, a number of American women lawyers participated – and both Cornelia Sorabji and Eliza Orme were invited to send papers for presentation, the first time that women joined male lawyers in a formal legal congress.[85] In addition, it may be

---

77 B Kercher, 'A Convict Conservative: George Crossley and the English Legal Tradition' (1999) 16:1 *Law in Context* 24

78 See GJ Clifford (ed), *Lone Voyagers: Academic Women in Coeducational Universities 1870–1937* (New York, Feminist Press, 1989).

79 See VG Drachman, above, n 25.

80 R Cooke (ed), *Portrait of a Profession: The Centennial Book of the New Zealand Law Society* (Wellington, AH and AW Reed, 1969) at 337.

81 L Frank, *La Femme-Avocat: Exposé Historique et Critique de la Question* (Paris, V Giard et E Brière, 1898) at 68.

82 See *Langstaff v Bar of Québec* (1915) 47 Rapports Judiciares de Québec 131 at 142; and (1916) 25 Rapports Judiciares de Québec 11 at 17 and 20.

83 'A Pioneer in Law' (15 October 1896) *Englishwoman's Review* (ns) at 217–18; and 'Women Barristers' (1896) 32 *Canada Law Journal* 84.

84 E Benjamin, Interview with Kate Sheppard (August 1897) 26 *White Ribbon* 1–2.

85 L Frank, above, n 81 at 133.

important to explore the precise connections between these first women lawyers and the organised women's movement in different jurisdictions: to what extent did women lawyers receive support from women's rights activists?

Indeed, in spite of some connections among the first women lawyers and with the organised women's movement, some of the first women lawyers appear to have embraced a primary identity as *lawyers*, ungendered. In addition, there is some evidence that it was women whose applications for admission to the bar were *unsuccessful* who chose to become active in the movements for women's equality at the turn of the twentieth century; by contrast, some women who became lawyers appear to have been more inclined to eschew connections with the women's movement in favour of strictly professional identities. Such observations raise important questions about the intersection of gender and legal professionalism in the lives of the first women lawyers. To what extent do historical assessments of changing ideas about gender help to explain the experiences of the first women who challenged male exclusivity in the legal professions? Are there insights in the history of the professions that explain the significance of women's claims for admission to the bar? And how are these historical assessments of gender and of professionalism enriched by an exploration of the ways in which women's aspirations for legal careers contributed to their experiences? In exploring these questions, this study reveals how the history of women lawyers may require us to 'reinvent the lives [of *women who first became lawyers*], discovering ... the processes and decisions, the choices and unique pain, that [lie] beyond [women's] life stories.'[86]

---

[86] CG Heilbrun, *Writing a Woman's Life* (New York, Ballantyne Books, 1988) at 31.

1

American Pioneers: The First Women Lawyers

A CENTURY OF STRUGGLE

The century of struggle for women to gain admission to the legal profession can only be understood by placing it in its historical context – with its roots in the struggle for women's rights in the United States. Only then can the question be answered as to why this struggle of women lawyers took place at this particular time in American history.[1]

D KELLY WEISBERG'S ASSERTION reflects two important aspects of the history of American women lawyers. One is her description of the history of women lawyers as a 'century of struggle': the one hundred years that began in the late 1860s, when women first began to attend university law schools and to gain formal admission to state bars, and that ended a century later when the last American law schools abandoned longstanding practices of gender discrimination in admission requirements. Thus, American women lawyers were the pioneers in entering the world's legal professions, gaining admission to a number of state bars almost three decades before women elsewhere. Paradoxically, they also remained excluded from a number of law schools for more than six decades of the twentieth century, long after women in many other jurisdictions had achieved admission to law schools and the bar. In such a context, both their success in gaining early access to the legal profession and the 'century of struggle' that followed must be understood in terms of the social conditions of nineteenth-century America.

Second, Weisberg's assertion identifies the roots of the history of women lawyers in the larger struggle for women's equality rights, particularly suffrage. And indeed, there is considerable evidence that women's access to paid work and the professions constituted an important goal of the

[1] DK Weisberg, 'Barred from the Bar: Women and Legal Education in the United States 1870–1890' (1977) 28 *Journal of Legal Education* 485 at 499; see also DK Weisberg, *Women and the Law: A Social Historical Perspective*, vol II (Cambridge, MA, Schenkman Publishing Company, Inc, 1982) 231.

women's movement both before and after the Civil War, so that the history of women lawyers is woven into the struggles of the nineteenth-century American women's movement. Yet, these connections are also complicated: women succeeded in becoming lawyers in several US states in the last decades of the nineteenth century, long before national suffrage was finally achieved after World War I, but even women's entitlement to vote did not eliminate discriminatory admission patterns in some law schools until later in the twentieth century. These paradoxes suggest that the history of women lawyers must be examined, not only in relation to the women's movement, but also in terms of the legal profession itself: how did nineteenth-century ideas about legal professionalism shape the conditions, both formal and more subtle, under which women first gained admission to state bars? And when these pioneering American women began to become lawyers, what was their impact on the tradition of male exclusivity in the legal profession?

These questions are important because increasing numbers of American women lawyers in the late nineteenth century fostered women's aspirations to join the legal profession elsewhere. By 1910, for example, Barbara Harris suggested that there were already 1500 women lawyers in the United States.[2] Their experiences, including their connections with the women's movement and also their expanding opportunities for work as members of the legal profession, often influenced strategies pursued by women elsewhere. In addition, judges in other jurisdictions, faced with women's claims to become lawyers, often looked to precedents in the United States, even though they were not binding elsewhere. Interestingly, Canadian judges tended to prefer US decisions which held that women were *not* eligible for admission to the bar without legislative intervention, virtually ignoring the lively debate about the respective roles of courts and legislatures that is evident in the early American cases of the 1870s and 1880s. In this context, the experiences of the first women lawyers in the United States shaped potential arguments and strategies for women who later initiated similar challenges elsewhere. In this way, the paradoxical 'century of struggle' for women lawyers in the United States established important patterns for women's admission to the bar.

Interestingly, although historical accounts of American women lawyers focus on the struggle to gain *formal* admission to state bars, there is evidence of women engaged in legal work as early as the colonial period; for example, Gerda Lerner suggested that women may have acted as 'attorneys-in-fact' in the American colonies before 1750.[3] Indeed, Karen

---

[2] BJ Harris, *Beyond Her Sphere: Women and the Professions in American History* (Westport, CT, Greenwood Press, 1978) at 110. See also VG Drachman, *Sisters in Law: Women Lawyers in Modern American History* (Cambridge, MA, Harvard University Press, 1998) at 173; and IM Pettus, 'The Legal Education of Women' (1900) 38 *Journal of Social Science* 234.

[3] G Lerner, 'The Lady and the Mill Girl: Changes in the Status of Women in the Age of

Morello identified the first woman lawyer in the United States as Margaret Brent; apparently, she arrived in the colony of Maryland in 1638, after her cousin, Lord Baltimore, had personally commended her to Governor Calvert.[4] Brent amassed some of the largest real estate holdings in the New World, and she was eventually appointed counsel to the governor. In addition, it seems that she was involved in assisting Calvert to regain possession of the colony after it was seized by two Virginian colonists, while Calvert was absent in England in 1643 during the English Civil War. When Calvert suddenly died after his return to Maryland, his final instructions named Brent his executor; her claim to act as his attorney was accepted and she subsequently engaged in a number of court proceedings to carry out Calvert's wishes. According to Morello, Brent's abilities were both legal and political, enabling her to break through 'all the existing restrictions facing seventeenth-century women.' Yet, this claim seems somewhat undermined by the fact that colonists, who did not have any precedent for a *woman* who engaged in such activities, 'frequently addressed her, in person and in court records, as "Gentleman Margaret Brent."'[5]

There is also evidence that some women pleaded their own cases before colonial courts.[6] For example, a slave woman, Elizabeth Freeman, successfully argued for her own freedom 'as a native-born American, free and equal' pursuant to the Massachusetts Bill of Rights in 1783; and a black woman, Luce Terry Prince, successfully defended a land claim (involving issues of ejectment, trespass and quieting title) all the way to the US Supreme Court in 1795.[7] In addition, Morello suggested that women may

Jackson, 1800–1840' in NF Cott and EH Pleck (eds), *A Heritage of Her Own: Toward a New Social History of American Women* (New York, Simon and Schuster, 1979) 182 at 188, citing SH Drinker, 'Women Attorneys of Colonial Times' (1961) 56 *Maryland Historical Society Bulletin*. See also DB Berry, *The 50 Most Influential Women in American Law* (Los Angeles, Lowell House, 1996) at 1; and W Prest, '"One Hawkins, A Female Sollicitor": Women Lawyers in Augustan England' (1994) 57:4 *The Huntington Library Quarterly* 353 at 355.

4 KB Morello, *The Invisible Bar: The Woman Lawyer in America 1638 to the Present* (New York, Random House, 1986) at 3. KB Morello reported, at 4–7, that Brent had attempted to cast a vote in the Maryland Assembly, based on her role as a landowner, and that she 'remained bitter' about the Assembly's refusal to permit her to vote. See also 'Margaret Brent,' Women's Legal History Biography Project, Stanford Law School, online [hereafter Stanford WLHP].

5 KB Morello, above, n 4 at 3. See also AM Bittenbender, 'Women in Law' in A Nathan Meyer (ed), *Woman's Work in America* (New York, Henry Holt and Company, 1891) 218 at 220–1; and M Minow, '"Forming Underneath Everything that Grows:" Toward a History of Family Law' [1985] *Wisconsin Law Review* 819 at 835–6. Minow argued that women in the colonial era 'held an important status and participated in the economic and public life of the community [more than in] later periods.'

6 KB Morello, above, n 4 at 8: Gertrude James of Maryland, Sarah Bland of Virginia, and Anna Meyanders of New York; the cases concerned property and estate settlements.

7 KB Morello, above, n 4 at 8, citing B Wertheimer, *We Were There: The Story of Working Women in America* (New York, Pantheon, 1977) at 36. See also JC Smith Jr, *Rebels in Law: Voices in the History of Black Women Lawyers* (Ann Arbor, University of Michigan Press, 1998) at 2, commenting on Luce Terry's excellent advocacy.

have practised law in the western states, far away from 'the restrictions of northeastern society,' without being formally admitted to a state or territorial bar. Thus, as the *Chicago Legal News* reported in February 1869, a woman was practising law in a small town in Iowa:

> ... in North English, Iowa County, there may be seen in front of a neat office a sign with the following inscription in gilt letters, 'Mrs Mary E Magoon, Attorney at Law.' We understand that Mrs Magoon is having a good practice and is very successful as a jury lawyer.[8]

Certainly, westward expansion in the United States provided women with opportunities previously closed to them, and law practice on the county level may not have required formal admission to a state or territorial bar. As Morello noted, this information about Mary Magoon 'leaves open the question of how many other women lawyers were practicing in small towns throughout the Midwest and West.'[9] In this context, moreover, it may be more than coincidental that the first successful application for *formal* admission to the bar occurred in 1869 in the state of Iowa, the same state in which Mary Magoon was already practising law.

Thus, Weisberg's 'century of struggle' for women lawyers in the United States began in 1869, when Arabella Babb Mansfield achieved formal admission to the Iowa bar. Mansfield, a skilled debater and classics student who had graduated from Iowa Wesleyan College, apprenticed with her brother in a law firm and then succeeded in passing the Iowa bar examinations. Significantly, the attorney who interviewed her recommended her admission to the bar, not only because she was 'the first lady' who had applied, but because her proven ability in the examinations offered 'the very best rebuke possible to the imputation that ladies cannot qualify for the practice of law.'[10] When the Iowa court approved her application in 1869, Mansfield became the first woman in the United States to achieve formal admission to the bar of any state.[11] Moreover, at the same time,

[8] KB Morello, above, n 4 at 11. As Morello noted, women were first entitled to vote in the western state of Wyoming in 1869, and the first female justice of the peace, Esther H Morris, was appointed there in 1870. See also M Matsuda, 'The West and the Legal Status of Women: Explanations of Frontier Feminism' (1985) 24 *Journal of the West* 47 at 50.

[9] KB Morello, above, n 4 at 11. See also MJ Matsuda (ed), *Called from Within: Early Women Lawyers of Hawai'i* (Honolulu, University of Hawaii Press, 1992); and 'Almeda Hitchcock,' Stanford WLHP, above, n 4.

[10] KB Morello, above, n 4 at 12. See also T Federer, 'Belle A Mansfield: Opening the Way for Others,' Stanford WLHP, above, n 4; and LA Haselmayer, 'Belle A Mansfield' (1969) 55 *Women Lawyers Journal* 46.

[11] KB Morello, above, n 4 at 12–14. According to Morello, Mansfield later accompanied her husband to Europe, where she continued to study law, and attended courtrooms in London and Paris to observe their practices; on her return, she accepted a faculty position at Iowa Wesleyan University. Later on, both she and her husband became faculty members at DePauw University in Indiana. See also T Federer, above, n 10; J Hoff, *Law, Gender, and Injustice: A Legal History of US Women* (New York, University Press, 1991) at 162–3; and

women were beginning to gain admission to law schools. After studying law in her husband's office for a time, Ada Kepley enrolled in the one-year law course at Union College of Law (now Northwestern University); when she graduated with the LLB degree in 1870, Kepley was the first woman to graduate from a law school in the United States.[12]

And Kepley was not the only woman law student at this time. For example, two women were admitted to study law at Washington University in St Louis in 1869. One was Lemma Barkaloo who became the first woman to try a case in an American court in 1870, although she had still not completed her course work when she died a few months later of typhoid fever. The other was Phoebe Couzins who graduated in law and was the first woman lawyer admitted to practice in the courts of Missouri, Kansas and Utah; however, she later became an important suffrage activist rather than engaging in the practice of law.[13] In the same year, moreover, a Black woman who had already had a long career as a teacher, began to study law at Howard University in Washington DC. Mary Ann Shadd had left Delaware in 1850 after the enactment of the *Fugitive Slave Act* in the United States resulted in large numbers of Black 'refugees' in Canada; she worked as a teacher for both escaped slaves and 'free persons' in Ontario. As well, she established, wrote, edited and published a newspaper, the *Provincial Freeman*, thereby becoming the first Black woman publisher in North America and the editor of the first abolition paper in Canada. After returning to the United States in 1868, she was among the first students at the newly-established law school at Howard University; however, although she completed her studies in 1872, it seems that she did not obtain a degree until the early 1880s.[14] By contrast with the admission of women to these law schools, however, Columbia University completely rejected applications from three women in 1868, and one member of the law school's

---

A Sachs and J Hoff Wilson, *Sexism and the Law: A Study of Male Beliefs and Legal Bias in Britain and the United States* (New York, The Free Press, 1978).

[12] However, Kepley was initially denied admission to the Illinois bar: see VG Drachman, *Women Lawyers and the Origins of Professional Identity in America: The Letters of the Equity Club, 1887 to 1890* (Ann Arbor, University of Michigan Press, 1993) at 235; and 'Ada Kepley,' Stanford WLHP, above, n 4.

[13] J Hoff, above, n 11 at 163. Couzins died in 1913, impoverished and bitter about the lack of recognition she had received as a pioneer in the suffrage movement and in the legal profession: see KB Morello, above, n 4 at 44–9.

[14] R Sadlier, *Mary Ann Shadd: Publisher, Editor, Teacher, Lawyer, Suffragette* (Toronto, Umbrella Press, 1995); and R Sadlier, 'Mary Ann Shadd' in R Sadlier (ed), *Leading the Way: Black Women in Canada* (Toronto, Umbrella Press, 1994) 16 at 23–4. According to Drachman, Mary Ann Shadd Cary ['Cary' was the surname of Shadd's husband whom she married in Ontario in 1856] was the first woman law student at Howard, an institution established in 1867 and open to both black and white students; the first woman law graduate was Charlotte Ray, and Shadd Cary graduated in 1883: see VB Drachman, above, n 2 at 44–6; JC Smith Jr, above, n 7 at 283; and S Sneed, 'Mary Ann Shadd Cary: A Biographical Sketch of the Rebel,' Stanford WLHP, above, n 4 at 20–22.

Board of Trustees firmly declared 'I think the clack of these possible Portias will never be heard at Dwight's moot courts.'[15]

Thus, in spite of the achievements of some women lawyers in the early 1870s, 'the battle was by no means over: in reality it had just begun;' indeed, as Kelly Weisberg noted, women initiated law suits in subsequent years to gain admission to the bar in seventeen states and in the United States Supreme Court.[16] In spite of further successes, moreover, there was continuing resistance to women students on the part of a number of university law schools well into the twentieth century. For example, Columbia University admitted women law students for the first time only in 1929; and women were not admitted to Harvard Law School until 1950, and to the law school at the University of Notre Dame until 1969. Indeed, 'the last male bastion,' Washington and Lee University, admitted women law students for the first time in 1972,[17] just over one hundred years after Arabella Mansfield had been admitted to the Iowa bar and Ada Kepley had graduated with the first LLB degree granted to an American woman.

This chapter focuses on the first women lawyers in the United States, whose pioneering efforts later influenced legal challenges presented by women who were seeking admission to the bar in other jurisdictions. The chapter first examines the context in which women in the United States began to seek entry to the legal profession in a number of different states, a context which included a strong women's movement, but also increasing concerns about professionalisation in law and new developments in legal work and in university legal education. The chapter then focuses on legal responses to women's claims to become lawyers, particularly in judicial decisions, beginning with Mansfield's case in Iowa in 1869. As a review of these decisions reveals, the arguments and strategies adopted by aspiring women lawyers in the United States reflected the goals of women's equality and they sometimes, but not always, succeeded in overcoming the tradition of male exclusivity to gain access to the legal profession. Yet, their arguments and strategies were not always successful, and even when they

[15] VG Drachman, above, n 2 at 41. Theodore W Dwight was professor of law, history, civil policy and political economy from 1847 and head of the Columbia School of Jurisprudence from 1858. See also Robert Stevens, *Law School: Legal Education in America from the 1850s to the 1980s* (Chapel Hill and London, University of North Carolina Press, 1983) at 22–3.

[16] DK Weisberg, above, n 1 at 485. According to VG Drachman, above, n 2 at 12 and 251 (Table 1), thirty-five states and territories and the District of Columbia granted permission to women to practice law between 1869 and 1899. See also RL Abel, *American Lawyers* (New York, Oxford University Press, 1989) at 90, citing WP Rogers 'Is Law a Field for Women's Work?' (1901) 24 *American Bar Association Reports* 548 at 564.

[17] DK Weisberg, above, n 1 at 486. According to Auerbach, the Dean of Columbia Law School, pressured by suffragists to admit women during World War I, predicted that, 'if women were admitted, his school soon would be swarming with "freaks or cranks": see JS Auerbach, *Unequal Justice: Lawyers and Social Change in Modern America* (New York, Oxford University Press, 1976) at 295.

did succeed, women sometimes gained admission to the profession without challenging underlying norms of male exclusivity in professional culture. All the same, these legal challenges were important precedents for cases later presented in other jurisdictions, even though American cases often focused specifically on provisions of the US Constitution. As Joan Hoff concluded, however, American constitutional arguments did not often lead to different outcomes in women's rights cases litigated in the United States and in England in this period – a conclusion which arguably applies to other jurisdictions too. As Hoff stated, judges in all of these cases were 'expressing roughly similar sentiments and arriving at substantially the same results,'[18] suggesting that ideas about gender roles may have been just as important as legal and constitutional jurisprudence. In this context, the chapter examines the reflections of some women who became lawyers in nineteenth-century America, and particularly their relationships with the women's movement and the legal profession, to assess their experiences in confronting male exclusivity in the legal profession.

THE CONTEXT FOR THE FIRST WOMEN LAWYERS: NEW IDEAS ABOUT WOMEN'S EQUALITY AND LEGAL PROFESSIONALISM

What marked them [women professionals] as special, and so suitable for their pioneering roles, was a belief that they could forge a synthesis between the Progressive sense of burgeoning opportunities and the separate, more constricted world of female endeavor. It was to be education ... that would allow them to play new roles and exercise their social, moral, and intellectual concerns in new arenas.[19]

Women's formal admission to the bar in the United States in the nineteenth century occurred in a reformist context characterised by aspirations for women's equality, including access to higher education and the professions, particularly after the Civil War. However, even prior to the War, women had increasingly become involved in public campaigns, especially in relation to the movement to abolish slavery. Indeed, Christine Bolt suggested that it was the refusal by organisers of the 1840 World Anti-Slavery Convention in London to give delegate status to women, which prompted Elizabeth Cady Stanton and others to vow to hold a convention in the

---

[18] J Hoff, above, n 11 at 170; according to Hoff, 'judges in the United States articulated policy issues far more freely than did their English counterparts.... Consequently, the inconsistency and judicial confusion over female citizenship ... were more readily apparent in this country than in Britain....'

[19] PM Glazer and M Slater, *Unequal Colleagues: The Entrance of Women into the Professions, 1890–1940* (New Brunswick and London, Rutgers University Press, 1987) at 210.

United States to advocate the rights of women.[20] As well, the temperance movement in the United States, initially launched with strong Church backing and male direction in the early part of the nineteenth century, gradually included women in its campaigns as they, along with children, 'were presented as enslaved by the male vice of drinking.'[21] And, in the years just prior to the Civil War, the enactment of the first statutes reforming married women's property rights in some states may have encouraged women to seek other egalitarian reforms of family law.[22] In addition to these changes, Harris argued that it was the constrained roles assigned to women by the Victorian ethos, which emerged in the middle of the nineteenth century, that created women's revolt and energised the women's movement.[23] Thus, even prior to the Civil War, American women were becoming involved in reformist ideas and campaigns.

In this context, a newspaper announcement which appeared on 14 July 1848 for a Convention to be held on 19–20 July in Seneca Falls, New York 'to discuss the social, civil, and religious condition and rights of women' attracted three hundred participants.[24] A young nineteen-year-old glove maker, Charlotte Woodward, described how she abandoned her tasks that day and climbed on the family wagon to make her way to Seneca Falls: 'before we travelled many miles we came upon other wagonloads of women, bound in the same direction ... and long before we reached Seneca Falls we were a procession.'[25] Discussion at the Convention focused on a Declaration of Sentiments, a document consciously modelled on the American Declaration of Independence, which defined comprehensive reform objectives for women, including: '*equal rights in the universities, in the trades and professions*; the right to vote; to share in all

20 C Bolt, *The Women's Movements in the United States and Britain from the 1790s to the 1920s* (Amherst, University of Massachusetts Press, 1993) at 68. See also E Flexner, *Century of Struggle: The Woman's Rights Movement in the United States* (Cambridge, MA, Belknap Press of Harvard University Press, 1959); WL O'Neill, *Everyone Was Brave: A History of Feminism in America* (Chicago, Quadrangle Books, 1971); and I Kugler, *From Ladies to Women: The Organized Struggle for Woman's Rights in the Reconstruction Era* (Westport, CT, Greenwood Press, 1987).

21 C Bolt, above, n 20 at 69.

22 Although married women's property statutes were not intended to be women's rights statutes, they may have influenced aspirations for legal reform: see N Basch, *In the Eyes of the Law: Women, Marriage and Property in Nineteenth-Century New York* (Ithaca, Cornell University Press, 1982).

23 BJ Harris, above, n 2 at 75, examined a number of competing theories for the rise of the American women's movement in the 1840s and 1850s; she concluded that 'the initial stages of feminism are best seen ... as a cry of protest against intolerable confinement,' citing J Demos, 'The American Family in Past Time' (1974) 43 *American Scholar* 435.

24 See C Bolt, above, n 20 at 87. See also E Griffith, *In Her Own Right: The Life of Elizabeth Cady Stanton* (New York, Oxford University Press, 1984); and K Barry, *Susan B Anthony: A Biography of a Singular Feminist* (New York, Ballantine Books, 1988).

25 Quoted in I Kugler, above, n 20 at 10; according to Kugler, Woodward was the only person who attended the 1848 Convention who lived to see the nineteenth amendment ratified and to vote in a national election after World War I.

political offices, honors and emoluments; to complete equality in marriage, to personal freedom, property, wages, children; to make contracts; to sue and be sued; and to testify in courts of justice.'[26] From the perspective of later developments in the women's movement at the end of the nineteenth century, the sheer breadth of reform goals identified in the Declaration of Sentiments in 1848 was highly significant for women's equality in the new republic. As Hoff argued, the Declaration of Sentiments represented 'a feminist demand for the long-overdue reconciliation of republican theory with republican practice.'[27]

Clearly, the right to vote was just one among many other demands for equality included in the 1848 Declaration of Sentiments.[28] For women like Elizabeth Cady Stanton, a formidable American advocate for women's rights, all the goals identified in the Declaration of Sentiments were essential to achieving women's equality. Her egalitarian principles also included strong support for the emancipation of slaves in the American south, and she argued that women's support for emancipation would eventually result in equal rights and opportunities for women in post-Civil War society. To her great disappointment, the struggle for women's rights did not end with the War; as she lamented: 'when the slaves were emancipated, and ... women asked that they should be recognized in the reconstruction as citizens of the Republic, equal before the law, all [expressions of women's] transcendent virtues vanished like dew before the morning sun....'[29] Partly as a result of the long and continuing struggle for women's equality in the decades after the War, the broader goals of many organisations in the American women's movement gradually narrowed by the end of the nineteenth century to focus simply on the achievement of women's suffrage, thereby sacrificing the ambitious programme set out in the Declaration signed at Seneca Falls. Opponents of this narrow focus on suffrage, including Stanton, increasingly found themselves a minority within the women's movement. Thus, as Harris noted in her analysis of the American women's movement, a significant gap emerged between women like Stanton who 'appealed to the egalitarian ideology of the Enlightenment

26 C Bolt, above, n 20 at 88 (emphasis added). According to J Hoff, above, n 11 at 136, the language of the Declaration of Sentiments looked back to 1776: 'it was steeped in the "ethical" and "humanistically" progressive language of the republican ideology of the American Revolution.'

27 J Hoff, above, n 11 at 136–7. According to Hoff, the Declaration's lasting significance lay in its challenges to the domesticity of the nuclear family and to the increasing privatisation of women's lives in the context of industrialisation and urbanisation.

28 According to C Bolt, above, n 20 at 88, the franchise resolution was successfully approved by *only* a very narrow majority of participants at the Convention in 1848.

29 EC Stanton, *Eighty Years and More, 1815–1897* (New York, Schocken Books, 1971) at 241, cited in BJ Harris, above, n 2 at 96. As Harris noted, at 122, not all members of the women's movement favoured linking the rights of slaves and women, and this difference resulted in a split in the movement in 1870: Stanton decided to support the war and abolition, deferring women's claims until it was over.

and aggressively assumed roles normally restricted to males' and, on the other hand, the majority of women reformers who 'advocated expanding the female role without challenging the domestic ideal.'[30] By the end of the nineteenth century, Harris argued, most women's groups were focused on 'a single-minded drive for the vote,' with much less concern about other issues of women's equality, championed for so long by women like Stanton. Moreover, arguments supporting women's right to the vote increasingly emphasised women's special talents as *moral guardians* of society, not their right to suffrage based on equality with men:

> Although the women's rights movement reduced itself to a demand for the vote by 1900, in the pre-Civil War period its program was much broader. *The Seneca Falls Declaration protested against the exclusion of women from the professions and trades and demanded equality in this area....* [In] the early years the right to work outside the home was a much more central concern than the right to vote. Furthermore, from the beginning there was a close connection between organized feminism and the victories of women trying to open the professions to themselves and their sex. [31]

This gradual transformation in the goals of the women's movement in the late nineteenth century United States is important to the history of women's entry to the legal professions. In the 1860s, for example, the aspirations of women who wanted to become lawyers were quite consistent with the overall goals of the women's movement, including the opening up of educational opportunities and equal access to the professions identified in the 1848 Declaration of Sentiments.[32] Indeed, Harris argued that 'the nineteenth-century feminist movement provided the major impetus for women [professionals].'[33] Moreover, women's participation in the abolition movement, as well as political challenges after the Civil War, accelerated opportunities for American women to enter the professions earlier than women in other countries; as Kugler explained, the end of the Civil War meant that American women looked 'forward to the postwar Reconstruction as the dawn of a new era of equal rights for all Americans – blacks and whites, women and men.'[34] By the end of the nineteenth century, however, strategies within the women's movement had

---

30 BJ Harris, above, n 2 at 85.

31 BJ Harris, above, n 2 at 86, citing J Demos, above, n 23 (emphasis added). J Hoff, above, n 11 at 145, identified the passage of constitutional amendments after the Civil War as influencing the development of individual litigation and single-issue politics among the equal rights women's group. See also O Banks, *Faces of Feminism: A Study of Feminism as a Social Movement* (New York, St Martin's Press, 1981).

32 As J Hoff noted, above, n 11 at 146, constitutional amendments fostered legal challenges.

33 BJ Harris, above, n 2 at 87, citing MR Walsh, *'Doctors Wanted: No Woman Need Apply': Sexual Barriers in the Medical Profession, 1835–1975* (New Haven, Yale University Press, 1977) at 276.

34 I Kugler, above, n 20 at 25.

changed; in this context, although many individual women lawyers supported suffrage, their aspirations for work outside the home and for economic independence in the practice of law were no longer so congruent with majority views in the organised women's movement. Thus, the fact that the first women lawyers in the United States began to enter the legal profession at a time when the women's movement included goals of equality in a wide variety of contexts, including access to the professions, may have significance not only for their connections to the women's movement, but also for their identities as *professional women.*

Women's entry to the legal profession was also encouraged in the 1860s and 1870s by increasing access to higher education for women generally. As Harris noted, 'the four decades after the Civil War witnessed a dramatic expansion of higher education for women,' related in part to pressures from the women's movement; it was also fuelled by economic needs on the part of colleges and universities as a result of economic depression, falling enrollments during the Civil War, and increasing enthusiasm for reforming traditional curricular arrangements.[35] As early as 1870, there were co-educational institutions at Wisconsin, Michigan, Missouri, Iowa, Kansas, Indiana, Minnesota and California, although Harris concluded that they tended to educate women for 'marriage and appropriate female jobs, such as public school teaching; ... college experience [for these women] discouraged them from challenging accepted ideas about women, developing strong motives for pursuing independent careers, or trying to break into "masculine" fields.'[36] By contrast with these coeducational institutions, however, separate women's colleges were also established during and after the Civil War: Vassar in 1861; Smith and Wellesley in 1875; Bryn Mawr in 1885; and Radcliffe in 1893: 'the goal of all these schools was to give females the first-rate education that men received at Harvard and Yale.'[37] As Glazer and Slater concluded, these separate women's colleges provided employment for women intellectuals as well as high standards of education for future generations of female scholars.[38]

A similar separatist model of education was adopted early on for women who wanted to enter the medical profession. As Virginia Drachman noted, they 'entered medicine through their own medical schools and

35 BJ Harris, above, n 2 at 98, citing P Graham, 'Women in Academe' in A Theodore (ed), *The Professional Woman* (Cambridge, MA, Schenkman Publishing Co, 1971) at 720–1.

36 BJ Harris, above, n 2 at 99, citing JK Conway, 'Perspectives on the History of Women's Education in the United States' (1974) 14 *History of Education Quarterly* 5–7.

37 BJ Harris, above, n 2 at 99. BJ Harris analysed data about women workers in the early twentieth century, and concluded, at 104–5, that only a small percentage were professional women; there were few women in medicine, law and the ministry. See also J Rendall, *The Origins of Modern Feminism: Women in Britain, France and the United States 1780–1860* (Chicago, Lyceum Books, 1985).

38 PM Glazer and M Slater, above, n 19 at 15. MR Glazer and M Slater examined the lives of women professionals in academia, medicine, research science and psychiatric social work to reveal the range of different professional possibilities for women; as they concluded, at 210–11, the range of options for women was actually quite narrow.

hospitals;' by contrast, she argued that the first women lawyers entered the legal profession with 'immediate integration' into the norms and culture of the profession.[39] Whether as apprentices or as students in law school programmes, women who wanted to become lawyers pursued their goals as a small minority alongside much larger numbers of men. In addition, while women supported their claims to enter the medical profession on the basis that medicine was a logical extension of women's nurturing role and that women doctors were essential to protect the modesty of women patients, women who wished to become lawyers could not rely on either of these arguments. As Drachman explained, Victorian American society 'saw law as a profession that demanded not only cold objectivity and the mastery of facts, but also cunning, toughness, and the ability to deal with a sordid world;' by contrast with the hospitals in which women doctors worked, women lawyers had to enter boisterous courtrooms 'where criminals and individuals of ill repute were brought to justice for their deception, greed, and crime.'[40] As a result, women like Corinne Douglas, an early graduate in law from Michigan in 1887, concluded that 'there does not exist the same urgent need of lady-lawyers, as lady-physicians.'[41]

It seems that one of the results of these differences between medicine and law as professions for women was that women obtained medical qualifications several decades before women sought formal admission to the legal professions. Even prior to the Civil War, for example, Elizabeth Blackwell became the first woman doctor in the United States, graduating in 1849. After further medical studies in London and Paris, Blackwell returned to the United States in 1851 to discover that she was barred from hospitals and dispensaries in New York and snubbed by her colleagues; eventually, she established a part-time dispensary for poor women which became a full fledged hospital, the New York Infirmary for Women and Children.[42] Significantly, the Civil War created an enormous need for hospitals and doctors, and Mary Putnam Jacobi, another nineteenth-century woman doctor, claimed that the war enlarged the medical sphere for women.[43] As well, the War effectively created the profession of nurs-

39 VG Drachman, above, n 2 at 5 and at 149, citing MR Walsh, above, n 33. See also the Flexner Report, *Medical Education in the United States and Canada* (1910); R Stevens, above, n 15 at 102–3; and R Chester, *Unequal Access: Women Lawyers in a Changing America* (Mass, Bergin & Garvey Publishers, Inc, 1985).

40 VG Drachman, above, n 2 at 73–74, citing 'Modern Portias in Practice,' *New York Times*, 11 March 1894 at 16.

41 V Drachman, above, n 12 at 48–9. According to Drachman, at 219–22, Douglas was finally called to the bar in Georgia in 1920, along with her daughter.

42 BJ Harris, above, n 2 at 88–9. Similarly, Marie Zakrzewska graduated in medicine in the 1850s, with the help of Elizabeth Blackwell, and later founded the New England Hospital for Women and Children, which also provided female doctors with practical training.

43 BJ Harris, above, n 2 at 105–6. See also MR Walsh, above, n 33 at 132–3; and Jacobi, 'Woman in Medicine' in AN Meyer (ed), above, n 5 at 170–1.

ing, although there remained concerns about the moral temptations facing young women working among male soldiers; one of the women in charge of army nurses solved this problem by requiring that nurses be 'over thirty, plain, and thick waisted.'[44]

Thus, by the end of the Civil War, when the first women were beginning to seek formal admission to state bars in the United States, women had already begun to attend colleges and universities and some of them were succeeding in obtaining qualifications in the medical profession. As a result of the War, moreover, the country was experiencing a 'dramatic shift in values ... a time in which everything that had been familiar was now changing;' as Nancy Cott noted, high rates of mortality on both sides of the Civil War significantly changed the demographic circumstances so that 'the assumption that every woman would be a wife became questionable, perhaps untenable.'[45] Yet, even in these promising conditions, aspiring women lawyers faced particular kinds of barriers when they sought to enter the legal profession.

According to Drachman, most lawyers in the mid-nineteenth century gained admission to the profession by means of the apprenticeship process; thus, for example, it was by apprenticing in the same firm with her brother that Arabella Mansfield had qualified to take the bar examinations in Iowa in 1869. Similarly, although she also attended lectures at Union College of Law for a year, Ada Kepley had been trained in the office of her husband, a well known attorney, prior to going to law school.[46] However, as Robert Stevens explained, the history of apprenticeship as a means of entering the legal profession in the United States had begun to be seriously undermined in the early years of the nineteenth century. As he argued, 'the guild feeling within the legal profession and the somewhat mystical view with which the common law was regarded by learned lawyers' were increasingly challenged, so that apprenticeship requirements were abolished in Massachusetts in 1836, in Maine in 1837, and in New Hampshire in 1838. Indeed, although fourteen out of nineteen jurisdictions had required a period of apprenticeship in 1800, only eleven out of thirty did so in 1840; by 1860, apprenticeship was required in only nine of thirty-nine jurisdictions.[47] The informality, even laxity, of processes for gaining

---

[44] BJ Harris, above, n 2 at 97, referring to a comment by Dorothea Dix, superintendent of army nurses in 1861.

[45] NF Cott, *Public Vows: A History of Marriage and the Nation* (Cambridge, Mass, Harvard University Press, 2000) at 78–9. According to Cott, the Civil War killed more Americans than any other war in which the United States has been involved. See also MR Glazer and M Slater, above, n 19 at 4.

[46] HB Kepley was described by VGDrachman, above, n 12 at 235–8, as a well known attorney in Effingham, Illinois. He encouraged Ada to study law, perhaps as a result of a 'need for a clerical assistant with some legal knowledge.' See also KB Morello, above, n 4 at 49–51.

[47] R Stevens, above, n 15 at 7–8, citing AZ Reed, *Training for the Public Profession of the Law: Historical Development and Principal Contemporary Problems of Legal Education in the United States with Some Account of Conditions in England and Canada* (New York, 1921) at 86–7.

admission to the profession was captured in Burton Bledstein's account of a young would-be lawyer who was examined 'in a desultory way' by Abraham Lincoln in the latter's hotel room while he was dressing. According to Bledstein's account, the would-be lawyer was asked by Lincoln to define a contract, as well as two or three other basic questions. The rest of the 'examination' consisted of Lincoln's 'recollections – many of them characteristically vivid and racy – of his early practice and the various incidents and adventures that attended his start in the profession.' On this basis, Lincoln recommended the young man to the judge who was also a member of the committee appointed by the Board of Examiners in Illinois, and the judge gave the young man a certificate without further inquiry.[48] By the 1850s, however, 'the pendulum began to swing back.' As Stevens noted, even Lincoln concluded that more systematic training in law was desirable; in a conversation in 1855, Lincoln explained that he was going back to law school to ensure that his position at the Illinois bar would not be eroded by 'college-trained men.' By this time, according to Stevens, 'law was beginning once more to be seen as a learned profession.'[49]

Indeed, new ideas about standards of professionalism in law and new requirements for a good legal education began to emerge after the Civil War. Although scholars have offered different explanations for the increasing professionalisation of legal services in the United States in the latter part of the nineteenth century,[50] there is agreement that the model of legal practice began to change in the 1860s and 1870s from the 'circuit-rider–office lawyer' to include the new type of law firm, 'with several partners and assistants, catering to the needs of the developing corporation.'[51] The numbers of lawyers also increased significantly between 1850

[48] BJ Bledstein, *The Culture of Professionalism: The Middle Class and the Development of Higher Education in America* (New York, WW Norton & Company, Inc, 1976) at 164. See also JW Hurst, *The Growth of American Law: The Law Makers* (Boston, Little Brown and Company, 1950) at 282; and RL Abel, above, n 16 at 40–41.

[49] R Stevens, above, n 15 at 10 and 19, citing NW Stephenson, *An Autobiography of Abraham Lincoln* (Indianapolis, The Bobbs-Merrill Co, 1926) at 118.

[50] In her influential study in 1977, Larson examined the structural development of the legal profession in England and the United States in the context of the rise of capital markets in the nineteenth century, and concluded that two features defined a profession: a body of exclusive knowledge, and control over the process of entry: see MS Larson, *The Rise of Professionalism: A Sociological Analysis* (Berkeley, University of California Press, 1977). See also BJ Bledstein, above, n 48; GL Geison (ed), *Professions and Professional Ideologies in America* (Chapel Hill and London, University of North Carolina Press, 1983); E Freidson, *Professional Powers: A Study of the Institutionalization of Knowledge* (Chicago and London, University of Chicago Press, 1986); RL Abel, above, n 16 at 14; Andrew Abbott, *The System of Professions: An Essay on the Division of Expert Labor* (Chicago, University of Chicago Press, 1988); and Eliot Freidson, *Professionalism: The Third Logic* (Chicago, University of Chicago Press, 2001).

[51] R Stevens, above, n 15 at 22. Stevens' examples included the Cravath firm, which had emerged in upstate New York in 1820, and came to prominence after the Civil War, doing work for banks and railroads in New York City. Shearman and Sterling was created in 1873, and Sullivan and Cromwell in 1879.

and 1880; according to Stevens, there were just over 20,000 lawyers in 1850 but more than 60,000 in 1880.[52] In this context, some lawyers expressed concern about admission procedures and standards; indeed, when the American Bar Association was established in 1878, the raising of standards in the profession was high on its agenda.[53] Even more significantly, interest in making the study of law more rational and 'scientific' resulted in the establishment of systematic programmes of legal education, especially in university law schools. As Bledstein reported, the number of professional law schools doubled between 1870 and 1890, part of the success of new developments in American higher education.[54] In the same period, the case method of instruction, initially pioneered at Harvard Law School, was increasingly recognised as *the* major innovation in legal education, confirming the elite status of Harvard and similar law schools; as Stevens concluded, widespread acceptance of the case method resulted from its claims to 'science, apparent practicality, elitism, financial success, and "thinking like a lawyer".'[55]

In this context, aspiring women lawyers with family connections to the legal profession often apprenticed as part of their process of qualifying for admission to the bar. However, expanding opportunities for university legal education may have been more useful for those without such family connections, and its promise of more systematic educational programmes may have been more appealing to some women students. Yet, in spite of increasing numbers of university law schools and creative innovations in legal education, not all law schools welcomed women as law students; indeed, women were not even eligible for admission to programmes in several of the most prestigious law schools in the eastern states, including Harvard and Columbia. Although Alice Jordan managed to graduate from Yale Law School in the 1880s, as a result of her persistence in pointing out that there was no written policy which excluded her, Yale expressly

---

[52] R Stevens, above, n 15 at 22, citing AZ Reed, above, n 47 at 442.

[53] R Stevens, above, n 15 at 27. Stevens reported, at 28, that Lewis Delafield, President of the American Social Science Association, recommended a programme of legal education which included the study of legal principles in a law school, one year in an office, and a public bar examination; according to Stevens, 'the modern law school movement accelerated' in response to this recommendation.

[54] BJ Bledstein, above, n 48 at 190. Bledstein argued (at *x*) that the American university came into existence 'to serve and promote professional authority in society' and that the development of higher education after the Civil War 'made possible a social faith in merit, competence, discipline, and control that were basic to accepted conceptions of achievement and success.' See also TL Haskell, 'Power to the Experts: A Review of Burton Bledstein's *Culture of Professionalism*' in TL Haskell (ed), *Objectivity is not Neutrality: Explanatory Schemes in History* (Baltimore and London, John Hopkins University Press, 1998) 63.

[55] R Stevens, above, n 15 at 63–4. Stevens argued that the case method was attractive because it enabled the universities to establish large classes for purposes of instruction. See also RW Gordon, 'Legal Thought and Legal Practice in the Age of American Enterprise 1870–1920' in GL Geison (ed), above, n 50 at 70.

amended its admission materials a year after she graduated, returning to its men-only status.[56] Some schools were more welcoming: for example, Boston University Law School was opened to men and women in 1872, and law schools in the western states more often admitted women students along with men; all the same, California's Hastings Law School in San Francisco was opened to women in 1879 only as a result of a lawsuit by two of its prospective women students.[57] Moreover, even when women students were admitted, they were not always accorded the same privileges as men: when Belva Lockwood graduated from National University Law School in the District of Columbia in the 1870s, she and the one other woman student were not permitted to sit on the stage with their male classmates. Lockwood did not receive her diploma until three years after completing her studies, and then only as a result of writing an angry letter to Ulysses S Grant, President of the United States as well as of National University.[58] For women like Charlotte Ray, the first Black woman lawyer to graduate from Howard University, moreover, the challenges were even greater; a trustee of the law school expressed amazement about the 'colored woman who read ... a thesis on corporations, not copied from the books but from her brain, a clear incisive analysis of one of the most delicate legal questions.'[59] Thus, as Drachman concluded, Ray and other women who were the first to attend university law schools were pioneers, 'breaking cultural taboos and institutional barriers to attend law school among men.'[60] And, in spite of all the well-documented reforms in the legal professions and in the universities, and both ability and persistence on the part of some applicants, it remained especially difficult for blacks and women to qualify as lawyers.[61]

Thus, the first women lawyers in the United States gained entry to the legal profession in a context in which a strong women's movement sup-

[56] VG Drachman, above, n 2 at 46–8. Interestingly, as Drachman noted, Boston University Law School was founded to preserve the traditional lecture method of legal education, thus resisting the case method at Harvard.

[57] VG Drachman, above, n 2 at 47: the students were Clara Shortridge Foltz and Laura de Force Gordon. Foltz was the first woman admitted to the practice of law in California: see BA Babcock, 'Reconstructing the Person: The Case of Clara Shortridge Foltz' in SG Bell and M Yalom (eds), *Revealing Lives: Autobiography, Biography and Gender* (Albany, State University of New York Press, 1990) 131; and BA Babcock, 'Clara Shortridge Foltz: Constitution-Maker' (1990–91) 66 *Indiana Law Journal* 849. See also 'Clara Shortridge Foltz' and 'Laura de Force Gordon' in Stanford WLHP, above, n 4.

[58] MB Stern, 'Belva Ann Lockwood' in MB Stern (ed), *We the Women: Career Firsts of Nineteenth-Century America* (Lincoln and London, University of Nebraska Press, 1962) 205 at 211.

[59] KB Morello, above, n 4 at 146. See also JC Smith Jr, above, n 7 at 90 and 277, for information about Lutie A Lytle, the first Black woman to hold a teaching position in a 'Black' law school in Tennessee in 1897.

[60] VG Drachman, above, n 2 at 50. See also H Garza, *Barred from the Bar: A History of Women in the Legal Profession* (New York, Franklin Watts, 1996) at 81.

[61] R Stevens, above, n 15 at 181. Stevens documented, at 83, the intransigence of Langdell and others to women's demands. See also JS Auerbach, above, n 17, concerning the exclusion of immigrants and ethnic lawyers.

ported a broad range of equality goals, including access to higher education and the professions, and at a time of expanding opportunities in the practice of law and a new emphasis on systematic programmes of legal education. Yet, if the women's movement provided encouragement to women to aspire to become lawyers, some law schools responded unenthusiastically, and sometimes with resolute opposition to women's interest in studying law. By contrast with the education of women doctors in the United States, moreover, there were no separate institutions for educating women lawyers until almost the turn of the century, too late to be of assistance to women aspiring to become lawyers in the last decades of the nineteenth century.[62] Thus, in the context of major transformations in legal practice and legal education, the legal profession remained resolutely gendered. As Grossberg argued, changes in legal practices in the late nineteenth century 'compelled lawyers to articulate more clearly than ever before the gender assumptions of their profession; ... [as well], legal science [epitomised by the case method] reinforced the idea of law as a hard, manly occupation grounded in seemingly objective, deducible rules.'[63] Indeed, according to Grossberg, it was women's legal challenges to the male exclusivity of the profession which substantially served to define masculinity in the nineteenth-century legal community in the United States.[64]

In this way, although women's aspirations to become lawyers were central to the movement for women's equality, their aspirations frequently met resistance from both universities and state bars. Significantly, it was often the universities and state bars that were most committed to institutional reform that were also the most resistant to the entry of women; for example, Harvard, Columbia and Yale remained closed to women until well into the twentieth century. Thus, it appears that reformist ideas about an elite legal profession were fundamentally inconsistent with the admission of women: elite legal education and its connection to elite corporate law firms remained steadfastly defined by traditional ideas of white, Protestant masculinity.[65] At least to some extent, this context helps to explain variations in courts' receptivity to women's claims to become lawyers in different states, as well as the barriers later faced by women who practised law. In addition, however, this context provides the

62 Washington College of Law was established in 1898 by two women lawyers, Ellen Spencer Mussey and Emma Gillett. Washington College of Law and Portia Law School (founded in Boston in 1908 as an exclusively all-women's law school) trained more women lawyers in the early twentieth century than any other law schools in the United States, except New York University; however, as part time institutions, their graduates entered law at the bottom of the professional hierarchy: see VG Drachman, above, n 2 at 149–52; and R Chester, above, n 39.

63 M Grossberg, 'Institutionalizing Masculinity: The Law as a Masculine Profession' in MC Carnes and C Griffen (eds), *Meanings for Manhood: Constructions of Masculinity in Victorian America* (Chicago and London, University of Chicago Press, 1990) 133 at 143–4.

64 Even after formal barriers were overcome, 'informal constraints continued to decree the law a man's profession': M Grossberg, above, n 63 at 145 and 148.

65 JS Auerbach, above, n 17 at 23–32.

background for the litigation concerning women's eligibility for admission to the bar, shaping the legal arguments presented to courts and legislatures on behalf of aspiring women lawyers not only in the United States but also in other jurisdictions where women sought admission to the legal professions.

CONSTITUTIONALISING (IN)EQUALITY FOR WOMEN LAWYERS

Late-nineteenth-century judges struggled to develop a judicial rhetoric to rationalize women's secondary status in a potentially egalitarian constitutional regime. Paradoxically, the jurisprudence of separate spheres was created in response to a jurisprudence of integration, a new and competing judicial rhetoric that assumed that *women were equal with men*.[66]

Women's efforts to gain entry to the legal profession in the United States occurred after the Civil War, when the 'Reconstruction' amendments were being added to the American constitution: the 13th amendment abolished slavery in 1865; the 14th amendment assured equal protection in 1868; and the 15th amendment guaranteed freed (male) blacks the right to vote in 1870. Yet, as Drachman noted, the hopes of women's rights activists at this time were dashed because all these constitutional amendments left 'the status of women as citizens or voters unchanged.'[67] Women activists responded with both individual legal actions and collective political campaigns in their efforts to gain recognition as equal citizens under the constitution. For women who sought entry to the legal profession as well, arguments based on equal rights for women and men (a 'jurisprudence of integration') were adopted in both court challenges and lobbying efforts to obtain amending legislation. Yet, by contrast with women's equality arguments, judicial responses to their claims often asserted a doctrine of 'separate spheres' for women and men, and this doctrine was later reflected in the suffrage movement's emphasis on women's special role in preserving moral standards. Clearly these legal claims did not exist in isolation; as Hoff suggested, women's efforts to achieve constitutional equality were characterised by a 'seesaw relationship between political and legal action.'[68] In this context, however, it was particularly significant that legal arguments presented by aspiring women lawyers sometimes drew clear distinctions between women's right to practise law and their right to vote; in making such distinctions, aspiring women lawyers enhanced their

---

66 VG Drachman, above, n 2 at 11 (emphasis added): women lawyers adopted the language of equality or 'integration' from activists in the women's movement.
67 VG Drachman, above, n 2 at 14.
68 J Hoff, above, n 11 at 152.

opportunities to gain admission to the bar, but they simultaneously constrained broader reform efforts to achieve the franchise for all women. In this way, although the interests of women lawyers and suffrage activists in the United States had been closely connected immediately after the Civil War, they increasingly diverged in the latter decades of the nineteenth century; indeed, it seems that a number of successful women lawyers gradually adopted a professional identity as *lawyers*, one that increasingly distanced them from other *women* activists.

In the context of the women's movement just after the Civil War, however, the first judicial decision about women's eligibility to practise law must have seemed auspicious: in 1869, an Iowa court held that Arabella Mansfield was eligible for admission to the bar, even though she was a woman. When her application was initially reviewed by the state's examining committee, the committee acknowledged that the statute governing eligibility for the legal profession expressly provided for the admission of only 'white male persons.' At the same time, however, the committee suggested that this statutory language should be interpreted in accordance with the principle (included in another statutory provision) that 'words importing the masculine gender only may be extended to females.' According to the committee, therefore, Mansfield was fully qualified for admission to the bar, 'not only by the language of the law itself, but by the demands and necessities of the present time and occasion.'[69] The committee's report was then presented to Justice Francis Springer, described by Morello as 'one of the most liberal and progressive judges in Iowa,' and Springer not only accepted the argument that masculine words should be interpreted to include females, but also provided an expansive view of gendered language; according to Justice Springer, the inclusion of an affirmative declaration of gender could never be construed as an *implicit* denial that the right extended to females.[70] The court's conclusion was reinforced the following year when amending legislation was enacted which eliminated both the race and gender requirements in relation to eligibility for the bar in Iowa.[71]

The inclusiveness of Justice Springer's statutory interpretation, as well as subsequent confirmation of this approach by the Iowa legislature, dramatically illustrate how a state might respond positively to women's claims to become lawyers. Yet, just a few months after Mansfield's

[69] See AM Bittenbender, above, n 5 at 222.

[70] Both J Hoff, above, n 11 at 162, and KB Morello, above, n 4 at 12, identified the statutory provision as section 1610 of the *Iowa Code* of 1851; AM Bittenbender, above, n 5 at 222, included an excerpt from the report of the examining committee, referring to section 2700 of the *Revised Code* of 1860. The provisions are identical.

[71] J Hoff, above, n 11 at 162–3, explained that the amending legislation was part of the 1870 *Iowa Code*, noting that 'the deletion [of the words "white male"] occurred fortuitously; 'it cannot be said that the intent of the legislature was to strike a blow against either racism or sexism within the legal profession.'

admission to the Iowa bar, an application submitted by Myra Bradwell for admission to the Illinois bar was firmly rejected. Bradwell had worked with her husband in his law office before the Civil War, assisting him with legal research and writing. In 1868, she established the first law journal in the West, the *Chicago Legal News*. With Bradwell as the journal's publisher and business manager as well as its editor-in-chief, the newspaper offered conventional synopses of judicial decisions and news of the Chicago legal community.[72] However, Bradwell also used the journal as 'a forum from which to lobby for reform in many areas – from renovating the local courthouse to streamlining the legal process to extending suffrage and full legal equality to women.'[73] When she decided to seek admission to the Illinois bar in 1869, she was interviewed in accordance with the usual procedures and submitted the required certificates of qualification. Recognising that the fact that she was a woman might be an issue, she also filed a memorandum of law outlining arguments which confirmed that women were not disqualified from obtaining a license to practise law in Illinois.[74] In addition, Bradwell cited Mansfield's case in Iowa as precedent for an inclusive interpretation of the male eligibility requirement in the Illinois bar statute.

However, as Morello noted, 'Myra Bradwell did not have the benefit of a Judge Springer to liberally interpret the Illinois statutes.'[75] Moreover, Bradwell was unsuccessful in her efforts to gain admission to the bar of Illinois, not only before the Illinois Supreme Court,[76] but also in her subsequent appeal to the Supreme Court of the United States.[77] Notwithstanding her lack of success, however, her case remains important because she used the guarantees of the American constitution, as well as arguments about common law disabilities and principles of statutory interpretation, to support her application to become a woman lawyer. As a result, her

---

[72] JM Friedman, *America's First Woman Lawyer: The Biography of Myra Bradwell* (Buffalo, Prometheus Books, 1993) at 29–30. Friedman suggested that Bradwell's role as editor of the *Chicago Legal News* confirmed her 'as the country's first and leading woman lawyer.' In addition, she argued Bradwell's claim to be the first woman lawyer on the basis that the Supreme Court of Illinois granted Bradwell a license to practise law in 1890, and the United States Supreme Court did so in 1892; both licenses dated from her original application. See also G Gale, 'Myra Bradwell: The First Woman Lawyer' (1953) 39 *ABA Journal* 180; and C Sanger, 'Curriculum Vitae (Feminae): Biography and Early American Women Lawyers' (1994) 46 *Stanford Law Review* 1245, at 1261–2.

[73] NT Gilliam, 'A Professional Pioneer: Myra Bradwell's Fight to Practice Law' (1987) 5 *Law and History Review* 105 at 106.

[74] NT Gilliam, above, n 73 at 108–9. According to KB Morello, above, n 4 at 15, Bradwell was examined by Judge ES Williams and Charles H Reed, the State's Attorney; they recommended that a license be issued.

[75] KB Morello, above, n 4 at 16.

[76] *In re Bradwell*, 55 Ill 535 (1869).

[77] *Bradwell v Illinois*, 83 US (16 Wallace's Supreme Court Reports) 130 (1873). According to NT Gilliam, above, n 73 at 105, *Bradwell* was the first case of sex discrimination heard by the US Supreme Court; it was resolved against the woman claimant, as 'every subsequent claim but one for the next ninety-eight years.' See also J Hoff, above, n 11 at 247.

case illustrates the variety of legal arguments used to decide the issue of whether women were eligible to become lawyers in the United States in the nineteenth century, arguments that were later adopted in other jurisdictions, particularly Canada.

Interestingly, the Illinois Supreme Court initially relied on Bradwell's status as a married woman to deny her application, even though her status as a married woman did not form part of the record in the case.[78] Moreover, Bradwell was clearly already involved in business as a married woman; indeed, before she published the first issue of the *Chicago Legal News* in 1868, she had 'successfully petitioned the Illinois legislature for a special act authorizing her to transact business independent[ly] of her husband.'[79] Incensed by the court's rejection of her application on the basis of her status as a married woman, Bradwell printed the clerk's letter confirming the court's decision on the front page of her journal; she then submitted a supplemental brief.[80] When the court released a further decision, the judges prudently limited their rejection of her application to the fact that Bradwell was a woman. In stark contrast to the reasoning in Mansfield's case in Iowa, however, the Illinois court concluded that the judges had no jurisdiction to admit persons 'not intended by the Legislature to be admitted, even though their exclusion [was] not expressly required by statute.' As Nancy Gilliam suggested, the judicial role in this case was one of deference to the legislature, particularly on a novel question such as women's roles in the professions: 'the temper of the times encouraged a passive, not an active, judiciary, at least in social matters.'[81] Thus, while Mansfield had successfully gained admission to the bar in Iowa in 1869, Bradwell's application was denied in Illinois just a few months later.

Significantly, while the same arguments about common law disabilities and statutory interpretation were presented in these two cases, the judges responded to them quite differently.[82] While the Iowa court illustrated a willingness to adopt an expansive interpretation of legislative language in the context of changing social roles for women, the Illinois court was more

[78] KB Morello, above, n 4 at 16: the clerk of the court wrote to Bradwell, advising that her application had been denied 'upon the ground that [Bradwell] would not be bound by the obligations necessary to be assumed where the relation of attorney and client shall exist, by reason of the disability imposed by your married condition – it being assumed that you are a married woman.'

[79] NT Gilliam, above, n 73 at 110.

[80] As NT Gilliam explained, above, n 73 at 109–10, Bradwell's supplemental brief was 'carefully crafted to provide the court with ample precedent to grant her application should the justices be inclined to make law.'

[81] NT Gilliam, above, n 73 at 111–12.

[82] NT Gilliam, above, n 73 at 110–13, examined the legal context in which the *Bradwell* decision was rendered, including the enactment of married women's property legislation in Illinois, and the courts' tendency to interpret this reform narrowly. See also A Sachs and J Hoff Wilson, above, n 11 at 97–8.

cautious, defining its role narrowly in relation to the legislature and the court's limited mandate for 'making law;' responding to this responsibility for legal change, the legislature enacted amending legislation a few years later, enabling a number of women to be admitted to the bar in Illinois over the next few decades.[83] However, the differing approaches of the courts in Iowa and Illinois were clearly reflected in subsequent challenges on the part of women who claimed eligibility for admission to the bar in other American states: sometimes courts granted their applications, and at other times, courts deferred to state legislatures.[84] Although Gilliam argued that even Bradwell herself could not have been surprised by the outcome of her application in Illinois,[85] Bradwell's response in the *Chicago Legal News* was scathing: 'what the decision of the Supreme Court of the United States in the Dred Scott case was to the rights of negroes as citizens of the United States, this decision is to the political rights of women in Illinois – annihilation.'[86] Bradwell later responded just as caustically to the argument that women were not eligible for admission to the bar in Illinois because female attorneys-at-law were then unknown in England, stating:

> According to our Canadian and English brothers it would be cruel to allow a woman to 'embark upon the rough and troubled sea of actual legal practice,' but not to allow her to govern all England with Canada and other dependencies thrown in. Our brothers will get used to it and then it will not seem any worse to them to have women practicing in the courts than it does now to have a queen rule over them.[87]

In addition to a deferential approach to the interpretation of women's common law disabilities and statutory principles in Bradwell's case in Illinois, however, the case assumed additional legal significance because Bradwell eventually appended constitutional arguments to her application for admission to the bar.[88] According to Drachman, the addition of these

---

[83] Alta Hulett's application for admission to the bar had been rejected in 1871; she then engaged in lobbying for a legislative amendment, supported by Myra Bradwell, Ada Kepley and the *Chicago Legal News*. The legislature passed the statute in 1872 (see 1871 Ill Laws 578); however, it imposed new requirements for admission to the bar, including an additional year of study. Hulett was admitted on 6 June 1873: see GH McNamee, 'Alta May Hulett,' in GH McNamee (ed), *Bar None: 125 Years of Women Lawyers in Illinois* (Chicago, Chicago Bar Association Alliance for Women, 1998) 7 at 8. See also NT Gilliam, above, n 73 at 128–9.

[84] See VG Drachman, above, n 2 at 251–3 (Table I); and KB Morello, above, n 4 at 37–8. See also IM Pettus, above, n 2 at 244.

[85] NT Gilliam, above, n 73 at 112–13, noted that Bradwell had also been denied an appointment as notary public in late 1869 because she was a married woman.

[86] KB Morello, above, n 4 at 18; see also *Dred Scott v Sandford*, 60 United States Supreme Court Reports 394 (1857); and J Hoff, above, n 11 at 173.

[87] KB Morello, above, n 4 at 18. See (June 1880) 16 *Canada Law Journal* 161; and (19 June 1880) *Chicago Legal News*. See also J Becker, 'Myra Colby Bradwell: Sisterhood, Strategy & Family,' Stanford WLHP, above, n 4.

[88] See NT Gilliam, above, n 73 at 114.

constitutional arguments occurred after the Bradwells met with Elizabeth Cady Stanton and Susan B Anthony in late 1869;[89] Bradwell's additional arguments included an equal rights claim pursuant to the 14th amendment's guarantee of equal protection, as well as a claim that the scope of the 'privileges and immunities' clause precluded the state from preventing her admission to the bar.[90] The Illinois court did not rule on either of these constitutional arguments, and even Senator Matthew Carpenter, Bradwell's counsel before the US Supreme Court, ignored the equal rights claim; as Gilliam suggested, Bradwell's emphasis on equality pursuant to the 14th amendment was 'generations ahead of her time.'[91] Moreover, as later commentators have generally explained, the 'privileges and immunities' arguments in Bradwell's case became entangled with an appeal by New Orleans butchers, the *Slaughter-House Cases,* which also concerned the scope of the 'privileges and immunities' clause and the extent to which the federal government could interfere with state legislation,[92] matters on which there was little jurisprudence in the early 1870s. Both in *Bradwell* and in the *Slaughter-House Cases,* the constitutional issue was 'whether the freedom to pursue an occupation was a privilege and immunity of United States citizenship which could be protected by the federal courts against state restriction.'[93] Just as the butchers claimed that the state had no right to force them to abide by a monopoly at the risk of being excluded from their occupation, so Bradwell claimed that the state of Illinois could not deny her the right to practise law if she were qualified. Ultimately, after numerous delays, a majority of five justices held that the scope of the privileges and immunities clause was not sufficient to negate the state monopoly legislation in the *Slaughter-House Cases.*[94] However, the decision was a narrow victory, and opposing views were clearly evident in the forceful opinions written by three of the four dissenting judges in favour of the butchers' freedom to carry on their trade. By contrast, in

[89] VG Drachman, above, n 2 at 17, citing EC DuBois, *Feminism and Suffrage: The Emergence of an Independent Women's Movement in America, 1848–1869* (Ithaca, Cornell University Press, 1978).

[90] The 14th amendment required that no state 'deny to any person within its jurisdiction the equal protection of the laws;' and precluded states from making or enforcing laws which 'abridge the privileges or immunities of citizens of the United States.' See NT Gilliam, above, n 73 at 114–16.

[91] NT Gilliam, above, n 73 at 114–15.

[92] *Slaughter-House Cases,* 38 US (16 Wallace's Supreme Court Reports) 36 (1873). See also VG Drachman, above, n 2 at 22 ff; J Hoff, above, n 11 at 165; and NT Gilliam, above, n 73 at 116.

[93] NT Gilliam, above, n 73 at 118.

[94] J Hoff argued, above, n 11 at 165, that the court's interpretation was so severely narrow that the clause 'has been virtually unused since.' Matthew Carpenter, who represented Bradwell, was counsel for the state monopoly in the *Slaughter-House Cases,* and thus opposed to the butchers; as a result, Hoff suggested, at 168–9, that 'Carpenter's victory as an attorney in the [*Slaughter-House Cases*] seems to have set the stage for the defeat in [*Bradwell*].' See also A Sachs and J Hoff Wilson, above, n 11 at 100.

denying that Bradwell's right to practise law was protected by the constitution, eight of the nine justices were in agreement, and the sole dissenting judge did not write an opinion.[95]

In spite of the disappointing outcome of her constitutional challenge, Bradwell continued to publish and edit the *Chicago Legal News* for two decades after 1873; the negative outcome of her case did not appear to affect her own life in any practical way.[96] Moreover, the decision did not prevent other women from gaining admission to the Illinois bar after the legislature enacted amending legislation; indeed, by 1900, about one hundred women had been admitted to the bar in Illinois.[97] Thus, the decision of the Supreme Court did not seriously impede the admission of women as lawyers in Illinois. Nonetheless, the *Bradwell* case was highly significant for women who sought to become lawyers in other states, and later on in other jurisdictions. As a decision of the highest court in the United States, it provided an important precedent confirming that there was no constitutional basis for the admission of women to the legal profession, even if later courts did not always take account of the precise constitutional principles which were at issue in *Bradwell*.[98] Certainly, the *Bradwell* decision utterly failed to extend the scope of equal protection in the 14th amendment to women's claims for admission to the legal profession.

Even more importantly, the *Bradwell* decision included a concurring opinion by Justice Bradley which confirmed that women were barred from the practice of law because women and men occupied 'separate spheres.' According to this view, 'it was the law of nature that women both lived in separate spheres from men and that the practice of law was closed to women':[99]

[95] According to NT Gilliam, above, n 73 at 125, the newly appointed Justice Ward Hunt sided with Justices Miller, Clifford, Davis and Strong in the *Slaughter-House Cases* against an expansive reading of the 13th and 14th amendments; Justices Chase, Field, Swayne and Bradley dissented, and all but Chief Justice Chase wrote opinions. By contrast, in *Bradwell*, the vote was 8:1, with Chief Justice Chase the lone dissenter, and he did not write an opinion. Although Justice Hunt had not yet been appointed to the Court when *Bradwell* was argued, Gilliam concluded that he had taken part in the decision. See also KB Morello, above, n 4 at 19.

[96] In an interview in 1889, Bradwell stated that her business had become so significant by the time the decision was handed down by the Supreme Court that she 'had no time to give to law practice,' and she didn't care to be admitted 'just for the privilege of putting "Attorney" after [her] name': JM Friedman, above, n 72 at 29, citing an interview with the *Chicago Tribune*, 12 May 1889 at 26. By that time, her husband, James Bradwell, had also been appointed to the bench. See also C Goddard and GH McNamee, 'Myra Colby Bradwell' in GH McNamee (ed), above, n 83; and J Becker, above, n 87.

[97] GH McNamee, above, n 83 at 32–3, lists 101 women lawyers *admitted to the bar* of Illinois by 1900; however, IM Pettus, above, n 2 at 244, notes only eighty-seven women lawyers *in practice* in 1900.

[98] J Hoff, above, n 11 at 170.

[99] VG Drachman, above, n 2 at 18.

... [The] civil law, as well as nature herself, has always recognized a wide difference in the respective spheres and destinies of man and woman. Man is, or
should be, woman's protector and defender. The natural and proper timidity
and delicacy which belongs to the female sex evidently unfits it for many of the
occupations of civil life. The constitution of the family organization, which is
founded in the divine ordinance, as well as in the nature of things, indicates the
domestic sphere as that which properly belongs to the domain and functions of
womanhood. The harmony, not to say identity, of interests and views which
belong or should belong to the family institution is repugnant to the idea of a
woman adopting a distinct and independent career from that of her husband....[100]

Thus, the *Bradwell* case not only provided a precedent from the highest
court in the United States, one which clearly denied women's right to
practise law, but it also confirmed that 'separate spheres' existed, *as a
matter of law*, for men and women. As a result, the *Bradwell* case firmly
entrenched a 'jurisprudence of separate spheres,' not only for women
in the United States, but also in other jurisdictions where judges used
Bradwell to deny claims submitted by aspiring women lawyers.

As Hoff argued, moreover, *Bradwell* was also significant because its
reasoning was used to deny broader claims concerning women's constitutional rights as citizens. Particularly in relation to the suffrage issue, the
narrow interpretation of the 'privileges and immunities' clause in *Bradwell*
severely limited the scope of federal review of state legislation that
precluded women from voting,[101] a problem which women activists tried
to address both in their political campaigns and in their subsequent court
challenges. Thus, after the *Bradwell* decision in the US Supreme Court,
Susan B Anthony wrote to Bradwell, asking for a detailed report of the
case; according to Jane Friedman, while prominent women activists
regretted the *Bradwell* decision, they hoped to be able to derive political
capital from the court's rejection of a woman of Bradwell's stature. In
promising to submit a report of Bradwell's case to an upcoming women's
rights convention, therefore, Anthony promised that the convention would
'pour hot shot into that old Court.'[102] However, in Anthony's celebrated
trial later in 1873 on the charge of voting without a right to do so, the
Bradwell decision proved to be a major barrier to women's claims to
equality in terms of the right to vote.[103] In this way, as Hoff argued,

[100] *Bradwell v Illinois*, above, n 77 at 141–2; and see KB Morello, above, n 4 at 20. As J Hoff
noted, above, n 11 at 165–6, Justice Bradley conceded that single women were not affected by
these duties and incapacities, but he regarded them as exceptions, since 'the paramount destiny
and mission of women [was] to fulfill the noble and benign offices of wife and mother': *Bradwell*
at 143.
[101] J Hoff, above, n 11 at 152.
[102] JM Friedman, above, n 72 at 27.
[103] *US v Anthony*, 24 Fed Cas 829 (CCNDNY 1873); *Bradwell* was also used to deny
women's right to vote in *Minor v Happersett*, 88 United States Supreme Court Reports 162
(1875). See also A Sachs and J Hoff Wilson, above, n 11 at 104–5.

Bradwell's effort to establish her constitutional right to practise law resulted in a negative precedent which was then used by judges to deny other women's claims to the right to vote.[104] Indeed, even Bradwell's counsel in the Supreme Court acknowledged opposition fears that permitting women to practise law would lead to female suffrage, 'which it is assumed, would overthrow Christianity, defeat the ends of modern civilization, and upturn the world.'[105] Thus, although Bradwell's claim was unsuccessful, it also emphasised the distinction between the 'reasonable' claims of women lawyers, by contrast with the more 'radical' efforts of women who were suffrage activists.

After the negative outcome of Bradwell's appeal to the Supreme Court blocked the possibility of further successful court challenges, many women activists turned to political action and lobbying efforts at state legislatures in their efforts to achieve suffrage and other women's rights goals, including the right to be admitted to the legal professions. However, women also continued to use the courts.[106] In some of these post-*Bradwell* cases, judges denied women's eligibility to practise law, citing *Bradwell* as a precedent for this conclusion. In addition, the jurisprudence of separate spheres, enunciated by Justice Bradley in *Bradwell* was often vigorously reasserted. Thus, when Lavinia Goodell applied for admission to the bar in 1875 in Wisconsin,[107] Justice Ryan's judgment denying her application fully reflected Justice Bradley's jurisprudence of separate spheres in *Bradwell*:

> There are many employments in life not unfit for female character. The profession of law is surely not one of these. The peculiar qualities of womanhood, its gentle graces, its quick sensibility, its tender susceptibility, its purity, its delicacy, its emotional impulses, its subordination of hard reason to sympathetic feeling, are surely not qualifications for forensic strife. Nature has tempered women as

104 J Hoff, above, n 11 at 173–5 and 187–91, suggested that the New York court which heard Anthony's case may have known that counsel for Bradwell in the US Supreme Court had clearly argued that women's right to practise law was quite different from women's right to vote: Matthew Carpenter had explained that voting was a 'political right,' while the right to an occupation was a right of citizenship. As a result, Hoff argued that after the decisions in *Bradwell*, above, n 77, and in *Anthony* and *Minor*, above, n 103, 'the only way that women could claim full citizenship was in a masculine voice.'

105 J Hoff, above, n 11 at 168. According to NT Gilliam, above, n 73 at 116–20, Carpenter was known as a superb orator, but his brief in *Bradwell* was not 'a model of legal consistency or adherence to the record;' it also 'disassociated Bradwell's quest for admission to the bar from the campaign for women's suffrage.' Carpenter was unopposed in the appeal to the Supreme Court.

106 See VG Drachman, above, n 2 at 251–3 (Table I).

107 *In re Goodell*, 39 Wisconsin Reports 232 (1875); see also KB Morello, above, n 4 at 22–4: Goodell was the daughter of the abolitionist, William Goodell, and apprenticed in a law firm known for its commitment to social reform. In 1874, she was admitted to practice in the local Circuit Court of Rock County. Bradwell supported Goodell's application to the Wisconsin Supreme Court in the *Chicago Legal News*, suggesting that the issue was whether Goodell would be 'allowed to continue [her practice], or be financially ruined because she [was] a woman.' See also DK Weisberg, above, n 1 at 487–91; and TM Derichsweiler, 'The Life of Lavinia Goodell: Wisconsin's First Woman Lawyer,' Stanford WLHP, above, n 4.

little for the judicial conflicts of the courtroom as for the physical conflicts of the battlefield. Womanhood is moulded for gentler and better things.... [By contrast, a court] has essentially and habitually to do with all that is selfish and malicious, knavish and criminal, coarse and brutal, repulsive and obscene, in human life. It would be revolting to all female sense of the innocence and sanctity of their sex, shocking to man's reverence for womanhood and faith in woman ... that woman should be permitted to mix professionally in all the nastiness of the world which finds its way into courts of justice....[108]

In thus concluding that Goodell was not eligible for admission to the bar, the court also warned that any conclusion that women were allowed to practise law would 'emasculate the constitution itself and include females in the constitutional right of male suffrage and male qualification. Such a rule would be one of judicial revolution, not of judicial construction.'[109] As a result of a legislative amendment to the Wisconsin statute a few years later, however, Goodell was admitted to the Wisconsin Supreme Court in 1879, with Justice Ryan still dissenting.[110]

A similar pattern occurred when Belva Lockwood applied for admission to a federal court, the Court of Claims. In denying her application in 1873, Justice Nott declared that even legislatures might not have authority over women's legal status because it was 'by an unwritten law interwoven with the very fabric of society;' certainly, the court had no jurisdiction to admit a woman to practise before it.[111] A few years later, when the Supreme Court also denied her admission, Lockwood addressed a Washington convention of women suffragists, arguing that it was not necessary to understand any of the technicalities of the law to explain the decision; the court had relied simply on the absence of a legal precedent that women were eligible for admission to the bar. In presenting this argument to the convention, Madeleine Stern described Lockwood's inimitable style as 'a Portia of the Venetian bar transposed to Washington' with her 'velvet dress and train, her eyes blazing with indignation, [marching] up and down the platform.'[112] With the help of male supporters in Congress and the Senate, however, Lockwood was eventually successful in obtaining a legislative amendment to permit women to be admitted to the federal courts of the

---

[108] *In re Goodell*, above, n 107 at 245–6.

[109] *In re Goodell*, above, n 107 at 242.

[110] *In re Goodell*, 48 Wisconsin Reports 693 (1879). See also J Hoff, above, n 11 at 163. According to a contemporary account, most reports favoured Goodell; and Goodell herself reviewed the decision in the *Chicago Legal News* 'and unquestionably had the better of him in the argument': see 'Women as Lawyers' (1879) 23 *Lippincott's Magazine of Popular Literature and Science* 386 at 387. However, Elsi B Botensak was the first woman to become a lawyer in Wisconsin in 1878: see VG Drachman, above, n 2 at 251.

[111] *In re Lockwood*, 8 Court of Claims Reports 346 (1873) at 355. See also VG Drachman, above, n 2 at 27; and KB Morello, above, n 4 at 33–4.

[112] MB Stern, above, n 58 at 216.

United States, including the Supreme Court.[113] In 1879, she became the first woman to be admitted to the Supreme Court of the United States. For at least one newspaper, this achievement was greeted with the confident assertion that 'the country was [nonetheless] still safe and the home was not in peril.'[114]

Thus, after the release of the *Bradwell* decision in 1873, the earlier pattern of women being admitted to the bar, at least in some cases, by the courts was replaced by the need to seek an amendment from state legislatures or Congress, as happened for both Goodell and Lockwood.[115] However, in the 1880s, a few courts once again began to grant women's applications for admission to state bars. In doing so, of course, judges could not ignore the impact of the binding legal precedent in *Bradwell*, and so legal arguments supporting women's right to practise law strategically changed.[116] In *In re Ricker* in New Hampshire in 1890, for example, the court held that a woman was entitled to practise law because the role of attorney did not constitute a public office; as such, the right to practise law could be distinguished from the right to hold public office, and more importantly, from the right to vote:

> The principle by which the question of judicial power to grant the petition in this case is to be determined seems plain and simple.... By our common law, women do not vote in town meeting. The reason is that voting is an exercise of governmental power. For the same reason, and by the same law, they do not hold public office. The reason of the rule does not exclude them from an occupation in which they would take no official part in the government of the country. The question is whether an attorney at law is an officer of government within the reason and purpose of the rule. If a licensed attorney, being a public officer in a special and limited sense, is not a public officer in the ordinary sense, and by virtue of his office takes no official part in the government, the

---

113 See MB Stern, above, n 58 at 214–20. The case started with Lockwood's application for admission to the Court of Claims, a federal court, in 1873; when she was denied admission, she appealed to the Supreme Court of the United States, which issued its decision in 1876. VG Drachman, above, n 2 at 27, reported that the Senate eventually passed the legislative amendment by a two-vote majority; as Stern noted, however, at 219, the two-vote majority on 7 February 1879 was actually created by 39 yeas, 20 nays and 17 abstentions.

114 MB Stern, above, n 58 at 220, citing JW Forney's *Progress*. Lockwood unsuccessfully appealed to the Supreme Court when Virginia refused to admit her to the state bar on the ground that the legislation contained only male pronouns: see *In re Lockwood*, 154 United States Supreme Court Reports 116 (1894); and A Sachs and J Hoff Wilson, above, n 11 at 105–6. In 1904, at the age of seventy-six, Lockwood appeared before the Supreme Court on behalf of the Eastern and Emigrant Cherokees to successfully claim payment of over $4 million in interest in a settlement of their land claims. See also FA Cook, 'Belva Lockwood: For Peace, Justice, and President,' Stanford WLHP, above, n 4.

115 See VG Drachman, above, n 2 at 251–3 (Table I).

116 According to VG Drachman, above, n 2 at 27, the 'rhetorical stridency of judges' natural law decisions' became muted, and judges reinterpreted the jurisprudence of separate spheres to be based on the inability of women lawyers to hold public office': see *Robinson's Case*, 131 Massachusetts Reports 376 (1881).

admission of women to the bar would not be a violation of our common law....
Giving due weight to history, tradition, and usage, it does not appear that members of the New Hampshire bar are public officers in any other sense than that
in which they are officers of the court....[117]

Even prior to *Ricker*, moreover, a court had admitted Mary Hall to the
bar of Connecticut in 1882 by characterising the role of an attorney as a
'lower' kind of public officer.[118] And, although a court in Massachusetts
had rejected this argument in relation to Lelia Robinson's application for
admission to the bar in the same year, Drachman rightly concluded that
the decision in the Connecticut court represented a new approach to
women's entitlement to become members of the bar.[119]

At the same time, Drachman's conclusion that the jurisprudence of
integration began to replace the jurisprudence of separate spheres in *Hall*
and later cases requires careful examination. In terms of the legal arguments adopted, for example, it was probably important that Hall's case
was litigated in 1882, almost a decade after the Supreme Court's decision
in *Bradwell*; moreover Ricker's case in 1890 was nearly two decades later.
By the time that Hall and Ricker were presenting their claims to become
lawyers, the courts' jurisprudence of separate spheres was increasingly
confronted with concrete evidence of women being admitted to a number
of different state bars and practising law, apparently with some success. As
the number of women lawyers steadily increased, Justice Bradley's views
about women's 'natural' domestic sphere would have appeared increasingly divergent from the reality of women practising law in a number of
states. Yet, even for judges who were inclined to respond more favourably
to women's applications for admission to the bar, the *Bradwell* precedent
represented a formidable legal barrier, requiring them to formulate an
argument which supported women's right to become lawyers but which
was not inconsistent with the reasoning of the Supreme Court. In this
context, the issue of whether attorneys were public officers assumed significance a decade after *Bradwell*, not only because the social context had
changed but also because these arguments were available to post-*Bradwell*
courts (not having formed part of the Supreme Court precedent). In this

---

[117] *In re Ricker*, 66 New Hampshire Reports 207 (1890); 29 A Rep 559 at 583–4. Marilla
Ricker's case was argued by Lelia Robinson, who had achieved admission to the bar of
Massachusetts in 1882 after the enactment of amending legislation. The lengthy judgment in
Ricker referred to older cases concerning the role of attorneys in England and the United States.

[118] *In re Hall*, 50 Connecticutt Reports 131 (1882). According to VG Drachman, above, n 2
at 31, *Hall* was 'one of five decisions between 1882 and 1893 [which] admitted women lawyers
by judicial decision rather than legislative statute': the other states were Pennsylvania,
Colorado, New Hampshire and Indiana.

[119] VG Drachman, above, n 2 at 27–32; see also *In re Hall*, above, n 118 at 137, and *In re
Robinson*, 131 Massachusetts Reports 376 (1881). Significantly, when Robinson had earlier
sought entry to the bar of Massachusetts, she had argued that the right to practise law need not
include the right to vote.

way, courts in the 1880s adopted legal arguments about whether the role of attorney constituted a 'public office' so as to accomplish a legal outcome that was more congruent with social facts. All the same, the *Bradwell* precedent was not overturned; indeed, it remained in place to support arguments against the admission of women to the bar decades later in a number of Canadian cases.

Similarly, the negative outcome in Lelia Robinson's case in Massachusetts in 1882 revealed the strength of continuing judicial opposition to women lawyers in a large Eastern state. Indeed, there were a number of states like Massachusetts, in which legislation rather than judicial discretion was needed to permit women's entry to the legal profession in the 1880s and 1890s. Significantly, moreover, the success of women's claims in the courts in the 1880s created increasing problems within the women's movement because of the arguments adopted in these later cases. By arguing that women could practise law because attorneys were not public officers, so that the right to practise law was distinguishable from 'public' acts, *including voting*, women lawyers succeeded in their individual court actions – but they did so, at least to some extent, by undermining legal arguments that supported women's right to vote. The success of women lawyers' arguments may also suggest that courts were content to accept the claims of *the few* women who wished to practise law, simultaneously forestalling claims on the part of *the many* women for the vote and the right to hold public office. Thus, by using the argument that an attorney was not a public office, individual women lawyers succeeded in gaining access to the legal profession, but they simultaneously distanced themselves from the broader goals of the women's movement, and especially from its suffrage campaigns. Indeed, it seems that woman lawyers consciously failed to respond to requests from women activists to delay their efforts to gain admission to the bar until 'women had gained equal citizenship with men.'[120] Certainly, admission to the bar on the ground that the role of attorney did not constitute a public office hardly represents a strong claim about women's equality with men. In this way, it seems that the first women who became lawyers in the United States chose arguments that were effective in achieving their immediate objective of admission to the legal profession; in the process, they also created problematic legal precedents for the broader goals of equality within the women's movement.

In addition, it is arguable that these first women lawyers were beginning to forge a 'professional identity' as lawyers; emphasising that they were *lawyers* rather than *women*, they claimed the right to practise law as

---

[120] VG Drachman, above, n 2 at 36, quoting MP Jacobi, *'Common Sense' Applied to Woman Suffrage* (New York, G P Putnam's Sons, 1915) at 55–6. According to Drachman, women lawyers disagreed with Putnam Jacobi's views on the basis that 'the practice of law was only a part of a broad movement to achieve equal rights, one that also encompassed gaining admission to law schools [and to the practice of law] on a par with men.'

professionals, without regard to either gender or the broader goals of women's equality. Indeed, Nancy Cott argued that although the first women who entered male professions like law saw their attempts as part of 'the cause of women...,' it was also clear that 'professional ideology ... was increasingly magnetic' by the end of the nineteenth century;[121] indeed, ideas about 'dispassionate professionalism' were to become increasingly attractive to women in the early twentieth century,[122] especially after the franchise was achieved at the end of World War I:

> The professional ethos, with its own promise of freedom from sex-defined constraints, was released to flourish in aspiring women's minds. Women professionals in the 1920s did not deny the instrumentality of feminism in breaking down barriers to women's first entry to the professions, but they assumed that since women had been admitted to professional ground and no formal bar remained, the professions' supposedly neutral and meritocratic ideology was not only their best armor but their only hope. As the scientific areas ... led the way, emphasizing that the professions' hallmarks were objectivity, empiricism, rationality, impersonality, and collegially determined standards, feminism seemed more openly to conflict with those hallmarks. The intensification of the perceived conflict between feminism and professionalism was part and parcel of a larger process of purging politics, advocacy, or reform from within professional definition....[123]

Cott's analysis suggests that it was the combined effect of achieving the longstanding suffrage goal after World War I, coupled with the rise of a dominant professional ideology, which resulted in women lawyers adopting a primary identification as *lawyers* in the early twentieth century. That is, since the goals of the American women's movement had narrowed to an almost exclusive focus on the achievement of suffrage, the successful enactment of the 19th amendment of the US constitution after World War I rendered the women's movement almost redundant. And, simultaneously, a new professional ideology was encouraging professional women to see 'a community of interest between themselves and professional men and a gulf between themselves and nonprofessional women.'[124] Moreover, in the

---

121 NF Cott, *The Grounding of Modern Feminism* (New Haven and London, Yale University Press, 1987) at 232. As Cott reported, 'there was a lively debate among the few women lawyers in the 1880s whether a woman should pursue her profession *because* of her sex ... or must *forget* her sex in order to pursue her profession.' (emphasis in original).

122 According to a report in 1896, women lawyers were being 'received and recognized by their brother members of the profession': see 'Women Lawyers' (1896) 83 *Leslie's Illustrated Weekly* 363.

123 NF Cott, above, n 121 at 233–4; according to Cott, 'the professional credo, that individual merit would be judged according to objective and verifiable standards, made a promise so potent to women professionals that they upheld the ideal even when they saw it travestied in practice.' See also F Stricker, 'Cookbooks and Law Books: The Hidden History of Career Women in Twentieth-Century America' in NF Cott and EH Pleck (eds), above, n 3 at 476.

124 NF Cott, above, n 121 at 237.

early years of the twentieth century, the professions' claim to 'a dis-passionate search for truth,' judging practitioners on merit as persons, not as men or women, was essential to the professions' new self-definitions.[125] Thus, for women in the legal profession, their gender became irrelevant: they were simply *lawyers*.[126] Even Belva Lockwood, the first woman candidate for President in two elections in the 1880s and a tireless reformer, declined to describe herself as 'a New Woman' or as someone who directly attacked the 'conventionalities' of society: 'I do not believe in sex distinction in literature, law, politics, or trade; or that modesty and virtue are more becoming to women than to men; but wish we had more of it everywhere.'[127] Moreover, although some features of legal profession-alism were not fully developed until the early decades of the twentieth century, women who were becoming lawyers in the last decades of the nineteenth century were already engaged in lively debates about their new roles as women in the legal profession.

WOMEN'S RIGHTS AND PROFESSIONAL IDENTITIES

... Just go quietly on, getting a start in some established office if possible, and make practical lawyers of yourselves. If some little matters seem unpleasant, merely take them as matters of course, and pay no attention to them. *Do not take sex into the practice.* Don't be 'lady lawyers.' Simply be *lawyers*, and rec-ognize no distinction – no existence of any distinction between yourselves and the other members of the bar. This will be your surest way to ... achieve success. Let no one regard you as a curiosity or a *rara avis*. Compel recognition of your ability and respect for your industry from all. You can take this stand and yet in no wise cease to be ladies – true ladies in every sense of the word.[128]

Lelia Robinson's letter to other women lawyers in 1887 reveals her firm commitment to legal professionalism and her rejection of the status of 'lady lawyer;' paradoxically, her letter also shows that she wished to retain

[125] NF Cott, above, n 121 at 237.

[126] For example, when Ellen Spencer Mussey, a law graduate of the 1880s and co-founder of the Washington College of Law, spoke to the International Council of Women meeting in Toronto in 1909, she encouraged women to study law to enable them to have opportunities for 'service to one's fellow-men': E Spencer Mussey, 'The Woman Attorney and Counsellor' in National Council of Women of Canada (ed), *Report of the International Congress of Women, Toronto: 24–30 June 1909*, vol 2 (Toronto, Geo Parker & Sons, 1910) 332 at 334.

[127] MB Stern, above, n 58 at 233. As Stern reported, at 222–7, Lockwood was a candidate for the Presidency of the United States, for the Equal Rights Party, in 1884 and again in 1888. One year after her admission to the US Supreme Court in 1880, Lockwood moved the admission of Samuel R Lowery, the first Southern Black to be admitted to the Supreme Court. In relation to 'new women,' see R Brandon, *The New Women and the Old Men: Love, Sex and the Woman Question* (London, Flamingo, 1991).

[128] V Drachman, above, n 12 at 66: letter of Lelia J Robinson, 1887 (emphasis in original). See also V Drachman, at 257–62; S Killingsworth, 'Lelia Robinson,' Stanford WLHP, above, n 4; M Nicol, 'Lelia Robinson Sawtelle: A Second Look,' Stanford WLHP, above, n 4; and LJ Robinson, 'Women Lawyers in the United States' (1890) 2 *The Green Bag* 10.

her identity as a 'lady.' Robinson's letter was one of a collection of annual letters, written by a number of women lawyers and circulated among the group for four years between 1887 and 1890. The group called itself the 'Equity Club' and the letters reveal how individual women lawyers in different jurisdictions were responding to the challenges of legal practice and forging their identities as members of the legal profession, after their sometimes strenuous efforts to gain admission to the bar. In defining their roles in a context that was without precedent, Drachman identified the issues that women lawyers necessarily confronted: 'how to dress as lawyers while retaining their femininity, whether women lawyers belonged in the courtroom, whether they could succeed in the business of law, while preserving their ties to charity and reform, how to balance marriage and career, and whether a woman had the physical constitution to withstand the demands of law practice.' As she concluded, their letters revealed how women lawyers 'grappled with this dilemma of how to strike a balance between femininity and professional identity....'[129]

Yet, even as they grappled with these dilemmas, some women lawyers were adamant that there was nothing 'strikingly peculiar' about their careers in law; as Mary Greene explained in 1891, 'our "brothers in law" ... receive us into their ranks as *lawyers*, not as feminine curiosities, and are more interested in the professional success of our efforts than in the manner in which we do our work.'[130] Moreover, as the Equity Club letters reveal, women lawyers were involved in the same kind of general legal practices as men in the legal profession. For example, Florence Cronise's 1888 letter from Tiffin Ohio described her work as including 'railroad suits, insurance, land, divorce and alimony (one, both or either,) bastardy cases, labor claims, libel suits, suits of all classes against corporations, settlement of estates, etc, etc, far too varied to recall;' moreover, as she concluded, she had enjoyed 'a success comparing favorably with that of the young men entering the profession at the same time.'[131] Belva Lockwood's 1887 letter from Washington DC detailed a number of different areas of her practice, but noted as well that she had established a 'Claim Agency' alongside her law office for 'the practice of all sorts of Claims against the Government, which has now grown into a large and prosperous business, and in which I am considered an expert.'[132] By

129 V Drachman, above, n 12 at 22. The Equity Club was a correspondence club whose membership and participation depended on annual letters which women lawyers wrote and circulated among themselves. There were also a few correspondents from Europe: Emilie Kempin from Switzerland, Marie Popelin from Belgium, and Eliza Orme from England.

130 MA Greene, 'A Woman Lawyer' (1891) 14 *Chautauquan* 218. See also M Strickland, 'Woman and the Forum' (1891) 3 *The Green Bag* 240.

131 V Drachman, above, n 12 at 95: letter of Florence Cronise, 1888. See also V Drachman at 217–9; and 'Florence Cronise,' Stanford WLHP, above, n 4.

132 V Drachman, above, n 12 at 59: letter of Belva A Lockwood, 1887. See also V Drachman, at 241–6; MB Stern, above, n 58; Cook, above, n 114; and M Evans, 'Belva Lockwood and the Mormon Question,' Stanford WLHP, above, n 4.

contrast with these reports of success in legal practice, it seems that some younger women lawyers may have experienced difficulty, at least at the beginning of their professional work. In a memoir written in the mid-1880s, for example, Catharine Waugh explained all her unsuccessful efforts to find a position in Chicago after her graduation from Union College of Law. As Cott argued, Waugh was among the small minority of women lawyers who were not wives, daughters, or other relatives of male lawyers, so that she experienced additional 'tribulations and frustrations in attempting to situate herself, a single, 24-year-old female lawyer, in the male legal establishment of Chicago.'[133] As a result of her difficulty, Waugh returned to her home in Rockford where she eventually achieved some success in her practice. Indeed, Waugh described how one male attorney had boasted that he would 'wipe the floor with her' when they met in court; however, as she then explained, 'we met and he didn't and we met again and still he didn't either literally or figuratively.'[134]

Interestingly, many of these same women lawyers wrote letters about their experiences to the Belgian barrister, Louis Frank, a few years later in 1896. Frank was probably already known to at least some women lawyers in the United States, because he had earlier forwarded copies of his 1888 treatise, *La Femme-Avocat*, to a number of them.[135] In a letter in October 1888, for example, Robinson thanked him for his treatise and declared it 'the most thorough and complete of anything that I have ever seen on the subject,' although she also confessed that it was a 'slow read' for her in French.[136] However, Robinson suggested that her colleague, Mary A Greene, who read French fluently, was interested in translating Frank's treatise for publication in the *Chicago Law Times*.[137] In a letter to Frank the following month, Greene confirmed that she was making good progress with the translation (and inserting a few corrections in relation to aspects of US law); the translated treatise appeared in installments in the *Chicago Law Times* in 1889.[138] Thereafter, Greene and Frank continued to collaborate in the early 1890s: for example, Greene willingly agreed to be

133 NF Cott, 'Women as Law Clerks: Catharine G Waugh' in DC Stanton (ed), *The Female Autograph* (New York, New York Literary Forum, 1984) 160 at 161.

134 V Drachman, above, n 12 at 175: letter of Catharine G Waugh, 1889. See also V Drachman, at 251–5; and JR Wilson, 'Catharine Waugh McCulloch: Attorney, Suffragist, and Justice of the Peace,' Stanford WLHP, above, n 4.

135 L Frank, *La Femme-Avocat: Exposé Historique et Critique de la Question* (Bruxelles, Ferdinand Larcier; and Bologne, Nicolas Zanichelli, 1888); the book included a letter from Lockwood.

136 Letter from Robinson to Frank, 19 October 1888, in Bibliothèque Royale, Brussels: *Papiers Frank* #6031 (file 2) [hereafter *Papiers Frank*].

137 Letter from Robinson to Frank, above, n 136. Robinson explained that the *Chicago Law Times* was 'a magazine on legal subjects published quarterly in Chicago ... by a woman lawyer, Mrs C V Waite.'

138 Letter from Greene to Frank, 22 October 1888, *Papiers Frank* #6031 (file 2), proposing a translation of his treatise for publication; Greene's translated text appeared in four installments in 1889: see (1889) 3 *Chicago Law Times* at 74, 120, 253, and 382.

the US correspondent for Frank's *L'Office Feministe Universel*,[139] and she may have translated Frank's article about women's higher education for publication in the United States in 1894.[140]

Thus, in 1896, Frank wrote to Greene and to other American women lawyers to request their help with a new book to appear in conjunction with Jeanne Chauvin's application for admission to the Paris bar. Frank's papers include a draft letter, clearly intended to be sent to women lawyers in a number of different jurisdictions, in which he requested information about the numbers of women lawyers, their status within the legal profession, and their treatment by other lawyers and by the courts. In writing to the American women lawyers, he explained that he would be engaged in Chauvin's case before the Paris court in the near future, and that he wanted to publish a larger work on the question of women lawyers (noting the first edition in 1888 and its translation in the *Chicago Law Times*); thus he needed information about the experiences of American women lawyers.[141] In response to Frank's requests, he received letters and photographs from a number of women lawyers, including several in the United States: Florence Cronise, Clara Foltz, Ella Knowles Haskell, Belva Lockwood, Nettie Lutes, and Catharine Waugh McCulloch; as well, Mary Greene provided an extensive review of the status and circumstances of American women lawyers and biographical details for several of them, including Myra Bradwell and Lelia Robinson, both of whom had recently died.[142]

Perhaps because they knew that Frank wanted to use the American experience as a precedent to support Chauvin's admission to the Paris bar, the letters written by these American women lawyers tended to emphasise their success and accomplishments, and to downplay any difficulties. For example, Waugh McCulloch (who had earlier found it impossible to find work in Chicago) explained that:

> There is no difference in the position which women lawyers occupy in relation to their clients, other lawyers or judges. The same civility, the same hard work meets both men and women. Our clientage is not restricted to women. Many

---

139 Letter from Greene to Frank, May 1895: *Papiers Frank* #7791–6 (envelope 2).

140 L Frank, 'University Opportunities for Women' (December 1894) *Educational Review* 471; see also L Frank, 'Les Femmes et L'Enseignement Supérieur' (1893) *Revue Universitaire* 234. In a letter to Frank in 1894, Greene thanked him for dedicating his recent book to her (*Le Grand Catéchisme de la Femme*, 1894), but advised against its translation because it dealt with 'subjects that had no existence in the USA': *Papiers Frank* #7791–4.

141 *Papiers Frank* #7791–3 (envelope 2). Frank's draft letter was in French, but it may have been translated by Greene for circulation to other women lawyers in the US. The same envelope includes a note in Frank's handwriting, entitled 'Femme-Avocats: Enquête, Correspondance, Réponses' and a list of portraits. *Papiers Frank* #7791–1 includes photos of women lawyers from several jurisdictions.

142 Letter from Greene to Frank, 9 September 1896: *Papiers Frank* #6031 (file 2); and #7793–2.

men care but little about the sex of their attorney, so long as their work is well done....[143]

Similarly, Clara Foltz (who had sued to obtain admission to law school in California) wrote about her experiences in the legal profession *almost* without complaint:

With very few exceptions my relations with my clients have been most cordial and satisfactory. I have sometimes lost cases I thought I would win, but so have my opponents, and I have certainly won quite my share. Losing clients are not always amiable, but their wrath has never been directed toward me.... Between myself and the members of the bar the most friendly relations have always been maintained. Sometimes one of the rifraf of the profession made himself obnoxious, but the cases were few and I feel assured that I have received quite as much of a welcome at the bar and been shown quite as much courtesy by its members, as any other member of the profession....[144]

Belva Lockwood's letter also reported favourably on the admission of women to the bar. In particular, she reported to Frank that the statute of 1879, which permitted women to be admitted to the US Supreme Court, had been favourable to women; she then continued:

It is my experience, and my opinion that women advocates have been kindly and favorably received as a rule by the male members of the bar, and well received by the Court in which they have practices.... The admission of women to the bar in our country has not been the cause of any abuse, or of any inconvenience, either to themselves or others.... I do not think the court has ever shown any difference between male and female attorneys, but all are treated with respect and must respect each other....[145]

Like other correspondents,[146] Mary Greene's lengthy letter also confirmed that women lawyers experienced no particular difficulties as members of the legal profession:

While prejudice still prevails, especially in the States bordering upon the Atlantic, it grows less, as women continue to prove their ability to perform the work, and to master the difficulties incident to the comprehension of legal principles and their application to actual practice.

[143] Letter from Waugh McCulloch to Frank, 28 October 1896: *Papiers Frank* #6031 (file 2).
[144] Letter from Foltz to Frank, 23 September 1896: *Papiers Frank* #6031 (file 2).
[145] Letter from Lockwood to Frank, 9 September 1896: *Papiers Frank* #6031 (file 2). Although Lockwood indicated that she would defer the matter of 'the opinion of male members of the bar' to a later letter, there is no record of another letter.
[146] Letters to Frank from Cronise (21 December 1896 and 26 June 1897); Foltz (23 September 1896); Haskell (12 September 1896); Lockwood (30 August 1896 and 9 September 1896); and Waugh McCulloch (28 October 1896) are all in *Papiers Frank* #6031 (file 2). A letter from Lutes (5 December 1896) is in *Papiers Frank* #7791–6.

The gentlemen of the bench and bar have been almost uniformly courteous and helpful. In the 15 States of the Union that do not yet admit women, their absence from the bar is simply due to the fact that no women have ever yet applied there for admission....

Neither is it true that women lawyers are limited to certain departments of legal practice. The special field of the woman lawyer is determined not by her sex but by her tastes, her talent, or her environment, just as it is with men. There are women lawyers like Miss Florence Cronise of Tiffin, Ohio, Miss Ellen A Martin of Chicago, and others who have built up a large and lucrative practice in the courts, trying all kinds of cases with success. Others, among whom Mrs Marilla A Ricker of New Hampshire and Mrs Clara Foltz of New York make a specialty of criminal law.... Mrs Catharine Waite of Chicago published for a time a review – the Chicago Law Times. Mrs Myra Bradwell, probably the most eminent of all American women lawyers established in 1868 a weekly paper entitled 'The Chicago Legal News,' which is now conducted by her husband and daughter, both lawyers, since Mrs Bradwell's death in 1894....[147]

Frank's *La Femme-Avocat* reflects the information forwarded by Greene and others, especially in relation to the details of women's admission to the bar and their legal work.[148] Relying on the positive tone of these letters, Frank concluded that women lawyers had been fully accepted as members of the legal profession in the United States.[149]

Interestingly, however, Frank also requested assessments of the role of women lawyers from 'official' sources in the United States. A short response came from the US Supreme Court, confirming that thirteen women had been admitted as members of the Supreme Court bar, and that their admission had created neither abuse nor inconvenience.[150] Another was a longer letter from the Office of the Attorney General in Washington, in which Judson Harmon reported that only a few of the women admitted to the bar had availed themselves of the right to practise; as well, his letter stated:

... There have been too few to afford any test of the fitness of women for the practice of law. The appearance of a woman at the bar is still, in all parts of the country, a subject of curiosity and remark, showing that the relations of that sex to the legal profession is still in an early stage of the experimental period. None of the women lawyers whom I have known or know of has achieved any distinction as lawyers. Few if any of them have had much to do in the way of practice....[151]

147 Letter from Greene to Frank, above, n 142.

148 L Frank, *La Femme-Avocat: Exposé Historique et Critique de la Question* (Paris, V Giard et E Brière, 1898) at 129 and 131.

149 L Frank, above, n 148 at 136.

150 L Frank, above, n 148 at 134; the letter is dated 4 September 1896 in *Papiers Frank*, but the year appears as 1897 in *La Femme-Avocat*, above, n 148 at 135–6.

151 Letter from Judson Harmon to Frank, *Papiers Frank* #6031 (file 2). Harmon responded to Frank's request in English, but his letter appeared in French in *La Femme-Avocat*.

Suggesting that women had generally been much more successful as members of the medical profession than as lawyers, the letter ended by concluding that it was necessary to wait for the time when women lawyers became more usual, and that women would then generally succeed as well as men in legal practice.[152] Not surprisingly, Frank emphasised the letter's conclusion, arguing that the fundamental point was to ensure that the professions were entirely open to women, a circumstance which would permit the public to become accustomed to women lawyers and that both men and women would then have similar opportunities for professional success.[153]

Yet, in spite of Frank's conclusion in *La Femme-Avocat*, the letter from the Office of the Attorney General is clearly different in tone from the letters forwarded to Frank by women lawyers. In particular, the confident assertion that women lawyers had made no significant impact as members of the legal profession in the United States appears jarring in the face of the women lawyers' reports of their acceptance and their increasing success. One possible explanation is that the Attorney General was taking into account that women still remained entirely excluded from the most prestigious law schools and that they were thus ineligible for jobs at the most elite corporate law firms and for important governmental positions at the end of the nineteenth century; even the involvement of women like Cronise and Lockwood in corporate and government work could not compete with the prestige of these activities. At the same time, the women's letters capture their hopefulness about the future, emphasising their roles as *lawyers*, ungendered. As Nancy Cott argued, one significant feature of women professionals' identity at the end of the nineteenth century was an abiding acceptance of professional norms, a feature that 'made the question of the relative power of male and female practitioners [in any profession] *unspeakable*.'[154] In such a context, gender was rendered invisible.

This sense of professional identity may also explain why some women experienced tensions between their commitment to the women's movement and their professional work; indeed, some women chose not to practise law at all in order to work for suffrage and women's rights causes. For example, Phoebe Couzins, the first woman to graduate from Washington University Law School in the early 1870s, devoted much of her life to the suffrage cause, and enthusiastically exhorted women to become lawyers to

Curiously, a sentence in the quoted excerpt (originally written in English and preserved in *Papiers Frank*) was rendered by Frank as '*Quelques-unes des femmes-avocats que j'ai connues ou que je connais, ont acquis une réelle distinction comme hommes de loi*': L Frank, above, n 148 at 135.

152 Letter from Harmon to Frank, above, n 151.
153 L Frank, above, n 148 at 136.
154 NF Cott, above, n 121 at 237 (emphasis added).

advance the broader goals of women's equality, saying that both the legal profession and the women's movement needed 'women's wit, women's fairness and women's sense of right and righteousness.'[155] In addition, Ada Bittenbender argued in her 1889 letter to the Equity Club that she had achieved a more successful professional career by taking up 'side issues' as attorney for the National WCTU than she would have experienced by sticking 'entirely to my office and the court practice which would have come to me through such sticking.'[156] Moreover, as Drachman noted, women who tried to combine legal practice with reform activities concerning family law, suffrage and temperance, sometimes experienced difficulty.[157] For example, in her 1889 letter to the Equity Club, Waugh McCulloch noted that she often received advice from other attorneys and from judges about the incongruity between practising law and working for women's rights.[158] For the most part, Waugh McCulloch seems to have ignored this advice, particularly when she decided to campaign for the Prohibitionists in the 1888 election; as she explained, 'way off in some benighted portions of the country were men who had never heard a woman speak and who supposed a woman lawyer had horns and hoofs or at least wore boots and breeches. My harmless, insignificant appearance amazed them.'[159]

Nonetheless, the narrowing of goals in the women's movement by the end of the nineteenth century, and the impact of the *Bradwell* decision in the US Supreme Court, clearly weakened the links between some women lawyers and suffrage activists. As Greene explained in a letter to Frank in 1895, she was not able to provide him with much information about suffrage in the United States, since:

> ... I do not know enough about the methods of the woman suffragists in this country to tell you much about them. My views on the subject differ in so many ways from those of the leaders that I cannot work with them. I do not believe that the ballot will cure all ills, nor do I believe that women are powerless without the ballot. I prefer to teach women how to use the power and the rights they already possess (which here in America are many) in order that they may know how to ask intelligently for changes in the laws. I do not like the way in which these leaders persistently misrepresent the present laws....[160]

155 H Garza, above, n 60 at 80–1. See also 'Phoebe Couzins,' Stanford WLHP, above, n 4.
156 V Drachman, above, n 12 at 153: letter of Ada M Bittenbender, 1889. See also V Drachman, at 211–13; and 'Ada Bittenbender,' Stanford WLHP, above, n 4.
157 Women lawyers sometimes experienced ambivalence about 'women's issues;'for example, Emma Gillett declined to write an article about divorce reforms because her ideas on the subject were 'so chaotic': V Drachman, above, n 12 at 185: letter of Emma M Gillett, 1890.
158 V Drachman, above, n 12 at 174: letter of Catharine G Waugh, 1889.
159 V Drachman, above, n 12 at 176–7: letter of Catharine Waugh, 1889. Waugh later reported that she and her new husband had organised their honeymoon around her commitments to speak in the suffrage campaign in South Dakota: Drachman, at 191: letter of Catharine Waugh McCulloch, 1890.
160 Letter from Greene to Frank, May 1895: *Papiers Frank* #7791–6 (envelope 1).

In another letter, moreover, Greene was scathing about Belva Lockwood's candidacy for President, asserting that it was a general sentiment in the United States that her candidacy was:

> ... most unfortunate both for herself and for the cause of her sex that Belva Lockwood allowed herself to pose as a candidate for the Presidency upon the nomination of a set of woman suffragists (*not* even a recognized political party).... I am simply telling you what the general sentiment in the United States is, in order that the value of your writing may not be impaired by giving prominence to those women who are more or less laughed at at home.... I do think that you ought to know what public opinion is here whether that opinion is just or unjust....[161]

Not surprisingly, Greene asked Frank to keep this letter confidential.

The variety of responses demonstrates how individual women lawyers chose to respond in different ways to the women's movement and the cause of women's suffrage. However, for some women lawyers, there may have been all too little choice: the stark reality was that they had to work hard as legal practitioners just to survive.[162] As Lockwood stated when she began her practice, she accepted 'every case, no matter how difficult, occurring in civil, criminal, equitable and probate law.'[163] Indeed, Drachman concluded that for many women lawyers, particularly those who were single or widowed, 'the hard realities of life, not the romantic notions of ideal womanhood, determined the direction of their professional careers.'[164] These factors meant that although individual women lawyers might become involved in the women's movement, they did not make a significant collective impact on its policies and programmes; moreover, some women lawyers were clearly opposed to, or at least ambivalent about, any involvement at all. In this context, it is hard to accept Drachman's conclusion that 'the women lawyers of the Equity Club did more than participate in the Woman Movement; they took their place at its very center.'[165] A more nuanced assessment suggests that women lawyers' relationships to the women's movement were not at all uniform.[166] Moreover, although it is difficult to assess precisely how emerging

---

[161] Letter from Greene to Frank, 10 August 1891: *Papiers Frank* #6031 (file 2). See also FA Cook, above, n 114 at 10–11; and J Norgren, 'Before it was Merely Difficult: Belva Lockwood's Life in Law and Politics' (1999) 23 *Journal of Supreme Court History* 16 at 32.

[162] VG Drachman, above, n 2 at 99, explained that a number of women lawyers had previously been teachers, and had left education for law 'in search of less arduous and more remunerative work.'

[163] V Drachman, above, n 12 at 58: letter of Belva A Lockwood, 1887.

[164] VG Drachman, above, n 2 at 99–100.

[165] V Drachman, above, n 12 at 21.

[166] DK Weisberg, above, n 1 at 502–3, asserted that there was a difference between the group of women who became lawyers in the two decades after 1870, by contrast with those who entered the legal profession in the later period between 1890 and the achievement of

ideas of professionalism influenced individual decisions, it appears that women lawyers' identities as professionals may have weakened ties between many women lawyers and other women activists.

At the same time, however, relationships between women lawyers and the organised legal professions reveal continuing patterns of male exclusivity. Although Ada Bittenbender reported in 1891 that 'women lawyers are welcomed as members of bar associations established by their brothers in the profession [and many women lawyers] have availed themselves of this privilege,'[167] women were not eligible to join the American Bar Association until 1918, and they were frequently excluded from local organisations, such as the Boston Bar Association as well.[168] Interestingly, women lawyers often seem to have responded by establishing their own organisations. Thus, in addition to participating in the Equity Club, for example, Robinson organised a Portia Club in Boston for dinner meetings of women lawyers.[169] Similarly, women lawyers who attended the first meeting of the International Council of Women in Washington DC in 1888 voted to create a Woman's International Bar Association that year.[170] Such organisations confirmed women lawyers' need for support and collegiality as *women* members of the legal profession; yet, they also demonstrated that women lawyers were becoming identified as lawyers, and gradually eschewing their connections with non-professional women. For example, at the time of the World's Columbian Exposition in Chicago in 1893, a group of professional women formed the Queen Isabella Association (honouring Columbus's patron) to distinguish their roles from more traditional women's activities, such as domestic, philanthropic and artistic work. Denied space at the Exposition, the Queen Isabella Association established its own club house nearby and thirty women lawyers attended a three-day conference there in August 1893;[171] the group also decided to create a National League of Women Lawyers.[172] In this way, women law-

suffrage at the end of World War I; according to Weisberg, it was the latter group which most clearly identified with the women's movement, but her conclusion may understate involvement in the women's movement on the part of the earlier group of women lawyers, some of whom were 'ardent suffragists.'

[167] AM Bittenbender, above, n 5 at 243. The corresponding secretary of the Equity Club, Martha Pearce, expressly confirmed that the Equity Club was not intended to take the place of bar associations: V Drachman, above, n 12 at 77–9: letter of Martha Pearce, 1888.

[168] R Stevens, above, n 15 at 84; and S Killingsworth, above, n 128 at 7.

[169] Letter from Robinson to Frank, 19 October 1888: *Papiers Frank* #6031 (file 2). See also Mary A Greene, 'Mrs Lelia Robinson Sawtelle – First Woman Lawyer of Massachusetts' (1918) 7 *Women Lawyers' Journal* 51.

[170] V Drachman, above, n 12 at 135: letter of Catherine Waugh, 1888. See also AM Bittenbender, above, n 5 at 243.

[171] Letter from Waugh McCulloch to Frank, 28 October 1896: *Papiers Frank* #6031; and draft programme for the meeting of the Queen Isabella Association, Law Department, Isabella Club House, Cor 61st Street and Oglesby Ave, Chicago III: #7791–6 (envelope 1).

[172] The League was established with Florence Cronise as President, Ellen A Martin as Secretary, and Catharine Waugh McCulloch as Treasurer. The League also named four

yers confirmed their identity as women members of the legal profession, separate and distinct from organisations of the women's movement on one hand and from male exclusivity in the legal profession on the other.

Yet, at the same time, women lawyers also wished to be included as full members of the legal profession, and they enthusiastically participated in the World's Congress of Jurisprudence and Law Reform, one of many congresses convened during the Exposition in Chicago. As the *Law Times* noted in September 1893, it was 'the first time in the history of the world [that] an international congress of lawyers has been held in which women lawyers have taken part.'[173] According to Greene, the credit for achieving the involvement of women lawyers in the main Congress belonged to Bradwell:

> Mrs Bradwell's latest triumph was secured in 1893, when she, as the Chairman of the Woman's Branch of the World's Congress of Jurisprudence and Law Reform, obtained recognition of women lawyers as speakers, on the same platform with the male jurists, rather than, as was desired by many of the Committee, that the women jurists should hold a separate Congress of their own. In this successful battle she was ably assisted by her brilliant daughter, Bessie Bradwell Helmer....[174]

As Frank reported in *La Femme-Avocat*, four women were selected to read papers at the Congress: two were Clara Foltz and Mary A Greene from the United States; the other two were Eliza Orme from England, the first woman law graduate from the University of London, who had been engaged in legal work since the 1870s although not admitted as either a solicitor or barrister in the UK; and Cornelia Sorabji, an Indian Parsi who had achieved prominence as the first woman to complete the BCL exams at Oxford in 1892.[175] In the end, the papers of all four women were published in the *Chicago Legal News*,[176] with Frank enthusiastically con-

women as honorary members of the League: Myra Bradwell, the founder of one of the principal legal journals in the US; Belle Mansfield, the first woman to gain admission to the bar; Phoebe Couzins, the first to undertake a law school course; and Ada Kepley, the first woman to graduate in law: see L Frank, above, n 148 at 132–3; according to Waugh McCulloch, Nettie Lutes was Vice-President: see *Papiers Frank* #6031 (file 2): letter from Waugh McCulloch, 28 October 1896. See also 'Women Lawyers at the Isabella Club House' 25 *Chicago Legal News*, 26 August 1893 at 451; and GH McNamee, above, n 83 at 16, 34 and 49.

173 *The Law Times*, vol XCV, 2 September 1893, at 402. See also *Albany Law Journal*, 19 August 1893.

174 Letter from Greene to Frank, 9 September 1896: *Papiers Frank* #6031 (file 2); see also letter from Waugh McCulloch to Frank, 28 October 1896: *Papiers Frank* #6031 (file 2).

175 L Frank, above, n 148 at 133.

176 Eliza Orme's paper, 'The Legal Status of Women in England' was read, in her absence, by Mary A Ahrens, of the Chicago Bar (see 25 *Chicago Legal News*, 12 August 1893 at 431); Clara Foltz read her paper, 'Public Defenders'(see 25 *Chicago Legal News*, 12 August 1893 at 431); Mary A Greene read her paper, 'Married Women's Property Acts in the United States

cluding that women lawyers had thus received official recognition from the most eminent jurists in the world.[177]

Such confident assertions were widely reported at the end of the nineteenth century. For example, *Leslie's Illustrated Weekly* asserted in 1896 that the work of women lawyers 'proves the falsity of the old belief that women have neither the inclination nor the ability to master the intricacies of the law.' Proudly, the *Weekly* stated that:

> The woman lawyer is largely a development of the last twenty-five years and of this country.... No other country has half as many women in the legal profession. The prejudice and opposition which so long obstructed their progress are rapidly disappearing. Women are now being received and recognized by their brother members of the profession... [178]

Clearly, the fact that increasing numbers of women were engaged in the practice of law suggested that such confidence was not misplaced. Yet, in spite of their increasing numbers, the situation for women lawyers remained contested, both as women and as legal professionals. As women, their traditional connections with the women's equality movement had diminished, in part as a result of women lawyers' strategic arguments in the courts and also because of their growing identity as professionals. Yet, even as professionals, the *Bradwell* precedent confirmed that women had no constitutional right to practise law, and women continued to be excluded from the emerging elite within law schools and the legal profession, as well as from many of the collegial activities of local bar associations. In addition, women began to practise law in the United States without the support of the 14th amendment's constitutional guarantee of equal protection, creating ongoing tensions between gender and professionalism. Nonetheless, the experiences of the first women lawyers in the United States fuelled women's aspirations in other jurisdictions. Moreover, as pioneers who first demonstrated to the world that women could become lawyers, women like Mary Greene espoused confidence in the future; as she reported to Louis Frank in 1896, 'The career of woman as a lawyer has passed beyond its experimental stage in the United States. She has made a place for herself, and is welcomed to the ranks of the bar.'[179]

---

and Needed Reforms' (see 25 *Chicago Legal News*, 12 August 1893 at 433); and Cornelia Sorabji's paper, 'Legal Status of Women in India' was presented by Bessie Bradwell Helmer (see 25 *Chicago Legal News*, 12 August 1893 at 434). See also BA Lockwood, 'The Congress of Law Reform' (1893) 3 *American Journal of Politics* 321. It seems that Lockwood also presented a paper at the Congress: see 'An International Arbitration Court and a Congress of Nations' 25 *Chicago Legal News*, 26 August 1893 at 447.

[177] L Frank, above, n 148 at 133.
[178] 'Women Lawyers,' above n 122.
[179] *Papiers Frank* at #7793-3: letter from Mary A Greene, 9 September 1896.

2

Women Lawyers in Canada: Becoming Lawyers 'On the Same Terms as Men'

WOMEN AS 'FELLOW LAWYERS'

'Women may be admitted as students-at-law on the same terms as men'

I imagine that very few of the students are aware that this neat little announcement appears in the Calendar of the Law School. Doubtless its original purpose was to inform ambitious young women who were so bold as to attempt to invade a field, formerly regarded as belonging exclusively to men, that the way was now thrown open to them.... Yet, [even if it has now outlived its usefulness], few of us would care to see these words removed from the calendar, because they form a rather fitting memorial to the woman who, only after a long struggle, was successful in having them inserted....[1]

MARY APPLEBY'S COMMENTS in 1934 in the law student newspaper at Osgoode Hall Law School in Toronto revealed two significant aspects about women lawyers in Canada. One was the confidence that women had been fully accepted as members of the legal profession. According to Appleby, at least eighty women had been called to the Ontario bar by 1934, and about forty of them were then practising; most of these women had received their call to the bar within the preceding fifteen years. In this context, Appleby confidently concluded that women lawyers were no longer regarded as curiosities, but 'accepted simply as ... fellow lawyer[s],' and her assertion was clearly consistent with the notice in the law school calendar that women lawyers were admitted 'on the same terms as men.' Yet, if this phrase was intended to emphasise the equality of male and female students, it also subtly revealed how law was fundamentally a male profession: women were welcome to join the

---

[1] M Appleby, 'The Entry of Women into the Profession of Law and Their Hopes' *Obiter Dicta*, 17 January 1934. See also P Axford, 'Portias of the Province' *Saturday Night*, 28 February 1948.

bar so long as they recognised that it was defined by men. In this context, Appleby suggested that 'it is only fair that a woman should not ask any special consideration because of her sex.'[2] As these comments reveal, women could become members of the legal profession – but only by accepting its (male) professional ethos, not by challenging it.

In addition to confirming this professional ethos, Appleby's comments also drew attention to Clara Brett Martin, the first woman to be admitted to the Ontario bar in 1897; since no other woman was admitted to a provincial bar until after 1900, Martin remains Canada's only nineteenth-century woman lawyer.[3] Thus, unlike the history of women lawyers in the United States, women in Canada did not begin to study or practise law until almost the end of the nineteenth century. Interestingly, Appleby characterised Martin's efforts as a 'long struggle;' it lasted six years in all, and included the enactment of two legislative amendments.[4] Yet, a much greater struggle arguably occurred in Québec, where a court challenge was initiated by Annie Macdonald Langstaff at the beginning of World War I;[5] significantly, neither her court challenge nor subsequent efforts to obtain a legislative amendment had yet succeeded when Appleby's article appeared in 1934. As Elizabeth Monk recounted, the legislative amendment was not enacted in Québec until April 1941, and even then, only as a result of Premier Godbout's courage in the face of 'almost violent opposition' from some members of the Québec bar, and 'eloquent attacks' on the part of the leader of the provincial opposition, the Honourable Mr Duplessis.[6] By contrast, although there had been earlier court challenges in New Brunswick[7] and in British Columbia,[8] both initiated by Mabel Penery French, legislation to permit women to become lawyers was enacted in

2 M Appleby, above, n 1. Appleby also suggested that 'in the not too distant future ... women will win equal distinction with men in every phase of the practice of law.'

3 See C Backhouse, '"To Open the Way for Others of my Sex": Clara Brett Martin's Career as Canada's First Woman Lawyer' (1985) 1 *Canadian Journal of Women and the Law* 1 [hereafter Backhouse]; C Backhouse, 'Lawyering: Clara Brett Martin, Canada's First Woman Lawyer' in C Backhouse (ed), *Petticoats and Prejudice: Women and Law in Nineteenth-Century Canada* (Toronto, The Osgoode Society, 1991); T Roth, 'Clara Brett Martin – Canada's Pioneer Woman Lawyer' (1984) 18 *The Law Society Gazette* 323; and S Ryan, 'A Pilgrim's Progress: Clara Brett Martin's Campaign for Admission to the Bar of Ontario' (unpublished study on file). See also L Scotton, 'A Quiet Revolutionary' *The Toronto Star*, 14 September 1989, at L-1.

4 See *An Act to Provide for the Admission of Women to the Study and Practice of Law*, SO 1892, c 32; and *An Act to Amend the Act to Provide for the Admission of Women to the Study and Practice of Law*, SO 1895, c 27.

5 *Langstaff v Bar of Québec* (1915) 47 Rapports Judiciares de Québec 131 (CS) [hereafter *Langstaff* (CS)]; and *Langstaff v Bar of Québec* (1916) 25 Rapports Judiciares de Québec 11 (CBR) [hereafter *Langstaff* (CBR)].

6 Memorandum prepared by Elizabeth C Monk, and reproduced in C Harvey, 'Women in Law in Canada' (1970–71) 4 *Manitoba Law Journal* 9, at 18–20; and *An Act Respecting the Bar* SQ 1941, c 56, s 1. See also G Gallichan, *Les Québécoises et le Barreau: L'Histoire d'une Difficile Conquête, 1914–1941* (Québec, Septentrion, 1999) at 28.

7 *In re French* (1905) 37 New Brunswick Reports 359 (SC) [hereafter *French* (NB)].

8 *Re French* (1910–12) 17 British Columbia Law Reports 1 (CA) [hereafter *French* (BC)].

these and most other Canadian provinces between 1906 and 1918, generally with little controversy.[9]

Thus, although the history of women's admission to the bar in Canada spans four decades from the end of the nineteenth century to World War II, women in provinces other than Québec became eligible to enter the legal profession between the last decade of the nineteenth century and the end of World War I.[10] These two decades were generally characterised by reformist ideas and a 'spirit of expanding opportunity'[11] in Canada, perhaps especially for women. According to Linda Kealey, the appearance of the 'new woman' in the 1890s was reflected in experiments in 'dress reform, bicycle riding, spiritualism and women's rights,' issues which were eventually transformed into a variety of reform initiatives and new ideas about women's citizenship and voting rights.[12] In this context, women's entry to the legal profession occurred as part of the 'progressive-reform impulse that gripped North America between the years 1880 and 1920,'[13] a wave of new ideas which sanctioned increased activism and awareness for Canadian women about reform goals, including women's suffrage, along with aspirations for higher education, opportunities for participation in public life, and economic independence.

Nonetheless, these new roles for women were still contested in the decades when women were first becoming lawyers in Canada. As Cook

---

[9] New Brunswick: *An Act to Remove the Disability of Women so far as relates to the Study and Practice of Law*, SNB 1906, c 5; British Columbia: *An Act to Remove the Disability of Women so far as relates to the Study and Practice of the Law*, SBC 1912, c 18; Manitoba: *An Act to Amend 'An Act to Amend the Law Society Act'* SM 1912, c 32; Saskatchewan: *An Act to Amend the Statute Law* SS 1912–13, c 46, s 27 (amending the *Legal Profession Act* RSS 1909, c 104); Nova Scotia: *An Act to Amend Chapter 164, Revised Statutes of 1900, 'The Barristers and Solicitors Act'* SNS 1917, c 41, s 2; Prince Edward Island: *An Act to Amend an Act to incorporate a Law Society and amending Acts* SPEI 1918, c 14, s 6. See also Alberta: *The Sex Disqualification (Removal) Act, 1930*, SA 1930, c 62; and Newfoundland: *An Act to amend Chapter 54 of the Consolidated Statutes...*, S Nfld 1910, c 16, s 1.

[10] The Canadian census for 1891 recorded 4308 men and 24 women whose occupations were 'lawyers and other legal pursuits;' since women were not yet eligible to practise law, these 24 women were likely involved in subordinate legal roles as law clerks, etc. The 1901 census included three categories: 'lawyers,' 'lawyers' clerks,' and 'notaries and conveyancers,' but it did not record any women lawyers in Canada, even though Clara Brett Martin had been practising law by then for four years: see also M Kinnear, *In Subordination: Professional Women, 1870–1970* (Montréal and Kingston, McGill–Queen's University Press, 1995) at 179 (table 12). See also DF Coyle, 'Women in the Legal Profession in Canada' (1952) 38:3 *Women Lawyers Journal* 14 (published by the National Association of Women Lawyers in the United States); D Stager (with HW Arthurs), *Lawyers in Canada* (Toronto, University of Toronto Press, 1990) at 20–21; and J Brockman, '"Better to Enlist their Support than to Suffer their Antagonism": The Game of Monopoly Between Lawyers and Notaries in British Columbia, 1930–81' (1997) 4:3 *International Journal of the Legal Profession* 197.

[11] J Errington, 'Pioneers and Suffragists' in S Burt, L Code and L Dorney (eds), *Changing Patterns: Women in Canada* (Toronto, McClelland and Stewart, 1988) 51 at 65.

[12] L Kealey, 'Introduction' in L Kealey (ed), *A Not Unreasonable Claim: Women and Reform in Canada, 1880s–1920s* (Toronto, The Women's Press, 1979) at 1.

[13] J Errington, above, n 11 at 65.

and Mitchinson noted, the idea of women's 'proper sphere' represented a significant constraint for Canadian women at the beginning of the twentieth century:

> A woman could not enter into any sphere of temporal society without being accused of being a proponent of 'woman's rights' whose ultimate goal was the destruction of the family. If women adhered to their role they became observers not participants. If they tried to participate, in fact, compete with men, they were ridiculed....[14]

These views about women's roles are reflected in archival records that reveal how some male lawyers and provincial law societies responded to the challenge of women's entry to the legal profession, disdainfully expressing their opposition to a 'Blackstone in petticoats.'[15] In addition, legal journals in Canada published editorials with disparaging comments about women lawyers as early as 1869, in response to news of Arabella Mansfield's admission to the legal profession in Iowa.[16] By contrast, there were expressions of editorial support a few years later for decisions by the Law Society and the Inns of Court in Britain which rejected applications submitted by women. As the editor of the *Canada Law Journal* concluded, women might succeed as conveyancers or as textbook writers, 'but to refuse to allow them to embark upon the rough and troubled sea of actual legal practice, is ... being cruel only to be kind.'[17] Although somewhat more muted, judicial reasoning in reported decisions concerning women's eligibility for the legal profession in Canada similarly reflected these traditional ideas about women's 'proper sphere.'

There were just three reported decisions in Canada: in New Brunswick, British Columbia and Québec; all three decisions were rendered in the decade between 1905 and 1915, and they all held that women were not

---

[14] R Cook and W Mitchinson (eds), *The Proper Sphere: Woman's Place in Canadian Society* (Toronto, Oxford University Press, 1976) at 5–6. See also R Cook, *The Regenerators: Social Criticism in Late Victorian English Canada* (Toronto, University of Toronto Press, 1985); and E Brunet, 'The 19th-Century Case against Women Becoming Lawyers' *Ontario Lawyers Gazette*, March/April 1998 at 24.

[15] Oscar Bass, secretary of the Law Society of British Columbia, responded to an inquiry about the admission of women lawyers, clearly indicating his opposition: see WW Pue, *Law School: The Story of Legal Education in British Columbia* (Vancouver, Faculty of Law of the University of British Columbia, 1995) at 223. Similarly, forty lawyers in Nova Scotia forwarded a petition to the legislature in 1917, 'praying that women be not enabled to practise law in the province': see C Cleverdon, *The Woman Suffrage Movement in Canada* (Toronto, University of Toronto Press, 1950) at 173. See also J Brockman, 'Exclusionary Tactics: The History of Women and Visible Minorities in the Legal Profession in British Columbia' in H Foster and JPS McLaren (eds), *Essays in the History of Canadian Law: Vol VI, British Columbia and the Yukon* (Toronto, The Osgoode Society, 1995) 508.

[16] 'Women's Rights' (Nov 1869) 5 *Canada Law Journal* 307; see also (1879) 15 *Canada Law Journal* 146 (reporting on the admission of women to the Supreme Court of the United States).

[17] 'Female Attorneys' (June 1880) 16 *Canada Law Journal* 160 at 161.

eligible *in law* to be admitted to the bar.[18] At the same time, the judges in these cases seemed aware of women's increasing aspirations for professional work, explaining that they were not expressing their own opinions 'as to the advisability of extending the right [to practise law] to women,' but simply stating 'the law of this country as we now find it.'[19] In fact, the judiciary's staunch opposition to women's applications for admission to the bar tends to confirm the ever-increasing strength of their claims. Moreover, in spite of judicial opposition to women's claims for admission to the legal profession, women claimants frequently enjoyed the support of male lawyers and of the organised women's movement, particularly in seeking statutory amendments from all-male legislatures, and often before women became entitled to vote. In this way, the stories of the first women lawyers in Canada offer insights about changes in women's roles and about differing responses to them in the courts, in the legal profession, and in provincial legislatures in the early twentieth century.

As well, since the timing of women's admission to the bar occurred alongside turn-of-the-century debates about professionalism, women's aspirations to practise law intersected with new ideas about the practice of law and the role of university legal education. As Wes Pue suggested, issues about the eligibility of women for admission to the legal professions in Canada were intertwined with professional debates concerning 'important questions [about] just what sort of person from what sort of background could properly embody law in a new British Dominion.'[20] Clearly, many of the challenges posed by industrialisation and improvements in transportation and communication were creating demands for new kinds of legal services in Canada, as in the United States, at the end of the nineteenth century, and these changes fostered new ideas about professionalism on both sides of the border. Indeed, Pue argued that the 'dominant cultural influence on Canadian lawyers in this period' came from the United States:

> By the early twentieth century a ready-made template of professionalisation had been developed there, drawing upon conceptions of social ordering which resonated with contemporary concerns.... On both sides of the border an intensely *moral* professionalism developed.... It mattered deeply ... that lawyers be gentlemen.... In developing a 'moral' vision of professionalism Canadians looked south for inspiration rather than 'home' to Britain....[21]

18 See above, n 7 (New Brunswick); above, n 8 (British Columbia); and above, n 5 (Québec).
19 *French* (NB), above, n 7 at 363, *per* Hanington, J.
20 WW Pue, 'Cultural Projects and Structural Transformation in the Canadian Legal Profession' in W Wesley Pue and David Sugarman (eds), *Lawyers and Vampires: Cultural Histories of Legal Professions* (Oxford and Portland, OR, Hart Publishing, 2003) 367 at 379–80.
21 WW Pue, above, n 20 at 387–8. See also WW Pue, 'In Pursuit of Better Myth: Lawyers' Histories and Histories of Lawyers' (1995) 33:4 *Alberta Law Review* 730.

Pue's thesis about the impact on Canadian lawyers of emerging ideas concerning legal professionalism in the United States reflects the factors of geographical proximity and increasing cross-border activities for lawyers in the early twentieth century. As Pue noted, these factors converged with similarities in the recent experiences of the two countries: both were confronted with the challenges of industrialisation and immigration, as well as by ideas about democratic egalitarianism and the frontier spirit. Yet, if members of the legal profession in Canada were influenced by emerging ideas of professionalism in the United States, it is clear that they were much less receptive, for several decades in the late nineteenth century, to American precedents that permitted women to become lawyers; on the issue of women lawyers, Canadian courts and law societies looked steadfastly to Britain, where women were formally excluded from becoming either solicitors or barristers until after World War I. In this context, it is important to assess whether the history of women's admission to the legal profession in Canada reveals a fissure in current theories about a common professional project in law in North America, or whether there is some other explanation for this divergence between the United States and Canada on the issue of women in law.

This chapter begins with an examination of the turn-of-the-century reform context in Canada, one that included new ideas about legal professionalism and about women's roles and that may have influenced individual women to pursue legal education and admission to provincial bars. It then explores the arguments presented in the three litigated cases, and in the judicial decisions rejecting women's claims to become lawyers. As noted, earlier challenges in the United States were often cited, so that there are echoes of American jurisprudence in these Canadian decisions, even though they were being presented to Canadian courts several decades later. In addition, the Canadian decisions reveal how courts continued to defer to jurisprudence in Britain, a jurisprudence of male exclusivity for both barristers and solicitors. Yet, when Canadian women claimants turned to provincial legislatures, their claims were almost always successful; male members of provincial legislatures seemed less inclined to be deferential than male judges in Canada. Significantly, however, a number of these provincial legislatures drafted amending legislation to permit women to become lawyers 'on the same terms as men,' an approach which simultaneously granted women admission to the bar and also confirmed the profession's fundamental maleness.[22] Moreover, because Canadian women were becoming lawyers at almost the same time that women were gaining the right to vote, their professional identities may have been strengthened in a context in which it seemed that the goals

---

[22] For example, see above, n 9: statutory amendments in Nova Scotia, New Brunswick, Newfoundland and British Columbia.

of the women's movement, particularly suffrage, had been substantially accomplished; in this context, it may have appeared increasingly irrelevant that they were *women* lawyers. As their stories reveal, these first women lawyers in Canada provide connections between the history of legal professionalism and the campaigns of women's reform movements in the late nineteenth and early twentieth centuries.

THE CONTEXT FOR THE FIRST WOMEN LAWYERS IN CANADA: REFORMIST IDEAS ABOUT PROFESSIONALISM AND WOMEN'S ROLES

> Ten years ago people were much more content to lead a vegetable life, troubling heads but little over what are now considered to be the burning questions of the day. There was a stifling air of 'laissez-faire' in those times, and a strong tendency towards the suppression and ridiculing of all women's higher aims and ambitions; but in this *fin-de-siecle* much of that is changed, and the ability of the gentler sex to cope with and successfully master many of the deeper problems of life is becoming an established and recognized fact.[23]

When Clara Brett Martin became a law student in 1891, and then succeeded in becoming Canada's first woman lawyer in 1897, the new Canadian federation of seven provinces had been in existence for just three decades. However, the formation of the Canadian federation in the years after 1867 appears to have encouraged lawyers to expand their horizons, especially in relation to burgeoning commercial activities, including railway construction and the spread of utilities. Not surprisingly, there was increased demand for lawyers' services in relation to these activities 'to incorporate limited-liability companies, to draw up more complex contracts with employees and business associates, and to devise the legal infrastructure for an increasingly complex array of securities instruments.'[24] As Carol Wilton suggested, lawyers were also needed to protect businesses from intrusive government regulation, and to provide legal representation in the courts: the 'needs of industry, not less than of railways and utilities, [demanded] effective litigators.'[25] Moreover, it was not only legal work, but also the organisation of law firms, which was changing. Although most lawyers at the end of the nineteenth century still practised as generalists, either alone or in small firms, some lawyers were

---

[23] *Victoria Times*, 7 November 1895; quoted in V Strong-Boag, '"Setting the Stage": National Organization and the Women's Movement in the Late 19th Century' in SM Trofimenkoff and A Prentice (eds), *The Neglected Majority: Essays in Canadian Women's History* (Toronto, McClelland and Stewart, 1977) 87 at 95.

[24] C Wilton, 'Introduction' in C Wilton (ed), *Inside the Law: Canadian Law Firms in Historical Perspective* (Toronto, The Osgoode Society, 1996) at 13.

[25] C Wilton, above, n 24.

already beginning to establish specialisations, as new commercial enterprises increasingly required specialised expertise.[26]

Some of these changes contributed to a greater sense of professional
identity and the need for enhanced prestige for the legal profession; indeed
the first meeting to consider establishing a national bar association was
held in Montreal in 1896.[27] Canadian lawyers were also becoming more
mobile. As Elizabeth Bloomfield demonstrated, some of this mobility
occurred within provincial boundaries: more than a hundred communities
in Ontario attracted their first lawyers between 1870 and 1900, for
example.[28] In the next few decades, however, the numbers of communities
in which lawyers practised fell, leading Bloomfield to conclude that there
was 'contraction and concentration of legal services between 1900 and
1920, including an increase in the size of firms.'[29] In addition, there was
expanded movement from one province to another, with lawyers from the
Maritimes and central Canada ever more frequently migrating to 'newly
opening areas of the prairie West and British Columbia.'[30] And while firms
had traditionally reflected homogeneity in the ethnic backgrounds and
religion of their members, Wilton suggested that there is evidence in the
early twentieth century of the beginnings of greater diversity in firm
membership, another kind of increased mobility.[31]

This description of the legal profession in Canada at the end of the
nineteenth century suggests a time of expanding opportunities, greater
mobility and increasing confidence for lawyers. In this context, new ideas
about legal education in the United States may have inspired the legal
profession in a number of Canadian provinces. Indeed, the need to
improve legal education on a national scale was one important rationale
for the creation of a national bar association in 1896; as the well-known
Nova Scotian lawyer, John Bulmer, immodestly lamented at that time,

26 For example, see JD Honsberger, 'Raymond and Honsberger: A Small Firm That Stayed
Small, 1889–1989' in C Wilton (ed), above, n 24 at 430.
27 See (1896) 32 *Canada Law Journal* 534, announcing that the first meeting was to take place
in Montréal. See also P Girard, 'The Roots of a Professional Renaissance: Lawyers in Nova
Scotia 1850–1910' in D Gibson and WW Pue (eds), *Glimpses of Canadian Legal History*
(Winnipeg, Legal Research Institute, 1991) 155.
28 E Bloomfield, 'Lawyers as Members of Urban Business Elites in Southern Ontario, 1860 to
1920' in C Wilton (ed), *Beyond the Law: Lawyers and Business in Canada 1830 to 1930*
(Toronto, The Osgoode Society, 1990) 112 at 119.
29 E Bloomfield, above, n 28 at 120–21. See also E Brunet, 'The Law Office at the Turn of the
Century' *Ontario Lawyers Gazette*, May/June 1999, at 32.
30 C Wilton, above, n 24 at 15. As Wilton noted, at 16, Ontario lawyers moved to Manitoba
in significant numbers in the 1870s, overwhelming the original contingent of Québec trained
lawyers; and increasing numbers of senior members of the Nova Scotia bar were migrating to
the west of Canada.
31 Wilton recorded instances in Toronto of a Roman Catholic in an Anglican dominated firm
in 1897, and Protestants and Catholics in partnership in late nineteenth century Halifax, as well
as a few examples of prestigious Toronto firms with Jewish junior lawyers and articling
students: see C Wilton, above, n 24 at 16.

'there was not much use trying to raise the standard in Nova Scotia with the low averages all about us of New Brunswick, Prince Edward Island, Québec and Ontario.'[32] By the time of the founding meeting of the Canadian Bar Association in 1896, of course, both McGill University in Québec[33] and Dalhousie University in Nova Scotia[34] had been offering law degrees for several decades. However, in New Brunswick and Ontario, as well as in western Canada, entry to the legal profession in the late nineteenth century was still based primarily on a period of apprenticeship or articling, a process which was both unsystematic and often unmonitored. An anonymous letter from a Saint John law student in the early nineteenth century captured many of the problems associated with the articling process: 'If I were asked ... which of the *learned* professions one could become a member of, with the least *learning*, and with the least labour, I would unhesitatingly answer – the profession of law.'[35] By contrast with medicine and theology, which required systematic study, the student's letter suggested that law students needed only to pay an entrance fee, take a desk in a barrister's office, and be registered in the 'Student's Book;' and then, so long as the student could read and write, and had 'walked in and out of an office door for four or five years,' he would be enrolled 'as a Lawyer.'[36]

Although the legal profession in Ontario had attempted to provide lectures to supplement the articling process on several occasions in the nineteenth century, it was only in 1889 that compulsory classroom instruction was finally established on a permanent basis.[37] Curtis Cole

32 P Girard, above, n 27 at 155. As Girard noted, Bulmer's remarks 'predictably ... were less than well received in the rest of the Dominion, and attendance "from the other provinces, and especially from Ontario, was noticeably weak" at the 1896 inaugural meeting.'
33 IC Pilarczyk, *'A Noble Roster': One Hundred and Fifty Years of Law at McGill* (Montréal, McGill University Faculty of Law, 1999) at 4–5. According to Pilarczyk, there were occasional lectures as early as 1829; but it was only in 1848 that a class of twenty two men began their studies at McGill under the guidance of William Badgley; in 1850, five of these students received McGill's first BCL degrees.
34 Dalhousie Law School opened in 1883, characterised by John Willis as 'a time of ferment in [common law] legal education;' by contrast with arrangements for law studies in England at that time, the programme at Dalhousie mirrored the newly established 'university law schools' in the United States, combining professional knowledge with the study of law as a liberal education: see J Willis, *A History of Dalhousie Law School* (Toronto, University of Toronto Press, 1979) at 7 and 20.
35 DG Bell, *Legal Education in New Brunswick: A History* (Fredericton, University of New Brunswick, 1992) at 19.
36 DG Bell, above, n 35. See also C Wilton, above, n 24 at 10–11, who reported that articling students often occupied 'an inordinate amount of time performing routine chores,' quoting ML Smith, *Young Mr Smith in Upper Canada* (Toronto, University of Toronto Press, 1980) at 17. See also IA MacKay, 'The Education of a Lawyer' (1940–42) *Alberta Law Quarterly* 103 at 110, quoted in WW Pue, 'Common Law Legal Education in Canada's Age of Light, Soap and Water' (1996) 23 *Manitoba Law Journal* 654 at 676; similar criticisms were evident in British Columbia: see WW Pue, above, n 15 at 9.
37 C Cole, *A History of Osgoode Hall Law School 1889–1989* (unpublished MS on file, 1995) at 51. See also GB Baker, 'Legal Education in Upper Canada, 1785–1889: The Law Society as Educator' in DH Flaherty (ed), *Essays in the History of Canadian Law*, vol 2

argued that the Law Society's decision to provide compulsory lectures was a response to changes in the economy and in society initiated by industrial-isation, urbanisation, and immigration; and that the institution of regular law lectures in 1889 represented the beginning of an important transition in legal education in Ontario: the transition from apprenticeship-based legal training to modern law school instruction.[38] Historians of legal education in Canada have traditionally noted the practitioner/academic dichotomy in different parts of the country: some provinces provided training for apprentices under the auspices of the profession (in Ontario and Manitoba, for example), while others offered lectures in university law schools (such as Dalhousie and McGill).[39] Interestingly, however, the introduction of systematic lectures (*either* by the profession *or* at university law schools) may have provided *the* significant catalyst for women's decisions to become law students. For a number of aspiring women lawyers in Canada, perhaps including Clara Brett Martin, who did not have fathers or other relatives who were legally trained, the necessity of obtaining full-time articles for three to five years might have created a substantial barrier to entering the legal profession.[40] In this context, it may be more than coincidental that Martin began her legal studies just a few years after Osgoode Hall introduced compulsory lectures in 1889. And it is possible that a similar pattern existed in the western provinces: the first women were admitted to the bar in Manitoba, Saskatchewan and Alberta between 1915 and 1917, after systematic lectures had been introduced for law students a few years earlier: in Manitoba from about 1911,[41] in Saskatchewan from 1913,[42] and in Alberta from 1912.[43] Moreover, after

(Toronto, The Osgoode Society, 1983) 49; and BD Bucknall, Thomas CH Baldwin and J David Lakin, 'Pedants, Practitioners and Prophets: Legal Education at Osgoode Hall to 1957' (1968) 6 *Osgoode Hall Law Journal* 137.

[38] C Cole, above, n 37. See also C Cole, '"A Learned and Honorable Body": The Profession-alization of the Ontario Bar, 1867–1929' (PhD thesis, University of Western Ontario, 1987).

[39] See JPS McLaren, 'The History of Legal Education in Common Law Canada' and JEC Brierley, 'Historical Aspects of Law Teaching in Québec,' both in RJ Matas and DJ McCawley (eds), *Legal Education in Canada* (Montréal, Federation of Law Societies of Canada, 1987) at 111 and 146.

[40] According to V Drachman, some American women found it easier to article with fathers or brothers, but this pattern was less evident in Canada, where it seems that fewer aspiring women lawyers had legally trained male relatives: see V Drachman, *Sisters in Law: Women Lawyers in Modern American History* (Cambridge, MA, Harvard University Press, 1998) at 40. There is evidence that Martin experienced problems as an articling student: see C Backhouse, above, n 3.

[41] Lectures were first instituted for law students in Manitoba in 1911; a few years later, legislation providing for the creation of the Manitoba Law School was enacted and the three-year lecture course, leading to both the LLB degree and admission to practice, opened in October 1914: see D and L Gibson, *Substantial Justice: Law and Lawyers in Manitoba 1670–1970* (Winnipeg, Peguis Publishers, 1972) at 215–16. See also JR London, 'The Admis-sions and Education Committee: A Perspective on Legal Education and Admission to Practice in the Province of Manitoba – Past, Present and Future' in C Harvey (ed), *The Law Society of Manitoba 1877–1987* (Winnipeg, Peguis Publishers, 1977) 74 at 77; and L Gibson, 'A Brief History of the Law Society of Manitoba' in Harvey (ed), 28 at 33.

[42] The Law Society in Saskatchewan established a law school in Regina in 1913; in the

French's controversial challenge in British Columbia, the admission of a second woman lawyer there occurred following the introduction of systematic lectures for law students.[44]

In addition to these changes in the legal profession, there were new ideas about women's roles in the latter decades of the nineteenth century, especially in relation to higher education. Perhaps inspired by women's increasing access to higher education in the United States, women entered Mount Allison University in New Brunswick as early as 1858, and a woman there received the first Bachelor of Science degree in the British Empire in 1875.[45] In the 1880s, Dalhousie, McGill, Manitoba College, and both Trinity and University Colleges at the University of Toronto all began to admit women students to courses in the Faculty of Arts.[46] As a supportive comment in the Dalhousie *Gazette* stated in 1882, women needed 'more education, not less,' and access to higher education for women was essential to bring 'a far-seeing wisdom to the service of their quick perceptions.'[47] Yet, as Veronica Strong-Boag argued, 'acceptance by the universities did not always include the right to enrol in professional

same year, the University of Saskatchewan in Saskatoon hired its first law professor, hoping to establish a university law school. In 1922, the Law Society entered into an agreement with the University of Saskatchewan and closed the school in Regina; according to Beth Bilson, the Law Society may have been motivated, not just by mounting debts, but also by the 1917 report of the Canadian Bar Association, which promoted university based legal education: see B Bilson, '"Prudence Rather than Valor": Legal Education in Saskatchewan 1908–23' (1998) 61 *Saskatchewan Law Review* 341.

43 The Law Society of Alberta initially promoted lectures alongside the law department of the University of Alberta, but 'financial pressures in a period of recession' in 1914 resulted in the Law Society ceding its responsibility for lectures in Edmonton and Calgary to the University of Alberta: see WW Pue, above, n 36 at 664–5. See also PM Sibenik, 'Doorkeepers: Legal Education in the Territories and Alberta, 1885–1928' (1990) 13 *Dalhousie Law Journal* 419, at 441–4; WH Johns, 'History of the Faculty of Law' (1980) *25th Anniversary Edition Alberta Law Review* 1; and WG Morrow 'An Historical Examination of Alberta's Legal System – The First Seventy-Five Years' (1981) 29 *Alberta Law Review* 148.

44 C Cleverdon, above, n 15 at 8. In 1909, law students requested the British Columbia Law Society to institute formal lectures; thus, the Vancouver Law School (1914 to 1943) and the Victoria Law School (1914 to 1923) came into existence: see WW Pue, above, n 15 at 44–64. Although lectures on law were offered at the University of British Columbia from 1920, the faculty of law was not established until 1945: Pue at 59–65. Comparing the British Columbia situation to other provinces, Pue concluded, at 62: 'the Vancouver Law School deserves to be recognised for what it was: a sustained, serious professional training school – no more; no less.'

45 F Bird, *et al, Royal Commission on the Status of Women in Canada* (Ottawa, Information Canada, 1970) at 164. See also J LaPierre, 'The Academic Life of Canadian Coeds, 1880–1900' in R Heap and A Prentice (eds), *Gender and Education in Ontario: An Historical Reader* (Toronto, Canadian Scholars' Press, 1991) 307; and G Davies 'The Literary "New Woman" and Social Activism in Maritime Literature, 1880–1920' in J Guildford and S Morton (eds), *Separate Spheres: Women's Worlds in the 19th-Century Maritimes* (Fredericton, Acadiensis Press, 1994) 233 at 236–7.

46 See *Royal Commission*, above, n 45; and M Dumont *et al, Québec Women: A History* (Toronto, The Women's Press, 1987) at 143. See also A Prentice, 'The Feminization of Teaching;' and DS Cross, 'The Neglected Majority: The Changing Role of Women in 19th-Century Montréal,' both in SM Trofimenkoff and A Prentice (eds), above, n 23 at 49 and 66.

47 H McInnis, 'For and About Women,' *The Dalhousie Gazette*, 7 April 1882, at 127–8.

faculties on the same basis as males,' and there was particular resistance from faculties of medicine, law and theology with 'their own traditions, which were rarely generous to women.'[48] Certainly, women were not initially welcomed in faculties of medicine. Indeed, Emily Stowe became Canada's first woman doctor in 1867 only after graduating from an American medical college. It was not until 1883 that her daughter, Augusta Stowe-Gullen, became the first woman doctor educated in Canada when she completed medical studies at the University of Toronto; and women faced similar challenges in medicine at both Queen's and McGill.[49]

In relation to law, however, it is more likely that resistance from professional bodies, not universities, may have discouraged women from becoming law students at McGill and Dalhousie until the early twentieth century. Certainly, the Dean of the Faculty of Law at McGill responded positively to Annie Macdonald Langstaff's application to attend law lectures in 1911,[50] and the Dalhousie *Gazette* appeared proud to record the admission of the first three 'good [and] earnest' women students in 1916.[51] Yet, since there is no evidence that women applied to study law at either university until just before World War I, the dearth of applications may itself confirm Strong-Boag's suggestion that Canadian women were not encouraged to seek university education in law in the last decades of the nineteenth century.[52]

In the decades after 1880, Canadian women were also becoming increasingly involved in organisations which sought to 'redress a host of social ills; [their goals included] temperance, religious instruction, improvements in the workplace, better housing, facilities for single women, and state-run public health and child welfare programs.'[53] As Jane Errington noted, women's organisations in different parts of the country

48 V Strong-Boag, 'Canada's Women Doctors: Feminism Constrained' in L Kealey (ed), above, n 12 at 109–10.

49 V Strong-Boag, above, n 48. See also C Hacker, *The Indomitable Lady Doctors* (Toronto, Clarke Irwin, 1982) at 17; V Strong-Boag (ed), *Elizabeth Smith: A Woman with a Purpose, the Diaries of Elizabeth Smith 1872–1884* (Toronto, University of Toronto Press, 1980); M Gillett, *We Walked Very Warily: A History of Women at McGill* (Montréal, Eden Press Women's Publications, 1981) at 279; and W Mitchinson, 'The Medical Treatment of Women' in S Burt *et al* (ed), above, n 11 at 237.

50 Dean Walton's letter of 28 September 1911, responding to an inquiry from Annie Macdonald Langstaff's employer, Sam Jacobs KC, suggested that no woman had ever sought entry to the law school but that 'there can be no objection to Mrs Langstaff following lectures in law': see M Gillett, above, n 49 at 304.

51 *The Dalhousie Gazette*, 1 December 1916, at 10.

52 John Willis concluded that women had been welcomed at Dalhousie as early as 1881, but that it was unclear whether they could be admitted to the bar, so no women registered: see above, n 34 at 76.

53 J Errington, above, n 11. See also W Roberts, '"Rocking the Cradle for the World": The New Woman and Maternal Feminism, Toronto 1877–1914' in L Kealey (ed), above, n 12 at 15; and M Dumont *et al*, above, n 46 at 241.

emphasised different kinds of reform goals, with women in the west less concerned about the urban problems which Ontario women more often addressed.[54] Nonetheless, it was in Stoney Creek, Ontario that the first Women's Institute was established in 1897; an organisation for farm women, Women's Institutes eventually spread throughout Canada and internationally.[55] Even earlier, women's missionary societies, as well as secular organisations like the Young Women's Christian Association, had been established.[56]

By 1900, however, it was the Women's Christian Temperance Union which was attracting 'the most publicity, the most criticism and the most support;' it had become 'a truly national organization,' located in both small towns and urban centres across Canada.[57] Although its major goal was prohibition, the WCTU also campaigned 'for Protestant missions, domestic science instruction for the poor, anti-tobacco legislation, stronger drug laws, social purity, school temperance textbooks, and ... suffrage.'[58] Eventually, the suffrage issue became the most prominent, since it appeared to provide the *means* of accomplishing the rest of the WCTU reform programme. This conclusion was reinforced when the WCTU was finally successful in persuading the federal government to conduct a national plebiscite on prohibition in 1898, and women then realised that they 'could only watch while men voted;' moreover, after a large majority of provinces had voted in favour of prohibition and the federal government nonetheless refused to enact legislation, the WCTU and other Canadian women aggressively focused their efforts on suffrage, believing that woman suffrage in Australia, New Zealand and some American states had been the catalyst for progressive changes in social laws.[59] As staunch

---

[54] J Errington, above, n 11 at 69. See also C Bacchi, 'Divided Allegiances: The Response of Farm Women and Labour Women to Suffrage' in L Kealey (ed), above, n 12 at 89; according to Bacchi, at 106–7, farm women tended to identify with issues of class rather than sex, distrusting urban, middle-class reform groups.

[55] See P Rankin, 'The Politicization of Ontario Farm Women' in L Kealey and J Sangster (eds), *Beyond the Vote: Canadian Women and Politics* (Toronto, University of Toronto Press, 1989) 309; and C MacDonald, *Adelaide Hoodless: Domestic Crusader* (Toronto and Reading, Dundurn Press, 1986) at 74.

[56] V Strong-Boag, above, n 23 at 88–9; and M MacMurchy, 'Women's Organizations, 1916' reproduced in R Cook and W Mitchinson (eds), above, n 14 at 216.

[57] V Strong-Boag, above, n 23 at 89–90. Strong-Boag identified Letitia Youmans, founder of the WCTU in Canada in 1874, as 'the single most important figure in the WCTU's early history.' By 1891, there were 175 unions in Ontario with 4318 members. See also W Mitchinson, 'The WCTU: "For God, Home and Native Land": A Study in Nineteenth-Century Feminism' in L Kealey (ed), above, n 12 at 151.

[58] V Strong-Boag, above, n 23 at 90–1.

[59] EG MacGill, *My Mother, The Judge* (Toronto, Ryerson Press, 1955) at 123; as MacGill argued, 'woman suffrage stood revealed as the keystone of the arch of domestic legislation.' W Mitchinson, above, n 57 at 158–9, argued that the federal government refused to enact legislation after the 1898 plebiscite because although almost every province voted in favour, Québec did not; and the federal government did not want to risk losing Québec support. See also JM Vickers, 'Feminist Approaches to Women and Politics' in L Kealey and J Sangster

WCTU campaigners like Nellie McClung explained, women's suffrage was necessary to accomplish moral reforms in Canadian society:

> If politics are corrupt, it is all the more reason that a new element should be introduced. Women will I believe supply that new element, that purifying influence. Men and women were intended to work together, and will work more ideally together, than apart, and just as the mother's influence as well as the father's is needed in bringing up of children and in the affairs of the home, so they are needed in the larger home, – the state.[60]

For McClung and other temperance reformers, women's suffrage was the means to enable women to play a role in society and politics, an extension of their role in the home; it was not intended to change women's fundamental responsibility for moral guidance, nor alter traditional relationships between men and women.

However, as Mitchinson noted, suffrage campaigns could not always rely on these arguments about the extension of women's 'purifying influence' outside the home. In the Maritimes, for example, the argument that women needed the vote to achieve temperance goals was relatively unpersuasive because prohibition had been substantially achieved there already by 'local option;' indeed, the Maritime provinces had the lowest *per capita* rate of alcohol consumption in Canada. As a result, suffragists were forced to use other more radical arguments about 'women's rights to equality and justice;' according to Mitchinson, such arguments presented more of a challenge to the established order, forcing women out from behind 'their concerns of home and family into the world.'[61] Clearly, these arguments were more controversial than those advocated by women like Nellie McClung;[62] perhaps for this reason, there were many women in the Maritimes (and in Québec) who declared that they 'did not want the vote and would not use it if they had it.'[63] Moreover, these more challenging arguments in support of women's suffrage reveal how claims by aspiring women lawyers, which were also based on principles of 'equality and

(eds), above, n 55 at 16 and 20–21. A bill had been introduced in the federal Parliament in 1885, extending the franchise to unmarried women and widows, but it did not succeed: see *Debates of the House of Commons*, 3rd session, 48–49 Victoria, 1885.

60 Quoted in Sylvia Bashevkin, 'Independence versus Partisanship: Dilemmas in the Political History of Women in English Canada' in Veronica Strong-Boag and Anita Clair Fellman (eds), *Rethinking Canada: The Promise of Women's History* (Toronto, Copp Clark Pitman Ltd, 1986) 246 at 252.

61 W Mitchinson, above, n 57 at 159.

62 See V Strong-Boag, '"Ever a Crusader": Nellie McClung, First-Wave Feminist' in V Strong-Boag and AC Fellman (eds), above, n 60 at 184.

63 C Cleverdon, above, n 15 at 7. Female suffrage proposals were considered in different parts of Canada in the nineteenth century, in addition to the federal bill of 1885: for example, see L McCann, 'The 1890s: Fragmentation and the New Social Order' in ER Forbes and DA Muise (eds), *The Atlantic Provinces in Confederation* (Toronto and Fredericton, University of Toronto Press and Acadiensis Press, 1993) 119 at 152–3.

justice' rather that women's 'purifying influence,' may have appeared very radical indeed in the late nineteenth century. In addition, women lawyers' aspirations for economic independence may have appeared to undermine women's role in the family, championed by the WCTU as the foundation of Canadian society.

At the same time, however, Canadian women were beginning to experience increasing opportunities to participate in reform efforts, both locally and in international reform organisations. For example, the Association for the Advancement of Women, an American organisation, held conventions in Canada on two occasions in the 1890s: in Toronto in 1890 and in Saint John in 1896; and Carol Bacchi reported that 'both meetings received wide and favourable press coverage.'[64] As well, the noted American suffragist, Susan B Anthony spoke in 1889 at a Toronto meeting held to launch the new Dominion Women's Enfranchisement Association, an organisation which eventually established branch societies in several Canadian cities.[65] In the 1890s, Canadian women also became active in the International Council of Women. Initially organised by the American suffragists, Elizabeth Cady Stanton and Susan B Anthony, the International Council had held its first meeting in Washington in 1888,[66] and several Canadian women were present, including Dr Emily Stowe.[67] The International Council met for a second time at the time of the World's Columbian Exposition in Chicago in 1893, and once again, a number of Canadians were present. Indeed, it seems that some American delegates were determined to influence the Canadians, whom they regarded as somewhat timid, to take up the suffrage issue more vigorously; as one Canadian delegate reported:

... a female shook her umbrella at me and bawled, (although I was very near her), 'You Canadians are indifferent. You must be aroused. You must vote!'[68]

At the meeting in Chicago, Lady Ishbel Aberdeen, the indefatigable wife

---

64 CL Bacchi, *Liberation Deferred? The Ideas of the English-Canadian Suffragists, 1877–1918* (Toronto, University of Toronto Press, 1983) at 17–18 and 148; she argued that 'female suffragists did not *fail* to effect a social revolution for women; the majority never had a revolution in mind.' See also C Whitton, 'Is the Canadian Woman a Flop in Politics?' *Saturday Night*, 26 January 1946.

65 C Cleverdon, above, n 15 at 16. According to Cleverdon, it was Dr Emily Stowe who arranged for Anthony to visit Toronto; she also invited other American women reformers to Toronto.

66 Fifty-three national women's organisations were represented at the 1888 meeting, along with representatives from other countries: see E Griffith, *In Her Own Right: The Life of Elizabeth Cady Stanton* (New York, Oxford University Press, 1984) at 192–3; and K Barry, *Susan B Anthony: A Biography of a Singular Feminist* (New York, Ballantine Books, 1988) at 283.

67 V Strong-Boag, above, n 23 at 97.

68 V Strong-Boag, above, n 23 at 97, citing 'Between You and Me,' *Saturday Night*, 8 January 1898, at 8.

of Canada's Governor General, became president of the International Council, and she then promoted the creation of Canada's own National Council of Women.[69] Canadian delegates attended the next meetings of the International Council in London and in Berlin, and then in 1909, Toronto proudly hosted the Council meeting.[70] In her presentation to a session at the Toronto meeting on 'Professions and Careers for Women,' Ellen Spencer Mussey, Dean of the Washington College of Law, reported that there were four women lawyers in Canada at that time.[71] Significantly, Mabel Penery French also presented a paper to this Council meeting, but the Council minutes noted that Clara Brett Martin 'sent her regrets.'[72] Later in the same year, Emmeline Pankhurst, the formidable British suffragist, spoke to the Toronto Club; according to the *Canadian Annual Review*, she 'impressed 500 thinking men with a vivid sense of the seriousness of the movement, a keen realisation of the sincerity of its advocate and her capacity as a leader, a sense of having listened to an appeal to reason as well as to sentiment.'[73] Thus, women's increased access to higher education and the existence of organised movements for reform may have contributed to some women's aspirations to seek admission to the profession of law.

Yet, even if a 'spirit of expanding opportunities' existed for women and for the legal profession, Clara Brett Martin experienced significant opposition from the legal profession when she applied to become a lawyer in Ontario in 1891. Indeed, although she stated in her application that, even though she was a woman, she was relying on the 'broad spirit of liberality and fairness that characterizes members of the legal profession' to be accepted, the Law Society reviewed her request for six months and then rejected it on the basis that neither the statutes nor the rules of the Society authorised the admission of women members.[74] The legal press

[69] See V Strong-Boag, above, n 23 at 98–9, citing W Thorpe, 'Lady Aberdeen and the National Council of Women' (MA Thesis, Queen's University, 1973) at 138; and D French, *Ishbel and the Empire: A Biography of Lady Aberdeen* (Toronto and Oxford, Dundurn Press, 1988) at 147. According to Sandra Gwyn, Lady Aberdeen's speech to the First Annual Meeting of the NCW in April 1894, which focused on the need for 'mothering' work on the part of Canadian women, revealed how Aberdeen's concern 'was not so much to reform the condition of women as such, but to reform society, employing women as a means to this end': see S Gwyn, *The Private Capital: Ambition and Love in the Age of Macdonald and Laurier* (Toronto, McClelland and Stewart Limited, 1984) at 279–80.

[70] The ICW meeting was held in Toronto from 24–30 June 1909 under the auspices of the NCW of Canada: see *Report of the International Congress of Women* (Toronto, Geo Parker & Sons, 1910), 2 vols.

[71] *Report*, above, n 70 (vol 2) at 333: Ellen Spencer Mussey, 'The Women Attorney and Counsellor.'

[72] See *Report*, above, n 70 (vol 1) at 173–4; and at 203.

[73] C Cleverdon, above, n 15 at 32. See also D Gorham, 'Flora MacDonald Denison: Canadian Feminist' in L Kealey (ed), above, n 12 at 47, distinguishing 'militant' *suffragettes* and more moderate *suffragists*. See also P Bartley, *Emmeline Pankhurst* (London and New York, Routledge, 2002) at 169–70 and 178–9; and J Purvis, *Emmeline Pankhurst: A Biography* (London and New York, Routledge, 2002).

[74] T Roth, above, n 3 at 326, citing *Ontario Sessional Papers*, 1892, vol 24, pt 6, no 75.

fully supported the Law Society's decision, with the *Canada Law Journal* stating succinctly that there was no known 'public advantage to be gained by [women] being admitted to the Bar.'[75] Apparently undaunted, Martin succeeded in having amending legislation enacted in 1893 to permit her to enrol as a law student. However, since the 1893 legislation authorised women to be admitted (on completion of the required programme) only as solicitors, she had to lobby again for the enactment of another legislative amendment authorising the Law Society to admit women as barristers; this legislation was enacted in 1895.[76] After some further intransigence, the Law Society finally passed the necessary rules to permit women to become members of the bar in November 1896, and Martin was admitted as a barrister and solicitor on 2 February 1897, the first woman lawyer in Ontario and in Canada.[77] In response to an inquiry from the Belgian barrister, Louis Frank, Martin forwarded a 'short sketch' of her career and a photograph in a letter dated 6 February 1897. She also noted that 'there are no other women studying law in Canada.'[78]

However, although she may not have known of other women law students, Martin was not the only one in Canada in the 1890s. According to Sandra Petersson, at least one woman was enrolled as an articling student by the Law Society of the Northwest Territories in 1896: Erella Laurena Leona Alexander of Calgary became an articling student and passed her intermediate examination in 1900, although there is no record of her sitting the final examination.[79] As Petersson noted, 'in contrast to the personal and political battles women faced in other provinces, women seeking to become lawyers in Alberta, formerly part of the Northwest Territories, encountered no formal opposition.'[80] In addition to these women students in Alberta, David Bell reported that two women, Edith Hanington and Isabel Mowatt, became students at the King's College of Law in Saint John in the years immediately after the College was established in 1892.[81] Isabel Mowatt was the daughter of a cobbler and had worked as a court stenographer; she was also a member of the Women's

---

75 (1896) 32 *Canada Law Journal* 423.

76 See above, n 4.

77 See above, n 3. Eva Maude Powley was admitted in 1902 and Geraldine Bertram Robinson in 1907. The fourth woman to be admitted was Mabel Penery French in New Brunswick in 1907.

78 Letter from Clara Brett Martin to Louis Frank, 6 February 1897, in Bibliothèque Royale, Brussels, *Papiers Frank* #6031 (file 3).

79 S Petersson, 'Ruby Clements and Early Women of the Alberta Bar' (1997) 9 *Canadian Journal of Women and the Law* 365 at 366–7.

80 S Petersson, above, n 79 at 366. Following Alexander, Grace McLeod enrolled in 1909, and then Bessie Hosking Nichols in 1910; neither of these women completed their articles.

81 DG Bell, above, n 35 at 95–7. In addition to women, Bell noted, at 92–4, that the first students included an Afro-Canadian lawyer, Abraham Walker, who already had a law degree and ten years' standing at the New Brunswick bar, a Jewish student, and several students whose families were not middle-class.

Enfranchisement Association, and may have been encouraged to attend the Law School as a result of her participation in the activities of the organised women's movement in Saint John in the 1890s.[82] However, neither Mowatt nor Hanington completed their studies. Although there is no information about Mowatt's reasons for discontinuing her studies, Hanington's decision may have been influenced by her embarrassing experiences as a law student. It seems that the Procedure lecturer, who was her uncle, routinely greeted her with a kiss at the beginning of each class, and then drew attention to her presence by addressing the class '*Lady* and Gentlemen.'[83]

Yet, although neither Mowatt nor Hanington became lawyers, it was only a few years later in 1902 that Mabel Penery French became a student at the King's College of Law. According to Bell, the leaders of the New Brunswick legal community had established the College to promote 'a dignified and deferential profession'; the Saint John Law School operated in conjunction with King's College in Windsor, Nova Scotia until 1923.[84] When French successfully completed her studies for a law degree in 1905, she petitioned the Barristers' Society to be admitted as an attorney, and as a result of a division of opinion about the propriety of admitting a woman, the Society referred the matter to the Supreme Court for an opinion.[85] After the court concluded unanimously that French was not eligible to be a lawyer, the issue was presented to the legislature, and an amending statute was enacted in 1906.[86] French was duly admitted as an attorney in March 1906, and after a mandatory year of satisfactory work in a law firm, she was formally admitted to the bar of New Brunswick on 22 November 1907. As Lois Yorke explained, French's success in gaining entry to the legal profession made her 'for a fleeting moment, the darling of the print media and the feminist movement.'[87]

---

[82] DG Bell, above, n 35 at 92 and 96–9. Bell noted, at 95, that a 'preemptive editorial' in the *King's College Record* in January 1893 had regretted the admission of women lawyers in the United States. Bell identified Mowatt as having entered the law school in 1893 (at 92) and then in 1896 (at 97); according to Yorke, however, Mowatt entered the law school in 1896: see LK Yorke, 'Mabel Penery French (1881–1955): A Life Re-created' (1993) 42 *University of New Brunswick Law Journal* 3 at 11.

[83] DG Bell, above, n 35, reported that Hanington had enrolled at the law school to please her father, who had been unsuccessful in encouraging her brother to enrol; when her brother enrolled the next year, Edith 'decided to retire from the field.' In addition, Edith experienced difficulty with night classes, since she was not permitted to walk home alone; according to Bell, at 97, Hanington concluded that she was not a 'pioneer.'

[84] DG Bell, above, n 35 at 47–50 and 55–6; according to Bell, at 67–9, the Saint John Law School was the beginning of the law faculty of the University of New Brunswick.

[85] See LK Yorke, above, n 82; C Mullins, 'Mabel Penery French' (1986) 44 *The Advocate* 676–9; and J Brockman and DE Chunn, '"A New Order of Things": Women's Entry into the Legal Profession in British Columbia' (2002) 60 *The Advocate* 385.

[86] See *French* (NB), above, n 7; and above, n 9.

[87] LK Yorke, above, n 82 at 4 and 18. According to Yorke, no other woman became a lawyer in New Brunswick until Muriel Corkery was admitted to the bar in 1921.

Thus, both for Martin in Ontario and for French in New Brunswick, the pattern was one of rejection of their petitions by the profession and the judiciary, and then, support for their claims on the part of provincial legislators. The same pattern was evident when French moved to Vancouver and submitted a petition for admission to the bar of British Columbia in 1911: the Law Society concluded that there was no authority for the admission of women members of the bar, and French thus applied for a writ of *mandamus*, an order compelling the Law Society to admit her. As before, her application was unsuccessful on an initial motion and again before a unanimous Court of Appeal, so that, once again, it was necessary to seek a legislative amendment. Eventually, the British Columbia legislature enacted an amendment authorising the admission of women to the bar; and after sitting the required examinations, French was admitted to the British Columbia bar on 1 April 1912.[88] In an interview with the media just prior to being called to the bar of British Columbia, French stated:

> I imagine that most women who will enter the profession in the years to come will do so like myself, with the desire of seeking a useful and independent career. If so, they will find in it a work that stimulates the mind and supplies continual interest....[89]

A few years later, however, French abandoned the practice of law completely and moved to England, where she married and spent the rest of her life; she never practised law again.[90]

Significantly, even after women had gained admission to the bar in these three Canadian provinces, the numbers of women lawyers remained small. According to the 1911 census, for example, there were just over 5000 lawyers in Canada, but only *seven* were women.[91] Yet, it may have been the success of women like Martin and French that encouraged Annie Macdonald Langstaff, an Ontario native who had moved to Montréal; after working for a few years in a law firm, she entered the BCL programme at McGill University in 1911. Graduating in 1914 with first rank honours, an overall standing of fourth place, and a prize, Langstaff

---

[88] *French* (BC), above, n 8; and above, n 9. See LK Yorke, above, n 82 at 29 and 41–2. See also A Watts QC, *History of the Legal Profession in British Columbia 1869–1984* (Vancouver, The Law Society of BC, 1984) at 133–5. Watts reported, at 135, that the Law Society established the Mabel Penery French annual golf cup in 1966, 'to be competed for by the ladies....'

[89] LK Yorke, above, n 82 at 43, quoting JS Cowper, 'Confidences of a Woman Lawyer' (1912) 39 *The Canadian Magazine* 142.

[90] LK Yorke, above, n 82 at 44. Yorke reported that French went to England in 1913, as a travelling companion of Joseph Russell, her counsel in the litigation in British Columbia; French married Hugh Travis Clay in 1923. According to Yorke, at 47, 'little is known of Mrs Clay's subsequent activities, although it is certain that she was not active in any branch of the legal profession.'

[91] *Census of Canada 1931*, vol 1, table 83.

then applied to take the preliminary bar examinations.[92] Her application was refused; and her subsequent petition to the Superior Court for a writ of *mandamus* was denied, as was an appeal to the Court of King's Bench in 1915.[93] However, the established pattern was altered when Langstaff's efforts to obtain a legislative amendment were unsuccessful.[94] Nonetheless, she continued to work in a Montréal law firm until she retired; she described her work there as 'a little secretarial work, a little bookkeeping, and a little law.'[95] As a single parent, moreover, who had separated early on from her husband and never received financial support from him, Langstaff needed to work. As she argued in a speech at the time of her court challenge:

> It is all very well to say that women's sole sphere should be the home, but it shows most lamentable blindness to the economic conditions which one would think were potent. The plain fact ... is that many women have to earn their living outside the home, if they are to have homes at all.... [All] that is asked for women who desire to practise is that they shall prove [their abilities] as men have to prove them....[96]

In spite of the efforts of Langstaff and others, however, it was not until 1941 that the Québec legislature enacted the amendment which permitted women to become lawyers; moreover, since the 1941 amendment required both an undergraduate degree and a law degree, Langstaff remained inadmissible as she did not have an undergraduate degree. Thus, she was never 'afforded the opportunity to directly utilize her formidable talents in the practice of law.'[97]

French's cases in New Brunswick and British Columbia, and Langstaff's case in Québec, are the only reported judicial decisions in Canada about women's eligibility to enter the legal profession. All three cases attracted multiple judicial opinions about women's eligibility to become lawyers, and with a single exception, the judges in these cases were united in their view that the law did not permit women to enter the legal profession. However, in New Brunswick and British Columbia, efforts to obtain support for legislative amendments were successful. Moreover, by the second decade of the twentieth century, other Canadian provinces had

---

92 M Gillett, above, n 49 at 304; see also IC Pilarczyk, above, n 33.
93 See *Langstaff* (CS) and *Langstaff* (CBR), above, n 5.
94 See G Gallichan, above, n 6.
95 IC Pilarczyk, above, n 33 at 59. According to M Gillett, above, n 49 at 309, Langstaff retired in 1965 at age 78, and died ten years later, 'without having [her] "sanguine hopes" of 1911 ever fulfilled.' However, Michael Vineberg, a partner at the firm where Langstaff worked, explained that 'actually, she was in our office for some 67 years and retired at the age of 88': letter from Michael Vineberg (Phillips, Vineberg) to Dean John Brierley, 16 December 1981 in Annie Macdonald Langstaff file, Faculty of Law archives, McGill University.
96 Speech to the Insurance Underwriters' Dinner, 1915: M Gillett, above, n 49 at 306.
97 IC Pilarczyk, above, n 33 at 59; see also G Gallichan, above, n 6 at 110.

begun to enact legislation permitting women to become lawyers,[98] even though there had been no judicial challenges. Thus, a few years before Langstaff began her litigation in Québec, legislation was enacted in 1912 in Manitoba, enabling Melrose Sissons and Winnifred Wilton to become the first women lawyers in Manitoba when they completed their studies in 1915.[99] Similarly, as a result of legislation enacted in Saskatchewan in 1913, Mary Cathcart became the first woman lawyer there in 1917.[100] In 1915, the Law Society in Alberta admitted Lillian Ruby Clements to the legal profession – without enacting amending legislation at all; in due course, a retrospective statute was passed in 1930.[101] In 1917, Nova Scotia enacted amending legislation which enabled Francis Fish, a native of New Brunswick, to become the first woman lawyer in Nova Scotia in 1918.[102] In the same year, legislation was enacted in Prince Edward Island, although it was not until 1926 that Roma Stewart became the first woman lawyer there;[103] similarly, legislation had been enacted as early as 1910 in Newfoundland, although no woman was admitted to the legal profession until Louisa Saunders became a lawyer in 1933.[104] Thus, at the end of World War I, only the province of Québec remained formally closed to women lawyers. Finally in 1941, the government enacted amending legislation which permitted women there to become lawyers; as the Montréal *Star* reported on 17 January 1942:

History was made in Québec on Thursday, when two women were admitted to the practice of law. The administration of the oath to Miss Elizabeth C Monk and Mrs Suzanne Raymond-Filion marks the culmination of a long struggle for

98 For statutes, see above, n 4, above, n 6 and above, n 9.

99 C Harvey, above, n 6 at 17; and Kinnear, above, n 10 at 79. See also P Wilton, 'Inappropriate for Women...' *Law Now*, November 1992, at 23.

100 C Harvey, above, n 6 at 17.

101 As Petersson explained, the Law Society had no authority to admit women as lawyers in 1915, although *R v Cyr* [1917] 3 Western Weekly Reports 849 later concluded that women were not disabled from holding public office: see S Petersson, above, n 79.

102 C Harvey, above, n 6 at 17; see also LK Kernaghan, 'The Madonna of the Law' (Fall 1991) *Hearsay* (Dalhousie Law School) at 26.

103 C Harvey, above, n 6 at 17. See D Kessler, *A Century on Spring Street: Wanda Lefurgey Wyatt of Summerside, Prince Edward Island, 1895–1998* (Charlottetown, PEI, Indigo Press, 1999) at 196–9; Wyatt was the first woman to become a student at law in late 1919, but she was never admitted to practice. See also S Petersson, above, n 79 at 384, citing K Fisher, 'Sounding Down the Years: Roma Stewart Goodwin Blackburn's Journey in Law' (Edmonton, 1994, unpublished).

104 C Harvey, above, n 6 at 17. According to S Petersson, above, n 79 at 384, the Law Society of Newfoundland rejected an application presented by Janet Miller in 1910, and the colonial government then enacted legislation permitting her to enrol as a student at law; Miller's uncle was Attorney General of Newfoundland. Her studies were interrupted when she married during World War I, and then became an ambulance driver after her husband was killed with many other Newfoundlanders in the Battle of the Somme. She returned to St John's after the War and remarried, but did not continue her law studies; her papers are in the Centre for Newfoundland Studies Archives: see 'Janet Miller Helped Pave the Way' (unidentified clipping forwarded by Justice Leo Barry, on file).

recognition of women's right to an equal place in the professions alongside men. It is related, of course, to the fight for the franchise and the general question of releasing women from a tutelage that derives from an earlier concept of their place in the social structure....[105]

Interestingly, the timing of statutory amendments concerning women's eligibility for admission to the bar in Canada frequently coincided with the date of women's provincial enfranchisement.[106] Thus, the first women were admitted to the bar in Manitoba, Saskatchewan and Alberta between 1915 and 1917, and the provincial franchise had been achieved in all three of these western provinces by 1916.[107] Similarly, although there were university law programmes in Québec and in Nova Scotia much earlier, statutes permitting women's admission to the bar in both these provinces occurred close to the timing of women's right to the provincial suffrage: in 1918 in Nova Scotia and in 1940 in Québec. Suffrage legislation was enacted in Prince Edward Island in 1925, just a few years after the enactment of a statute to enable women to become lawyers.[108] Thus, the 'spirit of expanding opportunity' for women in the late nineteenth and early twentieth centuries may have encouraged both women's suffrage and women's admission to the bar, challenging the profession's male exclusivity. Yet, amending statutes which permitted women to become lawyers 'on the same terms as men' meant that women were required to embrace a professional identity as lawyers; the profession's traditional culture and the small numbers of women lawyers combined to render them invisible as women. In this context, when the minutes of the British Columbia Law Society recorded the admission in 1912 of 'twenty gentlemen, including Mabel Penery French,'[109] there was no irony intended. The Society was simply recognising that if women wished to become lawyers, they must do so 'on the same terms as men.'

[105] See C Harvey, above, n 6 at 18; and G Gallichan, above, n 6.

[106] Technically, some of these statutes 're-enfranchised' women. According to J Garner, *The Franchise and Politics in British North America 1755–1867* (Toronto, University of Toronto Press, 1969) at 155–8, women in British colonies in North America followed English precedent and did not vote; however, there is evidence of some women voting in Lower Canada and in Nova Scotia. Statutes later disqualified women from voting: in Lower Canada in 1834, in Prince Edward Island in 1836, in New Brunswick in 1843, in the Province of Canada in 1849, and in Nova Scotia in 1851.

[107] See C Cleverdon, above, n 15 at 46.

[108] C Cleverdon, above, n 15 at 156. Federal legislation in 1917 extended the vote to women who were relatives of members of the armed forces; and then to all women in May 1918.

[109] A Watts, above, n 88 at 134.

'PERSONS,' PRONOUNS, AND POLICY CHOICES: JUDICIAL
REASONING IN *FRENCH* AND *LANGSTAFF*

To my mind, having regard to the common law disability ..., this fact that no
woman has ever been admitted in England, is conclusive that the word 'person'
in our own Act was not intended to include a woman. The context of our Act
refers to a profession for men, and men alone.[110]

In the three reported cases involving women's claims to be admitted to the
bar, legal principles about women's common law rights and about the
meaning of the word 'person' were interpreted in the light of British jurisprudence to deny their claims. Even though women's claims to become
lawyers were presented to courts against a background of significant
change in social and professional life in Canada, the decisions focused on
technical interpretations of women's common law rights, principles of
statutory interpretation, and legal precedents denying their claims. At the
same time, the judges sometimes acknowledged the significance of the
claims, carefully pointing out that they were not expressing their own
opinions, but merely applying the law. In this way, the decisions appear to
recognise tensions between the narrowness of judicial reasoning and
women's larger aspirations within a rapidly changing social and professional context. All the same, by denying any legal foundation for women's
claims to enter the legal profession, courts were ensuring that the law, as
well as the legal professions, preserved their traditional male exclusivity.
Judicial views of law as a male preserve contributed to the conclusion that
women were not eligible to enter the legal profession in Canada because it
was a profession for men, and men alone; any lingering doubts were met
with the argument that women continued to be excluded from the legal
professions in Britain.

The first reported decision was French's application, presented by the
Barristers' Society as *amicus curiae* to the New Brunswick court in
1905.[111] The court reviewed two kinds of arguments about women's eligibility to become lawyers: first, that there was a right at common law for
women to be admitted to the bar; and second, that the language of the
statute, which authorised the Barristers' Society to make rules for the
admission of 'persons,' included women as well as men. In relation to the
argument about the existence of a common law right, counsel for the
Barristers' Society carefully presented a number of American precedents in
which courts had recognised women's eligibility to become lawyers, as well
as decisions which reached the opposite conclusion; although American
decisions were not legally binding on the court in New Brunswick, the

---

110 *French* (BC), above, n 8 at 6, *per* Irving, JA. The appellate report included the motions
judgment.
111 *French* (NB), above, n 7.

French decision revealed the judges' preference for cases which had *denied* that women could be lawyers.[112] In relation to the second argument, the judges considered the meaning of the word 'person,' taking into account the provincial *Interpretation Act*, which provided that the word 'person' included anyone to whom 'the context is capable of applying.' However, since the context included the fact that women had never been lawyers in the past, the court decided that the legislature had never intended that women be included as 'persons' in the bar statute.[113] Thus, rejecting all of the arguments, the five judges who heard French's case concluded that there were no legal principles which supported French's claim to become a lawyer. Rather, just as Martin had been qualified to be admitted to the bar in Ontario only after the enactment of appropriate legislation, the New Brunswick court concluded that French's application was also a matter for the legislature.[114]

These same arguments were again considered when French submitted her application for *mandamus* to the court in British Columbia in 1911, requesting an order compelling the Law Society to enrol her as an applicant for admission to the bar. On the initial application, the judge focused on the statutory language which authorised the Law Society to enrol 'persons,' concluding that nothing in this language or in the practice of the courts suggested that the legislature had intended to include women as members of the bar.[115] The Court of Appeal subsequently agreed with this interpretation of the statutory language. As well, all three judges in the appellate court held that women were under a common law disability which precluded their admission to the legal profession, and that this traditional exclusion of women constituted conclusive proof that the word 'person' was never intended to include women. In addition to citing American and English precedents, the Court of Appeal referred to Martin's experience in Ontario and to French's case in New Brunswick as further

---

112 Connell cited American cases which held that women were eligible for admission to the bar without statutory enactments: *Ricker's Case* 66 New Hampshire Reports 207 (1890); *In re Hall* 47 American Reports 625 (Conn 1882); *Re Thomas* 13 Lawyers' R 538 (Colorado Reports 1891); and *Cummings v Missouri* 4 Wallace's Supreme Court Reports 277 (US 1866). He also cited cases confirming that women were disqualified from being admitted to the bar: *Chorlton v Lings* (1868) LR 4 CP 374; *Beresford-Hope v Sandhurst* (1889) 23 QBD 79 (CA); *Bradwell v Illinois* 16 Wallace's Supreme Court Reports 130 (US 1872); *Robinson's Case* 131 Massachusetts Reports 376 (1889); and *In re Leonard* 53 American Reports 323 (Or 1885). Tuck, CJ and Barker, J focused on *Chorlton v Lings*, *Beresford-Howe v Sandhurst* and *Bradwell*.

113 See *Consolidated Statutes of New Brunswick*, 1903 c 1, s 8(31). Tuck, CJ concluded that the legislature intended to include only persons who were qualified at common law to become lawyers, that is, males; Hanington, J agreed. Barker, J compared statutory language to conclude that the legislature had no 'thought or intention of making the radical change' required by French's application: *French* (NB), above, n 7 at 371.

114 Martin's admission to the bar in Ontario was noted in the *amicus curiae* submission.

115 Morrison, J concluded that the legislature 'had not in mind the contingency that women would invoke the provisions of the Act, and I do not think it applies to them': *French* (BC), above, n 8 at 3.

support for their conclusions, and all the judges firmly stated that any change in the law required the intervention of the provincial legislature.[116] Moreover, although French's counsel had argued that she was entitled to be admitted as a duly qualified barrister and solicitor from another Canadian province, not just as a woman seeking to be admitted to the bar for the first time, the British Columbia courts made no distinction in its interpretation of the word 'person;' in neither case was a woman a 'person.'[117]

The similarity in judicial responses to French's applications in New Brunswick in 1905 and in British Columbia in 1911 was also reflected in Langstaff's application for *mandamus*, when her application was presented to the Québec court in January 1915 to compel the authorities to permit her to take the preliminary bar examinations.[118] The bar defended its rejection of her application on the basis of three arguments, two of which concerned technical aspects of the bar's organisational structure and discretionary authority.[119] Its third objection was that the relevant legislation, which used male pronouns to refer to candidates for admission to the bar, precluded the admission of a woman as an advocate. By contrast, Langstaff's counsel argued that the *Code Civil* declared that the masculine gender included both sexes, unless the context required application to only one of them. In examining the context of the bar statute as a whole, however, the judge surveyed the history of the legal profession and concluded that 'no woman either in literary France, or in practical England' had ever made any attempt to become a member of the legal profession prior to the enactment of the statute governing the bar in Québec in 1849.[120] He also examined English authorities and a number of American cases in which *married* women had been denied the right to practise law, and pointed out that Langstaff had not provided any proof that, in spite of her separation from her husband, she had obtained his authorisation to present herself for the preliminary examination as a

[116] Irving, JA referred to principles of statutory interpretation and legislative intent. Quoting Barker, J in New Brunswick, he agreed that the BC *Interpretation Act* should 'not be used to bring about so radical a change': *French* (BC), above, n 8 at 8.

[117] Counsel for the Law Society argued against women from other provinces obtaining 'a right and privilege denied to British Columbia women': *French* (BC), above, n 8 at 2–3.

[118] Technically, Langstaff needed judicial authorisation to bring an application for mandamus because she was married and did not have her husband's permission to sue. Lane J gave permission, stating that it was 'in the interests of [all] that the matter should come up upon its merits...': see *Evening News*, 31 July 1914; *Gazette*, 11 July 1914; and *Daily Mail*, 14 July 1914.

[119] The Bar first argued that it lacked authority as each board of examiners was a separate corporation, an argument upheld by Saint-Pierre, J. The second argument related to the scope of the Bar's discretion, and Saint-Pierre, J concluded that no authority to admit a woman to the bar existed at law: *Langstaff* (CS), above, n 5 at 132–6.

[120] *Langstaff* (CS), above, n 5 at 140. Counsel for Langstaff argued that the *Civil Code* (art 17, para 9) declared that the masculine gender included both sexes, unless by the context it was applicable to only one of them. Applying this rule to the *Bar Act*, RS 1909, masculine pronouns should be interpreted to include women: *Langstaff* (CS), above, n 5 at 137.

student at law.[121] In the appeal to the Court of King's Bench, four of the five judges agreed that the context in which the legislation governing the bar was initially enacted precluded any possibility that the use of the masculine pronoun was intended to include both sexes. They also noted that women had become eligible to enter the legal profession in France and in several American states only as a result of legislation; as a result, the appellate court concluded that legislation was necessary to achieve Langstaff's goal.[122] Interestingly, although Langstaff's claim was considered pursuant to the civil code in Québec, the court's reasoning was very similar to the conclusions in French's cases in New Brunswick and in British Columbia.

However, it is possible that the Québec legal context was significant to the appellate judgment of Justice Lavergne, the only judge who dissented in any of these three cases. For Justice Lavergne, the *only* law applicable to the issue was the law of the province of Québec. Thus, although he examined cases in the United States and in England, as well as in other Canadian provinces, he firmly asserted that the only relevant provisions in this case were those of the *Code Civil* and the provincial statute governing the bar of Québec. Accordingly, to those who suggested that the language of these provisions required that a member of the bar must be a male person, Justice Lavergne held that the law stated the opposite: the bar was open to both males and females; according to Justice Lavergne, if the legislature had intended that it apply only to males, it would have stated this exclusion *expressly*. In support of this conclusion, he referred to legislation concerning notaries, which had been enacted in the same year as the statute governing the bar; this legislation *expressly* stated that women were *not* eligible to be notaries. As well, he pointed to other legislation in Québec which *expressly* excluded women from being elected to the legislature and from serving as a member of a jury. In this context, Justice Lavergne concluded that the absence of a prohibition in the statute governing the bar meant that women were included: '*notre loi est la loi de la province de Québec; [nous] n'avons pas à aller plus loin et cette loi-là ne souffre pas d'interprétation parce qu'elle est claire.*'[123]

Thus, of the fifteen judges who decided these cases in New Brunswick, British Columbia and Québec in the decade between 1905 and 1915, all but one concluded that women were not eligible to become lawyers. In

---

121 The *Evening News*, 20 January 1915, reported that Langstaff did not consult her husband about studying law; as she stated, 'I did not know his address. He has a wandering spirit, and we have been separated for many years.' She also confirmed that she alone supported her daughter.

122 Pelletier, JA concluded that '*la loi française, comme la loi anglaise, [c']était alors à l'effet que la profession d'avocat était interdite aux personnes du sexe feminin;*' he also noted the enactment of legislation in France to permit women to become *avocats*. Archambeault, CJ focused on the context to conclude that the legislature had never intended to include women: *Langstaff* (CBR), above, n 5 at 15–20.

123 *Langstaff* (CBR), above, n 5 at 12–13.

New Brunswick and in British Columbia, the courts unanimously concluded that there was no common law right which entitled women to
become lawyers, and that the use of the word 'person' in their relevant
statutes, as interpreted in the context of each statute as a whole, was not
intended to include women as well as men. In Québec, all of the judges
except Justice Lavergne similarly concluded that the use of a male pronoun
in the statute regulating admission to the bar should not be interpreted as
inclusive of women, having regard to the context in which the legislation
was enacted.[124] In all three cases, all the judges except Justice Lavergne
relied on cases in other jurisdictions where women had been denied the
right to enter the legal profession; they also pointed to the necessity of
legislative amendments to permit women to gain admission to the bar.
Thus, in terms of legal reasoning, Justice Lavergne adopted a very different
approach to the issues. By suggesting that *only* the law of Québec was
relevant, he clearly distinguished Langstaff's application from cases in
jurisdictions outside Canada, and in Ontario, New Brunswick and British
Columbia, and he clearly rejected the need for a legislative amendment to
permit women to become lawyers. In addition, by applying a principle of
statutory interpretation that women were included unless they were
expressly excluded, he created a presumption of inclusivity.

In the end, it is clear that different approaches to legal reasoning resulted
in different outcomes. Yet, all of these approaches constituted recognised
and accepted principles of legal reasoning: the need to take account of
relevant judicial precedents and to consider context in the interpretation of
statutory language, including the word 'persons' and gendered pronouns.
As is evident, however, determining 'relevance' in relation to precedents
and the meaning of 'context' in interpreting statutes required *choices*
about which approach to adopt. In the end, all of the judges except Justice
Lavergne in Québec made choices which resulted in maintaining the status
quo of the (male) legal profession. In making such choices, the judges
offered two justifications. One was the need to recognise the more limited
role of a judge, by contrast with a legislature, in making 'new' law; the
other was that women's claims to become lawyers challenged fundamental
ideas about women's proper role. Interestingly, since these explanations
were not necessary to their legal reasoning about the meaning of the word
'persons' or the scope of male pronouns, the judges' *obiter* comments
revealed their awareness of tensions in early twentieth-century Canada
about new ideas in relation to women's roles and legal professionalism.

The limited role of courts was used by judges in all three cases to

---

124 See also the differing views in the *Persons Case* in the Supreme Court of Canada and the
Privy Council: *Reference re Meaning of the Word 'Persons' in S 24 of the BNA Act* [1928]
Supreme Court Reports, Canada 276, and *Edwards v AG of Canada* [1930] AC 124. See also
MJ Mossman, 'Feminism and Legal Method: The Difference it Makes' (1986) 3 *Australian
Journal of Law and Society* 30.

suggest that the issue of women's eligibility to become lawyers should be referred to provincial legislatures.[125] Thus, in French's case in New Brunswick, Justice Hanington stated succinctly that 'the remedy in this case is with the legislature and not with this court.'[126] Similarly, when French sought admission to the bar in British Columbia, Chief Justice MacDonald concluded that while there might be 'cogent reasons for a change based upon changes in the legal status of women,... [the court would be] usurping the functions of the Legislature rather than discharging the duty of the Court, which is to decide what the law is, not what it ought to be.'[127] In Langstaff's case in Québec, moreover, Justice Saint-Pierre noted that his role was not to decide whether it would be 'more fair and more reasonable' to permit women to become lawyers, but only whether the legislature had intended to include women when it used the male pronoun in the statute. In the Québec Court of Appeal, Chief Justice Archambeault also concluded that the matter was for the legislature, not for the court.[128] Thus, with the exception of Justice Lavergne, the judges in all three cases adopted the view that women's claims to become lawyers constituted a major challenge to existing law; in the words of Justice Barker in French's case in New Brunswick, the women's claims represented a 'radical change.'[129] And because these were 'radical' claims, they were beyond the jurisdiction of courts: legislative action was necessary.

In concluding that women's claims to become lawyers were 'radical,' a number of the judges demonstrated an awareness of new ideas about women's roles, but also their firm rejection of them. For example, responding to counsel's suggestion that there was no need to 'delve into the dark ages for a precedent' to find that women were disqualified from becoming lawyers, Chief Justice Tuck in New Brunswick curtly stated his utter rejection of ideas based on 'the advanced thought of the age and the right of women to share with men in all paying public activities;' in his view, women should not compete with men, but should attend to 'their own legitimate business.'[130] It was Justice Barker in the same court, however, who invoked earlier American decisions which denied applications for admission to the bar presented by Myra Bradwell in 1872 and Lelia Robinson in 1889. Quoting Justice Bradley in *Bradwell* in the US Supreme Court, Justice Barker agreed that:

125 Prior to the *Canadian Charter of Rights and Freedoms* in 1982, judges often identified their role as 'interpreters, not makers' of law to distinguish it from the role of legislatures; this approach was defined as the 'myth of judicial neutrality' by A Sachs and J Hoff Wilson, *Sexism and the Law: A Study of Male Beliefs and Legal Bias in Britain and the United States* (New York, The Free Press, 1978) at 40.

126 *French* (NB), above, n 7 at 363, *per* Hanington, J. Hanington, J was the uncle of Edith, one of the first woman law students at Saint John Law School: see DG Bell, above, n 35 at 78 and 97.

127 *French* (BC), above, n 8 at 4–5.

128 *Langstaff* (CS), above, n 5 at 137–8; and *Langstaff* (CBR), above, n 5 at 20.

129 *French* (NB), above, n 7 at 371.

130 *French* (NB), above, n 7 at 360–2.

[The] civil law, as well as nature herself, has always recognized a wide difference in the respective spheres and destinies of man and woman. Man is, or should be, woman's protector and defender. The natural and proper timidity and delicacy which belongs to the female sex evidently unfits it for many of the occupations of civil life. The constitution of the family organization, which is founded in the divine ordinance as well as in the nature of things, indicates the domestic sphere as that which properly belongs to the domain and functions of womanhood. The harmony [of family life] is repugnant to the idea of a woman adopting a distinct and independent career from that of her husband....[131]

For Justice Barker, women's roles were entirely separate from men's. Thus, the change contemplated by French's application to become a lawyer was 'radical' indeed: it challenged the fundamental ideal of separate spheres for men and women, and the traditional view of law as a 'gentleman's profession.'

In French's case in British Columbia, the judges generally refrained from discussion about women's proper roles, although they relied on precedents that supported the view that women could not be lawyers.[132] In Langstaff's case in Québec, however, there are further references to the proper sphere for women in the judgment of Justice Saint-Pierre. In exploring the interpretive context to determine whether women were included within male pronouns pursuant to the *Code*, Justice Saint-Pierre used graphic contemporary examples of women's efforts in World War I to show how such work constituted *exceptions* to women's proper role:

A woman may be as brave as any man, and scenes which are in the present time, daily depicted to us, show that many of them are proving their usefulness as nurses on the field of battle; but the physical constitution of woman makes it plain that nature never intended her to take part along with the stronger sex in the bloody affrays of the battle field.... I would put within the range of possibilities though by no means a commendable one, the admission of a woman to the profession of solicitor or to that of *avoué*, but I hold that to admit a woman and more particularly a married woman as a *barrister,* that is to say, as a *person who pleads cases at the bar before judges or juries in open court and in the presence of the public*, would be nothing short of a direct infringement upon public order and a manifest violation of the law of good morals and public decency.[133]

As is evident, Justice Saint-Pierre's views about women's proper role were

---

131 *French* (NB), above, n 7 at 365–6. See also *Bradwell v Illinois* and *Robinson's Case*, above, n 112.

132 *French* (BC), above, n 8 at 4; MacDonald, CJA (referring to *Bradwell*, above, n 112) stated, 'In the United States the cases are conflicting, but the one which was decided by the highest authority there – the Supreme Court – and which is based upon the common law of England, is against the appellant.'

133 *Langstaff* (CS), above, n 5 at 139 (emphasis in original). Note the similar language in *In re Goodell* 39 Wisconsin Reports 232 (1875).

not significantly different from those adopted by Justice Barker in French's case in New Brunswick in 1905, views which were first enunciated in *Bradwell* in the United States more than forty years before Langstaff's application in Québec.

Clearly, these cases reflected ideas about separate spheres for men and women, views which were frequently invoked in Canada and elsewhere to explain, and also to justify, limitations on women's roles in the latter part of the nineteenth century. Yet, there are subtle differences between the ideas in the quotation adopted from *Bradwell* in French's case, and in the views expressed in Langstaff's case a decade later. In the *Bradwell* quotation, women were confined to their own sphere by being 'elevated to a superior position,' a typical argument used to justify the idea of separate spheres in the United States, and also in England. As a British member of Parliament explained during the debates on the Second Reform Bill in 1867, women did not need the vote because, by contrast with men who were ennobled by possession of the vote, a voting woman would be degraded; she would lose her admirable attributes: gentleness, affection and domesticity. As the MP explained, women's legal disabilities thus demonstrated 'how great a favourite the female sex was to the laws of England.'[134] However, as Sachs and Hoff Wilson pointed out, this image of women was highly idealised, even 'mythical,' in the context of real women's lives in late Victorian England, where 'more than a million unmarried women alone were employed in industry while a further three quarters of a million were in domestic service.' Indeed, Sachs and Hoff Wilson concluded that 'for the great majority of Victorian women, as for ... Victorian men, life was characterised by drudgery and poverty rather than by refinement and decorum.'[135]

By contrast with Justice Barker's view of women's 'superior position,' Justice Saint-Pierre's comments focused on the consequences of women's participation in the paid workforce; he was less concerned to exalt women's virtues in the home than to preserve public order and decency, both of which would be violated if women were permitted to participate in public life by practising law, particularly 'before judges or juries in open court and in the presence of the public.' Justice Saint-Pierre was especially worried about rape cases in which a woman prosecutor or defence lawyer would have to put questions to the complainant in relation to proof of the crime. In his view, 'no woman possessing the least sense of decency could possibly do so without throwing a blur upon her own dignity and without

---

134 Quoted in A Sachs and J Hoff Wilson, above, n 125 at 53.
135 A Sachs and J Hoff Wilson, above, n 125 at 53–4. These comments were also mythical in Québec: M Dumont *et al*, above, n 46 at 210, reported that in 1911, 27 per cent of factory workers were women: 'the exploitation of women workers was, in fact, an important element in the structure of the Québec economy.'

bringing into utter contempt the honour and respect due to her sex.'[136] In the appellate court, Justice Lavergne responded briefly to these comments, offering a differing perspective on the prospect of women at the bar. As he asked rhetorically: '*Est-ce une idée qui répugne que les femmes soient admises aux professions libérales?*' In response, he cited the examples of France, the Scandinavian countries, most Canadian provinces and many parts of the United States, where women were already entitled to practise law, and suggested laconically '*on ne dira pas que les Etats-Unis sont des pays barbares.*'[137]

As these comments make clear, the views of Justice Barker in *French* and of Justice Saint-Pierre in *Langstaff*, by contrast with those of Justice Lavergne in the *Langstaff* appeal, reflected different views about the continuing validity of separate spheres for men and women. Particularly as a result of women's experiences during World War I, ideas and expectations about proper roles for women were changing, even though for Justice Saint-Pierre, women's new roles were regarded as highly exceptional, acceptable *only* in the context of war. Yet, if the views of Justice Saint-Pierre appeared inconsistent with new ideas about women, they may nonetheless have reflected a view of law as a 'gentleman's profession.' In their study of professionalism in nineteenth-century Ontario, for example, Gidney and Millar examined the doctrine of separate spheres as well as the economic interests of male professionals; significantly, they suggested that while any 'new' entrants to the professions (including women) created additional competition for male lawyers, the entry of *women* to the legal profession was doubly challenging:

> The intrusion of women into the ... law office posed a threat to masculine identities simply because it challenged the power relations, economic and otherwise, embedded in the ideology of separate spheres.... The notion of the professional gentleman ... was a profoundly gendered concept ... [defining] the attributes of men of a certain class as against those of women....[138]

Thus, Gidney and Millar argued that the language adopted by professional men at the end of the nineteenth century (such as that used by Justice Barker and Justice Saint-Pierre) was often designed to keep women in their 'proper sphere.' In addition, however, Gidney and Millar suggested that such comments provide an '*entrée* to the language and behavioural codes by which professional men construed their own masculinity' out of their shared life experiences: education which provided men with intel-

---

[136] *Langstaff* (CS), above, n 5 at 139–40. Saint-Pierre, J noted the lower court decision denying Lavinia Goodell's application; he made no reference to her later appeal: see above, n 133 and 48 Wisc 693 (1879).

[137] *Langstaff* (CBR), above, n 5 at 14.

[138] RD Gidney and WPJ Millar, *Professional Gentlemen: The Professions in Nineteenth-Century Ontario* (Toronto, University of Toronto Press, 1994) at 329.

lectual initiative and disciplined rationality, workplaces which were exclusively male (whether craft based or professional), continuing connections with university life and all-male clubs, and opportunities for debate in courts, legislatures and public meetings. In this context, women's efforts to enter the professions at the end of the nineteenth century intruded into both 'the physical and psychic spaces that men claimed as their own.' Thus:

> It was not simply the threat of economic competition, though that is not to be discounted. The ideal of the professional gentleman incorporated, among its other elements, images about a particular form of masculine identity, about the gendered distribution of knowledge and authority in both the 'public' and the 'domestic' sphere, which the entry of women on equal terms necessarily challenged. And the consequences of that challenge could not be foreseen.... [The] entry of young women might change the nature of an occupation fundamentally and forever.... [Such concerns could not help] but raise anxiety among professional men themselves about their own future and their place in the social order.[139]

In this context, the judges' comments in the three cases about women's eligibility to become lawyers represent a debate not only about the nature of women's roles, but also about the fundamental character of (male) legal professionalism. If judicial comments did not conform to the reality of women's lives, that was not the point. Instead, the judges were engaged in a debate about the nature of professionalism, an idea that was fundamentally challenged by the prospect of women lawyers: how could women ever be part of a 'gentleman's profession'? Thus, these decisions illustrate how the legal process reflected contested social and political ideas about women and about professionalism. As Pue demonstrated, 'progressive' ideas about professionalism envisioned that the goal of legal education was to produce 'not only competent practitioners, but men (sic) who by their wise and sympathetic handling of the problems of our national life, [would] add to the dignity and influence of the great profession of the law.'[140] Such language tends to emphasise that professionalism, at least in its highest sense, remained exclusively male, so that women who entered the legal profession 'on the same terms as men' were required to become legal professionals in the same (male) mould. In this way, these cases about women's eligibility to become lawyers reveal how issues about women's aspirations for change intersected with emerging ideas about professionalism that were firmly embedded in the concept of law as a gentleman's profession. Thus, as Margaret Hyndman, a woman lawyer who achieved prominence in Ontario in the mid-twentieth century, asserted in 1949:

---

[139] RD Gidney and WPJ Millar, above, n 138 at 331–2.
[140] WW Pue, above, n 36 at 687; see also RW Lee, 'Legal Education: A Symposium' (1919) 39 *Canadian Law Times* 138 at 141.

Only the fact that I am a lawyer matters. That I am a woman is of no consequence. I make a point of not knowing how many women lawyers there are in Canada.[141]

CONTESTED IDEAS: NEW WOMEN AND LEGAL
PROFESSIONALISM

Oh, Judge St Pierre! Judge St Pierre! In the Neolithic Age,
You would have seemed, I make no doubt, a most instructive sage,
But in the twentieth century, you really seem to me,
Well, let us 'draw it mild' and say – a sad anomaly![142]

In this final stanza of a long, ironic poem about the initial decision in the *Langstaff* case, published in a Montreal newspaper in 1915, Frances Fenwick Williams heaped scorn on the decision of Justice Saint-Pierre. Williams was a journalist, and her public support for women lawyers was part of a vigorous campaign, in which prominent male lawyers, several male politicians, and leaders of the organised women's movement in Québec joined forces. Indeed, support for Langstaff clearly demonstrated how the issue of women's admission to the bar was not merely a struggle between male judges and individual aspiring women lawyers, but rather a continuing public debate in which new ideas about women's roles were being contested and shaped alongside new ideas about legal professionalism in early twentieth-century Canada.

These patterns of public support for women who aspired to enter the legal profession were established early on. For example, when Martin first sought to become a lawyer in Ontario, she requested support from the Dominion Women's Enfranchisement Association as early as 1892;[143] and the International Council of Women organised 'a volley of letters in the daily, weekly, and monthly journals, all recommending Miss Martin, and censuring the Benchers, until the old gentlemen were fairly worn out.' There were also letters to the newspapers in Toronto, some of them quite militant about men's 'tyranny' in preventing women from 'opportunity and freedom of choice in the world of work and duty.'[144] In addition,

---

141 'The Legal Lady,' *Maclean's Magazine*, 1949 at 23.

142 *Gazette*, 20 February 1915. The 'lay' had eight verses plus a chorus, to be sung to the tune of 'The Wearing of the Green.' Williams also published an article about women lawyers in other jurisdictions in *Beck's Weekly*, 20 February 1915; and a letter to the editor, *Gazette*, 26 February 1915.

143 T Roth, above, n 3, at 328. Charlotte Gray characterised Martin as a 'bluestocking' rather than a suffragist like Dr Emily Stowe; as Gray explained, respectable families tried to ensure that their daughters did not 'earn the wrong sort of reputations, as anti-men troublemakers': see C Gray, *Mrs. King: The Life and Times of Isabel Mackenzie King* (Toronto, Viking, 1997) at 152.

144 T Roth, above, n 3, at 328, citing *The Womans Journal*, 1 and 15 October 1900 at 3; and see also C Backhouse, above, n 3 at 17 and 26. C Cleverdon, above, n 15 at 26, also argued that Martin's achievement furthered suffrage reform.

Martin gained the support of Ontario's Premier and Attorney General, Oliver Mowat, who not only introduced the necessary legislative amendments but was active as an *ex-officio* Bencher in his role as Attorney General; his support was crucial to Martin's eventual success.[145] Significantly, Constance Backhouse concluded that Mowat may have agreed to support women's entry to the legal profession, as requested by the National Council of Women, rather than respond to the Council's more 'radical' request for women's enfranchisement.[146] In this way, women may have succeeded in becoming lawyers in Ontario by suggesting that their aspirations were reasonable, at least by contrast with more 'radical' suffrage goals; as in the United States, such arguments may have created some tensions between women lawyers and leaders of the women's suffrage movement.

By contrast, French's support in New Brunswick seems to have come mainly from male lawyers, three of whom presented arguments before the New Brunswick court. A B Connell, president of the Barristers' Society, presented relevant precedents from the United States, England and Ontario as *amicus curiae*; and Stephen Bustin, a partner in the firm where French was then working as a law student, argued in support of French's admission to the bar.[147] In addition, Charles N Skinner KC, Recorder of the City of Saint John, argued for a progressive view of French's application:

> The trend of recent legislation, both political and judicial, is to remove the disabilities of women and open to them every avenue leading to avocations which may enable them to earn a livelihood. Why delve into the dark ages for a precedent to justify holding them incompetent or by law disqualified from exercising a calling to which we have every reason to believe, from their successes in our universities and in the professions which have been opened to them, they will bring to bear equal intelligence, greater diligence and devotion to duty than men?...[148]

---

[145] It was Mowat who proposed the motion at the Law Society in 1892 that the Benchers frame rules for the admission of women as solicitors; the motion was approved on a vote of 12 in favour and 11 against: see C Backhouse, above, n 3 at 17. Mowat's Division Courts Act of 1880 was also a 'flash-point' for lawyers, as it increased the range of cases conducted in the lower courts by lay representatives, thus creating competition for lawyers: RD Gidney and WPJ Millar, above, n 138 at 298. See also MA Banks, 'Evolution of the Ontario Courts 1788–1981' in DH Flaherty (ed), above n 37 at 492.

[146] C Backhouse, above, n 3 at 26; and C Cleverdon, above, n 15 at 26–7. S Petersson, above, n 79 at 379–80, suggested that Alberta's Attorney General Oliver Mowat Biggar, grandson of Ontario's Premier Mowat, welcomed women lawyers.

[147] As DG Bell noted, above, n 35 at 99, French (like Isabel Mowatt) had started work as a secretary – at Bustin's law office; the daughter of humble parents, she hoped in this way to get 'a foothold in a law office.'

[148] *French* (NB), above, n 7 at 360–61. DG Bell stated, above, n 35 at 80, that Skinner was a politician at the municipal, provincial and federal levels, and had served as a judge of the Probate Court prior to being appointed Recorder; he had no legal training, but was a member of the faculty of the Saint John Law School.

And, in response to Chief Justice Tuck's expressed concern that if women were admitted to the bar, they would eventually become eligible to be appointed to the bench, Skinner replied confidently: '... if that be the inevitable consequence, worse things might happen.'[149] Significantly, although no one appeared to argue against French's application, all five judges had no difficulty in rejecting it unanimously. Yet, French then received support from Attorney General Pugsley, who introduced amending legislation as the first bill after the throne speech in February 1906. Yorke identified Pugsley as a supporter of legal reforms on behalf of women; and his comments in the legislature clearly demonstrated his understanding of women's needs for economic independence:

> Others may hold that women's sphere is the domestic circle. That might carry force were all provided with happy comfortable homes, but when we find them driven out by force of circumstances to earn their livelihood ... and find them doing so with honour and credit to themselves, why should a man stand up and say they shall not engage in the practice of law?[150]

After the legislation was enacted, French was admitted to the bar and entered into partnership with Stephen Bustin. According to Yorke, Bustin's partnership with another male lawyer was dissolved at the time when French was admitted to the bar; perhaps Bustin's views about women's new roles may not have been shared by his former partner? In any event, Yorke concluded that 'the firm of Bustin & French no doubt created a minor sensation within Saint John legal circles.'[151] Interestingly, there is no evidence of French's involvement in the organised women's movement until *after* she had gained admission to the bar in New Brunswick, when she became involved in lobbying for suffrage. As noted, she also presented a paper about child custody at the International Council of Women at its meeting in Toronto in 1909, and it is possible that she encountered other women lawyers there: it seems that a few American women lawyers were present, as well as Marie Popelin, who had unsuccessfully sought entry to the bar in Belgium in the 1880s.[152] All the same, it appears that French's

149 *French* (NB), above, n 7 at 361. As Bell noted, the comments of Tuck, CJ are interesting because his wife, Sarah, held office for several years in the Local Council of Women: DG Bell, 'William Henry Tuck,' *Dictionary of Canadian Biography*, vol 14 (Toronto, University of Toronto Press, 2000) at 1012–13.
150 LK Yorke, above, n 82 at 17, quoting the *Synoptic Report of the Proceedings of the Legislative Assembly of the Province of New Brunswick for the Session of 1906* (Saint John, 1906) at 25. Yorke reported Pugsley's support for reforms of the *Married Women's Property Act* and women's suffrage at school meetings.
151 LK Yorke, above, n 82 at 18. Yorke characterised French, at 18–19, as an anomaly, since 'the usual path for women barristers would be an independent practice with specialisation in probate, marital or property law;' or employment in a large legal firm or a corporate legal department.
152 LK Yorke, above, n 82 at 21–6. Yorke concluded that French's involvement in the women's movement was a 'means of establishing credibility with the upper-middle-class

success as a woman lawyer in New Brunswick depended primarily on 'professional gentlemen' like Bustin.

After she moved to British Columbia, she initially found work as a legal assistant in the firm of Russell, Russell and Hannington; all the partners were originally from New Brunswick, part of the 'Maritime Mafia' who had moved west in the first decade of the twentieth century.[153] It was the senior partner Joseph Russell, a 'flamboyant but respected criminal and civil liberties lawyer,' who presented her application for admission to the bar of British Columbia.[154] Yet, although Russell presented a number of arguments in support of French's admission to the bar, the Law Society strenuously opposed her application. Indeed, the Society's secretary, Oscar Bass, an 'arrogant and doctrinaire misogynist,' described Russell's argument as 'a verbose composition.'[155] There was a similar hint of antipathy to Russell's arguments in the motions judge's conclusion that he should take his 'gallant argument' to the legislature.[156] Interestingly, it was a social encounter between Russell's partner, Robert Hannington, and a leading member of the University Women's Club in Vancouver, Evlyn Farris, which seems to have been critical to legislative success for French.

After the appellate court denied French's appeal, a discussion between Hannington and Farris resulted in the University Women's Club taking up French's campaign. The Club was involved in issues of social and legal reform concerning women and children, and it may be that French's participation at the International Council of Women meeting in 1909 commended her to the Club; in addition, it is possible that Farris's roots in the Maritimes may have engendered sympathy for French's predicament.[157] In any event, it was Farris who persuaded WJ Bowser, the Attorney General of British Columbia, to introduce the legislative amend-

conservative constituency....' See also *Report*, above, n 70; ES Mussey, above, n 71; and L Frank, *La Femme-Avocat: Exposé Historique et Critique de la Question* (Paris, V Giard et E Brière, 1898).

[153] LK Yorke, above, n 82 at 27–8. Hannington's father was Hanington, J, one of the New Brunswick judges who had rejected French's application there; his son had changed the spelling of his name: see LK Yorke at 88.

[154] LK Yorke, above, n 82 at 28. Russell was also a wealthy lover of race horses, a founder of the Vancouver Hunt Club and the Vancouver Horse Show. According to the *Saint John Globe*, 4 May 1914, French won the championship of the Vancouver Horse Show in 1913 on a splendid white horse, 'Schweitzer.'

[155] LK Yorke, above, n 82 at 29 and 33. Pue also suggested that Bass might be described as a 'woman-hating, unenlightened, bombastic ...' individual: see WW Pue, above, n 15 at 223–4.

[156] *French* (BC), above, n 8 at 4.

[157] See *Report*, vol 2, above, n 70 at 203. Sylvie McClean reported that it was Hannington, who brought French's situation to Farris's attention, while playing bridge at her home; Farris then arranged for the University Women's Club to establish a committee: see S McClean, *A Woman of Influence: Evlyn Fenwick Farris* (Victoria, Sono Nis Press, 1997) at 81. According to one report, Mrs Farris's efforts on behalf of French showed how women 'rallied in support of and to maintain the cause of a sister woman....': see Antoinette, 'My Lady's Realm,' 28 February 1912.

ment to permit French's admission to the bar. According to Sylvie McClean, Bowser initially wished to postpone introducing the legislation, but 'family lore has it that [Evlyn Farris] refused to move from his office until he promised to bring the bill to the legislature before the end of the [current] session.'[158] Thus, in British Columbia, French received support from the women's movement and from two partners in the law firm where she worked; in addition, the Attorney General, perhaps somewhat more reluctantly, assisted her. Once again, these actions reveal the existence of at least some support for women lawyers, not only among members of the legal profession, but also in the political and public sphere.

Yet, it was Langstaff's case in Québec which most dramatically revealed how the issue of women lawyers was attracting increasingly strong support from a wide spectrum of public opinion and from prominent members of the legal profession. Langstaff's application was presented to the court by Sam Jacobs KC, senior partner in the firm in which Langstaff had been employed since before her years at McGill.[159] According to a report in *The Canadian Magazine* in 1914, Jacobs was 'one of the ablest lawyers at the Bar' and 'in the front rank of the profession;' after explaining that he was engaged in a wide range of reform activities, and had established a special reputation as a result of his legal and philanthropic efforts on behalf of the Jewish community in Canada, the report asserted (somewhat incongruously):

[Jacobs] is virtually the father confessor of the Jewish race in Canada.... Born in this country, Mr Jacobs is intensely Canadian, and his influence during a general election extends far beyond his own Province. He has travelled extensively, speaks several languages, and is well read. He is a familiar and popular figure in Quebec courts, where his eloquence, subtlety of argument and profound knowledge of the law have more than once called down the encomiums of the Bench. Will the honour be his of opening to woman the locked and bolted door of the Quebec Bar?[160]

Jacobs's eloquence was conceded by Justice Saint-Pierre, who noted that arguments on behalf of Langstaff had been 'urged with much force and

158 S McClean, above, n 157 at 82.
159 Langstaff initially worked as a secretary at the firm of Jacobs, Hall, Couture and Fitch: biography of Annie Macdonald Langstaff, Langstaff file, Faculty of Law Archives, McGill University.
160 L Crawford, 'Current Events,' *The Canadian Magazine*, November 1914, at 85. Jacobs was elected to the Canadian Parliament in 1917, representing Montréal-Cartier for the Liberals until his death in 1938: see G Gallichan, above, n 6 at 26. He was the second Jew elected to the House of Commons; the first was Henry Nathan, elected in Victoria BC in 1871: see B Figler, QC, *Sam Jacobs, Member of Parliament* (Ottawa, Private Pub, 1959) at 65. See also G Tulchinsky, *Taking Root: The Origins of the Canadian Jewish Community* (Toronto, Lester Publishing Ltd, 1992) at 271–2; and G Tulchinsky, *Branching Out: The Transformation of the Canadian Jewish Community* (Toronto, Stoddard, 1998).

ability' by her counsel. In arguing that the male pronoun should be understood to include females, for example, Jacobs had asserted that 'the tendency ... the world over [was] towards a larger measure of liberty for all classes and for both sexes,' and that it would be 'contrary to the spirit of the Canadian system of law [to permit the continuation of] antiquated rules and usages' which prohibited women from engaging in the professions; such prohibitions constituted both unfair discrimination and positive injustice.[161] Nonetheless, although Justice Saint-Pierre agreed that 'the field of labour for persons of the female sex should be enlarged and their means of earning their livelihood increased whenever the thing is within the range of possibility,' he concluded that his responsibility was not to determine whether it was fair and reasonable for women to become lawyers, but whether this possibility had been contemplated by the legislature when it enacted the statute creating the Québec bar.[162]

Justice Saint-Pierre's decision to deny Langstaff's application provoked an outburst of criticism in Montréal. As the *Gazette* reported on 18 February 1915, 'the leaders of the suffragist movement in Montréal are expressing themselves freely in regard to Justice Saint-Pierre's decision excluding Mrs Langstaff from the practice of law,... and there is no disposition to accept the matter as definitely settled.' In fact, the Equal Suffrage League had passed a resolution a few months earlier, part of which stated the League's 'earnest hopes that the proceedings so taken by Mrs Langstaff will result in a decision declaring that in the eye of the law women are entitled to have the same privileges and rights as men to practice the profession of law, to which they are as well suited temperamentally and otherwise as persons of the male sex.'[163] Both English and French language newspapers carried letters about Justice Saint-Pierre's decision, with *La Presse* reporting that Langstaff intended to appeal.[164] In the face of this criticism, it seems that Justice Saint-Pierre was moved to give an interview to explain the legal basis for his decision; focussing particularly on the outspoken views expressed by women, he stated firmly:

> Evidently these ladies do not understand my judgment. I have not the power of a Turkish Pasha. My powers are limited. What I, as judge have to do, is to follow the law and its precedents.[165]

---

161 *Langstaff* (CS), above, n 5 at 137. According to the *Daily Mail*, 21 January 1915, Jacobs noted that Lord Haldane was then introducing a bill to permit women at the Inns of Court in Britain.

162 *Langstaff* (CS), above, n 5 at 137–8. According to G Gallichan, above, n 6 at 31, Saint-Pierre, J, at the age of 72, was not up to date with the twentieth century; similarly, a note in the *Toronto Saturday Night*, 27 February 1915, stated that the decision 'might have [come from] the Old Testament.'

163 *Gazette*, 19 November 1914.

164 *La Presse*, 13 February 1915.

165 *Evening News*, 19 February 1915. In a report in the *Gazette*, 19 February 1915,

In response, on the following day, the *Gazette* printed the long poem, 'The Lay of Mrs Langstaff,' by Frances Fenwick Williams.

A week later, moreover, the Local Council of Women sponsored a mass meeting in support of Langstaff on 26 February. Over six hundred people (five hundred women and one hundred men)[166] crammed into the main hall of the YMCA on Dorchester Street: 'two sexes, speaking two languages, and with all kinds of enunciation in both French and English, ... registered an emphatic protest against the exclusion of Mrs Langstaff from practicing the profession of law.'[167] The meeting was chaired by the former mayor of Montréal, JJ Guerin, who spoke in favour of Langstaff's application for admission to the bar. Other speakers who supported Langstaff's application included Senator Dandurand,[168] and Gonzalve Desaulniers, KC, Syndic of the Montréal Bar; the latter seconded the motion that women should be permitted to enter the learned professions in Québec 'on the same terms as men.'[169] Similarly Carrie Derick, Canada's first woman university professor, declared at the meeting that 'the professions should be open to men and women alike.'[170] Although Langstaff was present, she did not speak publicly; however, a few weeks later, when she was invited as a dinner speaker on the topic, 'Women's Place in the Liberal Professions,' she argued that women should have the same rights as men in their chosen occupations: 'This is supposed to be a free country, but for women alone the freedom of opportunity is curtailed.'[171]

Public discussion of Langstaff's case continued until the appellate court's decision several months later in November 1915; arguably, Justice Lavergne's dissenting opinion may have been influenced by newspaper articles as well as by the legal arguments presented to the court. Moreover, even though the court rejected Langstaff's application by a 4:1 decision, Gilles Gallichan argued that the dissenting voice of Justice Lavergne was

Saint-Pierre, J suggested that his doubts about the intellectual unfitness of women for law practice were entirely confirmed by the recent criticisms of his judgment by outspoken women, as they were totally unable to 'seize the main point of [the] case.' The *Gazette* printed a response from Langstaff the next day.

166 *Evening News*, 27 February 1915. Several prominent women were present, including the suffrage advocate, *Mme* Gerin-Lajoie, and E Hurlbatt, warden of Royal Victoria College, McGill. Sam Jacobs, KC, counsel for Langstaff, was also on the platform and spoke at the meeting.

167 'Be a Queen but not Lawyer,' *Gazette*, 27 February 1915.

168 Senator Raoul Dandurand was one of two Senators who later escorted Cairine Wilson to her place in the Senate of Canada in 1930, after the Privy Council decision in the *Persons Case*, above, n 124: see V Knowles, *First Person: A Biography of Cairine Wilson, Canada's First Woman Senator* (Toronto and Oxford, Dundurn Press, 1988) at 88–91.

169 *Gazette*, 27 February 1915. According to *Le Devoir*, 27 February 1915, Me Désaulniers, speaking in French, stated: '*Le vingtième siècle est celui de la femme. Elle a des droits égaux à ceux de l'homme.*'

170 M Gillett, above, n 49 at 306. See also M Dumont *et al*, above, n 46 at 244.

171 Langstaff was present at the mass meeting: see Montréal *Star*, 27 February 1915. Her presentation was made to the Insurance Underwriters' Dinner: M Gillett, above, n 49 at 306; and Montréal *Star*, 20 March 1915.

significant: for the first time, a person in high authority had espoused the right of women to become lawyers in Québec:

> *C'est la preuve que la controverse a maintenant atteint les plus hautes sphères de pouvoir et que la candidate y a trouvé des alliés. Le cas Langstaff et le principe qu'il soulève ne sont donc plus une simple cause bizarre que l'on classe en souriant, une lubie de virago qu'il faut vite retourner à ses casseroles. En fait, ... la dissidence de Joseph Lavergne [permet] à Mme Langstaff de garder un peu d'espoir pour la suite des choses.*[172]

Moreover, in his representations to the legislative committee that was established to consider amending the law, Jacobs adopted some of Justice Lavergne's arguments; he appeared before the committee with two prominent representatives of the women's movement in Montréal, *Mme* Gérin-Lajoie and Dr Grace Ritchie England, and they made strong presentations on behalf of Langstaff. Nonetheless, the resulting vote in the legislature was twenty-one in favour and twenty-two opposed; as well, another bill, presented after the 1916 general election in Québec, was also unsuccessful. At this point, the issue apparently subsided in the face of the War, the conscription crisis, and the outbreak of Spanish flu; however, beginning again in 1920, there were continuing efforts to obtain legislative change in Québec, although there was no success until 1941.[173] By that date, Jacobs as well as all the judges involved in the *Langstaff* case were dead.[174] Nonetheless, Langstaff's case clearly demonstrated that, in spite of judicial support for the status quo, ideas about women's access to the legal profession had been increasingly accepted by male lawyers, as well as by leaders of the women's movement and the public.

All the same, women who were becoming lawyers in Canada faced many of the same challenges that had puzzled the American women lawyers who wrote the Equity Club letters in the late 1880s: whether to participate actively in the women's movement, how to obtain suitable legal work, and what to wear in the courtroom.[175] Indeed, even though these

---

[172] G Gallichan, above, n 6 at 35–6.

[173] See G Gallichan, above, n 6 at 40–42. Gérin-Lajoie was well known in Québec for her efforts to provide access to law: see N Kasirer, '*Apostolat Juridique*: Teaching Everyday Law in the Life of Marie Lacoste Gérin-Lajoie (1867–1945)' (1992) 30 *Osgoode Hall Law Journal* 427; and SM Trofimenkoff, 'Feminism, Nationalism, and the Clerical Defensive' in V Strong-Boag and AC Fellman (eds), above, n 60 at 127. Dr Grace Ritchie England was a pioneer woman doctor and noted suffragist: for example, see M Gillett, *Dear Grace: A Romance of History* (Montréal, Eden Press, 1986). See also G Gallichan at 37–59, above, n 6, and Annexes I and II.

[174] In 1915, all the judges except Carroll, JA were elderly; Archambeault and Pelletier were born in 1857, Lavergne in 1847, and Trenholme in 1837. All but Carroll died between 1918 and 1922; Carroll died in 1939: see G Gallichan, above, n 6 at 32–3. Jacobs died in 1938: see B Figler, above, n 160.

[175] See C Backhouse, above, n 3 at 31; and LK Yorke, above, n 82 at 19. The press always seemed interested in women lawyers' appearance; for example, Langstaff was described in the *Herald*, 9 July 1914: 'Attired in a blue summer dress with white stripes, a pretty white hat,

first Canadian women lawyers were entering the profession several decades later, there are similar patterns in their responses to these challenges. For example, like several of the first women lawyers in the United States, Martin practised law, initially in a small firm and then as a sole practitioner, until her death in 1923; her practice included conveyancing, mortgages, wills and family law, and she was elected as a trustee for the Toronto Board of Education for ten years.[176] Bacchi identified Martin as a suffragist as a result of her 'direct confrontation with sexual discrimination' by the legal profession,[177] and Roth reported that 'the women's movement found an eloquent voice in Clara Brett Martin;' Roth argued that Martin's commitment to women's rights and her vocation as a lawyer often overlapped, and that she was a lively speaker who provided audiences with information about the legal system, as well as arguments in favour of women's suffrage.[178] By contrast, Backhouse concluded that 'the demands of [Martin's] career seem to have prevented her from seeking and fostering a national image as a Canadian feminist leader.'[179] Indeed, both Backhouse and Yorke lamented that neither Martin nor French were more successful as leaders of the Canadian women's movement or as 'feminist' legal practitioners;[180] unlike the first women doctors in Canada, especially Emily Stowe, women lawyers did not achieve a national voice in relation to women's rights.

Yet, unlike the women who had first become doctors in Canada in the 1880s, women were gaining admission to provincial bars several decades later, prior to and during World War I; by that time, the women's movement was mainly the preserve of middle-class married women whose primary interests were social reforms and women's suffrage, not economic independence. Thus, while there were obvious connections between some goals of the women's movement and those of women lawyers, the middle-class women reform leaders probably had little in common with individual women lawyers: women like Martin, who wanted to achieve economic independence through professional work and who were prepared to forego marriage to do so. Indeed, such women lawyers directly challenged women reformers whose campaigns for the vote were founded upon women's virtues as wives and mothers and their special 'purifying influence' within the family. As Sylvia Bashevkin explained in relation to the organised

tilted just a shade to the right, with a black band and a white rose and sprays on the edge and carrying a small black handbag, Mrs Langstaff arrived at the offices in the Power Building this morning at ten fifteen.'

176 T Roth, above, n 3 at 335.
177 CL Bacchi, above, n 64 at 15: Bacchi also included Langstaff as a noted suffragist.
178 T Roth, above, n 3 at 336–7.
179 C Backhouse, above, n 3 at 37.
180 See C Backhouse, above, n 3 at 37; and LK Yorke, above, n 82 at 48–9.

women's movement in Canada, there was always 'an older "hard-core" minority which sought to challenge the discriminatory treatment of women [in employment, but they were marginalised by the] more moderate, reformist mainstream of "social feminism" [at least] in English Canada.'[181] Thus, while it seems that Martin participated in public meetings concerning law reform and suffrage, her role as a single professional woman who engaged in an independent career may have distinguished her from the majority of women reformers; from the reformers' perspective, moreover, Martin may not have been their preferred model for women in Canada.

Similarly, French's decision to abandon the practice of law in favour of marriage reveals a pattern that was evident earlier in the United States, where some women lawyers seemed to have to choose between a professional career and marriage. According to the records of the Law Society of Upper Canada, for example, nine of sixteen women lawyers who were called to the bar prior to 1920 were married, and only two of them were practising law; by contrast, five of the seven women who were unmarried were practising law.[182] Like Martin in Toronto, Emelyn MacKenzie and Grace Wambolt, two of the early women lawyers who graduated from Dalhousie Law School, chose to practise law full-time, and they never married.[183] By contrast, Winnifred Wilton, who worked in London and Paris during World War I following her admission to the Manitoba bar, eventually married an American and moved to New York; as the first British-born woman called to the New York bar, she opened her own law office on Madison Avenue in the 1920s, although she never built up a clientele and worked only part-time while raising her three sons.[184] In this context, it is possible that French chose marriage rather than the practice of law; however, since the facts suggest that she abandoned her Vancouver law practice nearly a decade *before* her marriage, it is hard not to agree with Yorke's conclusion that French was not deeply committed to either the legal profession or the woman's movement, but rather 'viewed her career chiefly as a means to social advancement.'[185] At the same time, it is

---

[181] S Bashevkin, above, n 60 at 249; and see D Gorham, 'Flora Macdonald Denison: Canadian Feminist' in L Kealey (ed), above, n 12 at 47. Similarly, Bacchi argued that the majority of suffragists were committed to strengthening the family rather than questioning the allocation of sex roles; by contrast, a minority 'demanded complete economic independence for women and their right to a choice of career;' such women remained isolated and unpopular: see CL Bacchi, above, n 64 at 11.

[182] Records of the Law Society of Upper Canada: 'List of Women Barristers and Solicitors in Ontario': Control Sheet (undated). The list included the name, address, and date of call for women lawyers in Ontario; a column labelled 'Remarks' showed whether the women were practising or not, and whether or not they were married (including their married names).

[183] For Grace Wambolt, see 'M Grace Wambolt' *Ansul* (Dalhousie Law School), vol 2, December 1977; and Grace Wambolt papers, Public Archives of Nova Scotia. For MacKenzie, see 'Emelyn MacKenzie' *Ansul* (Dalhousie Law School), 13 January 1976, at 5; and LK Kernaghan, above, n 102.

[184] See P Wilton, above, n 99.

[185] LK Yorke, above, n 82 at 48.

·clear that opposition to her admission to the bar had been openly hostile in Vancouver, so that she may not have had much of a legal practice to abandon.

Thus, the patterns for Martin and French generally reflect those adopted by American women lawyers some decades earlier: *either* a professional career *or* marriage. By contrast with these patterns, however, Langstaff had neither a career nor a marriage, although she worked all her life 'in law' to support herself and her daughter. Although there are fewer examples of this pattern in the US context, it was becoming increasingly common in Britain, where women who graduated from university law programmes were employed as legal assistants in solicitors' firms in the years before women became eligible to enter the legal professions there after World War I.[186] As a single parent, moreover, Langstaff clearly needed to work, although she apparently took up flying as a hobby; there is a report that on the occasion of the visit of Maréchal Foch to Montréal after World War I, Langstaff 'circled above the city for an hour to the delight of thousands of spectators.'[187] In later decades, Langstaff was recognised as a formidable manager in the law firm; a former junior lawyer recalled, with humour and respect, how Mrs Langstaff had responded to an expense claim for a client lunch by 'striking the martinis.'[188] Although archival records of her court challenges and her unsuccessful efforts to obtain a legislative amendment include little information about her subsequent activities, it seems that Langstaff provided loyal support to Jacobs and his firm; she managed the law firm while Jacobs practised in the courts and later while he engaged in practical politics after being elected to the House of Commons in 1917.[189]

In truth, however, the lives of Martin, French and Langstaff all remain somewhat mysterious. For example, Yorke reported that French left Vancouver in 1913, following a reorganisation of the Russell firm that resulted in Joseph Russell taking a year off to travel around the world; according to the firm's history, French accompanied Russell as a travelling companion. As horse-lovers, they ended up in Britain, and, according to Yorke, Russell returned to Vancouver in July 1914 while French remained in Britain, in spite of the impending war.[190] Yet, the *Saint John Globe* reported in May 1914 that Mabel French and her mother were then visiting Saint John, and that French was planning a short business trip to New York and would then return to Vancouver, where she was 'busily

---

[186] See M Birks, *Gentlemen of the Law* (London, Stevens & Sons Limited, 1960) at 248; and H Kirk, *Portrait of a Profession: A History of the Solicitor's Profession, 1100 to the Present Day* (London, Oyez Publishing, 1976) at 121.

[187] Biography of Annie Macdonald Langstaff, Faculty of Law archives, McGill University.

[188] Interview with Justice M Rothman, Montréal, 16 November 2000.

[189] Scrapbook of Annie Macdonald Langstaff, Faculty of Law archives, McGill University.

[190] LK Yorke, above, n 82 at 44–5.

engaged in a large practice;' her mother intended to remain in Saint John.[191] Unfortunately, there is no further trace of French until her marriage in London in 1923, and little information about her thereafter; nonetheless, Yorke confirmed that she never applied to any of the Inns of Court and that she was not involved at all in the practice of law. Significantly, her obituary did not mention her status as a colonial barrister.[192]

Similarly, there are intriguing questions about Langstaff. It appears that she enjoyed a warm relationship with Jacobs's young children after his marriage, and it is clear that she managed the law firm effectively while Jacobs was energetically involved in legal and political work; she also published a French-English/English-French Law Dictionary in 1937, probably the first in Canada.[193] According to the tributes presented in the House of Commons after his death, Jacobs was well-regarded as both a successful lawyer and a remarkable politician; indeed, he appears representative of progressive legal practitioners in early twentieth century Canada who believed that a new kind of 'professionalism' might offer 'a magic key capable of maintaining authority in a society rent by centrifugal forces.'[194] And it appears that Langstaff made a significant contribution to Jacobs's work; a few years after Langstaff's death, Jacobs's partner, Senator Lazarus Phillips described her role at the firm:

> Mrs Langstaff was an assistant to my late senior partner, S W Jacobs, KC, MP, and when I joined the firm on January 1, 1920 (after a stint in the Army), Mrs Langstaff was already there. She remained the alter ego of Mr Jacobs until the very day of Mr Jacobs' death in 1938 and, thereafter, I acquired, in a sense, this important legacy and privilege from Mr Jacobs. She remained my right arm in the practice of law until, of her own accord, she left me about 1970. My late wife would often say that she was the only lady that I feared in all respects. I respected her profoundly and we remained close friends for many years....[195]

Interestingly, the Board of Governors of McGill University voted in 1981 to name a seminar room in the faculty of law the 'Langstaff Seminar Room;' however, the plaque outside the seminar room makes no mention of her court challenge in 1914–1915, since, according to Dean Brierley, the 'proper form of words' did not come readily to mind.[196]

---

191 'Vancouver's Lady Barrister in Town,' 4 May 1914.
192 LK Yorke, above, n 82 at 46–8.
193 See B Figler, above, n 160 at 249 and 253; and A Macdonald Langstaff, BCL, *French–English, English–French Law Dictionary* (Montréal, Wilson & Lafleur, 1937). Langstaff also published 'Rights: Civil Status of Women' (November 1933) 1 *Woman's Circle* 2; and (February 1934) 1 *Woman's Circle* 5.
194 WW Pue, above, n 20 at 393; see also WW Pue, above, n 36.
195 Letter from Lazarus Phillips to Dean John Brierley, 19 May 1981, Annie Macdonald Langstaff archives, Faculty of Law, McGill University.
196 Memo from John Brierley to Michael Renshawe, Librarian (undated, circa 1981). Renshawe responded that the plaque should emphasise Langstaff's connection to the faculty of law, and then stated, 'As for the Bar, I suppose it would be diplomatic to leave it out.'

Langstaff's close connection to Jacobs and his firm is also interesting because there is some evidence that discriminatory views about his Jewish background may have prevented him from achieving appointments to the Cabinet or the Senate.[197] This possibility reveals how anti-semitism in Canada was all too common, particularly in the first decades of the twentieth century. Certainly, it affected the Toronto legal profession; as Cecilia Morgan reported, it was impossible for Jewish students (particularly women) to get articling positions in prestigious 'old Ontario' firms. As one student explained:

> Oh yes, you never walked inside a non-Jewish place, you just didn't. It was as if there was a big sign outside. I couldn't get a job when I graduated, I went into practice on my own because I couldn't get a job anywhere. I was Jewish and I was a woman.[198]

In this context, the discovery of a letter in the 1980s from Clara Brett Martin to the Ontario Attorney General, complaining about fraudulent conveyancing practices on the part of 'Jews and foreigners' in Toronto, created new controversies about the first woman lawyer in Canada. As Lita-Rose Betcherman argued, Martin's letter 'must be characterized as defamation on racist grounds,' and it clearly had potential to do considerable damage to a vulnerable community at the time.[199] While recognising that Martin's anti-semitism was all too common in Toronto in the first decades of the twentieth century, Betcherman nonetheless argued that:

> ... Clara Brett Martin's racism cannot be explained away simply by saying that it was in the air.... [Her] racist views were far from universal.... Other voices favourable to Jews and other immigrants were raised ..., and if they did not override the prevalent racism, they certainly provided an alternative mode of thinking for an intelligent, educated woman like Martin.... While it was open to her to espouse the tolerant attitude of a Sir John Williston, editor of *The Toronto News*, she chose instead to adopt the bigotry of a Goldwin Smith.[200]

Betcherman is surely right about Martin's choice of bigotry over tolerance, but it may also be important to take into account how such

---

197 See B Figler, above, n 160 at 259–62.

198 C Morgan, '"An Embarrassingly and Severely Masculine Atmosphere": Women, Gender and the Legal Profession at Osgoode Hall, 1920s–1960s' (1996) 11 *Canadian Journal of Women and the Law* 19 at 33.

199 See letter to Edward Bayly, Attorney General's Department, 26 March 1915, in Archives of Ontario, RG 4, Series 4–32, 1915, file no 503; and L-R Betcherman, 'Clara Brett Martin's Anti-Semitism' (1992) 5:2 *Canadian Journal of Women and the Law* 280 at 297. See also, in the same volume: C Backhouse, 'Clara Brett Martin: Canadian Heroine or Not?' at 263; B Cossman and M Kline, '"And if Not Now, When?": Feminism and Anti-Semitism beyond Clara Brett Martin' at 298; Lynne Pearlman, 'Through Jewish Lesbian Eyes: Rethinking Clara Brett Martin' at 317; and responses by Backhouse at 351 and Betcherman at 355. For a critical account, see R Martin, 'The Meteoric Rise and Precipitous Fall of Clara Brett Martin' *Inroads Issue* 4 at 182.

200 L-R Betcherman, above, n 199 at 296–7.

racist views were connected to ideas of legal professionalism. Like Myra Bradwell in the United States two decades earlier, who had aligned herself with elite members of the legal profession in her efforts to discourage Jews, foreigners, and divorce 'shysters' from entering the profession, Martin's views reflected her conformity to prevailing views of legal professionalism, based on race and class, in Canada. As Jerold Auerbach argued in a somewhat different context, the legal profession permitted some 'outsiders' to become lawyers 'in return for their loyalty to dominant professional values,'[201] a comment which may all too sadly reflect Martin's situation as a woman lawyer. As Betcherman argued, any such explanation remains uncomfortable; all the same, it may accurately reflect the context of Martin's challenge to the 'gentleman's profession' of law.

Overall, it is difficult to affirm that the challenges launched by Martin, French and Langstaff were fully successful in confronting male exclusivity in the legal profession. Moreover, few other women chose to follow them into the profession for several decades: the census for 1921 recorded sixty-four women out of a total of 7209 lawyers in Canada, but by 1931, the number of women had dropped to fifty-four, although the total number of lawyers increased to 8058. By 1941, the census recorded 129 women lawyers among a total of 7920 members of the legal profession.[202] Perhaps because their numbers were so small, there is no evidence of efforts to establish women lawyers' groups until the Ontario Women's Law Association was established as a social club at a meeting on Toronto Island in 1923; a chapter of the American-based women's legal sorority, Kappa Beta Phi, was also formed in Ontario, but not until 1937.[203] In this context, women lawyers did not envision themselves as radical reformers; as Morgan concluded about women who became lawyers in the decades before 1970:

> ... as both students and professionals, these women generally wanted acceptance from their male colleagues and recognition of their equal worth. Even those who wanted to make a difference in the profession did not seek sweeping changes as much as they desired more subtle and incremental shifts in lawyers' behaviour and image....[204]

In this context, it seems significant that the first women lawyers in Canada gained admission to the bar 'on the same terms as men;' as a result, they not only existed at the margins of the women's movement – they also remained virtually invisible within the legal profession.

201 JS Auerbach, *Unequal Justice: Lawyers and Social Change in Modern America* (Oxford, Oxford University Press, 1977) at 6.
202 'Lawyers and Notaries' in *Census of Canada, 1931*, vol 1, table 83; and Canada Dept of Labour, *Occupational Trends in Canada 1931–1961* (1963) 40 and 45.
203 C Harvey, above, n 6 at 28.
204 C Morgan, above, n 198 at 59.

3

'Sound Women' and Legal Work: The First Women in Law in Britain

<hr>

WOMEN'S ACCESS TO THE LEGAL PROFESSIONS IN BRITAIN

It must be acknowledged that the prejudice which existed against women enter-ing other professions or businesses has been gradually removed of recent years, as the conception of women's sphere has been widened, and it is to be hoped that man will soon grant to woman what he has always enjoyed – the unre-stricted choice of a career, and that any vague unbelief (sic) in the supposed unfitness of women to enter the legal profession may be superseded by a will-ingness to grant them full recognition.[1]

MARGARET HALL'S HOPEFUL comments about women's access to the legal professions in Britain were published in March 1901, at a time when women were not yet eligible to become either barristers or solicitors. Hall argued that educational reforms, which permitted girls and boys to sit for the same School Leaving Certificate, made it illogical to prevent girls from pursuing careers in law along with boys. She also referred to women who were already practising law in the United States, and in other jurisdictions, including Canada.[2] Sig-nificantly, her comments appeared shortly after Hall had applied to the Society of Law Agents in Scotland for permission to take its preliminary examination, arguing that the statute permitted 'persons' to become law agents.[3] However, the Society refused her application on the basis that the practice of law had traditionally been confined to men, and Hall then appealed to the court. In doing so, Hall undoubtedly hoped that the court

[1] M Hall, 'Women as Lawyers' (1901) 1 *New Liberal Review* 222 at 227. Hall was the unsuccessful litigant in *Hall v Society of Law Agents* (1901) 3 Sessions Cases, 5th ser 1059.

[2] M Hall, above, n 1 at 223 and 225–6.

[3] *Hall*, above, n 1; and *Law Agents Act* (1873). See also A Sachs and J Hoff Wilson, *Sexism and the Law: A Study of Male Beliefs and Legal Bias in Britain and the United States* (New York, The Free Press, 1978) at 27–8; and CA Corcos, 'Portia Goes to Parliament: Women and their Admission to Membership in the English Legal Profession' (1998) 75:2 *Denver University Law Review* 307 at 316–21.

would take account of women lawyers' success in other jurisdictions, particularly the United States, where it was reported that there were more than 275 women lawyers by the end of the nineteenth century.[4]

However, the court refused Hall's appeal on the ground that the word 'persons' in the statute did not include women; as the court stated, the word 'persons' had to be interpreted in accordance with its customary usage, and since women had not been eligible to become law agents when the statute was enacted in 1873, it was clear that the word 'persons' meant 'male persons.' As judicial decisions in Canada and in some American states had suggested, moreover, the court in *Hall* decided that if women were to become law agents in Scotland, express legislative authority was necessary.[5] However, it was not until nearly two decades after Hall first presented her case that the British Parliament enacted legislation to open the legal professions to women after World War I.[6]

Yet, Hall was not alone in seeking admission to the legal professions in Britain in the early twentieth century. In 1903, Bertha Cave applied for admission as a student at Gray's Inn, and the Benchers of the Inn exercised their discretion and 'politely declined her application.'[7] When Cave appealed to the courts, acting on her own behalf, she was granted five minutes to press her claim before seven justices of the House of Lords in a 'private meeting.' After a brief presentation by Cave, the judges decided at once that the Benchers were right. Lord Halsbury concluded the hearing by adopting the principle that 'there was no precedent for ladies being called to the English Bar, and the tribunal were unwilling to create such a precedent.'[8] In the same year, Christabel Pankhurst, daughter of the well-

---

[4] L Frank, *La Femme-Avocat: Exposé Historique et Critique de la Question* (Paris, V Giard & E Brière, 1898) at 129–30.

[5] *Hall*, above, n 1; and A Sachs and J Hoff Wilson, above, n 3 at 27–8. A Corcos, above, n 3 at 320, criticized the reasoning in *Hall* in relation to the *Interpretation Act*, 52 & 53 Vict, c 63. The Benchers in Ireland also rejected an application from Miss Weir Johnston in 1901: see I Bacik, C Costello, E Drew, *Gender InJustice: Feminising the Legal Professions?* (Dublin, Trinity College Dublin Law School, 2003) at 51. See also M Redmond, 'The Emergence of Women in the Solicitors' Profession in Ireland' in EG Hall and D Hogan (ed), *The Law Society of Ireland, 1852–2002: Portrait of a Profession* (Dublin, Four Courts Press, 2002) 97 at 100.

[6] *Sex Disqualification (Removal) Act*, 1919, 9 & 10 Geo 5, c 71. According to Michael Birks, the legislation was successfully enacted after the Khaki Election, when 'the profession had become resigned to the inevitable': see M Birks, *Gentlemen of the Law* (London, Stevens & Sons Limited, 1960) at 277. However, others reported that the professions maintained opposition to the entry of women members until the end: see R Pearson and A Sachs, 'Barristers and Gentlemen: A Critical Look at Sexism in the Legal Profession' (1980) 43 *Modern Law Review* 400 at 404–5. See also B Abel-Smith and R Stevens (with Rosalind Brooke), *Lawyers and the Courts: A Sociological Study of the English Legal System 1750–1965* (London, Heinemann, 1967) at 193.

[7] EM Lang, *British Women in the Twentieth Century* (London, T Werner Laurie Ltd, 1929) at 146. See also 'Lady Law Students' (January 1904) *Englishwoman's Review* 49.

[8] *The Times*, 3 December 1903, cited by A Sachs and J Hoff Wilson, above, n 3 at 28; and by EM Lang, above, n 7 at 146. See also 'Women and the Bar,' (12 December 1903) *The Law Journal* 620. The right of an applicant to appeal from the Inns of Court to the judges, and the Inns' agreement to be bound by the judges' decision, was established only in 1837, evidence

known suffrage leader Emmeline Pankhurst, applied for admission as a student at Lincoln's Inn. Apparently, her application was 'summarily dismissed on the grounds, among others, that there would be no point in admitting her, as women were not allowed to practise at the Bar anyway.'[9] Clearly, the summary disposition of applications presented to the Inns of Court by Cave and Pankhurst confirmed that the bar remained conservative, traditional, and steadfastly determined to preserve its male exclusivity.

However, women were no more successful in their efforts to become solicitors. In 1913, when Gwyneth Bebb and three other women, all with outstanding university qualifications, applied to the Law Society to take the preliminary examination to become solicitors, the Society refused their applications. Bebb and her colleagues initiated legal challenges.[10] In a letter to the press, one of the applicants explained that a great incentive for their legal claims was a 'desire to change public opinion of women's capacity – to have women regarded as ordinary competent human beings.'[11] Yet, in spite of being represented both at trial and on appeal by leading counsel,[12] both courts concluded that the language of the statutes should be interpreted in accordance with 'long usage' in the common law; as the Master of the Rolls concluded in the appellate court:

> In the first place, no woman has ever been an attorney-at-law. No woman has ever applied to be, or attempted to be, an attorney-at-law. There has been that long uniform and uninterrupted usage which is the foundation of the greater part of the common law of this country, and which we ought, beyond all doubt, to be very loth to depart from.... [The court's] duty is to consider, and so far as we can, to ascertain what the law is. And I disclaim absolutely any right to legislate in a matter of this kind. That is for Parliament and not for this court.[13]

of the Inns' traditional autonomy: see B Abel-Smith and R Stevens, above, n 6 at 64. For an argument that the Law Society should *not* follow the precedent established in Cave's case, see EA Bell, 'Admission of Women' (1912) 56 *Solicitors Journal and Weekly Reports* 814.

9 EM Lang, above, n 7 at 146. See also 'Lady Law Students,' n 7 at 50; and A Sachs and J Hoff Wilson, above, n 3 at 172–3.

10 *Bebb v Law Society* (1913) 29 Times Law Reports 634, 109 *Law Times* 36, 57 *Solicitors Journal* 664; affirmed [1914] 1 Ch 286 (CA), and also reported at (1914) 34 *The Canadian Law Times* 620 [subsequent references to the *CLT*]. The four women were Gwyneth Bebb and Karen Costelloe, both of whom had taken Firsts at Oxford; Maud Ingram, 'who had achieved Honours in History and Law Triposes at Cambridge and had already been working for six months with a firm of solicitors'; and Lucy Nettleford who was still at Newnham and had taken a First in Part I of the Law Tripos.

11 EM Lang, above, n 7 at 146–8, quoting K Costelloe, above, n 10.

12 Bebb was represented by Mr Buckmaster (later Lord Buckmaster), a staunch supporter of women's right to enter the legal professions; and by Lord Robert Cecil in the Court of Appeal.

13 *Bebb*, above, n 10 at 629–30; and EM Lang, above, n 7 at 147–8. See also A Corcos, above, n 3 at 362. Counsel for the Law Society claimed that women could not be attorneys because the profession was a public office, and women could not hold public office; in the appellate court, Cozens-Hardy stated that this argument was really 'beside the mark' since it was clear from long usage that women could not be attorneys: above, n 10 at 629. Some years later, a comment respectfully lamented the outcome of the *Bebb* decision: see H Paterson Gisborne, Solicitor, 'The Admission of Women to the Legal Profession' (March 1917) *International Law Notes* 46 at 46–7.

The court also concluded that it was clear that women were under a common law disability which had not been removed by the use of the word 'persons' in the *Solicitors Act, 1843*. Relying on the assertion of Lord Coke over three hundred years earlier that women could not be attorneys, Cozens-Hardy, MR conclusively stated that 'the opinion of Lord Coke on the matter of what is or what is not the common law is one which requires no sanction from anybody else.'[14]

In fact, the history of women and the legal professions reveals that women in Britain had been demonstrating an interest in widening the sphere of women's activities to encompass careers in law even before Margaret Hall, Bertha Cave and Gwyneth Bebb initiated their legal claims at the beginning of the twentieth century. For example, counsel in these cases cited early examples of women advocates such as Lady Crawford, who apparently represented an accused in 1563 and was successful in having him acquitted.[15] There are also reports of women practitioners in the courts of medieval Scotland,[16] and of a woman solicitor in a seventeenth-century treatise about the legal professions in England.[17] As well, there are reports that well before Hall's application to the Society of Law Agents in 1901, an unsuccessful application had been submitted by a woman to the Law Society in 1879;[18] in addition, a group of women had petitioned unsuccessfully for admission to Lincoln's Inn a few years earlier in 1873.[19] By the late nineteenth century, moreover, women's increasing access to higher education meant that a number of them had completed university degrees in law: Eliza Orme at the University of London in

[14] *Bebb*, above, n 10 at 629. The court considered arguments about the authority of *The Mirror of Justices*, from which Coke quoted the principle that *'fems ne poient estre attorneys;'* while expressing doubt about the *Mirror*'s authority, the judges did not hesitate to adopt Lord Coke's view: above, n 10 at 626–9.

[15] *Hall*, above, n 1. In *Bebb*, above, n 10 at 625, counsel for the appellant provided several examples of women holding public office, including Queen Eleanor who acted as Keeper of the Great Seal in 1253. Counsel for the Law Society relied on the decisions in *Hall* and *Cave*, as well as *Jex-Blake v Senatus of Edinburgh University* [1873] Scottish Law Reporter 549.

[16] E Ewan, 'Scottish Portias: Women in the Courts of Mediaeval Scottish Towns' (1992) 3 *Journal of the Canadian Historical Association* 27 (new ser).

[17] W Prest, '"One Hawkins, A Female Sollicitor": Women Lawyers in Augustan England' (1994) 57:4 *The Huntington Library Quarterly* 353, citing N Grew, 'The Meanes of a most Ample Encrease of the Wealth & Strength of England In a few Years' (unpublished: British Library, Lansdowne 691; and Huntington Library, HM 1264).

[18] H Kirk, *Portrait of a Profession: A History of the Solicitor's Profession, 1100 to the Present Day* (London, Oyez Publishing, 1976) at 110, citing (1879) 24 *Solicitors' Journal* 139. M Birks, above, n 6 at 276, identified the relevant date as 1876.

[19] Leslie Howsam identified a petition submitted by Maria G Grey and ninety-two 'ladies,' requesting admission to lectures at Lincoln's Inn; it was rejected 'out of hand' by the Benchers. As Maria Grey was the founder of the Women's Educational Union, Howsam concluded that the petition was a political gesture on the part of educational reformers: see L Howsam, '"Sound-Minded Women": Eliza Orme and the Study and Practice of Law in Late-Victorian England' (1989) 15 *Atlantis* 44 at 46, citing *The Records of the Honourable Society of Lincoln's Inn: The Black Books vol V 1845–1914* (London, Lincoln's Inn, 1968).

1888,[20] Letitia Walkington and Frances Gray at Trinity College, Dublin in 1889 and 1890,[21] and Cornelia Sorabji at Oxford University in 1892.[22] Yet, in spite of such qualifications, women continued to be excluded from the legal professions.

Clearly, the only solution was legislative action. Yet, although numerous bills were presented to Parliament to permit women to become barristers and solicitors in Britain in the years immediately after the *Bebb* decision, they were not successful.[23] Indeed, some observers have argued that women's claims to enter the legal professions became intertwined with suffrage claims, and that militant action by 'suffragettes' in March 1914 deflected support for a bill, then before Parliament, which would have permitted women to become solicitors before World War I.[24] As the war dragged on, however, the debate about women's fitness to become solicitors and barristers escalated, with supporters arguing that women's participation in the war effort refuted claims that women were 'unfit' for professional occupations; in addition, they argued that women needed economic independence through paid work, since 1,500,000 women would not be able to marry as a result of the male death toll during the War.[25]

Some members of the legal profession agreed with these arguments and supported women who were seeking admission to the bar and the solicitors' profession. For example, when Bertha Cave and Christabel Pankhurst were invited to address the Union Society in London after the rejection of their applications, 'they easily persuaded the assembled lawyers to carry a motion in favour of women being admitted to their profession.'[26] However, other members of the legal professions remained vehemently opposed to the admission of women. Thus, Elsie Lang reported on a vote at the general meeting of the bar in January 1917, which rejected a motion

---

[20] L Howsam, above, n 19 at 44; Orme was the first woman to obtain the LLB from the University of London.

[21] L Frank, above, n 4 at 66. See also I Bacik, C Costello and E Drew, above, n 5 at 51–61; and *Frost v R* [2000] 1 Irish Law Reports Monthly 479. Corcos reported, above, n 3 at 321, that the first two women were admitted to the bar in Ireland in November 1921, six months before the first women were admitted to the bar in England.

[22] V Brittain, *The Women at Oxford: A Fragment of History* (London, George Harrap & Co Ltd, 1960) at 84–5. Brittain reported that Sorabji obtained a special decree from Convocation to allow her to sit for the BCL examination, which Sorabji passed; however, she was not called to the bar until 1922.

[23] For a review of the Parliamentary bill after *Bebb*, see EM Lang, above, n 7 at 150; and A Corcos, above, n 3 at 379.

[24] C Rover, *Women's Suffrage and Party Politics in Britain 1866–1914* (London, Routledge & Kegan Paul, 1967) at 6; for suffrage bills, see at 211 (Appendix I). 'Suffragette' was a demeaning term applied to the militant wing of the suffrage movement, but it was defiantly adopted by the militants themselves; the suffragettes were members of the Women's Social and Political Union, formed in 1903. See also EM Lang, above, n 7 at 150–52.

[25] EM Lang, above, n 7 at 154; and C Rover, above, n 24 at 53–6.

[26] B Castle, *Sylvia and Christabel Pankhurst* (London, Penguin Books, 1987) at 43–4.

for women's admission to the bar, notwithstanding their wartime work, stating pointedly: 'The fact that women nurse and sew and wait at canteens is no indication of their capacity for the legal profession.' Lang also noted that the secretary of the Law Society had sent a letter to each member of the House of Lords, suggesting that it would be inappropriate to enact legislation for the admission of women as barristers and solicitors while 'the great majority of solicitors of military age, and of articled clerks in training to become solicitors, are now fighting for their country.'[27] Thus, when the *Sex Disqualification (Removal) Act, 1919* was finally enacted,[28] permitting women to become solicitors and barristers in Britain, and Ivy Williams became the first woman barrister, she recognised that 'she had gained entry not because of a fundamental change of heart among the barristers, but because Parliament had forced the way open.'[29]

The statute became law on 24 December 1919, and a number of women immediately signalled their interest in legal careers. According to Lang, Helena Normanton was the first woman to become a pupil at the bar; she obtained admission to the Middle Temple 'within a few hours' of the law taking effect, and was the only woman admitted as a pupil at the bar in 1919. However, several women dined for the first time in the Inns of Court in January 1920, even though 'the Benchers did not acknowledge their presence;' and twelve women registered articles of clerkship with the Law Society on 31 January 1920.[30] The first woman to be called to the English bar was Dr Ivy Williams of the Inner Temple, who was a law lecturer at Oxford; Williams was also among the first group of women to receive degrees at Oxford in October 1920, when she simultaneously obtained her BA, MA and BCL degrees.[31] Normanton was called to the bar in 1922 and was the first woman to be briefed at both the High Court of Justice and the Central Criminal Court.[32] According to Harry Kirk, the first woman admitted as a solicitor was Carrie Morrison; educated at Girton, she was admitted in 1922, an event which was apparently ignored by the legal press. Moreover, for some time, the *Law Society's Gazette* listed the names of women under the heading 'Gentlemen Applying for Admission.'[33] In addition, as Christine Corcos noted, women's formal admission as barristers and solicitors did not guarantee them admission to

[27] EM Lang, above, n 7 at 157–8; and (27 January 1917) 142 *The Law Times* 229–30.

[28] See above, n 6. See also EM Lang, above, n 7 at 154.

[29] R Pearson and A Sachs, above, n 6 at 405, citing V Brittain, *Women's Work in Modern England* (London, N Douglas, 1928).

[30] EM Lang, above, n 7 at 164.

[31] V Brittain, above, n 22 at 156. Since Williams did not practise, however, it was Monica Geikie Cobb who was the first woman to hold a brief.

[32] EM Lang, above, n 7 at 166; and obituary notice for Helena Normanton, QC, *The Times*, 16 October 1957. For a description of the practical arrangements for women's entry to the bar, see H Newton Walker, 'Women and the Bar' (June 1919) *The Englishwoman* at 129.

[33] H Kirk, above, n 18 at 111, citing 'The First Woman Solicitor' (1922) 86 *Just Peace* 647.

the Circuit and Sessions Messes. There was considerable controversy about this issue; several news articles argued for the protection of male lawyers' dining privacy, suggesting that women should form their own messes and 'adopt a Bar hotel of their own in each circuit town.'[34] As Pearson and Sachs suggested, 'the removal of legal impediments ... was not the same as creating equal opportunities.'[35]

Such comments reveal how women who entered the legal professions in Britain after World War I experienced many of the same challenges and frustrations that had confronted women lawyers in the United States and Canada several decades earlier. Indeed, the litigated cases demonstrate that courts in Britain generally adopted the same kinds of arguments that were presented in cases in North America. Moreover, women who completed university law programmes often faced challenges in finding legal work, and some turned to other pursuits; for example, one of the unsuccessful litigants in the *Bebb* litigation gave up law for medicine, while another went into business.[36] Pankhurst turned all her energy to the cause of women's suffrage. Decades later, Sachs and Hoff Wilson speculated that Pankhurst had been much more effective when she appeared on her own behalf, charged with offences arising out of the militant suffrage movement, because she was *not* a member of the bar: 'the courtroom became an arena in which she was far more effective as a feminist law-breaker than she would have been as a female barrister....'[37]

Other aspiring women lawyers similarly turned their energies elsewhere. Letitia Walkington, who obtained her BA and MA degrees in 1885 and 1886 from the Royal University of Ireland, went on to study law at the university as well; and she received her LLB in 1888 and her LLD in 1889.[38] In spite of these qualifications, her response to an inquiry from the Belgian barrister, Louis Frank, in January 1897, suggests the difficulties she faced in finding legal work:

> I have much pleasure in telling you anything you may wish to know about what I have been doing as regards the Law. I took my LLD in 1889, after completing my studies and passing the other necessary examinations. I had several offers from solicitors asking me to enter their offices, but did not accept them, as I found that although I could have done Chamber work I could not have proceeded any further. Besides the profession is here distinctly overcrowded and there did not seem to me to be any opening for women solicitors or judges.

---

34 A Corcos, above, n 3 at 396–7

35 R Pearson and A Sachs, above, n 6 at 405.

36 EM Lang, above, n 7 at 165, reported that Costelloe had become a doctor while Nettleford had become a manager in her father's business.

37 A Sachs and J Hoff Wilson, above, n 3 at 173. See also FW Pethick Lawrence (ed), *The Trial of the Suffragette Leaders* (London, St Clements Press, 1909).

38 I Bacik, C Costello, and E Drew, above, n 5 at 53. As the authors noted, the Royal University of Ireland became the National University of Ireland in 1908.

Since then I have been devoting myself to coaching others both men and women, and to trying to ameliorate the condition of the poor, especially of the Blind, and have just perfected a machine for embossing Braille.... Do you consider there is any opening for women lawyers either on the Continent or Abroad? Any information would oblige.[39]

In spite of its brevity, Walkington's letter reveals the difficulties she faced as a woman law graduate in Ireland in the 1890s. Although she explained her reluctance to enter solicitors' firms on the basis of the limited scope of work available to her, it is possible that she also feared not being fully accepted by members of the firm.[40] In this context, her charitable work on behalf of the poor and the blind is consistent with benevolent activities undertaken by many middle-class women at the end of the nineteenth century, and her letter suggests a commitment to providing significant practical assistance. However, her rather poignant query about openings for women lawyers in other jurisdictions indicates that she remained hopeful about finding an opportunity to practise law. Unfortunately, there is no evidence of a reply from Frank, and little information about Walkington's later activities.

Clearly, for many women at the end of the nineteenth century, rejection by the bar and the solicitors' profession resulted in decisions to look for other kinds of work. At the same time, a few women who aspired to do legal work after completing university degrees managed to accomplish this goal effectively in the last decades of the nineteenth century, long before legislation was enacted in 1919, and *without* gaining access to the bar or becoming solicitors. Among these women, Eliza Orme successfully established a law office in Chancery Lane in 1875, without seeking admission to the legal professions at all. In this context, Orme's decision to engage in legal work reveals a different strategy: rather than confronting the authority and culture of the legal professions directly, Orme chose to do legal work at the boundaries of professional jurisdictions, mainly as a conveyancer and patent agent. In addition, she was actively involved in writing and publishing, in the suffrage movement, and in a variety of public and political activities. Her experiences provide important insights about how a woman might engage in the practice of law without becoming a member of the legal professions in the late nineteenth century. Thus, in examining Orme's experiences in some detail, this chapter explores the context in which she engaged in legal work 'at the boundaries' of the legal professions in the late nineteenth and early twentieth

---

[39] Bibliothèque Royale, Brussels, *Papiers Frank* #6031 (envelope 3).
[40] A Sachs and J Hoff Wilson, above, n 3 at 172, described the hierarchy of solicitors' firms in England as 'a three-tiered structure, with men occupying virtually all of the top or professional sector, as well as most of the middle or managing layer, while women filled almost all of the bottom or clerical zone.'

centuries, the same period in which women in the United States and Canada were adopting litigation and legislative reform strategies to become lawyers. In assessing Orme's success in achieving her goal, this chapter reveals some of the fissures in traditional ideas about 'woman's sphere' and about law as a 'gentleman's profession' in Britain at the turn of the last century.

ELIZA ORME: CHALLENGING 'WOMAN'S SPHERE' AND A 'GENTLEMAN'S PROFESSION'

Susan Anthony..., happily recording her visit in 1883 with 'England's first and only woman lawyer,' was obliged to add: 'or as nearly one as she can be and not have passed the Queen's Bench' – women were not admitted to the legal profession until 1922.[41]

The American suffrage leader, Susan B Anthony, visited England and other parts of Europe for nine months in 1883, meeting with women reformers in France, Italy and Ireland as well as in England.[42] Her visit to the law office of Eliza Orme, 'England's first and only women lawyer,' occurred when Orme was thirty-five years old; by that time, she had been engaged in legal work for nearly a decade. At the time of Anthony's visit in 1883, Orme was already becoming a significant public figure, not only because of her professional work in law, but also as a result of her commitment to women's education and greater opportunities for paid work, as well as women's suffrage. As Leslie Howsam explained, she was a prosperous spinster who was opinionated, well-connected and formidably competent:

Such, at least, was George Gissing's impression when they were introduced by their publishers in 1894 and she smoked a cigar with the gentlemen. Beatrice and Sidney Webb's correspondence indicates that they found her to be a formidable political opponent, rating her as equal in importance to Millicent Garrett Fawcett. And George Bernard Shaw used her as a model when he created the character of a prosperous independent professional woman [Vivie Warren, the cigar-smoking actuary daughter in *Mrs Warren's Profession*].[43]

41 C Bolt, *The Women's Movements in the United States and Britain from the 1790s to the 1920s* (Amherst, University of Massachusetts Press, 1993) at 179.
42 K Barry, *Susan B Anthony: A Biography of a Singular Feminist* (New York, Ballantine Books, 1988) at 276–83; Elizabeth Cady Stanton was in England at the same time, and the two American women's rights advocates went sight-seeing together and engaged in discussions with British women.
43 L Howsam, above, n 19 at 44, citing P Coustillas (ed), *London and the Life of Literature in Late Victorian England: The Diary of George Gissing, Novelist* (Sussex, Harvester Press, 1978) at 353; N MacKenzie (ed), *The Letters of Sidney and Beatrice Webb, vol I, Apprenticeships 1873–1892* (Cambridge, Cambridge University Press, 1978) at 342 and 375–6; and M Holroyd, *Bernard Shaw, vol I, The Search for Love 1856–1898* (London,

Born in 1848, Orme grew up in the middle decades of the nineteenth century, a period characterised by energetic reform efforts and the emergence of new ideas about 'women's sphere.' She was just nineteen years old in 1867 at the time of the debate on the Second Reform Bill; along with several thousand other women, Orme's mother had signed the petition advocating women's suffrage, which was presented to Parliament by John Stuart Mill.[44] Mill's amendment to the Government's *Represen-tation of the People* bill focused on clause 4, 'to leave out the word "man" in order to insert the word "person" instead thereof;' on 20 May 1867, the House of Commons debated the amendment, rejecting it by a majority of 123.[45] After the defeat of Mill's amendment, suffrage societies sprang up in a number of cities, and their influence increased when they later federated in the National Society for Women's Suffrage.[46] In 1868, the year after Mill's amendment was rejected in Parliament, some women sought to register as voters, arguing that they were not expressly excluded as women, and that the use of the male pronoun in the 1867 statute was to be interpreted in accordance with the provisions of the *Interpretation Act* of 1850; it stated that 'words importing the masculine gender' included females 'unless the contrary be expressly provided.' Richard Pankhurst, a well-known progressive barrister and active member of the Manchester National Society for Women's Suffrage, argued the case of *Chorlton v Lings*, but the court rejected the women voters' application.[47] In the same period, there were public debates about expanded roles for women in family life, including legal reforms concerning divorce, and married

Chatto & Windus, 1988) at 295. Holroyd suggested, at 295, that Shaw may not have realised that Orme was working as a legal practitioner; he referred to the character of Vivie as 'partly based on a noted Liberal Feminist, Mrs Orme (sic), who lived in Chancery Lane, practising as an actuary and smoking huge cigars.' Interestingly, Holroyd also suggested that Beatrice Webb was the model for Vivie: 'It was after her [Beatrice] that Shaw created Vivie Warren in *Mrs Warren's Profession* – an "attractive ... sensible ... self-possessed woman ...."': see Holroyd at 266.

[44] 'Orme Family' in E Crawford, *The Women's Suffrage Movement: A Reference Guide (1866–1928)* (London, University College London Press, 1999) 479 at 480. According to Hirsch, the petition contained over 3000 signatures, and it was just one of several presented to Parliament: see P Hirsch, *Barbara Leigh Smith Bodichon 1827–1891: Feminist, Artist and Rebel* (London, Pimlico, 1999) at 223.

[45] C Rover, above, n 24 at 218. See also J Rendall, 'The Citizenship of Women and the Reform Act of 1867' in C Hall, K McClelland and J Rendall (eds), *Defining the Victorian Nation: Class, Race, Gender and the British Reform Act of 1867* (Cambridge, Cambridge University Press, 2000) 119.

[46] C Rover, above, n 24 at 6.

[47] (1868) LR 4 CP 374. Richard later married Emmeline: see P Bartley, *Emmeline Pankhurst* (London and New York, Routledge, 2002) at 25–6. See also *R v Harrald* (1872) LR 7 QB 361; J Purvis, *Emmeline Pankhurst: A Biography* (London and New York, Routledge, 2002); J Rendall, 'Who was Lily Maxwell? Women's Suffrage and Manchester Politics 1866–1867' in J Purvis and S Stanley Holton (eds), *Votes for Women* (London and New York, Routledge, 2000) at 57; and D Morgan, *Suffragists and Liberals: The Politics of Woman Suffrage in England* (Oxford, Basil Blackwell, 1975) at 12–17.

women's rights to property and custody of children;[48] and women were increasingly involved in organised efforts to confront social problems by promoting temperance and lobbying for legislation about 'contagious diseases.'[49]

Orme was undoubtedly aware of these reform activities, since artists and intellectuals such as Thomas Carlyle and John Stuart Mill were frequent visitors to her parents' comfortable home near Regent's Park in London, and Orme 'grew up in a cultured ... home, among women as well as men who discussed science and politics, art and literature.'[50] More significantly, Orme benefitted from these reforms because a 'focal point in the struggle' for women's equality was the goal of providing education for women, particularly higher education.[51] Orme's parents were supportive of education for women; indeed, her mother had been governess to Elizabeth Barrett Browning. In due course, therefore, Orme and two of her sisters attended Bedford College for Women; founded in 1849, it was one of the first of new institutions of higher education for women in England.[52] Then, in 1871, when Orme was twenty-three, University College London decided for the first time to permit lecturers to address mixed groups of men and women, and Orme became a student there, eventually obtaining awards and scholarships in Political Economy, Jurisprudence and Roman Law. After the University opened its degrees to women in 1878, Orme passed with honours the first of two examinations for the Bachelor of Laws degree. Then, in 1888, in the midst of an active practice and busy public life, Orme completed the requirements for the

[48] For legislative reforms, including the *Divorce Act* (1857), the *Married Women's Property Acts* (1870 and 1882), and the *Custody of Infants Acts* (1839 and 1873), see L Holcombe, *Wives and Property: Reform of the Married Women's Property Law in Nineteenth-Century England* (Toronto, University of Toronto Press, 1983).

[49] See C Bolt, above, n 41 at 127–32 and 226–7.

[50] L Howsam, above, n 19 at 45. Howsam identified Orme's Aunt Emily, the wife of Coventry Patmore, as the original 'angel in the house.' As well, David Masson, who married Orme's older sister Rosaline, became the first Professor of English Literature at University College London; another sister, Julia, married Henry Bastien, a physician and scientist who also taught at University College.

[51] WJ Reader, *Professional Men: The Rise of the Professional Classes in Nineteenth-Century England* (London, Weidenfeld and Nicolson, 1966) at 171. The University of London was described by Zimmern as 'the pioneer in this reform' of higher education for women: see A Zimmern, *The Renaissance of Girls' Education in England: A Record of Fifty Years' Progress* (London, A D Innes & Company, 1898) at 126. See also M Vicinus, *Independent Women: Work and Community for Single Women 1850–1920* (London, Virago, 1985) at 121; R McWilliams-Tullberg, 'Women and Degrees at Cambridge University 1862–1897' in M Vicinus (ed), *A Widening Sphere: Changing Roles of Victorian Women* (Bloomington & London, Indiana University Press, 1977) 117; and B Kanner, 'The Women of England in a Century of Social Change, 1815–1914: A Select Bibliography' in M Vicinus (ed), *Suffer and Be Still: Women in the Victorian Age* (Bloomington & London, Indiana University Press, 1973) 173 at 195.

[52] E Crawford, above, n 44 at 480. See also V Brittain, *Lady into Woman: A History of Women from Victoria to Elizabeth II* (London, Andrew Dakers Limited, 1953) at 79.

LLB degree at the University of London; according to Howsam, Orme was the first woman to graduate in law in Britain.[53]

Significantly, however, by the time that Orme obtained her degree in law in 1888, she had been engaged in legal practice for well over a decade. In fact, Orme had announced her interest in pursuing a career in law in 1872, and Helen Taylor, the step daughter of JS Mill, paid the fee of £75 for Orme to become a pupil at Lincoln's Inn. Although there is speculation that Orme's family did not pay the fee because they did not approve of her decision, there is also some evidence that Taylor was 'keen for women to test entry to the legal profession and may have insisted on paying.'[54] According to Elizabeth Crawford, Orme was introduced to a sympathetic barrister, Savill Vaizey, in Old Square, Lincoln's Inn by Alice Westlake, whose husband John Westlake was an enthusiast about women's equality, and Orme also received advice from John Stuart Mill and Leonard Courtney.[55] A few years later in 1875, Orme opened a practice as a conveyancer and patent agent with Mary Richardson, another law student at University College. A brief note appeared in the *Englishwoman's Review* in November 1875, followed by a longer description the following month:

> The two ladies who have lately opened an office in Chancery Lane, are not, it is true, entered as barristers at any of the Inns of Court. A woman may be capable of paying fees, but she is not yet considered qualified to 'eat her terms.' But the capacity of these ladies is already well proved, and so much work has already passed into their hands, that we are told they have been compelled from want of time to decline some. It is certain that there must be some cases in which women would rather consult a woman 'counsel learned in the law' than any man. There is nothing unfeminine in drawing conveyances, settlements, or wills, or even declarations, pleas, or rejoinders.... We may have our Portias yet at the English bar, and the thorough legal knowledge which these ladies possess entitle them to full reliance....[56]

[53] L Howsam, above, n 19 at 45; Orme graduated from the University of London in 1888, the same year that Letitia Walkington graduated with her LLB from the Royal University of Ireland: see above, n 38.

[54] E Crawford, above, n 44 at 480. Interestingly, Duman reported that the 'standard fee' for pupils or apprentices in the chambers of practitioners at this time was 100 guineas: see D Duman, *The English and Colonial Bars in the Nineteenth Century* (London & Canberra, Croom Helm, 1983) at 81. It is possible that Orme's fee was reduced because she was not eligible for admission to the bar.

[55] E Crawford, above, n 44 at 480. L Howsam, above, n 19 at 46 and 49, described Westlake as one of Orme's mentors; John Westlake had supported the Working Men's College, and was later one of five men who agreed to become a permanent suffrage committee after Mill's petition was presented to Parliament. Leonard Courtney was later a barrister and politician and member of the Royal Commission on Labour. John Savill Vaizey was a student of the Middle Temple and was called to the bar there on 26 January 1855; he was admitted as a barrister of Lincoln's Inn on 3 February 1863: John Foster, *Men at the Bar* (London, Reever and Turner, 1885). His obituary in 1916 stated that he kept chambers at 10 Old Square, Lincoln's Inn: *Law Journal*, 2 December 1916. See also 'Women and the Bar,' above, n 8.

[56] 'The Year "That's Awa"' (December 1875) 6 *Englishwoman's Review* at 533–4; and 'Women as Lawyers' (November 1875) 6 *Englishwoman's Review* 510.

Although Orme never did apply for admission to the bar or the solicitors' profession, she was engaged in legal work for twenty-five years.[57] Unfortunately, there are no surviving examples of Orme's conveyancing and patent work, but her published writing about higher education for women, women's access to paid work and the professions, women's suffrage, and contemporary legal issues, reveal her propensity for factual accuracy and analytical rigour.

Orme had attended the co-educational lectures at University College at a time when traditional ideas about 'women's sphere' were increasingly being challenged by reformers; it was also a time of changing economic and social conditions, some of which significantly undermined the traditional roles of unmarried middle-class women. As in the United States, women's rights reformers in nineteenth-century Britain used a number of different arguments to support the extension of women's legal rights and their access to education, paid work, and suffrage.[58] As Sandra Stanley Holton argued, early assertions of women's equality in the writings of Mary Wollstonecraft and John Stuart Mill were based on humanist principles of the Enlightenment and liberal political theory. However, without abandoning these principles, late nineteenth-century proponents of increased rights for women also stressed women's fundamental difference from men, emphasising how women's nurturing capacities would improve public life. Such arguments were useful in gaining support from other groups who were similarly committed to social and political reform in Victorian Britain.[59] At the same time, class issues in Britain sometimes created particular tensions in relation to suffrage proposals at the end of the nineteenth century: disagreements occurred between middle-class suffragists who wanted to extend suffrage to women on the same terms as men, even if only propertied women were thus entitled to vote, while socialist activists wished to achieve adult suffrage for all classes, even if it were initially confined only to men. These conflicts were, of course, often exploited by politicians who were all too content with existing requirements for voting based on property and (male) sex.[60] Yet, in spite of some

[57] 'Women and the Bar,' above, n 8.

[58] J Rendall, *The Origins of Modern Feminism: Women in Britain, France and the United States 1780–1860* (Chicago, Lyceum Books, 1985) at 4. As Rendall noted, however, women's arguments often reflected male political theories; thus, women's arguments had to 'combine both the demands that arose from the perceived needs of women, and the contemporary language of the male political world.'

[59] S Stanley Holton, *Feminism and Democracy: Women's Suffrage and Reform Politics in Britain, 1900–1918* (Cambridge, Cambridge University Press, 1986) at 9. Holton identified the origins of suffrage claims in Enlightenment philosophy and liberal theory, citing Mary Wollstonecraft and John Stuart Mill. See also J Rendall, above, n 58; and K Gleadle, *The Early Feminists: Radical Unitarians and the Emergence of the Women's Rights Movement, 1831–51* (New York, St Martin's Press, 1995).

[60] D Morgan, above, n 47 at 26, argued that the seeds of this problem were established under Gladstone in the 1880s and 1890s. See also B Harrison, *Separate Spheres: The*

differences, increasing recognition of political and civil equality for women, with opportunities 'to participate in public life, to take up employment, or to run a household' clearly supported changes in women's roles and 'women's sphere.'[61]

Significantly, however, the emergence of new ideas about women's roles coincided with changes in demography and in economic structures which, perhaps more than the ideas themselves, demanded major changes in 'women's sphere;' as a contemporary observer declared: 'Facts convince more speedily than theories.'[62] In particular, census figures for the latter half of the nineteenth century reveal an oversupply of middle-class women, partly the consequence of large numbers of eligible men emigrating to the colonies; as a result, it was increasingly evident that many middle-class women had no chance at all of ever marrying. Moreover, many of these women no longer had major household responsibilities, as the rise of factory industries removed from household labour, at least in middle and upper class households, such activities as spinning, weaving, sewing and some aspects of food preparation; and many households employed servants, including nurses, governesses and tutors. These factors all supported calls for better education and more opportunities for employment for middle-class women.[63] At the same time, changes in economic structures were affecting the ability of some middle-class men to make adequate financial provision for dependent women, including unmarried daughters and widows; and new commercial enterprises and governmental offices were creating greatly expanded needs for clerical workers, including unmarried women.[64] Thus, while changing ideas about 'women's sphere' undoubtedly influenced the creation of new opportunities for middle-class women in relation to higher education and paid work, demographic and economic changes were at least as significant in promoting reforms. As Lee

Opposition to Women's Suffrage in Britain (London, Croom Helm, 1978) at 39; and J Liddington and J Norris, *One Hand Tied Behind Us: The Rise of the Women's Suffrage Movement* (London, Virago, 1984) at 73. For analysis of the competing claims of 'adult suffrage' and 'women's suffrage,' see S Stanley Holton, above, n 59 at 53.

61 J Rendall, above, n 58 at 321. See also L Holcombe, *Victorian Ladies at Work: Middle-Class Working Women in England and Wales 1850–1914* (Hamden, CT, Archon Books, 1973) at 6–10, who argued that education and paid employment for women was encouraged not only to benefit individual women, but also to benefit society – by producing women who could administer workhouses, schools and hospitals.' See also J Harris, *Private Lives, Public Spirit: A Social History of Britain, 1870–1914* (Oxford, Oxford University Press, 1993) at 33–6.

62 L Holcombe, above, n 61 at 195, citing Georgiana Hill, *Women in English Life: From Mediaeval to Modern Times* (London, Richard Bentley, 1896) vol II at 88 and 92; Holcombe also noted concerns expressed at the meeting of the International Council of Women in London in 1899 about middle class women who were forced to earn a living without having any preparation to do so.

63 L Holcombe, above, n 61 at 4–15.

64 L Holcombe, above, n 61 at 11, citing *The Economic Foundations of the Women's Movement ... by M A* (London, Fabian Society, 1914) at 5–7.

Holcombe succinctly concluded, 'the Victorian women's movement witnessed but did not cause the widening of the avenues of employment for middle-class women.'[65]

In this context, Orme's opportunity to attend University College occurred at the same time as a number of other experiments in women's education were being implemented, including the founding of the first women's colleges at Cambridge and Oxford: both Girton and Newnham were founded at Cambridge in 1869, and Somerville College and Lady Margaret Hall were created a decade later at Oxford.[66] Yet, while women were entitled to be in residence and to attend lectures at both Oxford and Cambridge, full access to higher education was still limited by the fact that neither university admitted women to degrees until after World War I.[67] By contrast with the first women who attended all-women colleges at Oxford and Cambridge, however, Orme pursued her law studies at University College, a non-denominational, non-residential and co-educational institution, where she may have learned early on to face the challenges of working in a male environment. For example, Martha Vicinus noted that even after examinations at the University of London were opened to both sexes, fellowships were often awarded to men over women, and the women students at University College had only 'an awkward and inferior common room for many years.'[68] Such comments confirm that although women increasingly obtained greater access to higher education, they were still not regarded as equal to men when they pursued university studies.

In spite of these difficulties, women like Orme responded eagerly to new opportunities for higher education, even though the range of occupations generally available remained somewhat narrow: teaching,[69] nursing (transformed by Florence Nightingale's work in the Crimea in the 1850s into a respectable calling for middle-class women),[70] and clerical and other

---

[65] L Holcombe, above, n 61 at 198.

[66] G Sutherland, 'The Movement for the Higher Education of Women: Its Social and Intellectual Context in England, c 1840–80' in PJ Waller (ed), *Politics and Social Change in Modern Britain* (Sussex, The Harvester Press and New York, St Martin's Press, 1987) 91 at 93. See also V Brittain, above, n 22 at 49–50.

[67] See especially V Brittain, above, n 22 at 155–7; and R McWilliams-Tulberg, above, n 51. As McWilliams-Tulberg noted, at 120, Oxford admitted women students to degrees in 1920; Cambridge did so in 1948. For a personal account of a woman who studied law at Cambridge in the 1930s and was admitted to the bar, see T Lien-Li, *Life in Three Countries: China, Jamaica and England* (unpublished biography on file).

[68] M Vicinus, above, n 51 (*Independent Women*) at 135. According to Vicinus, the all women colleges tended to create loyalties to Oxford or Cambridge rather than to women's rights: 'Hedged in on all sides by social and economic constraints, they bought intellectual freedom at the price of political timidity....'

[69] L Holcombe, above, n 61 at 34. Legislation concerning primary and secondary education, for girls as well as for boys, also created a need for more teachers: see A Zimmern, above, n 51 at 234.

[70] See L Holcombe, above, n 61 at 69. As Holcombe reported, nursing attracted women from all classes; the number of nurses grew 210 per cent, compared to an increase of 44 per cent for all working women, between 1861 and 1911: see Appendix, Tables 2a and 2b.

employment in new fields including large retail shops, the civil service, and business offices; in particular, the invention of shorthand and typewriting machines created increasing work opportunities for large numbers of women.[71] Yet, in spite of these new developments, access to *professional* education and work continued to present significant hurdles. In medicine, for example, Elizabeth Garrett Anderson, inspired by the American woman doctor, Elizabeth Blackwell, finally succeeded in obtaining her licence from the Society of Apothecaries; although the Society was firmly opposed to granting a licence to a woman, its regulations referred to the qualifications required by 'persons' to obtain a licence, language which the Society reluctantly concluded required the issuance of a licence to Garrett Anderson.[72] Finally, in 1870, Garrett Anderson succeeded in gaining an MD, but she was forced to obtain the degree at the University of Paris since she was entirely barred from studying medicine at that time in Britain.[73] Moreover, just as Orme was beginning her studies at University College in the early 1870s, there was an 'uproar' in Scotland, when Sophia Jex-Blake requested permission to study medicine at the University of Edinburgh; the court's decision confirming the university's refusal in 1873 must have been disheartening to Orme – as well as to Jex-Blake.[74] Moreover, closer to home, even Orme's entitlement to attend lectures at University College in 1871 did not make her eligible for a degree; it was not until 1878 that the University of London opened its degrees to women.[75]

Thus, Orme's access to lectures at University College London in the

71 As D Morgan noted, above, n 47 at 21, it was the 'typewriter, telephone, department store' revolution which absorbed thousands of new women workers annually by the turn of the century. See also LA Tilly and Joan W Scott, *Women, Work, and Family* (New York, Holt, Rinehart and Winston, 1978) at 156.

72 WJ Reader, above, n 51 at 175–6, citing J Manton, *Elizabeth Garrett Anderson* (London, Methuen & Co, 1965). As Reader explained, at 40–41, the nineteenth century medical profession included physicians, surgeons and apothecaries; the apothecaries were the first to establish a system of qualification and registration in the *Apothecaries Act* of 1815. After Garrett Anderson's application for a licence, the Apothecaries amended their regulations to proscribe the granting of a licence to students who received 'private' training; women were forced to train privately since they had no access to universities.

73 Elizabeth Garrett Anderson obtained her MD at the University of Paris in 1870, two years after it began to accept women for medical degrees. She later obtained a degree from Dublin University, and was the originator of St Mary's Dispensary for Women, subsequently the New Hospital for Women and Children; she was also Dean of the London School of Medicine for Women, founded by Sophia Jex-Blake. Garrett Anderson was active in suffrage activities; she was the sister of Millicent Garrett Fawcett, leader of the National Union of Women's Suffrage Societies: see C Bolt, above, n 41 at 109.

74 *Jex-Blake v Senatus of Edinburgh University*, above, n 15. See also A Sachs and J Hoff Wilson, above, n 3 at 4–22. Twelve appellate judges participated; Jex-Blake's application was denied by a vote of 7:5. Parliament enacted the *Act to remove the Restrictions on the Granting of Qualifications on the Ground of Sex* in 1876; and teaching and examining institutions then began to admit women: see WJ Reader, above, n 51 at 179. Jex-Blake initially qualified in Berne and in Dublin; she founded the London School of Medicine for Women.

75 A Zimmern, above, n 51 at 127.

early 1870s presented her with an opportunity, but one which was none-theless limited by the lack of access to a degree. It is possible that this unsatisfactory situation resulted in her decision, on the advice of some of her instructors at University College, to become a pupil at Lincoln's Inn in 1872; in addition, of course, she did not require a university degree to undertake legal work.[76] All the same, Orme remained actively engaged in the ongoing debate about degrees for women at the University of London. For example, in 1874, just a year after the court's negative decision in Jex-Blake's case, Orme published two notes in *The Examiner* on the subject of degrees for women at London University. The first reported on a recent vote by a large majority of the university's graduates in favour of degrees for women.[77] In addition to commenting favourably on the fairness of the process adopted for voting on the question, and generally refuting the arguments of those opposed to granting women access to degrees,[78] Orme's approach is interesting because she stressed the need to 'keep as closely as possible to actual facts,' emphasising particularly the *fact* that some women were *required* to earn a living. As she suggested, if degrees were thought to be economically useful to men, they should similarly be made available to middle-class women, especially unmarried women, who might be required to provide their own financial support: 'It is not a question of whether women are to work or not to work. Many women must work. The question is, are women to have the assistance of a University degree in the work they are obliged to do?'[79]

As Orme was aware at the time when she published this article, the issue of degrees for women was about to be considered by the Senate of the University of London. Thus, when the Senate 'hastily' voted against opening its degrees to women a few months later, Orme's second note appeared in July 1874.[80] Unhesitatingly, Orme criticised the Senate's failure to obtain 'the facts' about women's education before voting on the issue, suggesting disdainfully that 'If the subject before the Senate had been the advisability of making Greek a compulsory subject for boys of sixteen we should have had to wait longer for its settlement.'[81] At the same time,

[76] B Abel-Smith and R Stevens, above, n 6 at 53, described efforts to reform recruitment, education, and discipline processes for both barristers and solicitors; however, admission to the bar remained within the authority of the Inns of Court, while admission as a solicitor was regulated by statute.

[77] E Orme, 'University Degrees for Women' (May 1874) *The Examiner* 508.

[78] Orme, above, n 77. In particular, Orme rejected the idea of women's incapacity for intellectual work; she also rebutted arguments that few women would take up degrees, and that a '*bachelor* of arts' degree was not appropriate for women.

[79] E Orme, above, n 77. Indeed, Orme suggested that women had *greater* needs for degrees than men, since the range of opportunities for paid work for women was so limited.

[80] E Orme, 'University Degrees for Women' (July 1874) *The Examiner* 707.

[81] E Orme, above, n 80 at 707. Orme was particularly critical that the Senate had relied for its 'facts' on an article in the *Fortnightly Review,* which cited a number of American examples; Orme argued that the Senate should have taken 'a little time and trouble' to collect statistics from English institutions.

she argued that the hastiness of the decision would at least prevent it from being regarded as 'the weighty expression of opinion ... on a question of such importance;' her comments demonstrated her concern about the process of decision-making, as well as her scathing wit:

> We are disappointed, because we find that such a body of men as the Senate of the University of London can treat the question of women's education with so little consideration. Men who know the full value of education in politics, in scientific pursuits, in professional life and in social intercourse, can allow a question of vital importance to women's education ... to be discussed and disposed of in one short debate, with no preliminary inquiries and no chances of reconsideration afforded by adjourned meetings. We venture to think that when a body of women acts in this way we shall hear many generalisations about the 'jumping at conclusions,' 'the feverish action,' and the 'want of scientific method' of the weaker sex.[82]

In the end, Orme encouraged women to decide to study 'with or without a degree,' arguing that 'nothing is so likely to make other people in earnest as to show that we are in earnest ourselves.'[83] It was undoubtedly gratifying to Orme when, just four years later in 1878, the University of London reversed its earlier decision and opened its degrees to women.[84]

Clearly, Orme had a personal interest in the issue of degrees for women; as Howsam concluded, Orme's views about women's access to higher education and paid work reflected her own experiences as an unmarried woman seeking financial independence.[85] In later writing as well, she continued to stress 'the facts' about women's circumstances and their consequential need to be educated and to obtain gainful employment. She also continued to use wit to respond to arguments; for example, in relation to a suggestion that women's clothing represented a barrier to their participation in intellectual work, she wryly commented: 'Why should it be more necessary for women to discard petticoats than for barristers to discard wigs? ... Wigs are extremely irksome, and even unhealthy, when worn in a heated court of justice, and during the performance of highly intellectual work.'[86] Orme also pointed out, in a careful analysis of the plight of the unmarried daughters of professional men (known as 'poor ladies'), that ladies who increased their incomes and their enjoyment of life by pursuing paid work contributed to the economy: 'earners of money are spenders of money, and the professional woman will very likely give employment to a dozen of her sex by paying for work which she would otherwise do herself

82 E Orme, above, n 80 at 707.
83 E Orme, above, n 80 at 707–8.
84 A Zimmern, above, n 51 at 127.
85 L Howsam, above, n 19 at 51; see also E Orme, 'How Poor Ladies Live: A Reply' (April 1897) The Nineteenth Century 613.
86 E Orme, 'Women's Work in Creation: A Reply' (1886–87) 9 Longman's Magazine 149.

without special skill or interest.'[87] Her comment seems to confirm her own experience of financial independence, achieved through education and paid work.

As is evident, however, Orme did legal work successfully for several years without a university degree. When she finally received the LLB degree in 1888, she was forty years old, and had been established as 'Orme and Richardson,' a conveyancing and patent agency office in Chancery Lane, since 1875. A contemporary description of her office at 27 Southampton Building fortuitously exists, as a result of a visit to the office by Jessie E Wright, a newly admitted woman lawyer from Massachusetts; in a letter to the Equity Club in the United States in 1888, Wright vividly described her impression of Orme's office. After knocking at the door with a sign that identified the office as 'Orme and Richardson,' Wright described how she was ushered into a room where 'the floors were carpeted, a blazing soft coal fire burned in the open grate, two large windows were lowered from the top, a book case stocked with reports was behind me' and there were good autotypes on the wall. She noted 'a good-sized office table' in the centre of the room, 'loaded with papers, pamphlets, books – a fine chaos,' with revolving chairs on each side.[88] Miss Lawrence, who had become Orme's partner after Richardson departed, was working at this table, while an office boy waited for her orders.[89] Wright vividly described her discussion with Orme about her work and her views about women in law:

Miss Orme is fine; a first-rate kind of woman, and nobody could have been more kind and cordial than she has been to me. She tells me that she has never applied for admission to the bar, but that when four or five women are ready to ask for admission they will do so. She says she thinks things look more hopeful now than ever, and that several of the benches are already in favor of their being admitted – not as solicitors, for which an act of parliament would have to be changed, as I now understand it, but as barristers. She now has a good business, working for barristers and solicitors, but getting their work as they do, she says, they only get half fees; though, of course, when they do what work they are

---

87 E Orme, above, n 85 at 617.

88 Letter from Jessie E Wright to the Equity Club, 23 April 1888, in VG Drachman, *Women Lawyers and the Origins of Professional Identity in America: The Letters of the Equity Club 1887–1890* (Ann Arbor, University of Michigan Press, 1993) 141 at 143–4. After briefly describing Orme's office, Wright explained that 'as, perhaps, Miss Orme herself will have a letter in this edition of the club's letters, I will say no more about it.' There is a cable message to the Equity Club from Eliza Orme, dated 18 June 1888: 'Cordial greetings. Will write letter next year.' However, no such letter has been found.

89 According to L Howsam, above, n 19 at 48, Mary Richardson left the office in the mid-eighties, and Orme then entered into partnership with another law graduate, Reina Emily Lawrence. Like Richardson, Lawrence was active in local politics: see R King, 'The Admission of Women to the Legal Profession' (Dec 1916) 2 *Law Journal*; King identified the partnership as 'Messrs (sic) Orme and Richardson.'

qualified to do – drawing of wills, for instance – for private parties, it is different....[90]

This description of the legal work being done in Orme's office in 1888 suggests that she and her partners were actively engaged in legal practice, although not admitted to the bar or the solicitors' profession. Most scholars who have noted the existence of her office have concluded that Orme worked as a legal assistant. For example, Birks described Orme and Richardson as 'legal assistants to solicitors and members of the Bar,'[91] even though they worked independently from their own office. Birks's suggestion that Orme was working as a legal assistant is consistent with the appearance of increasing numbers of women in law offices, both as legal assistants and even more often as 'typewriters' (a word used to describe both the machines and the women who used them); indeed, Birks quoted a solicitor who asserted at the end of the nineteenth century that 'no busy office [can] afford to be without typewriters.'[92] As Abel-Smith and Stevens confirmed, one result of opening the universities to women, while admission to the legal professions remained closed to them, was that women were increasingly employed as clerks in solicitors' offices in the 1880s. Even in this context, however, Abel-Smith and Stevens described Orme's independent office as a 'bold' enterprise.[93] Thus, it seems likely that while some women were increasingly involved as legal assistants to members of the bar or in solicitors' offices, there were few, if any, others who established themselves as independently as 'Orme and Richardson.'

In the early 1870s, when Orme first commenced her legal work, both the courts and the legal professions had been experiencing a period of reform for several decades; however, as Abel-Smith and Stevens concluded, the decade of the 1870s was the beginning of a 'period of stagnation' which would last until after World War I.[94] Certainly, the middle decades of the nineteenth century had witnessed considerable change and consolidation in relation to the reform of the courts.[95] In addition, there were a

[90] Wright in VG Drachman, above, n 88 at 144. Wright's description is similar to the stage directions for Act IV in GB Shaw's play, *Mrs Warren's Profession*, above, n 43: the chambers of Honoria Fraser in Chancery Lane, where Vivie was working as an actuary, were described as having 'a double writing table in the middle of the room, with a cigar box, ash pans, and a portable electric reading lamp almost snowed up in heaps of papers and books.... and is very untidy....' See also H Kirk, above, n 18 at 118–19.

[91] M Birks, above, n 6 at 276. Birks indicated that Orme and Richardson opened a legal office in the early 'eighties in Chancery Lane; however, it appears that the office had been established in 1875: see n 56.

[92] M Birks, above, n 6 at 248. According to H Kirk, above, n 18 at 121, women staff first appeared in law offices in the 1850s, but they were slow to be accepted; by 1891, there were only 112 women clerks in legal offices.

[93] B Abel-Smith and R Stevens, above, n 6 at 192–3.

[94] B Abel-Smith and R Stevens, above, n 6 at 51, indicating that 'many problems remained unsolved.'

[95] B Abel-Smith and R Stevens, above, n 6 at 29, referring to the six-hour lecture to the

number of reforms relating to the organisation of the legal professions and legal education: the incorporation of the Law Society as the professional organisation of solicitors in 1831 (leading to centralised responsibility for lectures and examinations, and eventually responsibility for maintaining the 'roll of solicitors' pursuant to the *Solicitors Act* of 1843);[96] proposals to re-introduce the study of law at Oxford and Cambridge; as well as an abortive effort to create a 'School of Law' in London with responsibility for educating both barristers and solicitors.[97] Yet, in spite of these changes, the Inns of Court had generally rejected proposals for reform, effectively managing to avoid Parliamentary regulation and remaining firmly in control of qualifications and educational requirements for admitting new entrants to their 'gentlemen's profession.'[98] At the same time, the prestige of the bar was beginning to be questioned by people who believed that 'it was absurd to accord superiority to a ... profession which could be entered by eating a number of dinners.'[99] As a result, the Inns began voluntarily to supplement the keeping of terms and dinners with some educational lectures, and they introduced compulsory examinations for admission to the bar in 1872.[100]

There were also economic changes which affected the practice of law. In the latter decades of the nineteenth century, relationships between the bar and solicitors fluctuated between cooperation and open competition; there was open competition, for example, in relation to advocacy in the newly created County Courts after 1846.[101] As well, some traditional arrange-

House of Commons by Lord Brougham in 1828. Significant criminal law reforms were accomplished; for example, 'the number of crimes for which the penalty was hanging was reduced from 200 in 1826 to 4 in 1861.'

[96] As WJ Reader noted, above, n 51 at 25, solicitors had originally been Chancery officials, while attorneys had practised at common law. The latter assumed the title of solicitors in 1874; after the Law Society was incorporated by Royal Charter in 1831, an earlier organisation, the Society of Gentlemen Practisers, amalgamated with it in 1832: see B Abel-Smith and R Stevens, above, n 6 at 53. Responsibility for administering the 'roll' of solicitors was granted to the Law Society by the Act of 1843; see also M Birks, above, n 6 at 132.

[97] See B Abel-Smith and R Stevens, above, n 6 at 68–9 and at 71, for discussion of the recommendations of the Select Committee on Legal Education in 1846 (including a combination of theoretical legal education provided by universities and practical training provided by the profession, 'a remarkably modern approach' to legal education). In 1846, law teaching was virtually moribund at Oxford and Cambridge.

[98] WJ Reader, above, n 51 at 47. Kirk noted that the idea of law as a gentlemen's profession derived from an order signed by Lord Coke in 1603, providing that 'none be hereafter admitted into the society of any house of court that is not of gentle descent': see H Kirk, above, n 18 at 169. In relation to solicitors, the purpose of a preliminary examination for entry, established in 1860, was to 'exclude from the profession all who are not gentlemen by birth and education': see B Abel-Smith and R Stevens, above, n 6 at 67–8.

[99] H Kirk, above, n 18 at 171. Louis Frank explained that the Inns '*ne sont pas seulement des collèges de droit, mais encore des sortes d'hôtelleries*': L Frank, above, n 4 at 66.

[100] B Abel-Smith and R Stevens, above, n 6 at 74–6. Acccording to Duman, the Bar Council (established in the late nineteenth century) did not threaten the hegemony of the Inns of Court: D Duman, above, n 54 at 71.

[101] B Abel-Smith and R Stevens, above, n 6 at 32 and at 35–7. As H Kirk noted, above, n 18 at 135–6, issues of demarcation for solicitors and barristers remained a challenge.

ments, including the practice of barristers following the circuits, were beginning to change as a result of the availability of cheap and frequent daily train service from London; thus, new developments were beginning to challenge the traditional ways of practising law.[102] There were also frequent allegations of overcrowding at the bar,[103] although Abel-Smith and Stevens pointed out that both solicitors and barristers often failed to take advantage of new opportunities presented by the growth of commercial activities in the late nineteenth century. For example, solicitors faced growing competition from banks (which increasingly provided financial advice), as well as from patent agents, house agents and brokers. Even more significantly, solicitors showed relatively little interest in the growth of limited liability companies and the increasing importance of taxation; indeed, the syllabus for solicitors' examinations did not include topics such as death duties, income tax or company law, areas increasingly taken over by accountants.[104] As Michael Burrage concluded, 'Neither [barristers nor solicitors ...] were much concerned to defend or extend the jurisdiction or market of lawyers as a whole or with any wider "system." Only their jurisdictions relative to each other mattered....'[105]

In this legal context, it was possible for Orme and her partners to take up work 'at the boundaries' of legal practice, providing clients with legal services that were outside the customary practices of the legal professions; in this way, they also avoided the necessity of seeking admission to the bar or to the solicitors' profession. As Howsam noted, for example, a patent agent required an ability to manage detailed and precise documents in the context of an increasingly complex registration process; Orme clearly undertook this work quite effectively, at least until the Institute of Patent Agents was established in the early 1890s.[106] Similarly, it was possible for

---

102 D Duman, 'Pathway to Professionalism: The English Bar in the Eighteenth and Nineteenth Centuries' (1980) 13 *Journal of Legal History* 615, at 623: '... by the 1880s it was clear that the circuit messes had lost much of their authority [especially the Southeastern, located near London.]'

103 B Abel-Smith and R Stevens, above, n 6 at 33–4, described the acrimony surrounding the enactment of County Courts legislation in 1846; since solicitors were granted a right of appearance, there may have been negative effects on junior barristers. See also D Duman, above, n 54 at 207; and WW Pue, 'Rebels at the Bar: English Barristers and the County Courts in the 1850s' (1987) 16 *Anglo-American Law Review* 303.

104 B Abel-Smith and R Stevens, above, n 6 at 58 and 209; and M Birks, above, n 6 at 229.

105 M Burrage, 'From a Gentlemen's to a Public Profession: Status and Politics in the History of English Solicitors' (1996) 3: 1 & 2 *International Journal of the Legal Profession* 45 at 56.

106 L Howsam, above, n 19 at 47, citing K Boehm, *The British Patent System, vol 1, Administration* (Cambridge, Cambridge University Press, 1967) at 30. M Birks, above, n 6 at 229, also noted concerns, expressed by the Law Society as early as 1848, about 'agents in soliciting Patents' who were encroaching on 'the province of professional men.' According to WJ Reader, above, n 51 at 165, an Institute of Patent Agents was established in 1891; see also *An Act to Amend the Patents, Designs and Trade Marks Act, 1883*, 51 and 52 Vict, c 50 (1888); and N Davenport, *The United Kingdom Patent System: A Brief History with Bibliography* (Hampshire, Kenneth Mason, 1979) at 26–7.

non-solicitors to do probate work; indeed, when the Law Society attempted in the early 1880s to prosecute a firm of law stationers for preparing documents for probate, and thereby infringing the *Solicitors Act*, the case was dismissed by the House of Lords.[107] Thus, in these areas of legal practice, Orme and Richardson were entitled to 'do [the] work they [were] qualified to do [for clients],' as Orme had carefully explained to Jessie Wright at the time of her visit to Orme's office in 1888.[108]

However, the situation with respect to conveyancing was more complicated. As a result of legislation enacted in 1804, the legal professions held a statutory monopoly on conveyancing.[109] According to Abel-Smith and Stevens, Sir William Pitt agreed to grant the monopoly on conveyancing to the legal professions in return for an increase in stamp duties, required to finance the war with Napoleon; moreover, the monopoly recognised that, at least in the early 1800s, conveyancing was time-consuming and involved a considerable amount of difficult travel.[110] Although the practical work of conveyancing transactions was generally regarded as the work of solicitors, the intricacies of English land law often required specialised knowledge and drafting skills, both of which were provided by the 'conveyancing barristers' of Lincoln's Inn. As J Stuart Anderson explained, conveyancing barristers provided opinions on title which established them as 'the lords of their segment of the lawyers' professions; [their] skill lay in adapting the underlying law to the property dispositions of the wealthy, devising documents to achieve the precise ends of their clients, resorting to creative private statutes where necessary.'[111] The expertise of the conveyancing barristers was highly regarded, even by judges; indeed, 'an opinion on the validity of a title by [one of the prominent conveyancing barristers] was as near to being final as makes no difference.'[112] The conveyancing barristers had established an Institute as early as 1815, and its members commented on reform statutes relating to land law throughout the nineteenth century; indeed, the Institute was still thriving in 1895, and its forty members who regularly dined together were by then known as the 'Forty Thieves.'[113]

---

[107] *Law Society v Waterlow Bros* (1883) LR 8 AC 407.

[108] Wright in VG Drachman, above, n 88 at 144.

[109] The monopoly was created by the *Stamp Act* of 1804; in response to increased stamp duties payable on articles of clerkship and admission certificates, Parliament inserted a clause providing for a penalty of £50 for unqualified persons who prepared conveyancing documents. See also H Kirk, above, n 18 at 130–31.

[110] B Abel-Smith and R Stevens, above, n 6 at 23.

[111] JS Anderson, *Lawyers and the Making of English Land Law 1832–1940* (Oxford, Clarendon Press, 1992) at 4: the conveyancing barristers included Tinney, Hodgson, Duckworth, Brodie, Sanders, Duval [and] Tyrell – 'their temperaments differed of course, so that what to one would be an unacceptable risk would to another be unjustifiable timidity.' See also H Kirk, above, n 18 at 173.

[112] JS Anderson, above, n 111 at 6.

[113] B Abel-Smith and R Stevens, above, n 6 at 211, citing (1895) 30 *Law Journal* 447. JS Anderson, above, n 111 at 262, stated that the Institute was 'a club of elite conveyancers,

Although there is no evidence that Orme attended dinners with the conveyancing barristers,[114] it appears likely that she was engaged by members of the Institute to provide legal opinions on land titles and to draft conveyancing documents, as a 'legal assistant;' such an arrangement would explain her receipt of 'half-fees,' as she had described her circumstances at the time of Jessie Wright's visit. Orme's acceptance as an assistant at the bar probably resulted from her ability to do highly competent and reliable legal work within this close-knit and highly specialised group of conveyancing barristers; indeed, her work for this group suggests that she was both accomplished and professional. An alternative theory is that Orme might have qualified as a 'certified conveyancer,' a specialised group at the bar who were primarily engaged in drafting documents, but who sometimes were also involved in conveyancing transactions; however, this possibility seems unlikely since the number of certified conveyancers was already declining in the 1880s.[115] Moreover, Orme's suggestion, in an interview in 1903, that women with legal training might band together and attempt to gain admission as specialised conveyancers before directly challenging their exclusion from the bar, appears to confirm that she had not taken this step on her own.[116]

Thus, in the end, it seems most likely that Orme was regarded as a legal assistant to the bar and to solicitors, providing legal opinions and drafting documents, even though she maintained her own independent office.[117] Although her secondary status must have been frustrating at times, the fact that conveyancing was highly lucrative may have tempered her concerns about obtaining only 'half fees.' As Abel-Smith and Stevens noted, 'the growth of railways, developments in agriculture and increasing industrialisation and urbanisation all led to more land changing hands;' moreover,

primarily social, which occasionally produced an opinion on matters of professional interest,' citing A Offer, *Property and Politics, 1870–1914* (Cambridge and New York, Cambridge University Press, 1981) at 33–4. There is no explanation for the reference to this group of barristers as the 'forty thieves,' but it may be a comment on how lucrative the conveyancing business was at the end of the nineteenth century: see M Birks, above, n 6 at 229. Abel-Smith and Stevens also identified barristers who specialized in patent work, so Orme may have done patent work as an assistant as well.

114 It is likely that the dinners took place in locations from which women were excluded. Even after World War I, there were no real cloakrooms for women at the Inns: see HN Walker, above, n 32.

115 According to M Birks, above, n 6 at 197, 'special pleaders and conveyancers' were 'gentlemen [who] were members of the Inns who devoted their lives to drafting pleadings and legal documents. English law and procedure had become so hag-ridden with futile technicalities that such specialists found a ready market for their services. Many of them were not called to the Bar and the growth of these two new professions was doubtless stimulated by the laws which prevented Catholics from practising as barristers or attorneys.' See also JS Anderson, above, n 111 at 6. According to H Kirk, above, n 18 at 134–5, there were thirty-seven certified conveyancers in 1870, ten in 1890, and only two in 1910.

116 See L Howsam, above, n 19 at 4. Orme's suggestion may not have been practical by 1903: see n 115.

117 See H Kirk, above, n 18 at 132; and B Abel-Smith and R Stevens, above, n 6 at 230–1.

the slow progress of bills in Parliament for the creation of a general system for registering interests in land meant that the process of drafting conveyancing documents remained technical and complex, and thus lucrative for its practitioners, until the end of the nineteenth century. Even changes in the method of charging for conveyancing and the establishment of schedules of fees for such transactions did not significantly diminish the financial returns for conveyancing.[118] As a result, Orme achieved economic independence by engaging in legal work, but without gaining admission to the legal professions. Yet, in spite of her success, the confident prediction which greeted the opening of Orme's office in 1875, that it would be the 'first step ... towards opening ... the [legal] professions to women,' remained unrealised for decades thereafter.[119]

A WOMAN IN LAW IN THE PUBLIC SPHERE

Miss Orme is regarded as one of the ablest women in England. She is one of the foremost leaders among women in politics, a field in which ... the women of England are far in advance of their American sisters. Her work on the English Labour Commission has been of great value. Miss Orme was the first woman to receive the degree of LLB from London University – that noble institution whose examinations are far more rigorous than those of Oxford and Cambridge, but which, unlike its antiquated neighbours, puts men and women upon a footing of equality, and confers its honours and degrees irrespective of sex....[120]

This tribute to Orme appeared in the *Law Times* in September 1893, announcing that she had been invited to participate in the Congress on Jurisprudence and Law Reform, held in conjunction with the World's Columbian Exposition in Chicago. Orme was one of four women who were included in the Congress; as the news report explained, her inclusion was auspicious because it was 'the first time in the history of the world [that] an international congress of lawyers has been held in which women lawyers have taken part.'[121] The other women invitees included

---

118 According to B Abel-Smith and R Stevens, above, n 6 at 59–60 and 196, changes in arrangements for conveyancing fees made conveyancing lucrative for the legal professions. See also JS Anderson, above, n 111 at 150–55.

119 'Women as Lawyers,' n 56.

120 'Women in the Law Reform Congress' (2 September 1893) 95 *The Law Times* 402.

121 *The Law Times*, above, n 120. A World's Congress Auxiliary arranged for major international congresses on religion, women's rights, and other topics, including Jurisprudence and Law Reform. Originally, there had been separate committees of male lawyers and female lawyers; but the women's committee decided to join with the men's committee (a total of nineteen men and four women), having concluded that 'the interest of women in the profession of law would be best conserved by a joint congress.' The Congresses were held in conjunction with the World's Columbian Exposition: see JE Findling, *Chicago's Great World Fairs* (Manchester and New York, Manchester University Press, 1994).

two Americans, Clara Shortridge Foltz and Mary A Greene, and a Parsi woman from India, Cornelia Sorabji, who had just become the first woman to complete examinations for the BCL degree at Oxford in 1892.[122] The report in the *Law Times* was reprinted verbatim from an article in the *Chicago Legal News*; significantly, while lauding Orme's role in politics, the report did not mention that women in England were also 'far behind' their American sisters in relation to access to the legal professions. Indeed, it seems that the *Law Times* reproduced the report without any need to note that Orme was not, in fact, a 'woman lawyer' at all. In this context, the tribute clearly demonstrates Orme's significance as a woman in the public sphere, a role that included professional legal work but which also encompassed activities beyond the office in Chancery Lane.

In fact, Orme had been involved in a variety of reform activities as early as the 1870s. For example, she participated actively in the Society for Promoting the Employment of Women. As Lee Holcombe explained, the Society promoted better educational opportunities for women, as well as a number of pilot projects to train women, employ them, or find employment in such fields as hairdressing, engraving, photography, house decoration, proof reading and, 'an especial favourite, the administration of charitable institutions;' it also established the Victoria Press, a printing business run by women trained by the Society as compositors.[123] The Society had been established in 1859 by the 'ladies of Langham Place,' a group which included Barbara Leigh Smith Bodichon and Bessie Rayner Parkes, as well as Anna Jameson. Orme was a member of the managing committee of the Society from 1873 to 1877,[124] and she acted as treasurer for a fund that was established by the Society to enable Sarah Marks (known as Hertha) to attend Girton College; Orme wrote to Helen Taylor, among others, to solicit funds, and Hertha later achieved renown for her scientific work on electric arcs.[125] It was the ladies of Langham Place who also established a journal which eventually became the *Englishwoman's Review*, and which published the notices of the opening of Orme's office in Chancery Lane in 1875.[126]

Increasingly, however, Orme became involved in the suffrage movement and the Liberal Party. She was a member of the London National Society

[122] The papers prepared by all four women were reprinted in (12 August 1893) 25 *Chicago Legal News* 431.

[123] L Holcombe, above, n 61 at 5–6 and 15–16. See also CA Lacey (ed), *Barbara Leigh Smith Bodichon and the Langham Place Group* (New York and London, Routledge & Kegan Paul, 1987).

[124] E Crawford, above, n 44 at 480. Although she worked with some members of the Group, Orme was not likely a member; in 1877, Orme was appointed to the London School of Medicine for Women's council.

[125] During World War I, she invented the 'Ayrton fan' for dispersing poisonous gases from the trenches; her daughter, Barbara Gould, was later elected a Labour MP in 1945: see P Hirsch, above, n 44 at 322–3.

[126] See above, n 56.

for Women's Suffrage, and an articulate speaker at suffrage meetings; in 1872, Orme became joint secretary of the London National Society. In 1885, she signed the petition to the House of Lords in support of a Woman's Suffrage Bill.[127] At the same time, she was active politically: at a meeting in Chelsea in June 1886, her topic was 'How Women Can Best Assist the Liberal Cause.'[128] In the 1880s, Orme became increasingly involved in efforts to strengthen women's involvement in the party through the Women's Liberal Federation, established as an umbrella organisation of local Women's Liberal Associations in 1887.[129] In 1888, the same year that she attained the LLB degree at the University of London, she became editor and manager of the *Women's Gazette*, the journal of the Women's Liberal Federation; according to the *Englishwoman's Review,* the journal had 'a direct political bias' and promised to give its 'attention to all questions affecting the social well-being and political position of women.'[130]

Yet, the decade between 1885 and 1895 was increasingly difficult and divisive for Liberals in Britain; as David Morgan suggested, it was a time when the Liberal Party 'was a prime recipient of the tensions generated by considerable societal pressures and a flux of ideas.'[131] In the election of 1885, for example, Parnell had directed Irish votes against the Liberals as a result of their failure to end coercion in Ireland and grant Home Rule; one consequence was that Richard Pankhurst, running as an Independent, lost his seat, a result which his wife Emmeline never forgot.[132] When Gladstone then reversed his position and supported Irish Home Rule in 1886, his decision split the party, with those opposed to Gladstone establishing the Liberal Unionists.[133] Even among those who remained Liberals, however, there were continuing differences, particularly on issues about state intervention to alleviate poverty and unemployment, the devolution of powers to Ireland, and imperial governance.[134] Interestingly, according

---

127 E Crawford, above, n 44 at 480. See also C Rover, above, n 24 at 217 (Appendix I) and at 219 (Appendix II).

128 L Howsam, above, n 19 at 49.

129 E Crawford, above, n 44 at 480. See also 'Eliza Orme' in CS Nicholls (ed), *Dictionary of National Biography – Missing Persons*, which identified Orme as a founding member of the Women's Liberal Federation in 1887, a federation of 40 Women's Liberal Associations, and editor of the *Women's Gazette and Weekly News* from 1889 to 1891. According to D Morgan, above, n 47 at 14, when Parliament enacted the *Corrupt Practices Act* in 1883, which banned paid election canvassers, parties established women's auxiliary organisations: the Primrose League (Conservatives) in 1885, and the Women's Liberal Federation in 1887.

130 Quoted in L Howsam, above, n 19 at 51–2.

131 D Morgan, above, n 47 at 25. Although Morgan was referring to the 1890 to 1914 period, he argued that the seeds of these difficulties were linked to the 1885 election. See also C Rover, above, n 24 at 117.

132 D Morgan, above, n 47 at 23–4.

133 D Morgan, above, n 47 at 24. Women supporters established the Women's Liberal Unionist Association.

134 Tensions were exacerbated in the early twentieth century by differing views within the Liberal Party about Britain's entry into the Boer War, and the election pact with the Labour

to Kirk, a large number of politicians also campaigned in the 1885 election in support of a national land registration system, directing considerable criticism against the legal professions for 'cost and delay in the transfer of land.' Moreover, among Liberals, land reform issues created some tensions as they began to respond to the changes in the Parliamentary franchise enacted in 1884, which expanded and redistributed the number of seats and included agricultural labourers among the electorate for the first time.[135]

In this context, women's suffrage was just one of a number of controversial public issues in the late 1880s. As a result, the suffrage issue never achieved a high priority for Parliamentary action while the Liberals were in power; as Morgan concluded, it was seen by many Liberal politicians as merely 'a peripheral question.'[136] Other Liberals were concerned that extending suffrage to women, without amending the property requirements for voting, would result in more votes for the Conservatives.[137] Moreover, a number of prominent women were publicly opposed to the extension of suffrage to women; among them were Mrs Humphrey Ward and Beatrice Potter (later Beatrice Webb), both of whom signed a women's anti-suffrage petition in 1889.[138] In such a context, there were undoubtedly some members of the Women's Liberal Federation, although probably a small minority, who did not support women's suffrage, and these differences were increasingly evident in meetings of the Federation. In the late 1880s, for example, motions in support of suffrage were presented and approved at meetings of the annual council of the Federation; in addition, a more controversial proposal to incorporate women's suffrage as a *specific* objective of the Federation gained increasing support, even though women's suffrage had not been adopted officially as Liberal Party policy. The issue came to a head in 1892, when a majority of Federation members voted to make women's suffrage part of the Federation's constitution; as a result, Orme and a number of other prominent members resigned from the executive of the Federation to establish their own organisation, the Women's National Liberal Association.[139]

Party; the latter resulted in the restoration of a Liberal government in 1905: see D Morgan, above, n 47 at 27. Orme was opposed to increased state intervention: as L Howsam noted, above, n 19 at 48, she lectured in March 1886 on the topic 'Are We Free? A Protest Against Over-Legislation and State Socialism,' countering Fabian arguments.

135 H Kirk, above, n 18 at 140, citing (1885) 29 *Solicitors' Journal* 322. See also JS Anderson, above, n 111 at 163–6.

136 D Morgan, above, n 47 at 25. Even after the Liberals returned to government in 1905, the suffrage issue was not a high priority, especially for Prime Minister Asquith.

137 C Rover, above, n 24 at 181.

138 L Radice, *Beatrice and Sidney Webb: Fabian Socialists* (New York, St Martin's Press, 1984) at 41. The petition, drafted by the novelist Mrs Humphrey Ward, was published in the *Nineteenth Century*. Beatrice Potter signed the petition, but it was 'a gesture she came to reject;' according to C Rover, above, n 24 at 171, Webb published her retraction as a letter to *The Times* on 5 November 1906.

139 See E Orme, 'A Commonplace Correction' (1892) 1 *Welsh Review* 467. Orme was

In response to public criticism for her action, Orme published a comment which, carefully and precisely, reconstructed the history of suffrage discussions at meetings of the Federation between 1887 and 1892, asserting that it was a matter of principle to refuse to make an issue, which was *not* a formal policy for the Liberal party, a positive requirement for membership in the Federation:

> To any person who can distinguish accurately between essentially different things, this outline shows that our Federation has always been opposed to making approval of Woman's Suffrage a test of membership. We desire that all Liberal women, whether they are in favour of that reform or not, should be able to join our ranks. Any local Association may make the reform one of its specified objects if the majority of its members wish to do so, but no local Association is bound to do so. The Federation remains open to all Liberal workers.... It seems to me so plain that I should have thought a little child could have seen it....[140]

As she put it bluntly, it was necessary to see 'the essential difference between believing in a reform oneself and kicking out of an organisation everyone who does not believe in it.'[141] In her approach, Orme associated herself with other members of the executive, particularly Lady Fry of Darlington, wife of a Liberal member of the House of Commons, who had worked tirelessly to create the Women's Liberal Federation.[142] When Lady Fry died suddenly in 1897, Orme published an account of her life, including Lady Fry's views about the focus of a Liberal women's organisation:

> She had never publicly advocated the political enfranchisement of women, but believed the time would come when a liberal measure would be accepted by the country, by means of which the responsibilities and interests of citizenship would be extended to women. On the other hand she considered that the great

responding to an assertion by Mrs Wynford Philipps, that 'Woman's Suffrage is the burning question in the Women's Liberal Federation at the present moment.' Orme firmly stated that 'the burning question in the Women's Liberal Federation at the present moment is how to win the General Election.'

140 E Orme, above, n 139 at 469–70.

141 E Orme, above, n 139 at 469. See also C Rover, above, n 24 at 141, who reported that Gladstone requested the Federation to 'shelve' the suffrage issue in 1892 in the interest of his Home Rule policy.

142 E Orme, *Lady Fry of Darlington* (London, Hodder and Stoughton, 1898) at 114 and 121–3. Lady Fry was the wife of Theodore Fry, who had served as mayor of Darlington in the 1870s; he was elected as a Liberal member of Gladstone's government in 1880 and again in 1885. After the 1885 election, Mrs Fry became 'the acknowledged centre of all those who approved of the education and active participation of women in practical politics.' At the second meeting of the Women's Liberal Federation, there were 40 associations with over 10,000 members, and Catherine Gladstone, wife of the Prime Minister, became honorary President. As Orme noted, the 'many ladies of rank and wealth' were seated at council meetings beside 'factory hands, Board School teachers, the wives and daughters of tradespeople and artisans....'

Liberal organisation which she had herself originated was not available for the promotion of reforms about which Liberals are in disagreement, and which are in fact not part of an accepted party programme.... [In] 1892 Mrs Fry, with several prominent members of the Federation, thought it best to retire from that body and work for the principles of Liberalism on the lines they could thoroughly approve....[143]

Orme's account of Lady Fry's views were, of course, thinly veiled statements of Orme's position as well. Indeed, it seems that, in a contest between her support for women's suffrage and her loyalty to the Liberal party, Orme clearly placed the party's well-being ahead of the advancement of women. However, this conclusion must also take account of Orme's longstanding commitment to 'the facts' and to 'fair processes,' a commitment which made it seem inappropriate to her for an organisation that had been established for purposes of advancing the Liberal party's interests to be 'taken over' by other interests, however laudable and however much she may herself have supported them. As well, her friendship with Lady Fry and her energetic organisational work with the other 'prominent' members of the Federation's executive may have motivated her to leave the organisation along with them. Thus, it must have been disconcerting that the Federation continued to flourish after 1892, under the leadership of two successive and dedicated presidents, the Countess of Aberdeen and the Countess of Carlisle; 'the latter, a celebrated temperance campaigner known as the "Radical Countess," was a fervent Liberal and an activist for social reform,' and guided the Federation through a period of growth which resulted in 1500 groups and 100,000 members by 1908. By contrast, the new organisation established by Orme and her friends languished.[144]

Yet, Orme's energetic work on the executive of the Federation had made her a public figure in London by the early 1890s, and her commitment to a rigorous analysis of 'the facts' must have been well known and respected, even by those who disagreed with her. Thus, it was not surprising that she was invited to assist, when the Conservative/Liberal Unionist government established a Royal Commission on Labour to inquire into controversial labour problems in 1891. As a result of crippling Dock Strikes in 1889, and later strikes and lock-outs in Durham, Lancashire and elsewhere, the Royal Commission was directed to 'inquire into the questions affecting the relations between employer and employed, the combinations of employers and employed, and the conditions of labour [arising out of the

---

[143] E Orme, above, n 142 at 131 and 135. Orme's account of Lady Fry's activities included her efforts to get women voters to the polls in all the elections in which they were able to vote, insisting 'upon this being the best and most practical way of leading up to that further enfranchisement': Orme at 140.

[144] P Gordon and D Doughan, *Dictionary of British Women's Organizations 1825–1960* (London, Woburn Press, 2001) at 173.

recent disputes].'[145] Leonard Courtney, formerly one of Orme's lecturers at the university and now a Liberal/Unionist politician, recommended Orme to the Commission when it was decided to expand the scope of inquiry to include working conditions for women.[146] Thus, Orme was appointed senior Lady Assistant Commissioner to the Royal Commission.[147] The Commission sat for three years, and cost £50,000; it was described as 'the most costly [commission] that has ever been undertaken.'[148] After releasing a very large number of background studies and summaries of evidence given by witnesses, the Commission eventually released its final reports in 1894. Unbeknownst to the majority of the Commissioners, a minority report was prepared by Sidney Webb, who was not a member of the Commission, but his report was adopted by four members of the Commission who were supportive of collective action.[149] Such action was being encouraged by trade unionists and the fledgling Independent Labour Party which had been formed in a meeting at Bradford only a year earlier in 1893.[150] Not surprisingly, the minority report was controversial; as one commentator stated, 'the Majority Report aspires at least ... to be judicial, [while] the Minority Report [reveals a bias which is] unmistakable, and [its] language is that of advocates rather than judges.'[151]

Orme had been appointed to assist the Commission in April 1892. Allegedly in response to a memo to the Commission from Beatrice Webb,[152] the Commission decided to appoint Lady Assistant Commis-

---

[145] Observer, 'The Labour Commission' (1894) 23 *The National Review* 201. The article described 'fierce conflicts' between shipowners and seamen in several parts of the United Kingdom.

[146] According to L Howsam, above, n 19 at 49, it was Leonard Courtney, by this time a Liberal/Unionist politician, who selected Orme; the Liberal Unionists were supporting the ruling Conservatives in 1891. Apparently, Courtney appointed Orme rather than Beatrice Potter, who was about to marry Sidney Webb; she was beginning 'to be identified as a socialist and supporter of cooperatives and trades unions.' By contrast, Orme was a supporter of women's employment, but did not favour women joining the same unions with men. Courtney was also the husband of Beatrice Potter's oldest sister, Catherine: see N and J MacKenzie (eds), *The Diary of Beatrice Webb 1892–1905: 'All the Good Things of Life'* vol 2 (London, Virago, 1983) at 62–3.

[147] Royal Commission on Labour, *The Employment of Women: Reports by Miss Eliza Orme et al (Lady Assistant Commissioners) on the Conditions of Work in Various Industries in England, Wales, Scotland and Ireland* (London, HMSO, 1893).

[148] LL Price, 'The Report of the Labour Commission' (1894) 4 *The Economic Journal* 444. The article further reported, at 444, that the Commission held 182 sittings with 583 witnesses.

[149] N MacKenzie and J MacKenzie (eds), above, n 146 at 45–7. The four members were Tom Mann, a trade unionist active in the Independent Labour Party, Michael Austin and William Abraham, both Liberal MPs, and James Mawdsley, a Conservative trade unionist. According to L Radice, above, n 138 at 95–6, the 'Minority Report' was a well-kept secret, 'which was suddenly sprung on the Commission in early March 1894.'

[150] L Radice, above, n 138 at 90–2. The election of 1892 was won by the Liberals, with a poor showing from the independent socialist candidates.

[151] LL Price, above, n 148 at 445. In her diary on 24 December 1892, Beatrice Webb recorded: 'Royal Commission on Labour a gigantic fraud': N MacKenzie and J MacKenzie (eds), above, n 146 at 25.

[152] G Drage, 'Mrs Sidney Webb's Attack on the Labour Commission' (September 1894) 36 *The Nineteenth Century* 452, at 457. Drage was responding to Beatrice Webb's critique of the

sioners to investigate working conditions for women. With the assistance of three other Lady Assistant Commissioners,[153] Orme proceeded to conduct intensive investigations; they submitted a detailed report on the employment of women and their conditions of work in England, Wales, Scotland and Ireland to the Commission in September 1893.[154] Orme was personally responsible for several reports: a report on barmaids, waitresses and bookkeepers in hotels, restaurants and public houses; another on women workers in Wales; and a further report on women workers in the nail, chain and bolt-making industries in the Black Country. In addition, she prepared the report on women's work in Scotland from investigations undertaken by another member of the investigative team, and she also collaborated in the investigation and preparation of the report on working women in Ireland.[155] Using printed sources as well as interviews with employers and employees, her reports meticulously documented hours of work, wages (including deductions and expenses), sanitary conditions, health and social issues for employees, trade union issues, and suggestions offered by interviewees for improving working conditions. Although one observer characterised these investigations as the reflections of 'wandering ladies' ascertaining 'the woes of female employees,'[156] others suggested that the report on working conditions for women represented 'a notable record of their labours' and 'a brilliant precedent' for the future; in particular, the latter reviewer noted 'the judicial balancing of evidence evinced by Miss Orme's legal culture.'[157] Even Beatrice Webb, who published a scathing indictment of the Report as a whole, concluded that the four 'accomplished' Lady Assistant Commissioners had produced, next to the Agricultural Reports, 'the most valuable [report] of the series.'[158]

Orme's report represented a formidable amount of work between April

---

Labour Commission: see B Webb, 'The Failure of the Labour Commission' (July 1894) 36 *The Nineteenth Century* 2. See also EFS Dilke, 'Women and the Royal Commission' (October 1891) *Fortnightly Review* 535.

[153] According to L Howsam, above, n 19 at 50, Clara Collet was a former teacher, and later worked with Beatrice Potter and Charles Booth on the latter's study, *Life and Labour of the People in London*; subsequently, she became Labour Correspondent with the Board of Trade and investigated women's industries. May Abraham was secretary to Lady Dilke, President of the Women's Trade Union League; she later became England's first woman factory inspector. Margaret Irwin was the Scottish Commissioner; she later became a factory inspector and wrote about employment and housing issues.

[154] See n 147.

[155] All reports, except the report on the nail, chain and bolt-making industries, were included in *The Employment of Women*, above, n 147; the report on the 'Black Country' industries was included in Volume II, Minutes of Evidence, Group A, at 569–75. See also L Holcombe, above, n 61 at 117.

[156] Observer, above, n 145 at 202–3.

[157] CA Foley, 'Review of the *Royal Commission on Labour: The Employment of Women*' (1894) 4 *The Economic Journal* 185 at 186.

[158] B Webb, above, n 152 at 9–10 .

1892 and September 1893.[159] Indeed, it appears that her commitment to the Labour Commission work prevented her from attending the Congress on Jurisprudence and Law Reform in Chicago. As Orme explained, however, invitations to present papers were forwarded to the four women only 'at the eleventh hour;' thus, Orme declined to write a paper 'because of the lateness of the invitation and because she was deeply engrossed with important work which she was under contract to perform, and could not, therefore, put aside;' in response to a further request, however, Orme produced a written paper for the Congress, which was subsequently published in the *Chicago Legal News* and elsewhere.[160] Her paper outlined the constitutional rights of women in England, identifying women's 'subordinate position, slightly improved by legislation during the past twenty-five years,' and their limited rights to vote.[161] She also reviewed personal rights, and the law of divorce and guardianship of children, harshly criticising the limited impact of legislation concerning the property rights of married women:

> Wealthy persons continue to protect their female relatives with settlements as before, while poorer classes derive but little benefit from the change of law. A poor woman earning a weekly wage is cajoled or coerced into giving it to her drunken husband and no law can prevent it. I do not believe that the Married Women's Property Acts have had any appreciable effect on our social system. The custom of settling women's property and appointing trustees to administer it ... is thoroughly bad [because the trustees have no personal interest and invest it poorly, while women remain 'mere children' in respect of their own property.] It would be a great advantage to England if property were always managed by those who spend the income. The wise owners would profit by having control over their own; the fools would become bankrupt and go to the wall.[162]

Orme also reported that women could not become barristers or solicitors, but she noted that 'two women have been for some years practicing conveyance (sic) but without legal qualifications;' in particular, she noted that they had drafted deeds for qualified practitioners, 'who have used the work in accordance with the maxim *qui facit per alium, facit per se*.'[163]

Orme's views in her paper for the Chicago Congress were expressed cogently and firmly. In this context, it is perplexing that, as Orme's intro-

159 For example, her report on the working conditions of barmaids, etc was based on 278 interviews, and visits to 91 public-houses, hotels and licensed restaurants, 20 railway, theatre and music hall bars, and 43 unlicensed places of refreshment: see n 147 at 197.

160 E Orme, 'The Legal Status of Women in England' (1886–1898) 25 *Chicago Legal News* 431; and (1897) 48 *Albany Law Journal* 145 [subsequent references to *Albany Law Journal*]. See also above, n 120.

161 E Orme, above, n 160. Orme cryptically began her review stating, 'The sovereign may be a woman.'

162 E Orme, above, n 160.

163 E Orme, above, n 160. The maxim means 'the acts of an agent are the acts of the principal': *Blackstone's Law Dictionary*.

ductory comments in her Labour Commission report explained, the Lady Assistant Commissioners presented their reports without any 'expressions of opinion as to proposed legislation and other matters.'[164] Clearly, she was deeply committed to her work for the Royal Commission; thus, in the context of public debates which were then current about whether to legislate an Eight Hour workday, the role of women in relation to trade unions, and especially the efficacy of prohibiting women from doing heavy and difficult work,[165] the absence of recommendations from the Lady Assistant Commissioners is initially puzzling. According to her published views, Orme was opposed to extensive governmental regulation of working conditions for women; and although she was supportive of trade unions, she believed that women should have their own unions, separate from men's.[166] In this context, Orme's report on the nail, chain and bolt-making industries suggested that there should be no 'further attempts to molest the women by Parliamentary enactments, restricting the hours and method of [women's] work;' nor did she believe that women should be precluded from choosing to do factory work along with men. Indeed, she concluded that 'any sudden prohibition [of women's work] would mean, in the present state of trade, the workhouse to many thousands.'[167] For Orme, liberalism meant the absence of state intervention and the freedom of women, like men, to choose work and economic independence.

It is possible that Orme's views were not shared by some of the other Lady Assistant Commissioners. In addition, Orme's reticence to offer recommendations may have been related to the fragile state of the new Liberal government, which had regained office in September 1893, just a year before the Royal Commission report was released. Certainly, other aspects of the report became highly controversial, particularly the involvement of Sidney Webb in the preparation of the Minority Report. As Beatrice Webb confided to her diary just before the release of the report:

> Another chicken hatched here last summer – Tom Mann's Minority Report – has not yet come off, though he has accepted it cordially and all promises well. Sidney has spent quite three weeks on it, one time or another, but, though we think it is of importance, we cannot help regarding it as a practical joke over which we chuckle with considerable satisfaction. Poor Labour Commission, having carefully excluded any competent Socialists from its numbers, having scouted the idea of appointing me as a humble assistant commissioner, will now

164 Orme's introduction explained that there were no recommendations because of the difficulty that each report had to be signed by two Lady Assistant Commissioners: see above, n 147 at iii.
165 See also O Schreiner, *Woman and Labour* (Toronto, Henry Frowde, 1911), written in the 1890s.
166 E Orme, above, n 85.
167 See 'Report by Eliza Orme, Senior Lady Assistant Commissioner, on the Condition of Women in the Chain, Nail and Bolt Making Industries in the "Black Country"' (April 1893) 24 *Englishwoman's Review* 73; and n 147 at 78.

find a detailed collectivist programme blazoned about as the Minority Report of its labour members! Poor old Leonard [Courtney], who told us with pompous superiority that they were all agreed, and that there was no prospect of any Minority Report, and we had it all the time lying on the table! – had been putting the last touches to it that very morning![168]

By contrast with these political manoeverings, Orme's report represented a highly professional investigation and summary of findings for the Royal Commission. Notwithstanding her strong views on some aspects of women's working conditions, Orme may have believed that lack of agreement among the four Lady Commissioners might have created problems for the government. In such a context, the presentation of a detailed report about the circumstances of women workers, without specific recommendations, may have seemed more judicious. In this way, it is possible that Orme's legal training ensured meticulous attention to 'the facts,' while her commitment to the Liberal party prevented the embarrassment of public disagreement about recommendations.

Clearly, Orme continued to have the trust of the Liberal Government; in 1894, she was appointed to a Departmental Committee on Prison Conditions, the only woman member of the committee. A few years later, she published her views about the need for reform of the working conditions of prison matrons and warders; she also made recommendations about conditions for women prisoners.[169] However, the defeat of the Liberals in the 1895 election resulted in a decade of Conservative government. As a result, it seems that Orme's reputation for meticulous fact-finding and judicious conclusions was no longer sufficient to create a need for her services. Yet, Orme remained a woman of independent views on matters of public policy. In 1897, when she was nearly fifty years old, she took up the issue of legal procedures in criminal trials in India, contributing a lengthy and critical preface to the report of a murder trial in the Howrah Sessions in 1894, *The Trial of Shama Charan Pal: An Illustration of Village Life in Bengal.*[170] In examining the case, Orme provided a persuasive but scathing critique of procedures adopted for collecting evidence and examining child witnesses, as well as suggestions for reform of British administration in India.[171] As Howsam suggested, Orme considered herself 'an educated

---

[168] N MacKenzie and J MacKenzie (eds), above, n 146 at 41.

[169] E Orme, 'Our Female Criminals' (1898) 69 (ns 63) *Fortnightly Review* 790. Orme argued for systemic reform of prisons for women, supporting the Prisons Bill, then before Parliament. According to Howsam, the Committee's recommendations 'marked a crucial stage in the evolution of penal policy' in Britain: see L Howsam, above, n 19 at 50, citing C Harding, 'The Inevitable End of a Discredited System? The Origins of the Gladstone Committee Report on Prisons, 1895' (1988) 31 *The Historical Journal* 592 at 608.

[170] Howrah Sessions, November 1894, *The Trial of Shama Charan Pal: An Illustration of Village Life in Bengal (with an Introduction by Miss Orme, LLB)* (London, Lawrence and Bullen, 1897).

[171] E Orme, 'Introduction' in *The Trial*, above, n 170 at *viii* and *x*; the defence counsel was an Indian barrister, Manomohan Ghose.

person, an authoritative expert, prepared to give her opinion on subjects ranging from Home Rule in Ireland to jurisprudence in India.'[172] She was both a Liberal and also a liberal individualist, a woman whose legal education had encouraged a commitment to objectivity, justice and equality, and who fully accepted a responsibility to make a contribution to public life. Her achievements in law and in public life were certainly due in part to the assistance of excellent male mentors, but she could not have succeeded without formidable intellectual ability, sound business practices and political acumen.

ELIZA ORME AND THE GENDER ISSUE

> Eliza Orme would be dismayed to know that she was being represented to posterity in terms of her gender.... The assumptions about objectivity, justice, and equality implicit in a legal education were the ideas with which Eliza Orme's mind was formed. She used them to achieve dramatic successes in university and, later, in professional and public life.[173]

In the late nineteenth century, women like Orme were frequently labelled 'strong-minded,' a description that was not complimentary: '"Strong-minded" was one of the most abusive terms that could be applied to a woman, and even the most dedicated [reformers] strove to avoid being so labelled.'[174] In a context in which Queen Victoria regarded women's rights agitation as a 'mad, wicked folly,'[175] women like Orme may have experienced a need to distance themselves from the negative connotations of 'strong-mindedness.' Characteristically, Orme firmly confronted this issue in an article published near the beginning of her career in 1874:

> 'Strong-minded' unfortunately suggests a host of weaknesses of which a very typical one is that peculiar taste which a few women have for trying to dress like men. The women who have been driven into notoriety by the refusal of just and moderate recognition, and those who try to enliven the dullness of a purposeless life by being uselessly eccentric, are generally called strong-minded. Society has adopted the word to describe the abnormal result of its own over-restrictions. How, then, can we speak of women who can take a journey by

172 L Howsam, above, n 19 at 53.
173 L Howsam, above, n 19 at 53.
174 L Holcombe, above, n 61 at 4. See also WJ Reader, above, n 51 at 178, who described Sophia Jex-Blake as an independent and strong-minded woman, 'as she was disapprovingly referred to.'
175 According to Holcombe, Queen Victoria wrote that 'The Queen is most anxious to enlist everyone who can speak or write to join in checking this mad, wicked folly of "Women's Rights" ... *with all its attendant horrors*, on which her poor feeble sex is bent, forgetting every sense of womanly feeling and propriety .... It is a subject which makes the Queen so *furious* that she cannot contain herself': L Holcombe, above, n 61 at 9, citing M Cole, *Women of To-Day* (London, Thomas Nelson, 1946) at 150–51.

railway without an escort, who can stand by a friend through a surgical operation, and who yet wear ordinary bonnets and carry medium-sized umbrellas?[176]

Although Orme clearly sympathised with 'strong-minded' women,
assigning blame for their 'notoriety' and 'useless eccentricity' to the
societal restrictions they experienced, she proposed the description of
'sound-minded' for women who were committed to new and independent
roles, but equally determined to pursue their goals by means of intelligent
and rational discussion; as Howsam concluded, Orme clearly regarded
herself as a 'sound-minded woman.'[177]

A decade later, Orme again published views that emphasised the need
for women to aspire to financial independence by obtaining education. As
she explained, the census figures clearly demonstrated that 'a large number
of Englishwomen must either remain unmarried and earn their own
livings, or else emigrate to the New World;' in this context, she argued that
parents should provide education for their daughters to become independent earners:

> To count upon a girl being provided for by marriage, and to teach her nothing
> but the duties of a married woman, is about as foolish as it would be to count
> upon a boy becoming heir to a fortune and to teach him nothing but the duties
> of a landed gentleman.[178]

Clearly, this subject was important to Orme because she returned to it
again in 1897. In response to published claims about the needs of 'poor
ladies', Orme argued that it was a good sign 'when the old boundaries
which separate class from class in the matter of work are seen to be breaking down;' in addition, she argued that:

> The increased employment of women encouraged by college training, and by
> the taking up of paid work by ladies in a good position, tends to make the life
> of an unmarried woman so interesting that she will be less likely to regard mar-
> riage as the only goal. The same effect is produced by breaking down
> conventional barriers and allowing each individual to do what natural talent
> prompts rather than what social status demands.[179]

As Howsam concluded, this article was 'the most autobiographical.'
Indeed, by 1897, Orme was entirely independent; her parents had died in
1892, and Orme had established a home at Upper Tulse Hill in south
London, with her sister, Beatrice, as housekeeper.[180]

---

[176] E Orme, 'Sound-Minded Women' (August 1874) *The Examiner* 820.
[177] L Howsam, above, n 19 at 53.
[178] E Orme, above, n 86 at 158.
[179] E Orme, above, n 85 at 615 and 619.
[180] L Howsam, above, n 19 at 51.

In fact, the year 1897 presented a different kind of challenge for Orme, when she became involved in the domestic turmoil of the novelist, George Gissing. Orme had been introduced to Gissing in 1894; one of his publishers was the younger brother of Orme's friend and law partner, Emily Lawrence. Orme was probably interested to meet the author of *The Odd Women*, a novel that explored ideas about women's independence and new relationships between men and women;[181] it was at this dinner meeting that Orme smoked a cigar with the gentlemen. Gissing was also a friend of Clara Collett, one of the Lady Assistant Commissioners who had worked with Orme to prepare the report on working women's conditions for the Royal Commission on Labour.[182] By 1897, Gissing was in despair, concluding that his (second) marriage was a failure and that he could not continue to write if he lived with his wife and young son; when he moved away from them for some months, both Orme and Collett became involved on his behalf in trying to assist his wife. Perhaps not surprisingly, Gissing's wife regarded these interventions with suspicion and hostility; as Gissing recorded: 'Miss Orme, one of the busiest women living, has given whole days to that paltry, wrong-headed creature [Gissing's wife],... and confesses herself hopeless in the matter.'[183]

In mid-September, when Gissing decided to travel to Italy to be able to write, Orme invited Gissing's wife and son to become boarders at Upper Tulse Hill. Gissing's letters to friends and his diaries are full of gratitude to Orme for this arrangement, but he was also well aware of his wife's acrimonious behaviour; as he explained a few years later, Orme was 'a very strong-minded (sic) woman, who [was] a good friend to me,... [but] she was insulted & abused & all the peace of her home ruined.'[184] As one Gissing biographer aptly concluded, the arrangement was impractical: Gissing could not afford to pay what Orme asked for board and lodging, and his wife did not wish to live with Orme.[185] Six months later, Orme arranged for Gissing to consult her solicitor to obtain a legal separation, and she moved his wife and son to other lodgings; in 1902, when this arrangement also disintegrated and Gissing's wife was lodged in an

---

[181] The publisher was HW Lawrence of Lawrence and Bullen: see PF Matteisen, AC Young, and P Coustillas (eds), *The Collected Letters of George Gissing* (Athens, Ohio University Press, 1995–1997) vol 6: 1895–1897 at 236. See also M Collie, *George Gissing: A Biography* (Hamden, CT, Archon Books, 1977) at 145; and J Halperin, *Gissing: A Life in Books* (Oxford, Oxford University Press, 1987) at 270–2. Gissing's *The Odd Women* was published in 1893.

[182] PF Matteisen, AC Young and P Coustillas (eds), above, n 181 (vol 5: 1892–1895) at xxix–xxx; and Collie, above, n 181 at 143–5.

[183] PF Matteisen, AC Young and P Coustillas (eds), above, n 181 (vol 6: 1895–1897) at 269: letter to Henry Hick, 13 April 1897.

[184] PF Matteisen, AC Young and P Coustillas (eds), above, n 181 (vol 7: 1897–1899) at 287: letter to Gabrielle Fleury, 6 February 1899. Gabrielle Fleury became Gissing's lover (and 'wife') in the last years of his life.

[185] M Collie, above, n 181 at 145.

asylum, it was Orme who arranged to place Gissing's son with a farm family in Cornwall, conveniently near the home of Orme's married sister who had agreed to look out for the child.[186]

It is difficult to define Orme's arrangement with Gissing, particularly because there are almost no surviving letters between them. From Gissing's correspondence to other friends, it seems clear that he was adamant that he could not live with his wife any longer, and that he was often frantic to achieve both a physical and legal separation. In this context, Orme's efforts on his behalf were described by Gissing in glowing terms: her objectivity, professionalism, and legal connections were extremely useful in helping him to sort out his unhappy domestic arrangements.[187] Indeed, their relationship often suggests a reversal of gender roles, with Gissing an emotional and highly intense man, who needed the advice and support of an objective and competent professional – who happened to be a woman. However, the situation may be more complicated, because Orme's decision to invite Gissing's wife and son to live at Upper Tulse Hill as boarders was also a financial arrangement.[188] While it is unclear that Orme needed additional income at the end of the 1890s, her governmental appointments were coming to an end by that time, and it appears that she ceased to engage in her legal work, at the latest at some point early in the twentieth century. When she was interviewed by the *Law Journal* in 1903, at the time of Bertha Cave's unsuccessful application for admission to the bar, she described how she had worked for conveyancing counsel and that 'for twenty-five years I found it both an interesting and profitable employment.'[189] Her statement suggests that she was no longer working in Chancery Lane, leaving open the possibility that her generosity to Gissing's family was partly motivated by financial need.

Yet, regardless of her financial circumstances, Orme's status as a consummate professional was well-established by the early twentieth century, and her willingness to assist Gissing was important to his ongoing literary

---

[186] PF Matteisen, AC Young and P Coustillas (eds), above, n 181 (vol 6: 1895–1897) at 340–1: Gissing's family stayed with Orme from September 1897 to 31 March 1898, when they moved into rental accommodation. Orme's solicitor was SNP Brewster: above, n 181 (vol 7: 1897–1899) at 137. His wife's insanity and admission to an asylum were described by Gissing: see above, n 181 (vol 8: 1900–1902) at 345: letter to Eduard Bertz, 24 February 1902; and Gissing's son was sent to live with Alfred James Smith and his family in Cornwall. Orme's sister was Mrs Howard Fox, wife of the consul for the USA, Belgium, Denmark: letter from Gissing to Gabrielle Fleury, 4 February 1902.

[187] PF Matteisen, AC Young and P Coustillas (eds), above, n 181 (vol 7: 1897–1899) at 21: letter to Clara Collett, 26 December 1897. Gissing wrote 'I grieve unspeakably over the trouble the Miss Ormes are having; it is monstrous that their quiet home should thus be disturbed. But I simply do not know what other arrangements to make....'

[188] M Collie, above, n 181 at 145, reported that Orme asked Gissing to pay £200 annually, which 'was beyond Gissing's means;' see also PF Matteisen, AC Young and P Coustillas (eds), above, n 181 (vol 7: 1897–1899) at 30.

[189] 'Women and the Bar,' above, n 8.

work. Since descriptions of his family problems survive only in Gissing's letters and diaries, it is not surprising that they reveal little sympathy for his wife; more significantly, although there are only a few references, it seems that Orme's sympathy lay entirely with Gissing – there is little evidence of any real understanding between these two women.[190] As Howsam noted, moreover, Orme's writing never addressed issues of contraception or child care, and her liberal values meant that she never considered the impact of recurrent pregnancies and family violence in the lives of married women.[191] Moreover, even when she was selected to present 'the woman's point of view' on the issue of Bertha Cave's application for admission to the bar in 1903, Orme's response reveals a measured, professional opinion, but one that is also not entirely consistent. Indicating that she did not think that 'the time was opportune for advancing the claim,' she suggested that 'the quiet life of the conveyancer is better suited to ordinary women than is the excitement of Court work.' At the same time, she explained that she would be glad to see the bar opened to women, pointing to the fact that 'no undesirable results ... followed the admission of women to the legal profession in America.' In the end, she recommended as a strategy that 'a number of women, acting in concert, should apply to the Benchers for admission as conveyancers under the bar,' and thereafter assert their claims for admission to the bar itself from this position of strength.[192] Yet, if Orme's views appear rather circumspect in the context of Cave's 1903 challenge, there is evidence that some women regarded her as highly unconventional. For example, when Cornelia Sorabji was struggling to gain entry to the legal profession in India, she carefully described her goal so that it would not be threatening to her middle-class friends, stating succinctly that she had no intention of becoming 'a Miss Orme.'[193]

By 1903, however, much had changed for Orme. In the course of her interview regarding Cave's application, for example, she explained that Miss Lawrence had assisted her during part of her twenty-five years in the office in Chancery Lane, but her comment suggests that the partnership had ended some time earlier.[194] Orme's decision to secede from the Women's Liberal Federation in the early 1890s had not prevented the organisation

---

190 PF Matteisen, AC Young and P Coustillas (eds), above, n 181 (vol 7: 1897–1899) at 23 and 161: letter from Orme to Collett, 29 December 1897. Orme described Gissing's wife as behaving like a 'disappointed child,' and her conduct as 'extraordinary;' she also explained that they had had some good laughs over her antics, 'but I cannot laugh at all when I think of [the little son].' Gissing's wife also wrote 'an insulting and threatening postcard to Orme,' addressed to 'Bad Eliza Orme.'

191 L Howsam, above, n 19 at 53.

192 'Women and the Bar,' above, n 8.

193 British Library MSS F 165/16: Cornelia Sorabji to Lady Mary Hobhouse, 16 October 1898.

194 'Women and the Bar,' above, n 8. According to Orme, Lawrence and Orme were the only two women who had obtained the LLB degree at the University of London.

from gaining both strength and influence; in addition, her friend Lady Fry had died, and the Liberal Party was out of government and wracked by factional disagreements. As Howsam suggested, Orme's liberal and egalitarian views about women and men were also increasingly being rejected by reformers in favour of claims about women's different and special nature, claims which were increasingly embraced within the women's movement, especially in relation to the suffrage agenda.[195] Indeed, her acknowledgement during the interview with the *Law Journal* that she had never made an application for admission to the professions, because her private inquiries had convinced her that any formal application would be 'useless,' ended rather poignantly: 'Perhaps I ought to have been more persistent.'[196]

Unfortunately, there is little information about Orme in later years. For example, when an auspicious meeting took place in London in April 1919, on Ladies Night of the Union Society at the Middle Temple, Helena Normanton argued for the proposition 'That all branches of the legal profession should be opened to women;' the proposition passed by a vote of 34 to 28. The report indicated that a number of women were present, including Cornelia Sorabji, 'a famous Indian law student in a flame-coloured gown with a scarf of the same colour over her dark hair.'[197] Significantly, Orme was not mentioned at all. By 1919, however, Orme was seventy-one years old; sadly, by the time of her death in 1937, at the age of eighty-eight, her obscurity was so complete that no one was available to write her obituary.[198] In the end, as Howsam concluded, Orme's egalitarian and intellectual approach had separated her from the mainstream of the women's movement; at the same time, as a woman, she had never fully achieved acceptance within the legal profession or the Liberal party.[199] Indeed, as a 'sound-minded' woman in law, Orme's independence had separated her from the worlds of both women and men.

---

[195] L Howsam, above, n 19 at 52.

[196] 'Women and the Bar,' above, n 8.

[197] EM Lang, above, n 7 at 163.

[198] L Howsam, above, n 19 at 52. Eliza Orme's will, dated 20 August 1885, appointed Reina Emily Lawrence as executrix; Orme bequeathed money and securities to her sister Beatrice, and devised all her real estate and residuary personal estate to her executrix: see Principal Probate Registry, London, Probate of the Will of Eliza Orme, 8 November 1937. The probate stated that Orme's gross estate at death was valued at 784 pounds, 15 shillings and 8 pence.

[199] L Howsam, above, n 19 at 53.

4

Colonies of the British Empire: The First Woman Lawyer in New Zealand

WOMEN LAWYERS IN THE COLONIES

Nowhere in the British Empire is conservatism more marked than in the legal profession, which renders the action of a woman seeking entrance to its ranks a bold undertaking, and one calling for exceptional qualities to make it successful. Not alone courage and persistence, but a more than ordinary careful professional preparation, and a resolve to win through, are essential....[1]

THESE EDITORIAL COMMENTS introduced a short article, published in 1909, on the subject of 'Law as a Woman's Profession.' The author of the article was Grata Flos Greig, the first Australian woman admitted to the legal profession in 1905. Greig had obtained an LLB degree from Melbourne University in 1903, and she and others had campaigned for the enactment of legislation to permit women's admission to the legal profession; in 1903, the *Women's Disabilities Removal Act 1903 (Vic)* was enacted.[2] In her 1909 article, Greig explained the nature of university studies in law, and the differences between the work done by barristers and solicitors, summarily dismissing the 'heaps of twaddle' that generally informed arguments against women's admission to the legal professions. Noting that law had been a recognised profession for women in America and France for many years, she concluded by asserting that 'the legal profession is likely to prove of increasing interest to women, not only for the facilities which it offers for earning a living, but also for the knowledge that is to be acquired thereby.'[3]

---

[1] Editor's Introduction to GF Greig, 'The Law as a Profession for Women' (1909) 6 *Commonwealth Law Review* 145. See also R Campbell, 'That Girl with the Terrible Name' (1975) 49 *Law Institute Journal* 502.

[2] The statute was also referred to as the *Flos Greig Enabling Bill*: see M Thornton, *Dissonance and Distrust: Women in the Legal Profession* (Melbourne, Oxford University Press, 1996) at 50–51.

[3] GF Greig, above, n 1 at 154.

However, Grieg's success in gaining admission to the legal profession in Victoria contrasted sharply with the experience of Ada Evans in New South Wales. Evans had been admitted to the University of Sydney law school in 1898, apparently when the Dean was absent on sabbatical; an inveterate opponent of women's entry to the legal professions, the Dean attempted on his return to convince Evans to transfer into medicine. However, Evans persevered and graduated in law in 1902. As Jocelynne Scutt reported, Evans then persevered again in efforts to obtain legislation to permit women to enter the legal professions in New South Wales: 'Every year following her graduation Ada E Evans lobbied the Attorney General for the passage of [legislation permitting women lawyers].'[4] Evans received support from the Feminist Club of New South Wales, an organisation formed in 1914, but it was not until 1918 that the New South Wales legislature passed the *Women's Legal Status Act*.[5] Once the legislation had been enacted, Evans still needed to complete two years as a student at law; she was finally admitted to the New South Wales bar in 1921. As a result of the long years between her university studies and her admission to the bar, however, Evans decided not to accept briefs 'on the ground that she considered herself incapable of handling them, not wishing women's standing in the profession to be undermined by a show of incompetence.'[6] As Margaret Thornton suggested, women's contribution to the war effort may have encouraged the enactment of legislation in New South Wales, as in Britain, at the end of World War I; by that time, 'the patience of women campaigners was clearly exhausted.'[7]

In the early years of the twentieth century, Edith Haynes was also unsuccessful in her efforts to gain admission to the bar in Western Australia. Although she was initially permitted to register as a student (articled to her father), she was refused admission to the intermediate examination by the Barristers' Board in 1904. Haynes launched a mandamus suit to compel the Board to permit her to sit for the examination, and her father argued the case; however, three judges of the Supreme Court of Western Australia held that women were not entitled to be registered pursuant to the *Legal Practitioners Act 1893 (WA)*.[8] As Thornton pointed out, the court's analysis in *Haynes* was very similar to

---

[4] JA Scutt, *Women and the Law: Commentary and Materials* (Sydney, The Law Book Co Ltd, 1990) at 17.

[5] JA Scutt, above, n 4 at 17–18, quoting G Griffith, 'The Feminist Club of New South Wales, 1914–1970: A History of Feminist Politics in Decline' (1988) 14:1 *Hecate* 56. The National Council of Women also participated in lobbying for this legislation.

[6] B McPaul, 'A Woman Pioneer' (1948) 22 *Australian Law Journal* 1. According to McPaul, Evans died in 1947 at the age of seventy-five.

[7] M Thornton, above, n 2 at 63. See also LJ Kirk, 'Sisters Down Under: Women Lawyers in Australia' (1995–96) 12 *Georgia State University Law Review* 491; and Kirk, 'Portia's Place: Australia's First Women Lawyers' (1995) 1 *Australian Journal of Law and History* 75.

[8] *In re Edith Haynes* (1904) 6 Western Australian Reports 209.

the arguments presented in the *French* case in Canada a few years later, and the status and expertise of the judges 'permitted them to uphold the prevailing gender order.'[9] It was not until 1923 that the *Women's Legal Status Act 1923 (WA)* was enacted; the first women were admitted to the bar of Western Australia in the early 1930s.[10]

In other Australian states, legislation was enacted prior to World War I: Tasmania in 1904, Queensland in 1905, and South Australia in 1911;[11] thus, ironically, it was New South Wales, the state in which Ada Evans became the first woman law student in Australia, which was the last to permit women access to the legal professions. However, even in states which enacted legislation earlier, there were continuing problems. For example, although Mary Kitson gained admission to the legal profession in South Australia in 1916, her subsequent application to be appointed a notary public was rejected on the ground that the office of notary public was not expressly included in the language of the statute enabling women to become lawyers.[12] Perhaps discouraged by such decisions, only a few women sought admission to the legal professions in Australia in the early twentieth century; in Tasmania, for example, no woman was admitted to the profession until 1935.[13]

Thus, the pattern for the first women lawyers in Australia was one of sporadic litigation and ongoing lobbying efforts to achieve legislation in each state, a pattern that was similar for women who aspired to become lawyers in other former British colonies, including Canada. Yet, as Thornton argued, suffrage had been achieved in most Australian states before women began to seek admission to the legal professions; indeed, the state of South Australia had enacted women's suffrage as early as 1894, and (white) Australian women obtained the federal franchise in 1902. In this context, ongoing judicial rejection of women's claims to become lawyers, as well as the intransigence of the legislature in New South Wales, suggest that the achievement of suffrage resulted in only a relatively minor change in women's legal status. As Thornton argued, citizenship for women meant the right to register a preference for an electoral candidate at the ballot box; clearly, '[it] did not mean that the rights and privileges of citizenship automatically flowed to women.'[14]

In addition, the interpretation of statutory language in the Australian cases about women's claims to become lawyers generally preserved the status quo.[15] This approach was also evident in challenges to the male

[9] M Thornton, above, n 2 at 59.
[10] M Thornton, above, n 2 at 53.
[11] See *Legal Practitioners Act 1904* (Tas); *Legal Practitioners Act 1905* (Qld); and *Female Law Practitioners Act 1911* (SA). See also M Thornton, above, n 2 at 51–3.
[12] *In re Kitson* [1920] South Australian Law Reports 230.
[13] M Thornton, above, n 2 at 53.
[14] M Thornton, above, n 2 at 62.
[15] M Thornton, above, n 2 at 56–63.

exclusivity of the legal profession in South Africa. Thus, in *Schlesin v Incorporated Law Society* in 1909, the Transvaal Supreme Court rejected an argument based on the requirement in the Interpretation of Laws Proclamation that 'words of the masculine gender shall include females;' the court relied on longstanding practices to conclude that the use of the word 'attorney' in the Proclamation created a 'contrary intention':

> I think that the mere use of the word 'attorney' indicates that the intention was that persons should be admitted as attorneys in accordance with what has been the universal practice, if not the law, for so long as the law on the subject has existed. The use of the word 'attorney' in my opinion indicates that the persons who are to be attorneys are to be of that class who have always been capable of being attorneys, and not of that class who, so far at all events as practice is concerned, have never been capable of being attorneys.[16]

In these circumstances, the court concluded that legislative action was necessary to permit women to become solicitors. Similarly, three judges of the Appellate Division of the Province of Cape of Good Hope overturned a lower court decision in 1912, after the lower court had ordered the Law Society to register the articles of a woman who wished to qualify as a solicitor. The Associate Chief Justice recognised that the case was one of 'utmost importance,' not only for the applicant but for other women who might wish to become solicitors, as well as for the profession and the public:

> If [the question] was rightly answered in the Court below, the result will be materially to widen the area of women's economic activities, though that be done by opening to a host of new competitors the doors of an already congested profession. If it was wrongly answered, then the law of the country will be denying to one-half of its citizens, on the mere ground of sex, the right of employing their natural abilities in the pursuit of an honourable calling....[17]

In spite of this sympathetic language, the court concluded that it had no choice but to deny women's entitlement to practise law. After an exhaustive review of Roman law, the scope of activity for legal officials in Holland, and the 1904 Scottish decision in *Hall v Society of Law Agents,* the court recommended that the applicant seek legislative relief; according to the court, only the legislature could hear representations 'for the

---

[16] *Schlesin v Incorporated Law Society* (1909) Transvaal Supreme Court Reports 363 at 364–5. In 1910, however, the Transvaal court held that it was not appropriate to refuse to admit an applicant as an attorney merely because he belonged to one of the native races: see *Mangena v Law Society* (1910) Transvaal Provisional Division Decisions 649; Leader Law Reports 458.

[17] *Incorporated Law Society v Wookey* (1912) Appellate Division Reports 623; WR 792 [subsequent references to AD].

bestowal of that equality of opportunity in regard to the practice of the legal profession which the applicant desires.'[18]

As these examples indicate, colonial courts often relied on British precedents, avoiding judicial responsibility for women's exclusion from the legal professions; as they concluded, it was only legislatures that could amend the relevant statutes. Even in jurisdictions where women had already attained the franchise, the same legal arguments prevailed. And, although a number of Australian states enacted legislative amendments before Britain did so at the end of World War I, as did some Canadian provinces, the paucity of women who chose to enter the legal professions suggests that 'the culture of masculinity ... remained resistant to ... women following the protracted attempts to exclude them.'[19]

In this context, this chapter focuses on Ethel Benjamin, the first woman lawyer in New Zealand. By contrast with aspiring women lawyers in Australia and South Africa, Benjamin gained admission to the bar quite readily. Indeed, she was admitted to the legal profession in New Zealand in 1897, just a few months after Clara Brett Martin had successfully gained entry to the legal profession in Ontario. However, Benjamin's circumstances were quite different from Martin's, because Benjamin applied for admission to the bar *after* the enactment of suffrage for New Zealand women, and also *after* legislation had been enacted to permit women to enter the legal profession. Thus, Benjamin was entitled to engage in legal work without having to launch a claim in the courts and without having to lobby the legislature; like Eliza Orme in Britain, Benjamin practised law without making her own challenge to male exclusivity in the legal profession, although Benjamin clearly had the advantage of formal membership in the New Zealand bar. Notwithstanding her advantageous legal position and relatively privileged family background, however, Benjamin's case reveals how the legal profession responded to a woman member of the bar at the end of the nineteenth century. There is evidence, for example, that the bar's prevailing culture limited her participation in collegial activities as a member of the profession and her access to legal work, and that her gender constituted a critical factor in shaping her experiences. At the same time, Benjamin's experience is interesting because two additional factors were interwoven: one was that she was not only a woman lawyer, but a *young* woman lawyer: she entered the legal profession at the age of twenty-two in 1897. And secondly, Benjamin was Jewish and thus part of the small Jewish community in Dunedin; although the community may have been reasonably prosperous, it appears that only a few Jewish lawyers were well established within the legal profession in Dunedin at the end of the nineteenth century. In these circumstances,

---

18 *Wookey*, above, n 17 at 635. See also (1913) 30 *South African Law Journal* 462; and M de Villiers, 'Women and the Legal Profession' (1918) 35 *South African Law Journal* 289.
19 M Thornton, above, n 2 at 49–50.

Benjamin's experience provides insights about how women confronted challenges *after* gaining admission to the legal professions. And, as a woman who was also young and Jewish, her experiences reveal some of the day-to-day struggles to 'succeed' as a woman member of the legal profession at the turn of the nineteenth century.[20]

ETHEL BENJAMIN

... I am the first lady lawyer south of the line, but not the first British woman lawyer. There is, you know, one in India and another in Canada. I always had a liking for the profession. I knew I should have to take up something in order to be self-supporting, and the Legal Profession had more charms for me than any other.[21]

Ethel Benjamin's comments during an interview in 1897, a few months after the ceremonies in which she received the LLB degree and then gained formal admission to the bar of New Zealand, suggest that she had chosen a career in law to achieve economic independence. As 'the first lady lawyer south of the line,' she acknowledged her pioneering role as one of the first women lawyers in the British Empire, and she seemed optimistic about her future. Benjamin practised law for a decade, initially in Dunedin and later in Wellington, and even for a short time after she married Alfred De Costa in 1907.[22] However, by 1908, she and her husband had left New Zealand to live in London, where some of Benjamin's family were resident – and where Benjamin was not entitled to admission to the bar or to the solicitors' profession. In the end, her career as New Zealand's first woman lawyer lasted only a decade, and after her departure for Britain in 1908, she never returned.

Benjamin was born in 1875 in Dunedin. Her parents were members of the small Orthodox Jewish community in Dunedin, and she was one of several children. According to Carol Brown, her father was Henry Benjamin, an entrepreneur who had emigrated from Britain to New Zealand in the late 1860s to set up a furrier business; later on, he worked in a mercantile business and in sharebroking.[23] The second half of the

---

[20] See C Brown, 'Ethel Benjamin: New Zealand's First Woman Lawyer' (Dunedin, University of Otago BA Hons Thesis, 1985).

[21] Interview with Kate Sheppard, published in (August 1897) 26 *White Ribbon* 1–2; the *White Ribbon* was published by the Women's Christian Temperance Union.

[22] Ethel Benjamin married Alfred De Costa on 23 July 1907 in Wellington: see C Brown, above, n 20 at 97. In *Colonial Cap and Gown* (Christchurch, University of Canterbury, 1979) at 109, WJ Gardner incorrectly stated that Benjamin had practised for some years and then married an unqualified law clerk and retired into private life at Gisborne: see Brown at 97. Benjamin was known after her marriage as Ethel De Costa, but her original surname has been used throughout this chapter.

[23] C Brown, above, n 20 at 3–4. Brown reported that Benjamin's mother was Lizzie (née

nineteenth century was a time of great economic prosperity in Dunedin. According to Cullen, 'Otago became the focus of the third great gold rush of the nineteenth century in the Pacific basin,' particularly after discovery of gold at Tuapeka in 1861; for a few decades, 'the steady stream of miners passing through Dunedin and the growth of business servicing the goldfields rapidly made the town the most prosperous of New Zealand.'[24] Beginning in the 1840s, British lawyers also began to arrive in New Zealand, and the first lawyer established a practice in Dunedin in 1848. As the economy grew in Dunedin, so did the legal profession; in one three-year period between 1862 and 1865, for example, fifty-three men were admitted to the legal profession in Otago, the district in which Dunedin was situated.[25] Interestingly, it was just a few years later, in 1869, that the first suffrage literature was published in New Zealand: Mary Müller's thirteen-page pamphlet, entitled *An Appeal to the Men of New Zealand*, argued in favour of women's suffrage, and indeed, for the complete emancipation of the female sex; John Stuart Mill sent Müller his congratulations.[26] Thus, by the time of Benjamin's birth in 1875, Dunedin was a place of economic prosperity with a thriving legal profession; in addition, the issue of women's rights, including suffrage, had already appeared on the public agenda.

In this context, Benjamin was fortunate that her parents encouraged her to pursue an education. According to Sandra Coney, it was middle-class parents like the Benjamins who were most often interested in higher education for their daughters; by contrast, working-class girls often experienced difficulty in attending school because they were required to work for a living, while upper-class families were more interested in social accomplishments than real educational achievements for their daughters.[27]

Mark), and she assumed that Ethel was the eldest of seven children. According to Louis Frank, Henry Benjamin held a significant position ('*une situation considérable*') in Dunedin, and Frank reported incorrectly that Ethel was one of twelve children: see L Frank, *La Femme-Avocat: Exposé Historique et Critique de la Question* (Paris, V Giard & E Brière, 1898) at 69–70. See also C Brown, 'New Zealand's First Woman Lawyer' (6 August 1985) *Critic* at 12; and K Findlay, 'Letters for a Lady' (unidentified clipping on file), which announced a documentary, 'First Lady of the Law,' screened on TV1 on 19 January 1988.

24 MJ Cullen, *Lawfully Occupied: The Centennial History of the Otago District Law Society* (Dunedin, Otago District Law Society, 1979) at 20.

25 P Spiller, J Finn and R Boast, *A New Zealand Legal History* (Wellington, Brooker's, 1995) at 240; the authors characterised Dunedin as the 'nursery' of the New Zealand legal profession, citing R Cooke (ed), *Portrait of a Profession: The Centennial book of the New Zealand Law Society* (Wellington, AH and AW Reed, 1969) at 331; and (1951) 27 *New Zealand Law Journal* 99.

26 S Coney, *Standing in the Sunshine: A History of New Zealand Women since They Won the Vote* (Auckland, Viking, 1993) at 16. See also A Zimmern, *Women's Suffrage in Many Lands* (London, Francis & Co, 1909) at 161.

27 S Coney, above, n 26 at 205. According to Brown, Presbyterians and Jews in Dunedin were particularly interested in education for their children, including girls: C Brown, above, n 20 at 5; and there is some evidence that Jewish parents encouraged their children to attend the University of Otago: see LM Goldman, *History of the Jews in New Zealand* (Wellington, AH and AW Reed, 1958) at 159.

Benjamin attended the Otago Girls' High School; first established in 1871, the school provided 'the most comprehensive education available for girls in New Zealand.' As Brown noted, the principal of the School from 1885 to 1895 was Alexander Wilson, a Scottish immigrant and an experienced educator. At the Girls' School, Wilson created high expectations for his students, and encouraged them to consider university education and professional careers in law and medicine; as a result, the school curriculum was directed to preparing students for examinations, a goal which was somewhat unusual at the time. Although Wilson believed in balancing work and other pastimes, his commitment to academic excellence remained firm; as he explained in his speech at the Otago University graduation in 1885, 'if parents enter their daughters for a race they must expect to see them hard driven.'[28]

Benjamin was an accomplished student at the Otago Girls' High School, winning prizes and scholarships,[29] and she was among the first group of New Zealand women to attend university. Kate Edger had obtained a BA degree in Auckland in 1877, the first New Zealand woman to receive a university degree. Then, in 1885, Caroline Freeman became the first woman to graduate from Otago University; she subsequently established her own private girls' school in Dunedin, named Girton College in honour of the women's college at Cambridge.[30] By the time that Benjamin passed the University Scholarship examinations in 1892, two women from her high school were already studying medicine at Otago University. In addition, a woman had previously entered the law programme at Otago, although she had then withdrawn without obtaining a degree. In the same period, Stella Henderson began to work as a law clerk in a firm in Christchurch, although she subsequently pursued a career as a Parliamentary journalist rather than in law.[31] In this context, Benjamin's decision to begin law studies at Otago occurred at a time when there were at least a few other women with aspirations for professional careers, both at Otago University and elsewhere in New Zealand. Nonetheless,

---

[28] C Brown, above, n 20 at 5–9, and citing *Otago Girls' High School Report* (1893) at 9. The Otago Girls' High School was the first state-funded secondary school for girls in Australasia, founded in 1871 by the efforts of Learmonth Whyte Dalrymple: see S Coney, above, n 26 at 200. Wilson's speech was reported in the *Otago Daily Times*, 28 August 1885, at 3.

[29] See C Brown, above, n 20 at 6; and Benjamin's interview in the *White Ribbon*, above, n 21.

[30] According to S Coney, above, n 26 at 205, New Zealand women gained access to universities without much opposition, because both American universities and the University of London were open to women by the late 1870s; all degrees were granted by the University of New Zealand until 1961.

[31] According to C Brown, above, n 20 at 9–10, Catherine Moss finished the BA degree and part of the LLB degree in 1891, but then discontinued her LLB studies. Margaret Cruikshank and Emily Siedeberg left the high school in 1892 to pursue medical education at the University of Otago; Benjamin graduated the next year. Gill Gatfield identified Stella Henderson as a legal clerk in the firm of William Izard at this time: G Gatfield, *Without Prejudice: Women in the Law* (Wellington, Brooker's, 1996) at 28.

Benjamin remained the only woman *law* student at Otago University for the four years of her studies. In late 1896, at the age of twenty one, she successfully completed the LLB degree, having achieved the highest marks in her class in constitutional history and law, jurisprudence, equity, and evidence, and sharing the highest marks in criminal law and in real and personal property; she also achieved the highest marks in New Zealand in Roman Law.[32] In the context of this academic success, one of her male classmates had cautioned at the end of Benjamin's first year, perhaps only partly in jest: 'Let the weaker sex – the men of course – look to it they are not eclipsed as happened last session, by the other representatives.'[33]

In the 1890s, legal education consisted almost entirely of independent study on the part of law students. Indeed, one description of New Zealand legal education in the late nineteenth century identified its limitations as merely 'university tuition [which] was generally limited and at times erratic, and ... conducted largely by part-time lecturers with poor library and other resources, who instructed overwhelmingly part-time students....'[34] In spite of these problems at the universities, however, the requirement of articling had been abolished in 1882; moreover, in 1888, New Zealand judges had delegated their responsibility for the examination of barristers and solici- tors to the University of New Zealand, then the only degree-granting university in the country. The University of New Zealand had established the LLB degree in 1877, and by 1888, the degree covered all the subjects specified in the judges' rules for admission to the profession.[35] At the same time, although the universities had responsibility for teaching, most of them had only a handful of law lecturers; in the 1890s, for example, Otago had a lecturer in property law for three years, and a lecturer on constitutional history and jurisprudence for a slightly longer period. Even this situation deteriorated by 1901, when disagreements between the Otago Law Society and the university about curriculum, the selection of lecturers, and most importantly, entitlement to examination fees, resulted in the abolition of all lectures on law; as Cullen noted, it was 'the end of the first, and somewhat inglorious, phase of the history of the University of Otago Law School.'[36]

---

[32] C Brown, above, n 20 at 14 and 17. According to M Thornton, above, n 2 at 56, Stella Allan also graduated LLB in 1896, but did not practise, becoming a journalist in Melbourne.

[33] C Brown, above, n 20 at 14, citing (May 1895) 8:1 *Otago University Student Review* 20.

[34] P Spiller, J Finn and R Boast, above, n 25 at 267. In 1925, a royal commission was appointed which made sweeping recommendations for the reform of legal education.

[35] See S Coney, above, n 26 at 205; and P Spiller, J Finn and R Boast, above, n 25 at 263–5 and 267–8. Initially, the *Supreme Court Ordinance* of 1841 provided for admission in New Zealand of barristers and solicitors who had qualified in England, Ireland and Scotland. Then, pursuant to the *Law Practitioners Act, 1861*, judges were empowered to make rules for the admission of barristers and solicitors; by 1882, the requirement for a period of articles for solicitors was eliminated 'when the view prevailed that no obstacles be placed in the way of any citizen who wished to become a lawyer.' See also MJ Cullen, above, n 24 at 119–21.

[36] MJ Cullen, above, n 24 at 124–5.

In this context, law students in the 1890s, including Benjamin, were forced to rely on individual study, supplemented occasionally by lectures. Yet, although access to legal materials in a law library was clearly fundamental to a student's progress in the LLB programme, the University of Otago had no law library at all. At the time, the main law library was the Supreme Court Library in Dunedin; in 1879, the Otago District Law Society had assumed responsibility for it, appointing a librarian to oversee it and collecting fees from practitioners to maintain it. However, until the mid-1880s, the Law Society firmly denied access to law students. By 1890, with increasing numbers of students studying on their own, the council of the Society was forced to relent and agree to admit students; all the same, the council attached conditions to student use, including requirements that the librarian be present when students used the library, and that there was to be no talking among students in the library.[37]

However, when Benjamin applied to the council for permission to use the library in March 1895, the council decided that there was 'no rule applicable to [her] case,' and that she could not use the library with other students. Nonetheless, the council granted permission to Benjamin to read in the Judge's Chamber Room, and to borrow books with the permission of the librarian or a member of council.[38] Benjamin's letter responding to the council's decision has been preserved:

> As 'there is no rule applicable to my case' I must ask you to convey my thanks to the Council for what is then their very liberal treatment of me. For the present it will answer every purpose and I am more than satisfied to be allowed to consult your many valuable Books even though apart from the Library and the Profession! [39]

Cullen concluded that Benjamin's response was a 'masterly tongue-in-cheek performance,' and that the council's decision was designed to ensure that male students were 'preserved from unnecessary and distressing contact with a woman.' Undoubtedly, Benjamin's letter demonstrated tact and pragmatism in acknowledging that the council's proposed arrangement would 'answer every purpose;' at the same time, she carefully qualified her acquiescence as only 'for the present.'[40] In March 1895, Benjamin was just beginning the third year of the LLB programme, and she may well have been grateful for any arrangement to gain access to materials essential to her law studies.

[37] MJ Cullen, above, n 24 at 51–2.
[38] MJ Cullen, above, n 24 at 52. See also G Gatfield, above, n 31 at 65, noting that a male lawyer in Christchurch asked a woman lawyer to leave the Supreme Court Library, thirty years after Benjamin's 1895 request.
[39] Ethel Benjamin to FJ Stilling, 26 April 1895, cited in MJ Cullen, above, n 24 at 52 and 217, in the correspondence file of the Otago District Law Society.
[40] MJ Cullen, above, n 24 at 52.

All the same, in the context of the New Zealand colony in the 1890s, it is clear that the council could have decided to reject her application altogether, especially as there was 'no rule applicable to [her] case.' In addition to the absence of a precedent, there was also little Parliamentary support for women lawyers; indeed, by 1895, several bills had been presented to Parliament to permit women to enter the legal profession, but none had yet succeeded.[41] In this context, the council might have relied on Britain's intransigent response to applications from aspiring women lawyers, and flatly refused Benjamin's request. Although the precise reasons for the council's decision in Benjamin's favour remain obscure, it has been suggested that the men who presided over the Law Society in the late nineteenth century were all 'highly active in a range of fields,' including politics, and that 'most of them were strongly orientated towards reform.' In addition, the Otago District Law Society was facing a number of challenges concerning the administration of its library, and also in relation to the collection of the Society's fees, the reporting of cases, and the establishment of a scale for conveyancing fees,[42] and these matters may have seemed much more important than whether a woman could use the library. Moreover, it seems that Benjamin had considerable support from her classmates; as Brown noted, law students at Otago unanimously confirmed their approval in 1894 of a bill to grant women the right to practise law, and suggested the need to make plans for a banquet in due course to celebrate the admission of 'our candidate.'[43]

In addition to the presence of reformist ideas within the legal profession, however, it is possible that the granting of women's suffrage in New Zealand in 1893 may have blunted some of the traditional arguments about 'women's sphere,' arguments which might otherwise have been invoked by the council to prevent Benjamin from using the library. Support for women's suffrage was promoted as early as the 1870s and 1880s in New Zealand, and the first Women's Franchise League had been established in Dunedin in 1892. According to Coney, it was 'the dedication and political skill of New Zealand suffragists' which ensured the success of the suffrage campaign,[44] but there were a number of factors that created a receptive environment for suffrage reform in New Zealand, factors which may have contributed to the acceptance of women in the legal profession as well. Not only were schools with excellent educational standards being established for girls, but there were also other new developments: women

[41] See G Gatfield, above, n 31 at 25–8, for discussion of the bills of 1891 and 1894.

[42] MJ Cullen, above, n 24 at 48.

[43] C Brown, above, n 20 at 15–16, citing (September 1894) 7 *Otago University Student Review* 120–124; this was the *Law Practitioners* bill of 1894: see G Gatfield, above, n 31 at 27–8.

[44] S Coney, above, n 26 at 13 and 30: the New Zealand suffragists were 'astute political lobbyists, who used connections, influence, public education and displays of massive public support to achieve their ends.'

were entering the paid workforce in larger numbers and beginning to join trade unions,[45] they were challenging the conventions and restrictions of marriage,[46] and they were beginning to take up cycling and other sports, requiring substantial changes in their traditional clothing. As the *New Zealand Graphic* commented in 1895, women could achieve independence with a bicycle, 'independence almost as glorious as the franchise.'[47]

Moreover, especially by contrast with Britain, the population of New Zealand was still relatively small and thus easier to organise, and New Zealanders were well educated by nineteenth-century standards: in 1890, seventy-six per cent of Pakeha women could read and write.[48] The suffrage movement in New Zealand was also less fragmented than in other jurisdictions, with support from working-class women such as the Dunedin-based Tailoresses' Union; suffragists also had support from Maori women since the fact that Maori men already had voting rights meant that there was never any question in New Zealand of the vote being a white woman's prerogative.[49] There was also strong support for women's purifying influence on public life from the Women's Christian Temperance Union, established in 1885 after a visit to New Zealand by its American representative, Mary Leavitt. In speeches all over the country, Leavitt advocated women's equal rights, expressing surprise that 'men governed by a Queen should argue against women taking part in government.'[50] As Coney argued, moreover, the campaign's links to temperance in New Zealand 'may have assisted the suffrage cause by tapping into a general concern about the socially damaging effects of alcohol abuse.'[51] As well, egalitarian ideals about democracy, equality, and liberalism were widespread among

[45] According to S Coney, above, n 26 at 220–21, twenty-seven per cent of Dunedin's workforce were employed in the clothing industry and eighty per cent of these workers were women; both the Women's Christian Temperance Union and the YWCA had become involved in the well-being of these women workers. The Dunedin Tailoresses' Union was formally established in a meeting on 11 July 1889; its declaration of support for suffrage was important in broadening the campaign.

[46] Legislation was enacted by Parliament in 1896 raising the age of consent; permitting a woman to live separately from her husband on the grounds of aggravated assault, desertion, persistent cruelty or wilful neglect; and prohibiting baby farming. As well, initial proceedings to establish the National Council of Women in New Zealand were undertaken in 1895 and the first 'Women's Parliament' was held in 1896: see R Nicholls, *The Women's Parliament: The National Council of the Women of New Zealand 1896–1920* (Wellington, Victoria University Press, 1996) at 16 and 28–30. See also P Spiller, J Finn and R Boast, above, n 25 at 94.

[47] The first ladies' biking club was established in Christchurch in 1892: see S Coney, above, n 26 at 116–7.

[48] S Coney, above, n 26 at 13: egalitarianism was fostered by the pioneering roles of women before 1880.

[49] S Coney, above, n 26 at 13.

[50] S Coney, above, n 26 at 19. Leavitt's visit to New Zealand was part of a world-wide tour; she established eighty-six new branches for the WCTU. Although prohibition was central to the WCTU, it adopted women's franchise as a central aim at its first convention in 1886: see Coney at 25.

[51] S Coney, above, n 26 at 13.

New Zealanders in the 1890s, a decade of liberal politics in which the state's interventionist role in regulating economic and social affairs was first becoming accepted.[52] All of these factors contributed to increasing support for women's suffrage, support which was confirmed by the presentation to Parliament of several suffrage petitions signed by women. During the debate on the Electoral Bill in July 1893, for example, Sir John Hall unfurled in the lower house a petition for female enfranchisement that was three hundred yards long and contained the signatures of 31,872 women, nearly one quarter of the adult female population of New Zealand. A long time supporter of women's suffrage, Sir John Hall was thereafter dubbed 'the carpet knight.' Although the bill's subsequent passage through the legislative council was fraught with controversy, it passed by two votes and the Governor then gave royal assent on 19 September 1893.[53] Thus, in the context of 'the first self-governing country to legislate for universal female franchise,' it may have appeared prudent to the Otago Law Society's council members in early 1895 to find a way to accommodate a 'lady law student' in their library.[54]

In fact, support for women's access to the legal profession in New Zealand was growing, and in 1896, two statutes were enacted, both of which confirmed that women were entitled to become lawyers.[55] Only thirty years earlier, just prior to the British court's decision in *Chorlton v Lings*, New Zealand had enacted legislation to bring the wording of its *Interpretation Act* into conformity with British legislation, so as to prevent women from voting or exercising other rights of citizenship.[56] In addition, in 1881, the New Zealand Parliament had expressly adopted language in

52 S Coney, above, n 26 at 13; and P Spiller, J Finn and R Boast, above, n 25 at 112. According to R Nicholls, above, n 46 at 22, the Liberal government which took power in 1891 and remained in office for over twenty years held reformist aspirations similar to those of the National Council of Women of New Zealand.

53 S Coney, above, n 26 at 28–31; and *The Electoral Act, 1893*, 57 Vict, c 18, s 6. Section 3 defined 'person' to include 'woman;' however, section 9 declared that women were not eligible to be nominated as a candidate, nor to be elected to the House of Representatives or appointed to the Legislative Council. Sir John Hall was a Conservative, whose career in public life spanned three decades in provincial and colonial government; he was also a former Premier: see Coney at 26. In relation to the Electoral Bill, the Liberal leader, Seddon, attempted to control voting in the legislative council; apparently, the result was that two council members, nominally opposed to suffrage, voted in favour of the bill. In the election, seventy-eight per cent of adult women were registered, and of those, eighty-five per cent voted: Coney, at 27 and 31–3.

54 According to P Spiller, J Finn and R Boast, above, n 25 at 113, 'politicians were loath to oppose openly measures which were seen as "women's issues"' for fear of political consequences; similar concerns may have animated the council of the Law Society. See also P Grimshaw, *Women's Suffrage in New Zealand* (Auckland, Auckland University Press, 1972) at *xiii*, reporting on women's suffrage in other jurisdictions.

55 See *The Female Law Practitioners Act 1896*, SNZ 1896, c 11 (royal assent 11 September 1896); and *The Law Practitioners and New Zealand Law Society Acts Amendment Act 1896*, SNZ 1896, c 22 (royal assent 12 October 1896). See also G Gatfield, above, n 31 at 25–40.

56 See G Gatfield, above, n 31 at 16. The word 'male' had been inserted before the word 'person' in several amendments of the *Law Practitioners Act* prior to 1896: see Gatfield at 19.

the *Legal Practitioners Act*, with the support of district law societies, to preclude women from becoming lawyers in New Zealand.[57] Interestingly, moreover, the women's movement in the 1880s offered little opposition to Parliamentary decisions which excluded women from becoming lawyers, particularly because of the strong influence of the Women's Christian Temperance Union; the Union's goals focused on women's higher sense of morality and their role in safeguarding the sanctity of the family, not on women's equality in public life and the professions.[58] Thus, with opposition from the law societies and no real support from the women's movement, Parliament continued to exclude women from legal practice, both in legislative debates in the 1880s, and again in 1891 and 1894.[59]

However, once suffrage was achieved in 1893, a number of reformists mounted increased pressure for the enactment of legislation to permit women to practise law. Thus, in 1896, the liberal MP George Russell introduced two bills: one to eliminate all women's common law disabilities and the other to permit them to practise law.[60] In the context of an election scheduled for the end of 1896, Roberta Nicholls suggested that Parliament may have wished to appear receptive to the interests of its newly enfranchised women voters.[61] At the same time, the enactment of legislation to permit women to practise law may have seemed less radical than the elimination of all women's common law disabilities, since the latter proposal would permit women to become Parliamentary candidates! As a result, with the help of the Otago MP, William Bolt, and in spite of opposition from politicians who feared an invasion of 'a great mass of Portias,' Russell succeeded in obtaining Parliamentary approval for his bill to permit women to enter the legal profession.[62] A month later, a government bill was enacted, and it also included a clause permitting women to become lawyers.[63] Apparently, the government had requested this clause in

---

[57] During debate on the 1881 *Law Practitioners Bill*, William Downie Stewart, later chair of the Otago District Law Society in 1895, proposed to restrict it to male persons only: G Gatfield, above, n 31 at 19.

[58] G Gatfield, above, n 31 at 24: the Women's Christian Temperance Union saw the vote as enabling women to safeguard 'the morality of the colony and the sanctity of the family,' not to invade the legal profession.

[59] See G Gatfield, above, n 31 at 19–22 and 25–8.

[60] See G Gatfield, above, n 31 at 29–37; and *Female Law Practitioners Bill 1895* and *Removal of Women's Disabilities Bill 1895*. According to R Nicholls, above, n 46 at 30–31, George Russell was a journalist and MP; he was among a small number of men who were invited to speak at the first convention of the National Council of Women in 1896 because women believed that liberal men might assist in achieving their goals. Russell enjoyed a varied career as a journalist, newspaper publisher and politician, rising to serve in the Cabinet during World War I: see GW Rice, 'George Warren Russell 1854–1937,' *Dictionary of New Zealand Biography* <www.dnzb.govt.nz> last accessed 29 Nov 2005.

[61] R Nicholls, above, n 46 at 27–8.

[62] Bolt, the Otago MP, arranged for the reintroduction of the bill in the legislative council after it had been rejected once: see C Brown, above, n 20 at 25; and G Gatfield, above, n 31 at 35. Gatfield noted that Russell's bill was passed with little media attention; only the *Evening Post* published a short notice.

[63] See G Gatfield, above, n 31 at 34–7; and R Cooke (ed), above, n 25 at 150. The

return for its support for legislative amendments proposed by New Zealand law societies. The societies were requesting a number of changes designed to strengthen the law societies' role in regulating and disciplining members of the legal profession, and to reinvigorate the New Zealand Law Society, an organisation originally established in 1869 but virtually moribund since that time.[64] In requesting the clause about women lawyers, the government was undoubtedly aware that the first convention of the National Council of Women in April 1896[65] had expressed support for Russell's bill and the opening of the professions to women.[66]

Thus, it was on the basis of *two* statutes permitting women to enter the legal profession that Benjamin wrote to the council of the Otago Law Society in October 1896 to request renewal of her library permit. In response, the secretary advised her that 'the Society recognize[d] her as a student and consequently [she was] entitled to use of the Library.'[67] When she had successfully completed all the requirements for admission in late 1896, Benjamin's success was noted in the *White Ribbon*, the publication of the Women's Christian Temperance Union, which proudly proclaimed that 'our New Zealand Portias have now a clear field for their powers.'[68] Finally, in May 1897, Benjamin was formally called to the bar of New Zealand, where Judge Williams congratulated her warmly and expressed the good wishes of the court. Several weeks later, Benjamin's graduation ceremony in the University library on 9 July 1897 also recognised her personal contribution to the achievement of this new role for women in law. The Vice Chancellor spoke positively about the need for women to enter the professions, an appropriate tribute on this occasion because there were four women graduates: one in medicine, two with BA degrees, and Ethel Benjamin in law.[69]

legislative council initially voted against the government bill, and also against Russell's bill. A week later, when the council decided to reintroduce the societies' proposed legislation, Russell's bill was also reintroduced. The council approved both bills, and after the societies' legislation obtained approval from the House of Representatives, it too became law.

[64] G Gatfield, above, n 31 at 34. See also MJ Cullen, above, n 24 at 60–61; and R Cooke (ed), above, n 25 at 149–50.

[65] The National Council of Women of New Zealand (which affiliated with the International Council in 1899) included a number of political organisations with ties to suffrage; the Tailoresses' Union affiliated in 1897 and the Wellington Workers' Union in 1898. Its members were often involved with the Women's Christian Temperance Union as well, and most were middle class; it was also firmly secular: R Nicholls, above, n 46 at 17 and 27.

[66] Russell's private members' bill faced problems in both the upper and lower chambers of Parliament. In his arguments in the House of Representatives, Russell identified Benjamin's progress in law at Otago, making women lawyers more than an abstract idea: C Brown, above, n 20 at 22 and 26.

[67] G Gatfield, above, n 31 at 37; and MJ Cullen, above, n 24 at 52.

[68] G Gatfield, above, n 31 at 37, citing 'In Parliament' (September 1896) 2:15 *White Ribbon* 8.

[69] C Brown, above, n 20 at 26; L Frank, above, n 23 at 70. According to Brown, at 18–19, the graduates included Margaret Cruikshank MB, BCh; MC Webster BA; and Margaret Smith MA, as well as Benjamin, LLB.

Significantly, it was Benjamin who was asked to speak at the ceremony, the first time that a current graduate participated in the ceremony in this way, and also the first occasion on which a woman made an official speech at the university. Benjamin reviewed the advances made by women's 'invasion' of a number of occupations, pointing to lady butchers, lady commercial travellers, lady auctioneers, lady opticians, lady dentists, lady watchmakers, and even lady blacksmiths, stressing women's need to become economically independent. However, she also suggested that women should not become 'mere thinking machines' and that 'the heart must be developed as well as the brain;' in this way, she predicted that women would succeed in overcoming the traditional unjust order of things.[70] Benjamin's hopefulness was evident again at the end of 1897, when she responded to an inquiry from the Belgian barrister, Louis Frank; in addition to forwarding her photo and two press cuttings about her career, she expressed warm support for Jeanne Chauvin's claim for admission to the Paris bar:

> The receipt of your letter afforded me much pleasure, and I must ask pardon for not replying to it sooner, but my time has been so much occupied that until now I have scarcely had a spare moment in which to write. I was much interested in reading your account of your advocacy of the claims of women to practise at law, and I sincerely trust that your efforts in this direction generally, and particularly those on behalf of *Mdlle* Chauvin will ere long be crowned with success. Only the other day a clipping from one of the London papers was sent to me announcing that *Mdlle* Chauvin was determined to demand admission to the Bar. It was said that the authorities would refuse to permit her to plead, but I trust that this prognostication will not prove correct and that the right of *Mdlle* Chauvin and of all duly qualified women to practise as advocates will before long be recognised by the Courts of France and of all civilized countries....[71]

As she acknowledged in correspondence a few years later, Benjamin believed that it was her 'progressive turn of mind' which encouraged her to study law even before she was eligible for admission to the bar;[72] she was fortunate that her individual aspirations coincided with liberal ideas about egalitarianism, women's access to higher education, and women's suffrage in New Zealand, all of which fostered her admission to the bar, the first woman lawyer in Australasia. Yet, if individual talent and a commitment to women's rights in New Zealand society assisted Benjamin to gain ad-

---

[70] C Brown, above, n 20 at 18–20, citing (September 1897) 11:3 *Otago University Student Review* 84; and *Otago Daily Times*, 10 July 1897, at 6. The 'new woman' emerged in the 1890s: see S Coney, above, n 26 at 15.

[71] Bibliothèque Royale, Brussels, *Papiers Frank* #7791–6 (envelope 1): (typed) letter from Ethel Benjamin, Dunedin, to Louis Frank, 21 December 1897.

[72] C Brown, above, n 20 at 26, quoting Benjamin to Stirling, 1 May 1899, Otago District Law Society Correspondence.

mission to the profession, her subsequent experiences suggest that success in the practice of law was much more elusive for women lawyers. As Brown succinctly noted, 'the law and the Courts were viewed as distinctly masculine fields of activity; ... [Benjamin's] distinctiveness as a woman thus set her aside from the other members of the profession who asserted their exclusiveness and homogeneity as a body of men.'[73]

Indeed, almost immediately, Benjamin began to encounter subtle distinctions in her treatment as a member of the bar. For example, only a few months after her admission in 1897, a resolution was proposed at a meeting of the Otago District Law Society that the judiciary should prescribe regulations for women lawyers' courtroom dress; in fact, the resolution proposed that the regulations should be similar to those adopted by the Law Society in Ontario, which indicated that women were to appear 'in a barrister's gown worn over a black dress, white necktie, with head uncovered.'[74] The Society's resolution was forwarded to Justice Williams, but when he declined jurisdiction, the matter was dropped.[75] Yet, even a decade later in 1907, a cartoon of Benjamin appeared in the *Exhibition Sketcher*, poking fun at Benjamin's appearance in courtroom dress. The cartoon showed Benjamin, dressed in her barrister's gown and preparing to put on her wig, and worrying about whether her petticoat was visible below her gown. She was talking to her maid, saying: 'Look after my clients, and give them lots of cream and heaps of cake. I'm counsel for the defence in the divorce case Smith v Smith, and intend giving old Smith taffy! Oh heavens, where are my wig pins! Now my brief. Does my jupon show below my gown? Right now for the court!'[76] As the cartoon suggested, women lawyers were still not to be taken entirely seriously.

Although it is possible that the Otago Law Society's attention to the professional appearance of 'lady barristers' before the courts was motivated by legitimate concerns about professional standards, rather than by any intent to condescend to Benjamin, any such ambiguity in the Society's motive was entirely absent from its treatment of Benjamin in relation to the profession's ceremonial occasions. For example, when a dinner was organised in 1898 to celebrate the fiftieth anniversary of the

---

73 C Brown, above, n 20 at 26 and 29, citing Benjamin's correspondence, 19 September 1907.

74 R Cooke (ed), above, n 25 at 337. See also C Backhouse, '"To Open the Way for Others of My Sex"; Clara Brett Martin's Career as Canada's First Woman Lawyer' (1985) 1 *Canadian Journal of Women and the Law* 1 at 29, citing W Riddell, 'Women as Practitioners of Law' (1918) 18 *Journal of Comparative Legislation* 201 at 204. Neither men nor women wore wigs in Ontario in 1897: see JC Hamilton, *Osgoode Hall: Reminiscences of the Bench and Bar* (Toronto, Carswell Co Ltd, 1904) at 120.

75 R Cooke (ed), above, n 25 at 337.

76 G Gatfield, above, n 31 at 76. Benjamin appeared in a divorce case, *Smith v Smith*, in 1906: see C Brown, above, n 20 at 44–5, citing *Otago Daily Times*, 10 November 1906, at 11. See also Gatfield, at 75, citing 'Women Barristers' Dress' (1961) 37 *New Zealand Law Journal* 77.

founding of the Otago settlement, invitations were sent to all legal practitioners, and Benjamin indicated that she would attend. According to Gill
Gatfield, Benjamin's name was at first included in brackets in the seating
plan for the dinner, and then struck off the final invitation list.[77] In the
end, Benjamin was not present for this dinner, at which thirty-five male
lawyers sat through 'five toasts (with four responses), five songs, one
pianoforte solo, oysters, soup, fish, entree, poultry or meat, dessert, and
fruit (plus champagne, sherry, claret, a fifty-year-old port, and liqueurs).'
The dinner must have been successful, as the Law Society made arrangements for a second dinner the following year, with the same menu – but
seven songs![78] This time, Benjamin was not invited at all. She sent a letter
to the Society, described by Cullen as 'tartly worded but beautifully
controlled':

> I wish to ask you why I was not notified of the Bar Dinner recently held under
> the auspices of the Law Society. I am exempted from none of the obligations
> imposed on members of the Profession, and I consider all privileges extended to
> them as such, should also be extended to me. Whether or not I avail myself of
> those privileges is surely a matter for me to decide. It may be, of course, that the
> omission of my name was an oversight, but, if purposely omitted on account of
> my sex, I have to enter a protest against such treatment.... I resent the omission
> of a courtesy which I consider my due. Moreover, I do not think that without
> protest I should allow a precedent to be established that may affect the rights of
> other members of my sex who will follow in my footsteps.[79]

As Gatfield reported, Benjamin's 'prescient protest was not heard,' and
she was not invited to the next bar dinner, held in 1902 in connection with
the opening of a new court building. Moreover, the fact that women lawyers were still protesting their exclusion from Otago District Law Society
bar dinners in the early 1960s underlines the profound masculinity of
professional culture which resulted in the Society's resistance to recognising
women as full members of the profession.[80] For Benjamin, such treatment
reinforced the extent to which gaining admission to the bar was just the
first step; the more difficult challenge was to be fully accepted as a member
of the practising bar.

In 1902, there was another ceremonial occasion in which Benjamin was
again singled out. When a new law court was opened in Dunedin that year,

[77] G Gatfield, above, n 31 at 71, citing correspondence from Benjamin to FJ Stilling, 2 March
1898, in the correspondence files of the Otago District Law Society.
[78] MJ Cullen, above, n 24 at 68.
[79] G Gatfield, above, n 31 at 71, citing correspondence from Benjamin to FJ Stilling, 1 May
1899, in the correspondence files of the Otago District Law Society. See also MJ Cullen, above,
n 24 at 68, who recorded this correspondence incorrectly as 1 May 1897.
[80] G Gatfield, above, n 31 at 71–3; as Gatfield noted, even in the 1950s, women lawyers had
to choose between staying away from bar dinners or 'being one of the boys.' See also MJ Cullen,
above, n 24 at 67.

the bar celebrated the occasion with a public procession from the old premises to the new court. The members of the legal profession assembled at the old premises, 'arrayed in wig and gown to proceed in a body to their new quarters,' attracting a large crowd as they processed in pairs down High Street to the vestibule of the new court to be greeted by the judges. Benjamin was part of the procession. However, as one account of this occasion noted, Benjamin 'again [sic] proved something of an embarrassment, as none of the profession was anxious to be paired with her in the procession;' eventually, however, 'JM Gallaway, who had always been a champion of her cause, came to the rescue and walked with her.'[81] It is hard not to conclude that such treatment on an important and public occasion, only five years after Benjamin's celebrated admission as a member of the bar, must have been humiliating. All the same, in the photograph which was taken on the steps of the new law courts to commemorate this occasion, Benjamin appears centre front; although it is difficult to be certain, of course, her position in the photograph may have reflected the profession's gallantry rather than its professional acceptance of a young woman lawyer.[82]

Yet, if she was not fully accepted within the male culture of the legal profession, Benjamin also did not fit comfortably into the women's movement in New Zealand. For example, when she sent a paper to be read at the third convention of the National Council of Women in 1898, the paper was rejected. Entitled 'The Inequalities of the Law Regarding Men and Women,' Benjamin's paper warned of the dire consequences which would ensue if women regarded men as their natural foes, a position with which the Council probably agreed. In addition, however, the twenty-three-year-old Benjamin went on to scoff at the pretensions of women members of the Council, suggesting that 'it [was] really absurd for a few women, as yet political infants, to meet and in a moment "carry unanimously" motions which few of them understand, which in all probability are quite impracticable, or which, if given effect to, might revolutionise society in a way that few of them thoroughly appreciate.'[83] In the context of the Council's lobbying for women's eligibility for political office, Benjamin's comments were unhelpful. In addition, the executive was displeased with the tone of her criticism, and thus returned her paper, informing Benjamin that they found it to be opposed to the spirit of the Council's work. In response to the executive's decision to reject her paper, Benjamin immediately notified

[81] I Gallaway, 'Otago' in R Cooke (ed), above, n 25 at 339. MJ Cullen, above, n 24 at 66–7, reported the procession to the new court. See also K Catran, *Hanlon: A Casebook* (Auckland, BCNZ Enterprises, 1985) at 92.

[82] C Brown, above, n 20 at 33, concluded that Benjamin was placed by the photographer in the centre front of the whole profession; the expression on Benjamin's face is enigmatic.

[83] R Nicholls, above, n 46 at 35, citing *Evening Post*, 30 April and 5 May 1898. Benjamin's comment about male support reflects her experiences; her attack on the National Council is less easily explained, but it was similar to criticisms expressed by the press and unsympathetic politicians: Nicholls at 33.

the press, protesting the tactics and censorship of the Council, and arguing that the Council should have permitted the paper to be read so that women could determine the merits of her arguments.[84] The Council's views on this matter were provided to the press by Margaret Sievwright, a nurse who had trained under Florence Nightingale before emigrating to New Zealand, and who was the founder of the Women's Christian Temperance Union in Gisborne, a vice president of the National Council, and wife of a solicitor. Labelling Benjamin a coward for not appearing in person to read her paper, Sievwright pointedly stated that it was Benjamin herself who had expressed views on matters she knew nothing about:

> ... does the poor child fully understand what she talks about – so 'glibly'? The 'political infants' – those of them, at least, who have taken a prominent part in the discussion – are grey-haired women, who for a quarter of a century or more (before Miss Benjamin was born) have been working for the emancipation of women, and, through them, of men – .[85]

There is no evidence that Benjamin attempted to participate again in the conventions of the National Council. Indeed, Nicholls reported that by the early twentieth century, 'there was a feeling among [Council] members that young feminists like Ethel Benjamin could take advantage of the gains made by the older generation yet dismiss the struggle that had gone before....'[86] As a result, it is likely that Benjamin received little, if any, further support from the Council for her work as a pioneering woman lawyer.

At the same time, it is not clear that the older generation's view that Benjamin 'could take advantage of the gains made by [them]' was true. In fact, in addition to being excluded from the profession's collegial events, Benjamin also faced challenges in obtaining clients and legal work. Unlike some early women lawyers, she had never worked as a law clerk,[87] and so she entered the legal profession without having had previous opportunities to establish working relationships with male lawyers. She had some support from one of her former classmates at university, and also from two successful Dunedin lawyers: Saul Solomon, a prominent Jewish lawyer,[88] and JM Gallaway, president of the Otago District Law Society in

---

[84] R Nicholls, above, n 46 at 35; according to Nicholls, Benjamin expressed sympathy with the goals of the women's movement, but she did not approve of the Council's tactics.

[85] R Nicholls, above, n 46 at 21 and 35–6. In 1899, Maud Pember Reeves was selected to give a paper from New Zealand at the meeting of the International Council of Women in London; when she fell ill, the paper was read by Beatrice Webb, who had visited New Zealand in 1898 and was a friend of Reeves.

[86] R Nicholls, above, n 46 at 78. Interestingly, Sievwright was committed to women's economic independence, having campaigned early on for equal pay: see Nicholls at 75.

[87] G Gatfield, above, n 31 at 62. Gatfield identified several early women lawyers who worked as law clerks, including Stella Henderson, above, n 31; and Geraldine Hemus and Ellen Melville in Auckland.

[88] According to G Gatfield, above, n 31 at 63, Solomon began his own practice in Dunedin in 1884; after 1900, there were several other partners. According to C Brown, above, n 20 at 33, Solomon and Benjamin both did divorce cases. See also MJ Cullen, above, n 24 at 198.

1898.[89] She also expressed a willingness to do any kind of legal work.[90] Yet, it seems that she continued to place her business cards in the papers well past the normal period allowed; when the law society objected, she replied that she would continue to do so until solicitors began passing her briefs.[91] Indeed, a decade after her admission to the bar, she responded firmly to the Law Society in Wellington, when it passed a resolution declaring her frequent advertising of her services as both 'unprofessional' and 'unacceptable':

> I know from experience that no business will be put my way by other Solicitors, and I must look to the Public for support.... I consider that it is imperative that I should make myself known by constant and attractive advertising.... I reserve the right to conduct my business as I think desirable.[92]

Benjamin's assertiveness confirms her strong personality, but it also suggests a serious need to advertise for work.

At the end of the nineteenth century, the work of lawyers in New Zealand was quite varied, and lawyers who met the appropriate requirements were entitled to practise as both barristers and solicitors.[93] According to Brown, Benjamin made some court appearances as a barrister. Indeed, when she appeared to represent a plaintiff in a case of debt recovery on 17 September 1897, the case was reported (incorrectly) in the *Otago Daily Times* as 'the first time that a female lawyer appeared as counsel in any case in the British Empire.'[94] In addition, however, Benjamin probably engaged in many of the activities identified at the end of the nineteenth century by the Otago District Law Society as solicitors' work: negotiating loans on commission, buying and selling of properties on commission, the collection of rents, interest and other monies on commission, the management of companies, including insurance companies, and land estate agency

---

[89] MJ Cullen, above, n 24 at 185.

[90] C Brown, above, n 20 at 34–5, quoting Benjamin's advertisement in the *Otago Daily Times*, 18 September 1897. See also G Gatfield, above, n 31 at 86, quoting Benjamin's view that women were entitled to choose areas of practice, like men, according to 'their individual ability': see E Benjamin, 'Women and the Study and Practice of the Law' *Press*, 13 September 1897 at 5.

[91] K Catran, above, n 81 at 93.

[92] C Brown, above, n 20 at 34–5, citing correspondence from Benjamin to Harrison, Secretary of the Wellington District Law Society, 19 September 1907. G Gatfield noted, above, n 31 at 89–90, that Benjamin offered to cease advertising if the Law Society guaranteed her a practice producing 2000 New Zealand pounds per year.

[93] P Spiller, J Finn and R Boast, above, n 25 at 235, explained that 'the realities of the New Zealand environment' required one profession, rather than the British model of two separate professions.

[94] C Brown, above, n 20 at 36, citing *Joseph Cox v John Andrew*, *Otago Daily Times*, 18 September 1897, at 4 (Magistrates Court); see also J Mayhew, 'Woman at Law' (1992) *New Zealand Law Journal* 85, and P Spiller, J Finn and R Boast, above, n 25 at 286. Brown recognised that the claim was incorrect because of the earlier appearance of Clara Brett Martin in Ontario.

work generally; as well, solicitors had a monopoly on conveyancing.[95] For example, early in her practice, Benjamin undertook legal and financial work for two well-to-do women, arranging tenants for their rental accommodation, collecting rents, and making investments on their behalf.[96] She also obtained some work from the Jewish community, and because her office was next door to the Wains Hotel, the hotel's owner became one of her most significant clients.[97]

In addition, when a number of legislative reforms at the turn of the nineteenth century created opportunities for women to challenge the traditional confines of unsatisfactory marriages, Benjamin acted for a number of women in family law matters; in this way, she was expressing her earlier views that women lawyers might usefully 'make a speciality of those branches of the law which especially affect their own sex.'[98] Thus, Benjamin obtained divorces for women clients pursuant to the *Divorce Act* of 1898, which made adultery a ground for divorce on the petition of either spouse; although this egalitarian reform was generally welcomed by the women's movement, organisations such as the Women's Christian Temperance Union were less enthusiastic when the same legislation expanded the grounds for divorce to include drunkenness, desertion and imprisonment, thus making divorce more accessible and undermining the traditional family.[99] However, even the reform legislation did not result in large numbers of divorce petitions because separation or divorce was practically impossible for many women who were economically dependent on men. As Brown explained, 'limited career options, low wages and the traditional obligations of home and family' made it difficult for women to support themselves; thus, they often tolerated unsatisfactory marriages.[100] In addition to divorce cases, Benjamin also provided advice and representation for women clients seeking legal separations, and in cases involving domestic violence,[101] orders for financial support, and adoptions.

Benjamin's experience in family law work resulted in her volunteering her services as honorary solicitor to the Society for the Protection of Women and Children in 1899, when a branch of the Society was formed in Dunedin. Initially established in Auckland in 1893, the Society's goal was

95 MJ Cullen, above, n 24 at 56; lawyers shared this work with land agents, moneylenders, etc.

96 C Brown, above, n 20 at 35.

97 C Brown, above, n 20 at 35–6.

98 G Gatfield, above, n 31 at 85, citing Benjamin, above, n 90.

99 The Union was concerned when women's petitions for divorce increased significantly after 1898; see C Brown, above, n 20 at 56 and Appendix II. See also R Phillips, *Divorce in New Zealand* (Auckland, Oxford University Press, 1981) at 65.

100 C Brown, above, n 20 at 64–5; as Brown noted, it was often difficult to enforce support orders.

101 Utilising the *Destitute Persons Act* of 1894, Benjamin obtained separation orders and financial support for women whose husbands assaulted them; the statute deemed the assault to constitute 'desertion': see C Brown, above, n 20 at 45–6.

to address social problems, including poverty, domestic violence and illeg-
itimacy, all of which were becoming more prevalent with increasing urbanisation in New Zealand.[102] In responding to a notice about the Society,
Benjamin stressed the need for a *woman* to handle legal cases, since
women who might need the Society's help 'would rather confide in a
woman than a man.' In due course, at the Society's inaugural meeting in
Dunedin, executive members were selected, including local government
and church leaders, and an honorary medical officer; along with two male
lawyers, Benjamin was named an honorary solicitor of the Society.[103]
Although Benjamin's work for the Society was voluntary, she received
annual acknowledgements for her contribution to its work. More importantly, her work for the Society helped her to establish a reputation for
family law work, thus attracting as clients other women who sought to
escape from unsatisfactory marriages.[104]

In her review of some of Benjamin's family law cases, Brown revealed
that Benjamin was firm and straightforward, and often quite tenacious, on
behalf of her women clients; she was also quite fearless in her dealings
with husbands, even when they were known to be violent. In one case, in
which Benjamin was acting for a wife who had been referred to her by the
Society, Benjamin sought a separation order on the basis of a husband's
severe cruelty to his wife.[105] There were several witnesses who described a
shocking incident in which the husband had used the crooked end of a
stick to beat his wife repeatedly on the head and shoulders; she finally
collapsed, covered in blood from her wounds. According to the witnesses,
moreover, this incident was merely one of a number in which the husband
had administered severe 'thrashings' to his wife. Yet, it seems that the
husband was successful in obtaining an acquittal on a charge of assault;
after denying the allegations, he explained: 'In a playful kind of way, I
caught me wife around the neck with the curved part of the stick to drag
her home, she struggled and the stick slipped and scratched her head....'[106]
Significantly, the husband was represented by Alf Hanlon, a prominent
Dunedin barrister, who had been president of the Otago District Law
Society the previous year, when the bar had celebrated the opening of the
new court with its procession of lawyers; at that time, while Benjamin had

---

102 C Brown, above, n 20 at 37–8. In 1899, the Society in Auckland merged with the Society
for the Prevention of Cruelty to Animals; however, the Society remained autonomous in
Dunedin: see Brown at 42.

103 C Brown, above, n 20 at 39–40, citing Benjamin's letter to the *Otago Daily Times*, 1
March 1899, at 3. The Society was non-denominational, but with strong Christian connections:
see MJ Cullen, above, n 24 at 64.

104 C Brown, above, n 20 at 41 and 53.

105 C Brown, above, n 20 at 46–7: *Parker v Parker* and *R v Parker*.

106 K Catran, above, n 81 at 94. According to Catran, the assault occurred outside a hotel;
however, Brown indicated that it took place outside the couple's home.

almost been forced to walk alone, Hanlon had presided by leading the whole procession.[107]

Apparently undeterred by Hanlon's success in having the husband acquitted, and frustrated with the husband's denial of the circumstances of the assault under cross-examination, Benjamin initiated proceedings to charge the husband with perjury. The perjury charge was heard in the Supreme Court in 1903, and Hanlon once again represented the husband. Benjamin sought out the witnesses to the assault, and when the evidence clearly revealed that the husband had beaten his wife, and lied about the incident in court, Hanlon resorted to criticising Benjamin's zealous efforts on behalf of her client.[108] He argued that domestic violence did not deserve the court's attention, and criticised Benjamin for instigating proceedings in a trivial matter involving a marital dispute; according to the newspaper account, Hanlon was scathing about Benjamin's conduct on behalf of the wife:

> After she [Benjamin] was defeated she hunted up the matter and instigated the police to bring a case for perjury. If Miss Benjamin is going to devote her time and attention to trying to make up perjury cases where there was a little exaggeration, she would find plenty to do, especially in marital cases. In those cases the wife naturally made things out against the husband to be as black as possible and the husband threw the blame on the wife.[109]

However, the presiding judge agreed with Benjamin, saying that she had been 'quite right to bring the charge,' and suggested that cases of male violence against wives were not brought to the court as often as they should be.[110] According to one report, the husband received three months with hard labour.[111] Moreover, the Society for the Protection of Women and Children continued to lament the prevalence of domestic violence in New Zealand society, and encouraged women to seek injunctions to prevent it. Yet, as Benjamin explained in correspondence in 1904, fears of 'public disgrace' as a result of dragging domestic concerns through the courts inhibited many women from seeking prosecutions against their husbands.[112]

In her capacity as honorary solicitor to the Society, Benjamin was also involved in acting for women who were experiencing difficulty in maintaining their children. Sometimes, her clients had been deserted by their

---

[107] MJ Cullen, above, n 24 at 66.

[108] K Catran, above, n 81 at 94.

[109] C Brown, above, n 20 at 47–8, citing *Otago Daily Times*, 21 July 1903, at 7.

[110] C Brown, above, n 20 at 48, citing AC Hanlon archives, No 1, Brief no 239; see also K Catran, above, n 81 at 96; Catran indicated that the judge at the perjury trial was Sir Robert Stout (a supporter of women's rights). See also Brown at 50–51.

[111] K Catran, above, n 81 at 96.

[112] C Brown, above, n 20 at 50–51, citing Benjamin's letter to Lee, 15 April 1904, Letterbook G, at 356.

husbands, but women who were widows often experienced the same financial problems. As well, women whose children were born outside of marriage usually had few economic resources. Moreover, as Brown noted, the limited support available pursuant to legislation 'did little to ease the long-term poverty of an unsupported woman and her child/ren.'[113] In the years between 1905 and 1907, Benjamin acted on behalf of the Society in legal cases to determine paternity and to force reluctant fathers to provide support for their children. She was also involved as an intermediary between biological mothers and prospective adoptive parents, particularly when children were born to unmarried mothers. As Brown explained, women who wished to have their children adopted made themselves known to Benjamin, either through the Society or independently; in addition, Benjamin responded to notices in the newspapers offering babies for adoption. Although adoption legislation had been enacted in New Zealand as early as 1881, there were no prohibitions concerning the exchange of money in adoptions, and a biological mother generally paid both the fee for filing the adoption application with the court and the legal fees, a not insignificant amount. In addition, however, until 1906 when it was subjected to regulation, a practice existed of paying an additional 'premium' to adoptive parents in lieu of the biological parent's continuing responsibility for maintaining the child.[114] Although Benjamin seems to have been actively involved in adoption work for a few years, it may not have offered long-term prospects for her, as the state became increasingly involved in regulating the adoption process in the early twentieth century.[115]

Benjamin's involvement in family law resulted, at least in part, from reforms promoted by the women's movement, and her work on behalf of women and children was generally consistent with these reform goals.[116] By contrast, Benjamin's involvement as an advocate for clients who were publicans was directly opposed to one of the most cherished objectives of the Women's Christian Temperance Union: prohibition. Even for Benjamin, a commitment to representing publicans must have seemed somewhat incongruous alongside her substantial commitment to defending women in cases of domestic violence, a problem which was very often linked to excessive drinking. According to Brown, there were a number of factors which encouraged Benjamin to advocate on behalf of licenses for publicans, and to oppose prohibitionists. One factor was Benjamin's fun-

---

113 C Brown, above, n 20 at 66, referring to limitations of the *Destitute Persons Act*.

114 C Brown, above, n 20 at 69–73; S Coney, above, n 26 at 76–7; and P Spiller, J Finn and R Boast, above, n 25 at 96–7. The practice of paying premiums was regulated in 1906 by the *Adoption of Children Amendment Act*: Brown at 75.

115 C Brown, above, n 20 at 76, reported that the Society favoured increased state regulation of adoption, and opposed 'baby-farming' practices.

116 G Gatfield, above, n 31 at 85, suggested that women lawyers were expected to work in family law.

damental commitment to women's economic independence; by contrast, the prohibition movement emphasised women's purity as a way of overcoming the evils of liquor, but these arguments about women's moral superiority tended to strengthen the view that women belonged in the home and subject to their husbands' control. Benjamin's spirited independence and commitment to paid work were not at all consistent with the Prohibitionists' view of women. In addition, of course, the Union was demonstrably Christian, so that it offered little appeal to a woman who was Jewish. And finally, Brown suggested that Benjamin clearly distinguished between the use of liquor 'in moderation' and the problems which it caused when used in excess; for example, Benjamin did not hesitate to seek judicial orders against men whose drunkenness was causing harm to others, particularly women and children.[117]

All of these factors provide useful explanations for Benjamin's choice to represent publicans. In addition, however, the availability of work for business clients who enjoyed considerable prosperity must have been attractive to Benjamin, who may have needed some well-paying legal clients to sustain the economic viability of her legal practice. More importantly, Benjamin herself was actively involved in the management of hotels in Dunedin and elsewhere. For example, she managed the business affairs of Wains Hotel, one of Dunedin's largest hotels, for the hotel's owner; Benjamin was responsible for settling accounts, obtaining the hotel's annual license and arranging publicity.[118] In addition, Benjamin was involved in managing hotels in Palmerston, Milton, Kaitangata and Wallacetown; she was a joint shareholder with another woman of the Wallacetown Junction Hotel, and, in the hotel in Palmerston, she was responsible for hiring and organising the staff, ordering provisions, deciding on the menu, and choosing the decor.[119] Thus, Benjamin was closely connected to the hotel business and the liquor trade in a personal capacity, as well as providing legal services to hotel proprietors between 1902 and 1905.

Benjamin's work on behalf of publicans involved some controversial and high-profile litigation. By the early twentieth century, the prohibition movement was gaining considerable momentum in Dunedin and the surrounding area. Legislation permitted voters to participate in 'local option

---

117 C Brown, above, n 20 at 78. Apparently, Benjamin encouraged husbands to take the pledge voluntarily: Brown at 78, citing correspondence: Benjamin to Peters, 15 May 1905, Letterbook G, at 956.

118 C Brown, above, n 20 at 78–9. Benjamin designed the advertisements for Wains Hotel, and they were placed in newspapers, in the programmes of touring groups, and in printed circulars: see Brown at 79, citing correspondence: Benjamin to Donne, 13 December 1903, Letterbook G, at 207.

119 C Brown, above, n 20 at 79; and at 78, citing correspondence: Benjamin to McLay, 5 September 1906, at 594. Benjamin was a joint shareholder with Mrs McLay in the Wallacetown Junction Hotel.

polls,' held in conjunction with general elections, to determine whether licenses would be 'continued,' 'reduced' or 'prohibited' in individual districts; however, to 'reduce' or 'prohibit' licenses, it was necessary to obtain a three-fifths majority of voters and to prove that at least half the electors on the roll had voted. Although prohibitionists had been actively campaigning throughout the 1890s, it was not until the general election of 1902 that five electorates near Dunedin achieved the requisite majority to prohibit licenses in the 'local option polls,' held in conjunction with the election.[120] However, a group of thirteen publicans in the Bruce electorate, one of the five where prohibition had been achieved, decided to challenge the result of the local option vote. As a result, Benjamin was retained by the Bruce Licensed Victuallers' Association, and immediately launched an inquiry into the local option poll procedures.

A few months later, Benjamin was present for a hearing before a magistrate in the Dunedin Supreme Court chambers. The publicans were represented by three barristers: Frederick R Chapman, who was appointed to the Supreme Court a few months later in 1903; WA Sim, a partner in Mondy, Sim and Stephens; and Donald Reid, who had been elected to the House of Representatives in 1892. The temperance supporters were represented by Alexander S Adams, a Baptist prohibitionist, who was also one of the honorary solicitors to the Society for the Protection of Women and Children; and JF Woodhouse, who had been president of the Otago District Law Society in 1893.[121] The requirements for local option polling were quite strict, and Benjamin's case on behalf of the publicans included evidence about improper closing of the polls and violations of secrecy in several polling booths. Thus, the magistrate concluded that he had no choice but to declare the poll null and void: '... however right or wrong it may appear to be, ... we have nothing to do but to obey [the law], and administer it as we find it'[122] The Bruce publicans were overjoyed!

However, the prohibitionists were outraged, claiming that 'the will of the people had unjustifiably been defeated by legal technicalities.'[123] They were critical of the government and its lax legislation, which permitted such technicalities to be used to defeat a poll. As one staunch prohibitionist argued in a speaking campaign condemning the magistrate's decision:

The publicans went scouring all over the country in search of irregularities ... having got hold of a lot of trivialities, they submitted these to the ingenuity of

---

[120] According to C Brown, above, n 20 at 80, the five electorates which voted for prohibition in 1902 were Newtown, Ashburton, Chalmers, Bruce and Mataura; as well, Clutha had achieved prohibition in 1894.

[121] C Brown, above, n 20 at 81.

[122] C Brown, above, n 20 at 82. See also PB Fraser, 'The Electors of Bruce versus the Law Courts of New Zealand' (Dunedin, *Otago Daily Times* Printing Co, 1903) at 6, cited in Brown. See also *Bastings v Stratford* (1900) 18 New Zealand Law Reports 513.

[123] C Brown, above, n 20 at 82, citing PB Fraser, above, n 122 at 4.

the ablest lawyers to see if by any technicality they could attack the verdict of the people.[124]

Their outrage made the prohibitionists as determined as the publicans to achieve their goals, and both sides engaged in clever strategies to outwit their opponents. Thus, when elections were held for membership on the Licensing Committee in Bruce, the prohibitionists put forward candidates, and successfully managed to get them elected. Then, when publicans applied for licenses, after the magistrate had invalidated the poll favouring prohibition, the Licensing Committee stated that it could not grant them because, in the absence of a valid poll, the committee had no jurisdiction to do so. In response, the publicans defiantly kept their bars open, without licenses. When the police intervened, charging the publicans with selling alcohol without a license, Benjamin filed a writ to compel the Licensing Committee to grant the licenses, claiming that there had been no valid poll preventing their issuance.[125]

However, Benjamin's application on behalf of the Bruce publicans was stayed, pending the outcome of a similar case in Wellington, in which a local option poll in Newtown had been similarly voided, and its committee had also refused to issue licenses. On 31 July 1903, the full court in Wellington decided that the Licensing Committee could not be compelled to grant the licenses, with the result that prohibition prevailed in Newtown.[126] Shocked by this result, the Newtown publicans decided to appeal to the Privy Council, a process which meant a delay for at least a year, and the publicans of Bruce were, of course, similarly constrained. As a result, publicans shifted their focus from the courts to the New Zealand Parliament, while prohibitionists were equally active in lobbying politicians to preserve their victory. Both sides sent deputations to meet with Premier Seddon, who attempted initially to avoid involvement in the controversy by claiming that no action was possible because the matter was before the Privy Council.[127] Eventually, however, the situation became so controversial that the Governor intervened, recommending to Seddon that his government should introduce a licensing bill.[128]

---

[124] C Brown, above, n 20 at 83, citing PB Fraser, above, n 122 at 4.

[125] C Brown, above, n 20 at 83. For the prohibitionists, the problem was that the legislation did not authorise a new poll immediately; thus, the publicans' victory at the hearing remained until the next general election.

[126] C Brown, above, n 20 at 84, citing the *Otago Daily Times*, 7 May 1904, at 7; and 1 August 1903, at 8.

[127] Interestingly, the MP for Bruce, James Allan, acting in support of the prohibitionists, introduced a bill to validate the Bruce poll, the *Bruce Licensing Poll Validation* bill; however, the government declined to support the bill, which did not proceed after second reading: see C Brown, above, n 20 at 86, citing *New Zealand Parliamentary Debates*, 12 August 1903, at 435–41.

[128] C Brown, above, n 20 at 87, citing AR Grigg, 'The Attack on the "Citadels of Liquordom": A Study of the Prohibition Movement in New Zealand 1894–1914' (Dunedin, University of Otago PhD thesis, 1977) at 216.

Benjamin's astute interventions in relation to the drafting of this proposed legislation reveal a pragmatic approach to promoting her clients' interests. In a letter to Premier Seddon, Benjamin proposed that the legislation provide for a 'fresh poll' to follow immediately after one that was voided; she also offered to withdraw the application of the Bruce publicans if the legislation were made retrospectively applicable to them. Benjamin also requested that draft legislation be forwarded to her for review.[129] As Brown noted, Benjamin's suggestion of a fresh poll in Bruce was entirely consistent with the interests of her publican clients in Bruce. Instead of having to wait for a decision from the Privy Council, a fresh poll could be conducted; since a valid poll required participation by at least fifty per cent of the electorate, the publicans' supporters could defeat the prohibitionists simply by staying away from the polls and not voting. However, Seddon wisely concluded that any legislative initiative would not affect either Bruce or Newtown because of the case before the Privy Council.[130] As a result, in a second letter to Seddon, Benjamin changed her strategy, suggesting that legislation grant temporary licenses to the Bruce publicans, pending the decision in the Privy Council. To support her request, she explained that such legislation would preclude governmental liability to compensate the publicans for financial losses, in the event that the Newtown appeal were successful in the Privy Council; she recommended that Seddon make this economic argument in Parliamentary debate on the legislation. In the end, Seddon's bill, introduced in 1903, did not meet the concerns of either the prohibitionists or the publicans, and it was eventually withdrawn.[131]

As a result, it was the Privy Council decision in 1904, allowing the Newtown appeal, which ordered the Licensing Committee to hear applications for renewal, thus permitting the reinstatement of licenses in both Newtown and Bruce.[132] However, even this decision did not end the struggle between the publicans and the prohibitionists. Thus, when Benjamin applied once again to the committee for license renewals for her clients, the committee ignored its obligations by refusing to meet at all. Firmly, Benjamin wrote to the committee's representative, warning against the use of such tactics: 'If the Committee wish it to be believed that they

---

[129] Benjamin stressed the confidentiality of her letter, since it would be 'impolitic to make known the fact that the legislation for a fresh poll was introduced "at the request of the publicans"': see C Brown, above, n 20 at 87, citing correspondence: Benjamin to Seddon, 29 September 1903.

[130] C Brown, above, n 20 at 87–8.

[131] C Brown, above, n 20 at 88–9, citing correspondence: Benjamin to Seddon, 12 October 1903.

[132] See *Smith v McArthur et al* [1904] New Zealand Privy Council Cases 323; the appeal was from a judgment of the Full Court (1903) 23 New Zealand Law Reports 419, Stout CJ, Denniston and Cooper JJ; Conolly and Edwards JJ dissenting. The JCPC appeal included five actions, *sub nom Corby v McArthur and Others; Smyth v The Same; Barclay v The Same; Redmond v The Same; Halley v The Same*. See also *Otago Daily Times*, 17 May 1904, at 6.

are not animated by strong bias it will be well for them to meet forthwith and consider the applications in a fair and judicial manner.'[133] Although the committee then communicated its willingness to meet, Benjamin was not prepared to leave the matter to the 'sweet will' of its members, and she resolutely applied for mandamus to compel a meeting. Her instincts proved to be correct: the committee promptly resigned in order to avoid being compelled to meet. Benjamin then telegraphed the Colonial Secretary and Minister of Justice, requesting the appointment of a new committee, and suggesting the names of possible appointees; although the Minister did not appoint those suggested by Benjamin, a committee was established. In due course, the Licensing Committee met to consider applications, submitted by Benjamin on behalf of the Bruce publicans; all thirteen licenses were granted by the new committee.[134] Not surprisingly, the prohibitionists were devastated; as one stated: 'Of law we can have as much as we can afford to pay for, but of justice none.'[135]

The government was not unmindful of the prohibitionists' concerns, particularly because of the strength of support for prohibition from the Women's Christian Temperance Union and like-minded organisations in New Zealand.[136] Thus, once the Privy Council decision had been released, the government again introduced new legislation, the *Licensing Acts Amendment Act*, which eliminated many of the technicalities which Benjamin had earlier relied on to invalidate the Bruce poll.[137] Thus, although the Privy Council decision had favoured the publicans, the prohibitionists were successful in their efforts to obtain new legislation which undermined the potential for publican victories: particularly because the new legislation required proof that irregularities had 'materially affected the outcome of the poll,' not just that it 'tended to defeat its fairness' as required earlier, it was more difficult to challenge the validity of a poll. Thus, when a licensing poll in Invercargill in 1905 voted prohibition, Benjamin was retained to act for the publicans there, but her efforts to reverse the poll under the new legislation were unsuccessful.[138] As a result, three months later, the 'will of the people' resulted in the closing of sixteen hotels.

Other than this reversal in Invercargill, however, Benjamin's advocacy

---

[133] C Brown, above, n 20 at 90, citing correspondence: Benjamin to Adams, 20 May 1904.

[134] C Brown, above, n 20 at 90–91, citing *Otago Daily Times*, 30 June 1904, at 2.

[135] C Brown, above, n 20 at 91, citing correspondence in the *Otago Daily Times*, 29 June 1904, at 5.

[136] As G Gatfield noted, above, n 31 at 69, the early efforts of suffragists were 'closely aligned to the temperance movement.' In the first decade of the twentieth century, however, the influence of the National Council of Women declined, particularly because of differences over the Boer War: see R Nicholls, above, n 46 at 50.

[137] The legislation included new arrangements for reviewing disputes about polls, and provided for fresh polls, if needed, within forty days of an election: see C Brown, above, n 20 at 92.

[138] C Brown, above, n 20 at 94.

on behalf of her publican clients seems to have been astute and substantially successful. Yet, for some reason, she had great difficulty collecting the fees for her legal work from them; in fact, she was forced to threaten court action and reduce her fees in order to recover any payment at all.[139] Undoubtedly, her fees for all of this work were high, and many publicans had experienced financial difficulties during their long struggle with the prohibition movement. At the same time, the publicans' unwillingness to pay her legal fees may suggest that they did not take seriously the legal work done on their behalf by a young woman: is it possible that they engaged Benjamin because she was a woman, rather than because she was a lawyer, in order to demonstrate that they, like the prohibitionists, had the support of some women? In addition to this problem, moreover, Benjamin's advocacy for the publicans must have further exacerbated her position with other women reformers. As Brown concluded, Benjamin's actions 'as a politically active woman, working in the public sphere to defeat [the prohibitionist] cause ... must have riled prohibitionists who believed that a woman's place was in the home.'[140] More importantly, Benjamin's personal interests in the hotel trade meant that her economic interests were also fundamentally threatened by the prohibitionists. In this way, her work as a lawyer was intricately connected to her interests as a businesswoman.

In this context, it is possible that by 1906–1907, Benjamin was becoming disenchanted with legal practice. Clearly, while she was active in family law matters, it is likely that many of her family law clients had relatively little money. Moreover, as the experience in Invercargill had demonstrated, the new licensing legislation meant that her legal work on behalf of publicans was not likely to flourish in the future. By this time as well, Dunedin was experiencing a declining influence as power was increasingly centralised in the New Zealand Law Society,[141] and there are some signs that Benjamin was still struggling to obtain legal work. Thus, although she had ceased to advertise publically for clients by 1904,[142] she had obtained the retainer from the Invercargill publicans only after she wrote a letter to them, explaining her expertise in licensing matters and offering her services; her letter suggests a keen interest in finding legal work, even if she had to travel beyond Dunedin.[143] However, her enthusiasm for business opportunities, by contrast with law, was most clearly evident in her decision in December 1906 to leave Dunedin for several months to manage a restaurant at the Christchurch International Exhi-

---

[139] C Brown, above, n 20 at 93.
[140] C Brown, above, n 20 at 94–5.
[141] MJ Cullen, above, n 24 at 62.
[142] C Brown, above, n 20 at 35, citing Benjamin's letter to the advertising manager on 4 February 1904.
[143] C Brown, above, n 20 at 93–4.

bition. It is striking that, as a sole practitioner, Benjamin was able to move to Christchurch to take up a management position at the Exhibition, apparently without any problems in relation to existing client work in Dunedin; in such a context, it seems entirely possible that her law practice was not thriving.[144]

This conclusion is also consistent with her stated intention to move to London, which she announced on her return to Dunedin in April 1907. These plans were delayed when she met and married Alfred De Costa, also a practising Jew, and they moved together to Wellington. Benjamin practised for a brief period there, but her forceful letter to the Law Society about her intention to continue advertising her services in Wellington suggests that she needed publicity to find legal work because she was once again excluded from referrals within the profession.[145] And then, just one year later in 1908, at the age of thirty-three, Benjamin's career in law in New Zealand ended when she and her husband left for London. Although the evidence is not definite, it seems likely that Benjamin's decision to abandon her New Zealand legal career occurred, at least in part, because it was not the great success she had envisaged in 1897. Then, she had counselled potential women lawyers to persevere, even though they might face an uphill battle: 'If women are determined to succeed, if they are diligent and "pushing," if they make the most of every opportunity that presents itself, sooner or later success will crown their efforts.'[146]

Yet, if Benjamin did not fully succeed as a lawyer, in spite of quite prodigious efforts, it is possible that she consciously decided to use her formidable talent to pursue business opportunities as an entrepreneur rather than as a lawyer. For example, Brown reported that Benjamin engaged in property speculation in an office adjacent to her husband's after their move to Wellington,[147] and it appears that both Benjamin and De Costa were highly successful financially.[148] In this context, with Benjamin's parents already living in Britain, and in the expectation that both Benjamin and her husband would be able to engage in business activities there, the couple's decision to move to Britain in 1908 was obviously consistent with their mutual interests.[149] Moreover, after her experiences in a decade of

---

[144] It seems that Benjamin worked in a sole practice; according to G Gatfield, above, n 31 at 42, it was not until later in the twentieth century that large numbers of women were employed in law firms.

[145] See n 92.

[146] G Gatfield, above, n 31 at 80, citing Benjamin, above, n 90 at 5; Benjamin also suggested that women would need to be outstanding, so that 'average women with average ability' should not attempt to become lawyers.

[147] C Brown, above, n 20 at 98.

[148] C Brown, above, n 20 at 99, citing the will of Ethel De Costa, January 1944, Somerset House, London. Benjamin left an estate of £20,000, including shares and investments, to her siblings and their children.

[149] Unlike many first women lawyers, Benjamin was married; however, she did not have children.

legal practice in New Zealand, the fact that Benjamin would not be eligible to practise law in Britain may not have seemed very significant.

Unfortunately, much of Benjamin's later life in Britain remains relatively undocumented. According to Brown, Benjamin may have worked as a legal assistant in a law firm, and she reported that Benjamin managed a bank in Sheffield during World War I; in relation to this claim, Judith Mayhew suggested that Benjamin was probably 'the first woman bank manager in the United Kingdom.'[150] Significantly, there is no evidence that Benjamin was active in the suffrage movement in Britain; by contrast, Anna Stout (wife of Sir Robert) spent three years there after 1909, where she 'cultivated links with feminist leaders and liberal members of the aristocracy, spoke at meetings, marched in processions, had interviews with the press and published letters and articles in defence of the women's cause.'[151] Benjamin's husband seems to have continued his business activities in London, and the couple's financial security enabled them to spend extensive periods in France and Italy, both before World War I and again in the 1920s and 1930s. After her husband's death at the beginning of World War II, Benjamin apparently remained in their London flat, periodically escaping from the aerial bombing to her sister's home in Middlesex; she died in hospital in Northwood, following an accident, in 1943, leaving a substantial estate to her siblings and their children.[152]

A 'REBEL [EXTENDING] THE BOUNDARY OF THE RIGHT'?

... [N]ow women's lives are becoming fuller, freer. They have at last come forward and claimed their right to work as and how they will. The struggle for their rights has not yet ended. It is growing keener and keener day by day and year by year.... For centuries women have submitted to the old unjust order of things, but at last they have rebelled, and as Sarah Grand has it: 'It is the rebels who extend the boundary of right, little by little narrowing the confines of wrong and crowding it out of existence.'[153]

---

150 See C Brown, above, n 20 at 98; Mayhew, above, n 94 at 86; and Brown's entry about Benjamin in the *Dictionary of New Zealand Biography* (1993: vol 2) <www.nzhistory.net.nz> last accessed 29 Nov 2005

151 R Nicholls, above, n 46 at 89. For three years from 1909, Anna Stout remained in Britain to fight for suffrage there, 'painting the results of the franchise in New Zealand in glowing colours.'

152 Brown reported that Benjamin died after sustaining fatal injuries when the building in which she was residing collapsed in the midst of a blackout: C Brown, above, n 20 at 99; but Mayhew, above, n 94 at 86, stated that Benjamin was killed in a motor accident. In Brown's entry about Benjamin in the *Dictionary of New Zealand Biography*, above, n 150, she reported that Benjamin died of a fractured skull after being accidentally knocked down by a motor vehicle. See also above, n 148.

153 C Brown, above, n 20 at 20, citing *Otago Daily Times*, 10 July 1897 at 6. Sarah Grand was an English novelist and supporter of women's rights: see S Coney, above, n 26 at 27.

Notwithstanding these confident words at her university graduation ceremony in 1897, Benjamin's experiences reveal some perplexing questions. By contrast with women lawyers in other parts of the British Empire, she did not experience problems in gaining admission to the legal profession in New Zealand, and it appears that she was not personally engaged in the legislative debates about women lawyers while she was a student. Moreover, since Parliamentary legislation had resolved the issues about both women's suffrage and women's access to the legal profession before she completed her law studies, she had good reason to be confident about pursuing a career in law. Yet, in spite of her ability and hard work, it seems that she was never fully accepted in the Dunedin legal profession: she was excluded from some of its collegial activities and she appeared to have difficulty obtaining legal work. In such a context, her gender seems to provide an explanation for the treatment she experienced, and her exclusion from all-male professional dinners clearly supports such a conclusion. Moreover, the fact that it was many years before other women sought to enter the legal profession in Dunedin,[154] and in other parts of New Zealand,[155] confirms the extent of male exclusivity embedded in the legal profession.

Yet, this explanation may be more complicated. Benjamin was not only female; she was also young, and she was Jewish. Called to the bar at the age of twenty-two, Benjamin's years in practice occurred mainly while she was still in her twenties. Her outstanding achievements in high school and university may have encouraged her to be outspoken rather than discreet, particularly in relation to the women's movement. In addition, her religion clearly marked her as an outsider in the profession.[156] Although Goldman

[154] According to MJ Cullen, above, n 24 at 141, the second woman admitted to the Otago legal profession was Prudence Rose Collier in 1926; she never practised. Margaret Smith Mackay, from Oamaru, was admitted in 1929, Mary Moir Hussey in 1947, and Marion Thomson in 1961. In 1970, two women were admitted: Josephine Carpenter and Sharon Blaikie, and Carpenter was 'only the second woman to practise on her own account in Otago as a solicitor (the first being Ethel Benjamin)': Cullen at 190.

[155] According to G Gatfield, above, n 31 at 44–9, and at 88 and 94, Stella Henderson was a law student in Christchurch in the same period that Benjamin was studying at Otago University; she applied unsuccessfully for a post at Victoria University College of Law in January 1900, and campaigned for equal pay. Henderson was active in the National Council of Women, attending its conventions in 1898 and 1900 as a representative of the Christchurch Progressive Liberal Association: R Nicholls, above, n 46 at 125–6. The first law students in Auckland were Ellen Melville and Geraldine Hemus, admitted to the bar in 1906 and 1907 respectively; Melville was an unsuccessful candidate for Parliament seven times and was President of the National Council of Women in 1919: see S Coney, above, n 26 at 37 and 41, and R Nicholls, above, n 46 at 113. Harriet Vine, the first woman in New Zealand to obtain an LLM degree, was admitted to the bar in 1915 and was employed as a 'qualified clerk' in a Wanganui law firm for forty years; her title was intended to distinguish her from other women law clerks. The first Maori woman to work as a legal adviser was Rachel Zister, who entered a firm in 1917. Overall, there were three women lawyers in New Zealand in 1911 and four in 1921: see G Gatfield, at 48–9 and at Appendix, Tables A1, A5 and A6.

[156] MJ Cullen reported, above, n 24 at 144, that the religious affiliation of members of the

suggested that 'harmony and goodwill existed between Jews and Gentiles' in late nineteenth-century New Zealand, he also identified tensions that appeared in the 1890s as a result of plans to permit the settlement of Russian Jews (who were experiencing persecution in their homeland) in various parts of New Zealand.[157] By the last decade of the nineteenth century, moreover, the decline of the gold mines and other economic problems had resulted in the movement of Jewish families to the North Island, particularly Wellington; according to Goldman, there were 428 Jews in Otago in 1878, but their numbers had declined to 311 by 1901.[158] In such a context, Benjamin's Jewish faith may have created another barrier to her opportunities for work in the legal profession.

However, by contrast with Benjamin, Saul Solomon was a distinguished Jewish lawyer in Dunedin at the time, and he became one of the first ten appointees as King's Council in New Zealand in 1907.[159] Yet, Solomon already had an established practice by the time the Jewish community began to diminish in Dunedin; and he was more senior and also male. Thus, while it is impossible to isolate these different factors to explain the challenges confronting Benjamin, it is also difficult to avoid the conclusion that gender made a significant difference to Benjamin's legal career. Although it did not prevent her from gaining entry to the legal profession, it clearly contributed to the challenges she faced as a young woman who was a member of a minority religious community. In such a context, Benjamin's assertiveness on behalf of her women clients in family law matters may have appeared too brash, especially to more established members of the New Zealand legal profession; certainly, Hanlon's response to her efforts to bring perjury charges against his client suggests that her actions were out of the ordinary for Dunedin practitioners. At the same time, her unstinting efforts on behalf of publicans clearly distanced her from women who were actively involved in reform movements, especially temperance, even though they may have applauded her legal work on behalf of women in family law matters. Her willingness to go to the press to challenge a decision of the National Council of Women identified her early on as both confident and independent, qualities which may not have been easily

Otago legal profession between 1888–1907 included persons who were Anglican (12), Presbyterian (10), other Protestant (10), or Roman Catholic (4); only two persons were identified as having 'other' religious affiliations. However, since the religious affiliation of 51 members of the profession was 'not known,' it is difficult to determine how many Jewish lawyers practised in Otago.

157 LM Goldman, above, n 27 at 140–41. In 1891, the New Zealand Parliament unanimously agreed to send a memorial to the Russian Emperor supporting his 5 million Jewish subjects; when news arrived that 500 destitute Russian Jews were being sent from London to New Zealand, however, there were protests.

158 LM Goldman, above, n 27 at 91–2.

159 According to R Cooke (ed), above, n 25 at 181 and 324, the first group of King's Counsel in New Zealand was nominated by Chief Justice Stout; ten men were appointed in 1907, including two lawyers from Dunedin, John Henry Hosking and Saul Solomon.

accepted in a young, female, Jewish lawyer, either in the Dunedin profession or in the New Zealand women's movement at the end of the nineteenth century. As a result, it seems likely that Benjamin was increasingly isolated, both geographically and professionally, in her years in practice in New Zealand.[160]

In this context, Gatfield's assertion that Benjamin was a 'leading feminist'[161] does not fully capture the complexity of her experience. In particular, Gatfield's conclusion that Benjamin's legal activities were designed to promote women's equality needs to be qualified; clearly, while such a claim is amply supported by Benjamin's legal work on behalf of women in divorce cases, her work for the publicans in high profile prohibition litigation must have seriously damaged any continuing relationships within the women's movement in New Zealand.[162] Similarly, Brown's conclusion that even though Benjamin's career was brief, it 'proved that despite discrimination and isolation, women could compete and succeed in a "male world"'[163] fails to acknowledge the major barriers that Benjamin encountered, and never really overcame, in spite of her strenuous efforts to achieve professional success. Thus, without diminishing her significant accomplishment in the face of resistance from the legal profession and a lack of sympathy within the women's movement in New Zealand, a more nuanced assessment of Benjamin's experience as the country's first woman lawyer seems appropriate. Indeed, even though she aspired to be a 'rebel who [extended] the boundary of the right,' her overall experience as New Zealand's first woman lawyer vividly demonstrates the challenges which confronted a woman lawyer who passionately engaged in any such rebellion.[164]

---

[160] As G Gatfield noted, above, n 31 at 68, 'Until the mid-1950s each [woman lawyer] was usually the only woman in her law class and the only woman professional at her workplace. Even into the early 1970s, a woman lawyer remained a novelty, unusual, an oddity.'

[161] G Gatfield, above, n 31 at 331.

[162] G Gatfield, above, n 31 at 93.

[163] C Brown, above, n 20 at 99. Brown, at 37, compared Benjamin's level of 'feminist consciousness' on two levels: her own achievement of education and professional qualifications, and her work on behalf of the improvement of legal, economic and social well-being of other women; according to Brown, Benjamin fulfilled the requirements for both levels of feminist consciousness.

[164] See above, n 153.

5

The Empire and British India: The First Indian Woman 'In Law'

A WOMAN PLEADING IN A BRITISH COURT IN INDIA: 1896

For the first time in any land under the rule of the British flag, a woman has pleaded before a British judge, and, strange to tell, this new thing comes from Conservative India. Extremes meet – the very intensity of the seclusion of women in Indian life has been the cause of this reform.... Of course there was opposition to such a novel departure as a Portia in Conservative India, but she soon showed the great need for a woman lawyer.... The native Courts first opened their doors to her. She has pleaded several cases and won them all. But her last great achievement was in a *British* court in Poona, presided over by a Civil Service Judge.[1]

THIS ACCOUNT OF the first occasion when a woman pleaded in a British court was widely reported in different parts of the British Empire. The case involved an accused charged with murder, who was successfully defended by Cornelia Sorabji, a young Indian woman who had studied law at Oxford. As the report indicated, Sorabji had been practising successfully for some time in the native courts, but her appearance for the defence in a murder case in a British court, as well as her success in achieving an acquittal, fostered hopes that women might soon gain acceptance as members of the legal professions in other jurisdictions 'under the ... British flag.' Indeed, the report of Sorabji's appearance in the court in Poona in 1896 was particularly timely: Ethel Benjamin was then in her final year of the LLB programme in Dunedin, and the Law Society of Upper Canada was formulating rules for the admission of women to the

---

1 'A Pioneer in Law' (15 October 1896) *Englishwoman's Review* (ns) at 217–18. Poona is now Pune, but this study uses the spelling of Indian place names as of the late nineteenth century. See also J Uglow, *Dictionary of Women's Biography* (London, MacMillan, 1998) at 437; SB Gall and C Zilboorg (eds), *Women's Firsts* (Detroit, Gaile Research, 1997) at 339; ET Williams and HM Palmer (eds), *Dictionary of National Biography (1951–1960)* vol 6 (London, Oxford University Press) at 907; and S Gooptu, 'Cornelia Sorabji 1866–1954: A Woman's Biography' (University of Oxford, D Phil thesis, 1997).

Ontario bar as a result of the efforts of Clara Brett Martin. Notwithstanding the hopefulness that accompanied this news of Sorabji, however, the editor of the *Canada Law Journal* used the occasion to reproduce comments published in a British newspaper, expressing grave concerns about the potential impact of women lawyers invading 'the hallowed precincts' of the English courts: according to the report, 'the average legal mind shudders at the notion.'[2]

Sorabji's career as a legal practitioner demonstrates both the constraints and the opportunities that resulted from the application of British law in India. As long as women remained ineligible to become barristers and solicitors in Britain, she faced unyielding opposition to her applications for *formal* admission to the legal professions in India, with judges consistently deferring to British precedents as they excluded her from the rolls. Nonetheless, because her legal skills were clearly useful, some native courts in India exercised discretion to permit her to appear on behalf of clients as early as 1894. And in July 1896, she became the first woman in the British Empire to provide legal representation for a client in a British court. Moreover, in permitting Sorabji to provide legal representation in this case, the judge interpreted a section of the *Criminal Procedure Code* applicable in India, which stated that an accused could be represented by a 'person,' thus confirming that an Indian woman was a 'person' in public life.[3] As a result, the court's decision in Poona in 1896 not only recognised a woman's right to provide legal representation in a British court; it also established that women were 'persons' in law.[4] In the context of women's exclusion from the legal professions and from legal 'personhood' in Britain, therefore, Sorabji's achievement for women and the law in the British Empire was highly significant.

Yet, like the judges who refused to grant any of her applications for formal admission to the legal professions, Sorabji herself was deeply committed to the traditions of 'British justice' and to the British imperial presence in India. For nearly two decades in the early twentieth century, she worked for the British administration in India as a professional legal advisor to women living in *purdah* in northern India;[5] in this work, she

---

2 'Women Barristers' (1896) 32 *Canada Law Journal* 84, quoting an unidentified English daily.

3 C Sorabji, *India Calling: The Memories of Cornelia Sorabji* (London, Nisbet & Co Ltd, 1934) at 34–5 and 59–63. This book was republished as C Lokugé (ed), *India Calling: The Memories of Cornelia Sorabji, India's First Woman Barrister* (New Delhi, Oxford University Press, 2001). See also *Code of Criminal Procedure* (25 of 1861), s 4.

4 Women's status as legal 'persons' was established by the Privy Council in a case concerning women's eligibility to be appointed to the Senate of Canada: see *Edwards v AG for Canada* [1930] AC 124.

5 Both Hindu and Muslim women lived in *purdah* in northern India in the late nineteenth century. Sorabji explained the nature of *purdah*, particularly for her British readers, in 'Safeguards for *Purdahnishins*' (Jan 1903) *Imperial and Asiatic Review* at 69. For a critique of Sorabji's relationship to the *zenana*, see Antoinette Burton, 'The *Purdahnashin* in Her Setting: Colonial Modernity and the *Zenana* in Cornelia Sorabji's Memoirs' (2000) 65 *Feminist Review* 145.

demonstrated both legal and practical skills, and a tenacious commitment to providing legal assistance to her Indian women clients, sometimes in spite of inadequate resources and disinterested officials. At the same time, it is clear that her opportunity to do this legal work was fundamentally dependent on the needs of her women clients for legal services, and the fact that they were precluded from obtaining advice from male lawyers; in this way, it was her women clients' need for legal services that defined the scope for Sorabji's legal work. As a result, it is important to take account of how gender defined her legal activity, both constraining her participation in legal work undertaken by male lawyers, and simultaneously providing her with a unique 'mission' and justification for her work on behalf of the *Purdahnashins*.

Moreover, Sorabji's work experiences reinforced her commitment to traditional ways in India; as she explained in her letter to a British friend in 1897, she was 'a Tory of the Tories,' who only reluctantly yielded to 'the rush of Time.'[6] Thus, even as she was striving to establish a career as a woman lawyer, Sorabji paradoxically idealised traditional roles for Indian women, and publicly criticised some reformist efforts designed to enhance their equality.[7] In addition, her identification with the ideals of imperial administration meant that she was deeply committed to a role for India *within* the British Empire, advocating a gradual transformation to dominion status; indeed, Sorabji was widely known in the 1920s and 1930s for her persistent criticism of the goals and tactics of the nationalist movement inspired by Gandhi.[8] Thus, even though Sorabji's life coincided with 'two great and successful struggles for freedom [equality for women and

6 British Library, Oriental and India Office collection [hereafter BL] F165/20: letter to Mrs A Darling, 17 October 1897. Mrs Darling was the sister-in-law of Lady Ford, who adopted Sorabji's mother.

7 Early in her career, Sorabji cautioned against rapid reform for Indian women: see C Sorabji, 'Stray Thoughts of an Indian Girl' (Oct 1891) *The Nineteenth Century* 638. See also A Burton, '"Stray Thoughts of an Indian Girl" by Cornelia Sorabji, The Nineteenth Century, October 1891' (1996) 3:2 *Indian Journal of Gender Studies* 249. For Sorabji's reviews of Indian women, see 'The Legal Status of Women in India' (Nov 1898) *The Nineteenth Century* 854; 'English and Indian: A Study' (1902) *The Monthly Review* 133; and 'Portraits of Some Indian Women' (March 1905) *The Nineteenth Century* 481.

8 See C Sorabji, 'Gandhi Interrogated: An Interview' (April 1932) *Atlantic Monthly* at 133; 'Comments' in *India: Discussed by Dr Haridas T Muzumdar, Miss Cornelia Sorabji, CF Andrews and CF Strickland* (New York, Foreign Policy Association, 1930) at 8; 'Prospice: The New India' (Feb 1931) *The Nineteenth Century* 176; 'India: The Sympathy which Debilitates' (2 July 1932) *The Saturday Review* at 6, and (9 July 1932) at 35; 'Temple-Entry and Untouchability' (June 1933) *The Nineteenth Century* 689; 'A Bengali Woman Revolutionary' (Nov 1933) *The Nineteenth Century* 604; 'An Indian Looks at the New Proposals' (Jan 1935) *The National Review* 63; 'Where Stands India?' (26 Jan 1939) 52 *Great Britain and the East* 102; 'Stocktaking in India' (April 1939) *Asiatic Review* 218; 'Salute to Loyal India! Answering the Congress Grievances' (2 Nov 1940) 55 *Great Britain and the East* 387; 'Congress Party in India' (9 Jan 1941) *Great Britain and the East* 36; 'The Situation in India' (4 Sept 1942) *The Spectator* at 216, and (18 Sept 1942) at 264; and 'Majority Community in India' (3 Oct 1942) *Great Britain and the East* 21. See also J Morris, *Farewell the Trumpets: An Imperial Retreat* (London, Penguin Books, 1979).

national liberation for India],' her views on both issues were sidelined in the sweeping changes which occurred in India in the first half of the twentieth century. As Vera Brittain concluded in 1960, Sorabji had chosen 'the wrong direction at an important moment in history, and [had thus been] repudiated by the currents of her time with a completeness which tends to withhold from her the status that is her due.'[9]

Brittain's comments confirm that Sorabji was a woman of some importance in her lifetime. Certainly, her role as a pioneering woman lawyer is clear. In Britain, she was the first woman to study law at Oxford University and, in 1892, the first to sit for the BCL examinations there, even though women were not then entitled to Oxford degrees nor eligible for admission to the bar. In India, Sorabji was the first woman student at Deccan College in the 1880s, and also the first woman to graduate with the LLB degree from Bombay University in 1897. Although her applications for formal admission to the legal professions in India were repeatedly rejected in the 1890s, she was permitted to plead in criminal and native courts, whenever judges exercised discretion to permit her to provide legal representation. As well, her expertise in providing advice to women living in *purdah* was recognised formally in 1904, when she was appointed Lady Assistant to the Court of Wards of Bengal, Bihar and Orissa, and Assam, an administrative post within the imperial government in India.[10] Eventually, when women became entitled to degrees at Oxford after World War I, Sorabji returned to Britain to receive her BCL degree in 1922, a full thirty years after completing the required examinations for it. In addition, after six months as a pupil at Lincoln's Inn, she was called to the English bar in June 1923. By that time, Sorabji was fifty-five years old, and had recently retired from her governmental post.[11] For a few years, she practised at the bar in Calcutta, and then moved permanently to London, where she continued to write and to do some legal work; in the years before World War II, she travelled back to India regularly, and she visited the United States and Canada.[12] By the end of the War, however, a combi-

[9] V Brittain, *The Women at Oxford: A Fragment of History* (London, George G Harrap & Co Ltd, 1960) at 84–5. See also P Adams, *Somerville for Women: An Oxford College 1879–1993* (Oxford, Oxford University Press, 1996).

[10] See obituary notices in *The Times*, 8 July 1954; and *Manchester Guardian Weekly*, 15 July 1954.

[11] In relation to her Oxford degree, see V Brittain, above, n 9 at 152–3, 156 and Table 2; and BL F165/116. Sorabji retired from her government appointment as of 15 November 1922 at the age of fifty-five: see BL F165/129, letters dated 22 January 1924 and 19 September 1924. The Bar Books of Lincoln's Inn show Sorabji's admission to the bar on 13 June 1923; the register of terms kept indicates that she was at Lincoln's Inn for six terms from Easter 1922 to Trinity 1923, a shortened period because she was a *Vakil* of the High Court of Judicature at Allahabad (admitted in August 1921). See also JJ Paul, *The Legal Profession in Colonial South India* (Bombay, Oxford University Press, 1991) at 160.

[12] Sorabji visited North America in 1930, speaking on several occasions in the United States and in Ottawa and Toronto: see *India Calling*, above, n 3 at 290–97; BL F165/179; and *The*

nation of old age, declining eyesight, and the trauma of the bombing of wartime London seemed to affect her health. In October 1945, she was moved to a hospital for mentally ill patients, and then to a nursing home, where she died in 1954 a few months before her eighty-eighth birthday.[13] At the time of Sorabji's death, Helena Normanton QC, who was the second woman admitted to the bar in Britain, recounted in a letter to *The Times* the celebrated debate on the subject of women barristers, organised by the influential Union Society in the Old Hall of Lincoln's Inn in April 1919; Normanton had argued in favour of the proposition that women should be eligible for admission to the legal professions. In her letter to *The Times* after Sorabji's death, Normanton confirmed Sorabji's pioneering role:

> [At the debate,] the only woman speaker who supported my motion was Miss Cornelia Sorabji; and this she did by a speech so eloquent, relevant, and telling, illustrated by analogies from her own legal work in India, that a handsome majority resulted in the end, in spite of much opposition; an opposition by no means unfair, or unchivalrous, but very serious in tone. She was the only woman who came forward to support me and I desire now to say how largely the victory, that night in the debate, and subsequently in [the legislation of 1919] was due to her career and her advocacy.[14]

Thus, the history of Cornelia Sorabji and her efforts to become a woman lawyer, both in India and in Britain, provides an important record of relationships between gender and law at the end of the nineteenth century. This chapter focuses on her efforts to gain formal admission to the legal professions in India, and then on some aspects of her work as Lady Assistant to the Court of Wards, and other activities later in her life. In examining these challenges, there are formal documents and reports, as well as lively collections of correspondence with friends and family members;[15] in addition, her legal work often provided inspiration for her

---

Undergrad (University of Toronto), 30 October 1930. In April 1930, the IODE in Toronto donated funds for a new building at St Helena's School in Poona, where the Kaiser-i-Hind had been established as a chapter of the Canadian IODE; Susie Sorabji, Cornelia's sister, was in charge of this school until her death in 1931: see C Sorabji, *Susie Sorabji: Christian-Parsee Educationalist of Western India, A Memoir by Her Sister* (London, Oxford University Press, 1932) at 32; *India Calling*, above, n 3 at 291; and *Saturday Night*, 5 April 1930 at 44.

13 Sorabji leased three ground floor rooms at 22 Old Buildings, Lincoln's Inn in March 1940, where she lived during the war: Archives of Lincoln's Inn; and BL F165/51: letters to Elena Rathbone, 11 Sept 1940, 16 Nov 1940, and 18 April 1941. On 24 October 1945, a Master appointed Cornelia's sister, Dr Alice Pennell, as Receiver: see BL F165/114. According to S Gooptu, above, n 1 at 289, she was moved to Northumberland House in 1947, where she died in 1954, a 'terribly lonely, and distressed woman.'

14 Undated cutting from *The Times* in BL F165/19; and (12 April 1919) 146 *The Law Times* 428–9. See also Elsie M Lang, *British Women in the Twentieth Century* (London, T Werner Laurie Ltd, 1929) at 163.

15 In *India Calling*, above, n 3, Sorabji described her family background and education at Oxford, her efforts to establish herself as a legal practitioner in India, and her legal work on behalf of women and children. See also C Lokugé, above, n 3 at xxxiii.

other writing: family biographies, personal memoirs, collections of stories set in India, and articles and comments for journals and newspapers on contemporary political and social issues in Britain.[16] Indeed, recent studies of her writing have explored how colonial culture in India shaped, and was shaped by, her experiences in these two connected worlds.[17] As Antoinette Burton concluded, Sorabji was an Indian in the late nineteenth century, but her identification with 'Englishness' functioned to make her an *imperial* citizen.[18]

BECOMING A WOMAN IN LAW IN INDIA

> I am more than ever convinced that the profession I have chosen is nicer than any other, & that women could find in it, as many interests & as much work as would satisfy any ambition & appease any thirst for usefulness....[19]

Sorabji's confidence about the opportunities for women lawyers is clearly evident in this comment to a friend in the mid-1890s. By that time, Sorabji had been pursuing her goal for almost a decade. As she explained in her

---

[16] Sorabji's books included *Love and Life Behind the Purdah* (London, Freemantle & Co, 1901); *Sun Babies* (London, John Murray, 1904) and (London, Blackie 1918 and 1926); *Therefore: An Impression of Sorabji Kharsedji Langrana and his Wife Francina* (London, Oxford University Press, 1924); and *Susie Sorabji*, above, n 12. She also published *Between the Twilights: Being Studies of Indian Women by One of Themselves* (London and New York, Harper and Bros, 1908); it was reviewed by Virginia Woolf in *The Times Literary Supplement*, 11 June 1908 at 190–91. In addition, Sorabji wrote *Indian Tales of the Great Ones* (Bombay, Blackie and Son Ltd, 1916), *The Purdahnashin* (Calcutta, Thacker Spink & Co, 1917), and *Gold Mohur Time: 'To Remember'* (London, De La More Press, 1930). In 1934, C Sorabji published her autobiographical study, *India Calling*, above, n 3, followed in 1936 by *India Recalled* (London, Nisbet & Co Ltd, 1936), a collection of remembrances and stories; this book was republished as Cornelia Sorabji, *India: Ancient Heritage* (New Delhi, SBW Publishers, 1992). Her last book was an edited collection, *Queen Mary's Book for India* (London, George G Harrap & Co, 1943) published in support of the Indian Comforts Fund during World War II.

[17] A Burton, *At the Heart of the Empire: Indians and the Colonial Encounter in Late-Victorian Britain* (Berkeley, University of California Press, 1998). See also S Vasudevan, 'Spatial Subjectivities: Gender in Indian Narratives, 1900–1940' (Austin, University of Texas, PhD Thesis, 1997); E Boehmer (ed), *Empire Writing: An Anthology of Colonial Literature 1870–1918* (Oxford, Oxford University Press, 1998); S Tharu and K Lalitha, *Women Writing in India 600 BC to the Present, vol 1* (New York, The Feminist Press, 1991); S Sarker, 'Unruly Subjects: Cornelia Sorabji and Ravinder Randhawa' in S Sarker and E Niyogi De (eds), *Trans-Status Subjects: Gender in the Globalization of South and Southeast Asia* (Durham and London, Duke University Press, 2002); CL Innes, *A History of Black and Asian Writing in Britain, 1700–2000* (Cambridge, Cambridge University Press, 2002) at 142; RS Ash, 'Two Early Twentieth-Century Women Writers: Cornelia Sorabji and Sarojini Naidu' in AK Mehrotra (ed), *A History of Indian Literature in English* (New York, Columbia University Press, 2003) at 126; F Gandevia, 'Cornelia Sorabji Recalled' in NB Mody (ed), *The Parsis in Western India: 1818 to 1920* (Bombay, Allied Publishers Ltd, 1998) 182; and S Banerjee, 'Imperial Diasporas and the Politics of Nation-Space: Indian Identities and Metropolitan Englishness (1855–1935)' (University of California, PhD thesis, 2001).

[18] A Burton, above, n 17 at 115 (emphasis added).

[19] BL F165/16: letter to Lady Hobhouse, 27 February 1896.

autobiographical memoirs in *India Calling*, she was born 'into a post-Mutiny world' in the Bombay Presidency at Nasik in 1866.[20] Her childhood occurred during a time of administrative reconstruction and social and educational reforms in India after 1857. Indeed, British administrators became increasingly involved in India after 1857, although British courts had been established decades earlier in the three Presidency towns of Bombay, Calcutta and Madras, as well as in some provincial (*mofussil*) areas.[21] In addition, while British policies had initially attempted to respect traditional aspects of Muslim and Hindu religious laws, Archana Parashar suggested that such deference tended to decrease with the passage of time because of the pressures of 'humanitarian considerations, public policy and demand[s] by the public.'[22] Moreover, as British judges increasingly presided over Indian courts, the result was an anglicisation of indigenous law, a process that was reinforced by the Privy Council's decision in 1887 which held that the rules of British law applied in India to the extent that they were relevant to Indian society and circumstances.[23] Indeed, by the 1880s, legal and social reformers were actively engaged in proposals for legislation to alter a number of indigenous religious practices, including child marriage,[24] the prohibition of widow remarriage,[25] the custom of *sati*

---

[20] *India Calling*, above, n 3 at 1. In 1857, Indian soldiers in the British army mutinied and their resistance spread to a large area of North India, involving large numbers of peasants as well; the British crushed the rebellion. Thereafter, the *India Act* of 1858 abolished the authority of the East India Company and established the direct rule of the British government in India: see *Government of India Act, 1858 (UK)*, 21 & 28 Vict, c 106. See also K Jayawardena, *Feminism and Nationalism in the Third World* (London, Zed Books Ltd, 1986) at 76–7; and Mrs EF Chapman, *Sketches of Some Distinguished Indian Women* (London, W H Allen & Co Ltd, 1891) at 113.

[21] A Parashar, *Women and Family Law Reform in India: Uniform Civil Code and Gender Equality* (New Delhi, Sage Publications, 1992) at 61–76. In the 1860s, an additional High Court was established at Allahabad: see D Duman, *The English and Colonial Bars in the Nineteenth Century* (London & Canberra, Croom Helm, 1983) at 131. 'British India' represented three fifths of India's territory, but the Viceroy also exercised authority over 600,000 square miles of 'Indian India,' composed of 565 independent states that owed allegiance to the British Crown.

[22] A Parashar, above, n 21 at 71–2; see also the *Caste Disabilities Removal Act* (21 of 1850), the *Hindu Widows Remarriage Act* (15 of 1856), and the *Native Converts Marriage Dissolution Act* (21 of 1866).

[23] A Parashar, above, n 21 at 72–3, citing the Privy Council decision in *Waghela Raysanji v Sheikh Masludin* (1887) LR 14 IA 89, and the interpretation of the principles of 'justice, equity and good conscience.'

[24] According to K Jayawardena, above, n 20 at 83, the *Marriage Act* (3 of 1872) set higher age limits for marriage: fourteen for girls and eighteen for boys; and the *Age of Consent Act* of 1891 raised the legal age of consent to sexual intercourse for girls from ten to twelve. The issue of child marriage became a major public issue in 1885 in both India and Britain in relation to the case of Rukhmabai: see S Chandra, *Enslaved Daughters: Colonialism, Law and Women's Rights* (Delhi, Oxford University Press, 1998) at 37–9; and (1885) Indian Law Reports 9 Bom 529 and (1886) Indian Law Reports 10 Bom 301.

[25] The *Hindu Widows Remarriage Act*, above, n 22, had been enacted in 1856, but Borthwick argued that it was 'more theoretical than practical': see M Borthwick, *The Changing Role of Women in Bengal 1849–1905* (Princeton, NJ, Princeton University Press, 1984) at 49.

which required a Hindu widow to perish on her husband's funeral pyre,[26] polygamy,[27] and unsatisfactory rules concerning Hindu married women's property.[28] Eventually, in relation to many of these practices, reform legislation was enacted, although it was not always fully effective throughout India. However, as Kumari Jayawardena suggested, most of these legislative reforms affected women's roles within the family, so that they tended to strengthen the idea that the family was women's proper sphere. Thus, even though reformers were often motivated by liberal values, legislative reforms tended to have relatively little effect in promoting careers or economic independence for Indian women.[29] In this way, reform proposals and traditional practices frequently co-existed in India, perhaps especially for women.

However, in addition to administrative and social reforms, nineteenth-century India witnessed new developments in education. Among both British and Indian social reformers, education was viewed as a way of promoting 'civilisation' in India, and many reformers regarded the improved position of women as an integral part of the idea of civilisation.[30] Particularly for Christian missionaries in India, who believed that 'progress in civilization was directly equated with conversion to Christianity,' women's education was essential to achieving their goal of establishing Christian families.[31] Among British administrators, the idea of civilisation was increasingly understood in terms of western liberal education. Thus, in 1835, the British government had adopted as policy the promotion of western knowledge, rather than traditional learning, in Indian schools; and administrators began to implement a system of English education, consciously designed to educate Indians in western literature and science through the medium of the English language.[32] As Lord Macaulay

[26] See L Mani, 'Contentious Traditions: The Debate on *Sati* in Colonial India' in K Sangari and S Vaid (eds), *Recasting Women: Essays in Indian Colonial History* (New Brunswick, NJ, Rutgers University Press, 1990) at 88. See also A Burton, above, n 17 at 35–6.

[27] According to K Jayawardena, above, n 20 at 83, 'polygamy in India was practised by both Muslims and Hindus of "high" caste and class.' See also A Parashar, above, n 21 at 204–13.

[28] See K Jayawardena, above, n 20 at 83–4, referring to the *Married Women's Property Act* (3 of 1874).

[29] K Jayawardena, above, n 20 at 80. See also A Parashar, above, n 21 at 18, who argued that Indian women's equality was substantially compromised in the twentieth century when the Constitution failed to bring religious personal laws into conformity with its equality provisions.

[30] See M Borthwick, above, n 25 at 27, citing James Mill's influential *History of British India* which asserted that among 'civilized people,' women were exalted; for Mill, the state of dependence of Hindu women marked them as completely 'uncivilized.'

[31] M Borthwick, above, n 25 at 28. As C Lokugé noted, above, n 3 at 222, missionary activities increased after 1813, when restrictions on their entry to India were lifted; missionaries began many of the first girls' schools in India.

[32] C Lokugé, above, n 3 at 221. Viswanathan argued that English language and literature were used in India to reproduce the values, traditions and authority which were disseminated in England by the church: see Gauri Viswanathan, *Masks of Conquest: Literary Study and British Rule in India* (New York, Columbia University Press, 1989) at 7 and 164. See also Sara Suleri, *The Rhetoric of English India* (Chicago and London, University of Chicago Press, 1992).

explained in his Minute on Education, the content of the curriculum as well as the medium of instruction was to be wholly English, with the aim of producing 'a class who may be interpreters between us and the millions whom we govern: a class of persons, Indian in blood and colour, but English in taste, in opinions, in morals, and in intellect.'[33] In this context, girls' schools were established mid-century,[34] many of them with the help of middle-class British women who believed that women's influence was essential to a flourishing Empire.[35] Education for middle-class girls spread rapidly; in Bengal, for example, where there were ninety-five girls' schools in 1863, the number had increased to 2,238 schools by 1890.[36] Women also began to pursue university education; two women graduated for the first time from Calcutta University in 1883,[37] and both Madras and Bombay Medical Colleges had opened their doors to women by that year.[38] All the same, the tradition of female education in India, both for reformers and conservatives, remained primarily directed to achieving fulfilment in family life; for example, even among nationalist reformers like Gandhi, 'the image of the modern independent career woman' was beyond conception.[39]

In the context of nineteenth-century India, Chandani Lokugé identified three influences which shaped Sorabji's life: British, Indian and Parsi.[40] The

[33] Quoted in M Borthwick, above, n 25 at 29. According to Borthwick, both British and Indian reformers 'saw women as passive objects of educational reform,' and women were not generally consulted about the reforms: see Borthwick at 41. C Lokugé, above, n 3 at xv–xvi, asserted that the Parsis were an important segment of 'the alienated subgroup that the Raj devised for their purpose' to fulfil the functions identified by Macaulay. See also H Bannerji, 'Attired in Virtue: The Discourse on Shame (*lajja*) and Clothing of the *Bhadramahila* in Colonial Bengal' in B Ray (ed), *From the Seams of History: Essays on Indian Women* (Delhi, Oxford University Press, 1997) at 67.

[34] For example, the Bethune School was established in Calcutta in 1849: see M Borthwick, above, n 25 at 73–5.

[35] A Burton, 'The White Woman's Burden: British Feminists and the Indian Woman, 1865–1915' (1990) 13:4 *Women's Studies International Forum* 295 at 306. See also B Ramusack, 'Cultural Missionaries, Maternal Imperialists, Feminist Allies: British Women Activists in India, 1865–1945' (1990) 13:4 *Women's Studies International Forum* 309; M MacMillan, *Women of the Raj* (London, Thames and Hudson, 1988) at 200; M Fowler, *Below the Peacock Fan: First Ladies of the Raj* (Toronto, Penguin Books, 1987); and A Burton, *Burdens of History: British Feminists, Indian Women, and Imperial Culture, 1865–1915* (Chapel Hill & London, University of North Carolina Press, 1994).

[36] P Chatterjee, 'The Nationalist Resolution of the Women's Question' in K Sangari and S Vaid (eds), above, n 26 at 233 and 245–7.

[37] According to M Borthwick, above, n 25 at 93–4, the University of Calcutta established rules for the admission of women to degrees in 1878, *prior* to a similar decision at the University of London later the same year.

[38] K Jayawardena, above, n 20 at 89; Jayawardena's statement that 'Cornelia Sorabjee ... was the first Indian woman to *graduate in law at Oxford in 1882*' is inaccurate: Sorabji did not graduate until after World War I, and she completed the requirements for the degree in 1892, not 1882.

[39] Jarawardena, above, n 20 at 97, citing M Mies, *Indian Women and Patriarchy* (New Delhi, Vikas, 1980) at 126. See also 'Introduction' in K Sangari and S Vaid (eds), above, n 26 at 20–21.

[40] C Lokugé, above, n 3 at ix.

first two of these influences were woven together in the childhood up-bringing of Sorabji, her six sisters and one brother;[41] as Sorabji herself later explained, they were 'brought up English,' with English nursery tales and English discipline, using the English language, and living in a home furnished like an English home.[42] However, at the same time, they learned local languages, and 'from [their] earliest days ... were taught to call [themselves] Indians, and to love and be proud of [their] country of adoption.'[43] Sorabji's reference to India as her family's 'country of adoption' confirmed her identity as a member of the Parsi community in western India; her father's family was descended from Persian Zoroastrians who had migrated to western India in the seventh century and who included about one million inhabitants by the late nineteenth century. In *India Calling*, Sorabji suggested that the Parsis compared favourably with the British in their great interest in the development of trade; and she claimed that 'being, as a community, rich, prosperous and generous, [Parsis were] responsible for many public benefactions.'[44] She always identified herself as 'Parsee by nationality,' a claim which was subtly intended to demonstrate her superiority to Hindus and Muslims in India: as she repeatedly emphasised, Parsi women were *not* secluded, and the Parsis had 'no social customs to which the West would take exception.'[45] Indeed, as early as 1893, Sorabji identified the role of Parsis as the 'bridge between the continents' of East and West. As she explained, they were 'an anomalous little body of people, with a history and a philosophy, planted in a small corner of Western India ... *Western* in progressive thought, in education, and in social customs; *Eastern* in location, in birth, in imagination, and religion....'[46]

41 A Burton, above, n 17 at 218, identified Sorabji's sisters as Lena, Mary and Susie (who were involved in teaching), Pheroze (who was a musician), Ailsa (later Alice Pennell, who became a doctor) and Zuleika; Sorabji's brother was Richard (or Dick), a graduate of Balliol and a barrister and educator.

42 C Sorabji, *India Calling*, above, n 3 at 7. Sorabji explained, at 8–9, that her family ate in the English manner off English plates, varying the simpler (duller) English pattern of food with 'lucious [Parsi] stews.'

43 C Sorabji, *India Calling*, above, n 3 at 7. The language of the Parsis was 'Parsee Guzerathi,' described by Sorabji, at 3–4, as a debased form of Guzerathi; in addition, according to her application for permission to plead in the court at Baroda in 1897, she had also passed the Bombay University matriculation test in Marathi as part of her BA degree: see BL F165/118, petition dated 28 August 1897. When Sorabji took the *vakil* examinations at Allahabad, she was required to pass a test in Urdu: see BL F165/20: letter to Mrs Darling, 20 January 1898.

44 C Sorabji, *India Calling*, above, n 3 at 3–4. See also C Lokugé, above, n 3 at xiv–xvi, who suggested that Sorabji celebrated an Indian-Parsi identity that was cosmopolitan and a bridge between Indians and the British.

45 C Sorabji, *India Calling*, above, n 3 at 4; and C Sorabji, 'The Parsees' (Oct 1893) *The Nineteenth Century* 605 at 611.

46 C Sorabji 'The Parsees,' above, n 45 at 612 (emphasis in original). Years later, the *Britannia and Eve* (February 1937) described Sorabji as 'Indian by birth, a Persian by descent, and an Englishwoman by adoption': see BL F165/197. See also TM Luhrmann, *The Good Parsi: The Fate of a Colonial Elite in a Postcolonial Society* (Cambridge, MA, Harvard University Press, 1996) at 107–8.

Yet, in claiming this strong Parsi identity to distinguish herself from Muslims and Hindus, Sorabji was ignoring both her mother's Hindu origins and the fact that her family was exceptional within the Parsi community because both her parents were converts to Christianity. Although Lokugé did not identify Sorabji's Christianity as a defining influence, it seems that Sorabji's faith was quite significant in creating her unique educational opportunity at Oxford and in defining her sense of 'mission' as a woman lawyer later on.[47] Sorabji's father, Rev Sorabji Kharsedji, had converted from Zoroastrianism to Christianity as a young man, and later became agent for the Church Missionary Society at Poona, where Cornelia spent her childhood.[48] Sorabji's mother, Francina, had been born into a Hindu family in south India, but after her mother's death, Francina had been adopted by Lady Cornelia Ford, wife of a British military administrator, and Francina was thereafter raised in the Christian faith.[49] Both of Sorabji's parents were dedicated to education and social service, and Francina had been in charge of the Victoria High School in Poona since 1876. Significantly, Sorabji remembered how her mother had asserted that daughters were just as important as sons in their potential to serve India.[50] Yet, while her faith may have consigned Sorabji to a religious minority in India, it probably fostered highly useful connections with British administrators in India and with friends and benefactors in Britain. In this way, it was not only her identification with 'Englishness' and the progressive reputation of the Parsi community, but also her adherence to the Christian faith, which seem to have been significant in rendering Sorabji a 'civilised' Indian woman.

In addition to these influences, however, it is also important to take account of gender, although her parents' progressive views about female education meant that Sorabji's gender posed few difficulties for her until after she graduated from Deccan College.[51] As the first woman student at

47 According to R Blackshaw, 'A Parsee Portia: Miss Cornelia Sorabji, Oxford Graduate, Lawyer and Author Too' (1903) 43 *Critic and Good Literature* 432, Sorabji was a Christian and 'a woman with a mission, though not a religious one.' Benjamin Jowett also described Sorabji's proposed work in India as 'missionary work': see BL F165/18, letter from Jowett to Sorabji, 21 September 1892.

48 In C Sorabji, *Therefore*, above, n 16, Sorabji told the story of Sorabji Kharsedji Langrana, his conversion to Christianity and later rejection by the Zoroastrian community. See also A Burton, above, n 17 at 115–16.

49 C Lokugé, above, n 3 at 226–8. Sorabji's mother provided evidence to the Education Commission in 1882, and addressed meetings in England, Scotland and Ireland in 1886 for the Zenana Bible and Medical Mission.

50 C Sorabji, *India Calling*, above, n 3 at 14. Sorabji also noted, at 2, that universities had been established in Bombay, Bengal and Madras in 1857, and that her father was instrumental in securing a resolution of the governing body of Bombay University providing that all degrees were open to women equally with men.

51 C Sorabji, *India Calling*, above, n 3 at 19–20. Sorabji's obituary in *The Times*, above, n 10, stated that she had lectured at Gujarat College while 'still in her teens;' however, Sorabji's BA degree from Bombay University (stating that she had graduated from Deccan College) was dated January 1888, when Sorabji was twenty-one years old: see BL F165/116.

Deccan College, Sorabji described the challenge of attending the college while living at home and commuting a distance of five miles each day to attend lectures with 'hundreds of Hindus and Moslems.'[52] In the final degree examination, however, Sorabji obtained the highest marks in Bombay Presidency, and was therefore automatically entitled to the Government of India Scholarship to attend an English university, including travelling and other expenses. However, because she was female, Sorabji was excluded from this prize. As she stated pointedly in *India Calling*, 'It was in fact impertinent of any woman to produce circumstances which were not in the mind of the Authorities as a possibility when they dangled a gilded prize before eyes that should have been male eyes alone!'[53] Yet, although Sorabji endured similar problems of exclusion in her subsequent legal work, simply because she was female, she never overtly embraced a female identity.[54] Indeed, when she was interviewed in Britain in 1903, in the process of promoting her plan to provide legal advice to women in *purdah*, she described her aim as one of securing recognition by the British courts in India of *'men of business' of her own sex*.[55] As Lokugé concluded, Sorabji always sought 'the promise of gender-free liberalism and individualism,' introduced to her in childhood by her parents, and independence to participate openly and equally with men in social and public life.[56] Nonetheless, as a woman who wanted to achieve independence through work, Sorabji was forced to engage with nineteenth-century ideas about gender, ideas which shaped her career in law.

Sorabji's description of her family life in Poona suggests that her parents were comfortable, but probably not wealthy. As a Christian missionary agent, Rev Sorabji may have had some prestige, but it is unlikely that he accumulated great wealth. In any event, when Sorabji was excluded from the scholarship to study in Britain, it appears that she had no alternative but to accept a teaching position for a year.[57] In due course, she contributed savings from her teaching salary to her expenses at Oxford, but the evidence suggests that she contributed only a small part of the total cost for her first year of study.[58] Although her father had also initially pro-

---

[52] According to her obituary in *The Times*, above, n 10, Sorabji 'encountered in the early days hostile and inconsiderate treatment from the 300 youths of that institution.'

[53] C Sorabji, *India Calling*, above, n 3 at 20.

[54] According to M Borthwick, above, n 25 at 58–9, negative views had been expressed about 'strong-minded' women in the Indian press as early as the 1870s.

[55] R Blackshaw, above, n 47 at 433 (emphasis added).

[56] C Lokugé, above, n 3 at xxxii.

[57] C Sorabji, *India Calling*, above, n 3 at 20. Sorabji accepted a post at Gujarat College in Ahmedabad, where she lectured to male students on English literature; in a letter to Lady Mary Hobhouse, she expressed her hope that 'it would greatly benefit the cause of women generally, for a woman, even once, to have been entrusted with directing in a measure men's intellects': see BL F165/16: letter to Lady Hobhouse, 10 May 1888.

[58] The pamphlet printed to obtain subscriptions indicated that Sorabji's expenses for a year (including travel to Britain) were estimated at £300; she had saved £60 from her teaching salary, and the pamphlet stated that she had borrowed £60 in India. By December 1889, a

vided some funding, his contribution appears to have been merely a loan, as Sorabji's letters expressed concern about the loan being repaid promptly out of the funds subscribed for her 'substituted scholarship,' established by Lady Hobhouse and others in Britain.[59] Lady Hobhouse and her husband were well known liberals who had lived in India in the 1870s, when Lord Hobhouse had been the law member of the council of the Governor General of India.[60] It appears that Lady Hobhouse had also become acquainted with Sorabji's mother, probably as a result of Francina's connections to Indian educational projects, and Lady Hobhouse had written a sympathetic letter to *The Times* in 1888 at the time of the decision to exclude Sorabji from the scholarship for study in Britain.[61] A year later, in August 1889, Lady Hobhouse again wrote to *The Times*, announcing the establishment of a special fund to permit Sorabji to study at Oxford and requesting subscriptions to the fund from others. Although there were eventually a number of subscribers, including Florence Nightingale and members of the Oxford University community, Lord and Lady Hobhouse provided a substantial portion of the total funding required for Sorabji's studies at Oxford and her subsequent training.[62] Indeed, even after Sorabji returned to India to establish a career in law, money was frequently a problem, and Lady Hobhouse continued to send sympathetic support as well as money from time to time,[63] at least until Sorabji obtained the government post at the Court of Wards in 1904. Thus, in spite of her 'Englishness' and her intellectual ability, it is unlikely that Sorabji would have studied at Oxford without the financial support

sum of £137 had been collected, in addition to a Somerville Hall scholarship of £25: BL F165/17 (undated pamphlet). See also BL F165/16: letters to Lady Hobhouse, February 1890 to October 1891.

[59] According to the subscription list, above, n 58, Lady Goldsmid and Lady Hobhouse each contributed £20; Lord Hobhouse contributed about £50 annually between 1891 and 1893.

[60] Lord Arthur Hobhouse (1819–1904) attended Balliol College, Oxford, graduating both BA and MA. He was called to the bar at Lincoln's Inn in 1845 and became a QC, and a bencher of Lincoln's Inn in 1862. He retired from practice to become a charity commissioner, and became law member of the council of the Governor-General of India in 1872. He returned to Britain in 1877, and was appointed to the Judicial Committee of the Privy Council in 1881, where he delivered decisions in 200 appeals over the next twenty years, of which 120 were from India. He was also influential in the reform of married women's property; Hobhouse was described as 'to the last an advanced liberal and constructive legal reformer.' His wife was Mary Hobhouse: *Dictionary of National Biography 1901–1911*, vol I (London, Oxford University Press) at 272.

[61] See A Burton, above, n 17 at 120; and C Lokugé, above, n 3 at 226–7. Sorabji wrote to Lady Hobhouse in 1888 to send her 'very grateful thanks' for her letter to *The Times*, reprinted in the *Bombay Gazette*; in this letter, Sorabji expressly stated that her mother 'sends you her very kind remembrances': BL F165/16: letter to Lady Hobhouse, 10 May 1888; and BL F165/17: letter from Lady Hobhouse to *The Times*, 13 April 1888.

[62] Madeleine Shaw Lefevre, Sir William Markby and Florence Nightingale each contributed £5: see n 58.

[63] There is evidence that Sorabji often experienced financial difficulties: see her pension correspondence in 1922: BL F165/121 and 129. When her sister Alice was appointed Receiver in 1945, Sorabji had a bank overdraft of £1200 and other debts: see BL F165/114, order of 24 October 1945.

provided by the Hobhouses and their friends in Britain. At the same time, Sorabji's educational achievements in India, her imperial values, and her Christian faith undoubtedly made her attractive to liberal social reformers with an interest in encouraging 'civilisation' in late-Victorian India.

In spite of these mutual interests, however, Sorabji may have experienced some tension between her own wishes and the well-intentioned advice of her benefactors when she arrived in Britain in 1889 to study at Oxford. Her interest in studying law had already been clearly defined[64] in a letter in June 1889 to Madeleine Shaw Lefevre, the first principal of Somerville College:[65]

> ... And now I must ask you something of the plans at which I hinted when I last wrote. I want eventually to read Law in England with a view to coming back to India to practise, which would, I believe, be allowed in our Presidency. It was a Ranee of one of the Kathyawar States who suggested the idea to me. She is a widow & completely at the mercy of her agents.... But ... she told me of the many Evils which arise in the native states for want of Lady Lawyers.... My certificate at Oxford plus the degree of my own University will entitle me to higher work here than were I not so qualified....[66]

In response to Sorabji's request to study law, Shaw Lefevre apparently made inquiries at Oxford, and a few weeks later, the Somerville principal received a letter of advice from Professor William Markby, Reader in Indian Law at Oxford;[67] Markby stated succinctly that 'Miss Sorabji had better at once begin to read Law.' Although he noted that she would have to learn some Latin, he thought that 'with her perfect knowledge of English,' it would not be difficult for her to complete the work within two years. As he concluded, moreover, 'I do not apprehend any difficulty about

---

64 In *India Calling*, above, n 3 at 15–18, Sorabji identified a childhood experience, in which a Hindu woman sought her mother's assistance as a result of having been defrauded by her male manager, as the basis for her decision to study law in order to help such women, the *purdahnashins*. C Lokugé, above, n 3 at xxii–xxvii, concluded that Sorabji's account rendered Indian subjects 'exotic' in ways that would reinforce imperial ideas about India. See also A Burton, above, n 17 at 116–17, who concluded that Sorabji had constructed the childhood story, when she was writing *India Calling* decades later, to justify her 'calling' to provide legal assistance to women living in *purdah*. However, Sorabji's 1889 letter to Shaw Lefevre confirms that, whether or not the childhood experience actually occurred, Sorabji was already considering law prior to her arrival at Oxford: see BL F165/17, letter dated 16 June 1889.

65 Madeleine Shaw Lefevre was appointed the first principal of Somerville College in May 1879, and remained in this position until 1889, when Agnes Maitland was appointed Principal: V Brittain, above, n 9 at 58–9 and 84–5. Another student at Somerville was Emily Penrose, who later became Principal; Penrose intervened to enable Sorabji to receive her degree in 1922: BL F165/116.

66 BL F165/17: letter to Shaw Lefevre, 16 June 1889.

67 Sir William Markby (1829–1914) graduated from Oxford and was called to the bar in 1856. He was appointed a puisne judge of the Calcutta High Court from 1866–1878 and became Vice Chancellor of Calcutta University; he was Reader in Indian Law at Oxford from 1878 to 1900: see CE Buckland, *Dictionary of Indian Biography* (New York, Greenwood Press, 1969) at 275.

opening the School of Jurisprudence to women.'[68] Yet, on arrival in Britain, it seems that Sorabji's plans changed, and she first contemplated studying medicine, and then her British sponsors apparently persuaded her to plan a teaching career. In fact, it was not until some months after her arrival in Oxford that, upon hearing about the possibility of a minor governmental legal post in India, Sorabji changed her studies to focus on law.[69] At the time, of course, no woman in the British Empire had yet gained admission to the bar, and Sorabji arrived at Oxford only a year after Eliza Orme had received her law degree at London University. By contrast, several women had already become doctors and teachers in different parts of the British Empire,[70] so that Sorabji's British sponsors may well have regarded these careers as more suitable for women than law; and Sorabji's wish for their approval may have deflected her plans at the outset. Significantly, however, she eventually followed precisely the plan of study which she had clearly articulated in her 1889 letter to Shaw Lefevre.

In *India Calling*, Sorabji described her student days at Oxford in glowing terms: the physical beauty of the colleges, the kindness of everyone, and the opportunity to learn that 'difference of opinion need not affect friendship or personal appreciation.'[71] Once she began to study law, she received warm support from several faculty members, including Benjamin Jowett, William Markby, Frederick Pollack, and AV Dicey;[72] and she was invited to social gatherings by Lord and Lady Hobhouse and their friends where she met prominent leaders of political and artistic life in Britain: William Gladstone, George Bernard Shaw, the Tennysons, and Margot

---

68 BL F165/17: letter from Markby to Shaw Lefevre, 12 July 1889.

69 In *India Calling*, above, n 3 at 26, Sorabji claimed that she was permitted to read law only after Jowett's intervention. See also C Lokugé, above, n 3 at xx–xxi; and A Burton, above, n 17 at 117–18 and 133–4. However, it seems that Markby wrote to Agnes Maitland, confirming that he would 'advise [Sorabji] what to read for the BCL examination': BL F165/116: letter to Maitland, 26 August 1890.

70 K Jayawardena, above, n 20 at 89.

71 C Sorabji, *India Calling*, above, n 3 at 22–3. Sorabji's letters to her parents confirm that she arrived in Britain in August 1889: see BL F165/1. However, Sorabji's obituary in *The Times*, above, n 10, and her biographical entry in the *Dictionary of National Biography*, above, n 1, incorrectly identified her arriving in 1888.

72 Benjamin Jowett was Master of Balliol College at Oxford, where Sorabji's brother Richard was a student. Jowett corresponded with Sorabji after her return to India and she published a tribute to him after his death in 1903: see C Sorabji, 'Benjamin Jowett – Master of Balliol College: Some Reflections' (1903) 54 *Nineteenth Century and After, A Monthly Review* 297; and BL F165/18. Sir Frederick Pollack became a lifelong friend and supporter of Sorabji and her work; he provided a guarantee when she applied for admission as a student at Lincoln's Inn in 1922: see BL F165/21, letter to H F Blair, 27 June 1901; and Admission Bond for Cornelia Sorabji, 1 May 1922, Archives of Lincoln's Inn. AV Dicey was known to Sorabji, although she was not fond of him: see BL F165/16: letter to Lady Hobhouse, 23 August 1896; BL F165/118: letter from AV Dicey to Sorabji, 1900; and AV Dicey, *Letters to a Friend on Votes for Women* (London, John Murray, 1909). For Markby, see above, n 67.

Tennant (later Asquith).[73] She was also presented formally to Queen Victoria.[74] At the conclusion of her studies in 1892, moreover, it was Benjamin Jowett who intervened on her behalf to obtain a special decree, which permitted Sorabji to sit for the BCL examinations.[75] Thus, as she noted in *India Calling*, the excellent quality of instruction at Oxford and the kind support from so many friends resulted in her feeling great disappointment with her results in the examinations: only *third*-class honours. As she wrote to Lady Hobhouse in June 1892, 'I do not attempt to conceal the fact that I have intensely disappointed myself.' Perhaps attempting to exonerate herself with her benefactor, however, she continued:

> ... It was of course a stiff Examination, and everybody is very kind, & says nice things about my having done in two years, what the men have taken over from 5 years upwards but I can't help bewailing that second. And I feel I have betrayed the faith which so, many of my friends were kind enough to put in me. Write and tell me that you are not very ashamed of – or disappointed in me: though if you are it will be only what I deserve.[76]

And indeed, Lord and Lady Hobhouse continued to support Sorabji in her work. When she decided that she wanted some practical legal experience before returning to India, she gave credit in *India Calling* to Lord Hobhouse for initiating the arrangements for her to work at a solicitors' firm in London.[77] However, it appears that it was Lily Bruce, the mother of one of Sorabji's school friends from Somerville College, who recommended Sorabji to her brother, Henry Whately, a partner at the firm of Lee and Pemberton in London:

> Do you think it would be possible for you to take her into your office, to work as a clerk, for a few months? She would agree to almost any arrangement you wished to make, provided she learnt the business. You would probably find her

---

73 See C Sorabji, *India Calling*, above, n 3 at 22–7; and C Lokugé, above, n 3 at 231–2. See also Sorabji's account of her play being reviewed by Mrs Patrick Campbell and George Bernard Shaw: *India Calling*, at 46–7.

74 In *India Calling*, above, n 3 at 38, Sorabji described being presented to Queen Victoria, wearing her azalea *sari*, 'something in colour between pink and yellow;' she was presented by Lady Gerald Fitzgerald, although she had specifically requested to be presented by Lady Hobhouse: see BL F165/16: letter to Lady Hobhouse, 28 June 1892. See also C Lokugé, above, n 3 at 235–6.

75 C Sorabji, *India Calling*, above, n 3 at 27–9; Sorabji believed she needed to write under the same conditions as men in order to be qualified for a degree in due course. Her degree was finally conferred in 1922: see BL F165/116, letter from E Penrose, 23 November 1922; letter to Penrose from C Leudesdorf, University Registry, 13 March 1922; and certificate of the Assistant Registrar, 27 June 1922.

76 BL F165/16: letter to Lady Hobhouse, 22 June 1892. V Brittain, above, n 9 at Table 2, explained Sorabji's third-class honours (probably incorrectly) on the basis that 'English was not her native language.' See also BL F165/116: letter from Thomas Raleigh to Maitland, 18 June 1892.

77 C Sorabji, *India Calling*, above, n 3 at 34–5.

infinitely more intelligent than the average clerk, & extremely zealous. She is very amiable and good-tempered – nothing oriental about her except her appearance – which no doubt would create some astonishment in the office – but she would only be a two days wonder. You could put her in charge of the chief accountant – or some Elderly respectable person of that type. If she cannot persuade a Solicitor to allow her to enter his office, she will be obliged to return to India only half-prepared for her work, & her career would be more or less spoilt – & the poor Zenana women have to continue in the old way.... I always imagine Solicitors to be a very conservative race – so perhaps you will not be able to overcome your partners' prejudices! But I expect you would find her quite businesslike in every respect....[78]

When the firm accepted Sorabji, it was Lord Hobhouse who paid the fee for her to 'article,' although the fee was discounted because, as a woman, Sorabji was not eligible to be formally articled nor to become a solicitor.[79] According to Whately, Sorabji did the ordinary work of articled clerks such as drawing settlements, wills and deeds during her six months as a student.[80] Indeed, it was Whately who eventually arranged to provide her with a special certificate from Lee and Pemberton, confirming that Sorabji had shown 'unusual industry and proficiency in mastering the details of conveyancing,' and was competent to pass the solicitors' examination.[81]

Thus, having completed the BCL examinations at Oxford and six months of practical work at Lee and Pemberton in London, Sorabji was ready to return to India in the spring of 1893. In the month before her departure, however, she again focused her attention on the issue of legal representation for women in *purdah*, responding to an invitation from Mary Haweis, an artist and wife of Rev Haweis, to present a paper on the subject of the law of women's property in India to a gathering at Queen's House in Chelsea.[82] In the handwritten text of her paper, Sorabji began by

---

[78] BL F165/19: letter from Bruce to Whately, 19 August 1892.

[79] See BL F165/19: letters from Hobhouse to Whately, 20 September 1892 and 22 September 1892; the usual fee of £300 was discounted because Sorabji worked for only six months (14 September 1892 to February 1893): BL F165/19: letter from Lee and Pemberton to Sorabji, 27 August 1892.

[80] Certificate re Cornelia Sorabji from Lee and Pemberton, Solicitors, 8 December 1893: BL F165/116. In *India Calling*, above, n 3 at 35–6, Sorabji said that the fee of £50 was returned to Hobhouse because she had detected a flaw in some title deeds, which 'had saved the firm more money than the cost of [her] training.' However, Whately later reported to Elena Rathbone, Sorabji's literary executor, that the firm returned the fee 'because she had given us little trouble & it was an uncommon venture & we knew that money was none too plentiful....': BL F165/19: letter from Whately to Elena Rathbone, 14 August 1954. See also BL F165/19: letter from Hobhouse to Whately, 23 February 1893.

[81] Certificate, above, n 80. Sorabji also applied for admission as a conveyancer; her application was rejected: BL F165/19.

[82] 'The Law of Women's Property in India in relation to her Social Position' read at Queen's House, Chelsea, 19 March 1893: see BL F165/117. There is correspondence from Sorabji to Mary Haweis about their efforts to find a date for this presentation: see University of British

professing herself to be 'ludicrously incapable of making speeches,' but her modest beginning was then followed by a well-organised and succinct outline of the property rights of Muslim and Hindu women in India. As she noted, their substantive rights sometimes actually exceeded those of English women, 'under even their Magna Carta of 1882.'[83] According to Sorabji, however, social customs that required Indian women to live in seclusion often made it difficult for them to *enforce* their substantive rights to property in practice. Quoting a representative of the legal profession in India, who had suggested that male lawyers were available to advise these women if they abandoned their seclusion, Sorabji asked rhetorically why Indian women should be required to renounce *purdah*, 'when there is such a much better way?' For Sorabji, the circumstances of Indian women living in *purdah* created a special task for women with knowledge of the law and a love for Indian women and their needs.[84] Yet, in defining this new role for women with legal training, Sorabji diplomatically suggested that they would pose no challenge to the work of male lawyers, saying: 'We need not *supplant* men. There is enough to do if we will *supplement* them.'[85] In her carefully chosen language, Sorabji was identifying legal work for which she was then the only qualified applicant. In addition, it was already clear that her aspirations for a career as a woman lawyer were completely entwined with the needs for legal services of more traditional, less 'civil-ised' Indian women.

However, when Sorabji returned to India in 1893, she found little support for her plan.[86] At that time, both the legal profession and the judiciary reflected the complex hierarchies of imperial administration in India. Thus, barristers trained at the Inns of Court, or in Scotland or Ireland, held a monopoly over practice before the High Courts in the three Presidency towns of Calcutta, Bombay and Madras, and also in Allahabad

Columbia archives, Haweis Family collection, letters from Sorabji to Haweis, 5 March 1893 and 25 March 1893. See also Sorabji's letter to Lionel Haweis, Mary's son, describing her fondness for Rev and Mrs Haweis: 4 September 1938. Sorabji's paper was later published: see above, n 7; and the account of this paper for the Congress on Jurisprudence and Law Reform, held in conjunction with the World's Columbian Exposition in Chicago in 1893, appeared in *The Law Times*, 2 September 1893, at 402–4. See also L Frank, *La Femme-Avocat: Exposé Historique et Critique de la Question* (Paris, V Giard et E Brière, 1898) at 133.

[83] See n 82 at 1 and 7. Sorabji's reference is to the legislation enacted in 1882: see *Married Women's Property Act, 1882*, 45 & 46 Vict, c 75; and L Holcombe, *Wives & Property: Reform of the Married Women's Property Law in Nineteenth-Century England* (Toronto, University of Toronto Press, 1983).

[84] Above, n 82 at 10.

[85] Above, n 82 at 10: Sorabji suggested that 'the man can do the pleading in the Courts of Law, but none but a woman can put in train for him the cases which come from behind the purdah....'

[86] See BL F165/19: letter to Whately, 13 November 1893. According to Paul, some members of the legal profession thought that Sorabji's proposal for women legal advisors was 'either insufficient or impractical because [it] would only serve a negligible percentage of the total litigant population': see JJ Paul, above, n 11 at 159.

where a fourth High Court had been permanently established in the 1860s.[87] Until 1862, when the first Indian barrister was admitted to the Inns of Court, all barristers were British, and even after Indians began to qualify for the bar at the Inns of Court, their numbers increased very gradually.[88] Indeed, according to Daniel Duman, Indian barristers continued to face disadvantages at the bar in India, not only because Europeans received most of the briefs on the original side in the High Court, but also because European barristers were generally preferred by solicitors, many of whom believed that Indian barristers were less likely to win their cases. Thus, at the end of the nineteenth century, business and other 'connections [were] crucial both for native and European barristers' to achieve success, particularly as a result of conditions of overcrowding at the bar.[89] In part, these conditions resulted from recognition of other advocates, particularly the *vakils*, who were similarly entitled to plead in some courts in India. These 'pleaders,' who were predominantly non-Europeans, were much more numerous than barristers, and provided some competition for the bar, even though *vakils* were regarded as inferior in both prestige and income.[90]

The processes for selecting judges for the courts in India also created tensions, especially between advocates and members of the Indian Civil Service. Although legislation enacted in 1861 had identified categories of appointees to the High Courts,[91] Duman reported that by the end of the nineteenth century, most candidates for chief justiceships were still being recruited from the practising bar in Britain, and three quarters of them had spent their entire judicial career in Britain as well. In fact, at that time, only three judges had practised in India prior to being appointed to the bench, and only one, Sir Charles Sargent at the Bombay High Court, had served as chief justice of another colony prior to his appointment in India.[92] Interestingly, it was Chief Justice Sargent at the High Court in Bombay who received Sorabji's initial request in September 1893 to become a legal practitioner for women in *purdah*. By that time close to retirement at the age of seventy-three, Sargent's long experience as an imperial judge may have reinforced his view that law was a profession for men and men alone. Thus, although he was cordial to Sorabji, Chief

---

87 D Duman, above, n 21 at 131. See also JJ Paul, above, n 11.

88 D Duman, above, n 21 at 131–2. The first Indian barrister was G M Tagore, called to the bar of Lincoln's Inn in 1862; by 1885, there were 108 Indian barristers who had been trained in Britain.

89 D Duman, above, n 21 at 132 and 134.

90 See D Duman, above, n 21 at 131. See also JJ Paul, above, n 11 at 5–6, suggesting that 'pleaders never commanded the respect usually accorded to barristers.'

91 See D Duman, above, n 21 at 134–5.

92 D Duman, above, n 21 at 137. Sir Charles Sargent (1821–1900) was educated at King's College, London and at Trinity College, Cambridge; he was called to the bar of Lincoln's Inn in 1848. He was a member (1858–1860) and then Chief Justice (1860–1866) of the Supreme Council of Justice of the Ionian Islands. Appointed a puisne judge of the Bombay High Court in 1866, he was Chief Justice from 1882–1895: see CE Buckland, above, n 67 at 374.

Justice Sargent was firm in his opposition to the idea of women practising law. As Sorabji explained in a letter to Lady Hobhouse:

> I find he is my Arch Enemy. He is a dear old man & very kind & nice socially; but in his profession he is a very Mephistoples (sic) of obstinacy and prejudice.... He owned the sense and need of what I purposed, & he also said that he knew if he but lent me the recognition & protection of the Courts the success of the scheme would be assured beyond doubt – but he baldly affirmed he meant *not* to give such protection or recognition: nothing would induce him.... and the refrain was ... 'You see you are not a man, & no woman should be allowed to meddle with the law....'[93]

This encounter with Chief Justice Sargent in 1893 represented just the beginning of Sorabji's long quest for formal recognition as a member of the legal profession in India.[94] Although individual judges exercised discretion to permit her to represent clients in their courts, Sorabji was unsuccessful in her efforts to gain formal admission as a member of the legal profession. In this context, she focused increasingly on the need to provide legal advice to women in *purdah*, a justification for her work as a lawyer; as she had diplomatically explained in her 1893 speech in Chelsea, women lawyers were needed to *supplement* the services offered by men, not to *supplant* them.[95]

In spite of her discouraging meeting with Chief Justice Sargent, Sorabji initially experienced some support for her legal work. In April 1894, she began work at the firm of Framji and Moss, a solicitors' firm in Bombay. As she reported to Lady Hobhouse, she was provided with two pleasant and private rooms for her work, and her name was added to the firm's listing; Sorabji was also pleased when she received a Muslim woman client in her first week at the firm, particularly when the client expressed satisfaction about being advised by a woman.[96] At the same time, however, Sorabji explained to Lady Hobhouse that her aspirations were changing as a result of her experiences in legal practice. In particular, she expressed dismay about the poor quality of pleading by male counsel, who appeared in court for her clients after she had prepared the files and evidence. Indeed, Sorabji acknowledged that she was now longing to plead cases *herself* in the High Court, a goal which required that she gain formal admission to the bar. Yet, Sorabji's letter reveals the subtle balance neces-

---

93 BL F165/16: letter to Lady Hobhouse, 16 November 1893; the interview with Chief Justice Sargent took place in September in Bombay. See also C Sorabji, *India Calling*, above, n 3 at 55–9; and BL F165/18: letter from Jowett to Sorabji, 6 August 1893.

94 Sorabji's requests were accompanied by personal interviews, and decisions rejecting her requests were communicated by letter, often without detailed legal reasons.

95 C Sorabji, 'The Law of Women's Property in India,' n 82 at 10.

96 See BL F165/16: letters to Lady Hobhouse, January 1894 and 16 February 1894. The timing of Sorabji's activities in *India Calling* is sometimes inconsistent with events described in her letters and diaries; where details conflict, this study relies on the letters and diaries.

sary to explain such ambition on the part of a woman in 1894: as she declared, she was determined to avoid being mistaken for 'An Advanced Woman!' Instead, Sorabji explained how admission to the bar was necessary to achieve her goal of representing women living in *purdah*; nonetheless, Sorabji's concern to avoid criticism for her plan is evident in her pleading tone:

> Should you hate me if things came to such a pass, & think of me instantly as in mental tights with a cigar between my fingers & a non-removable platform under my feet...? Though I have had 'advanced' and wicked yearnings in the direction of the High Court, I should really only be pleading as a *means* to my very legitimate end. Would that improve matters?'[97]

As Sorabji's questions reveal, she wanted to present her aspirations for admission to the bar in terms of her potential clients, *not* as mere personal ambition and *not* as a challenge to male lawyers. Clearly, the legal needs of women living in *purdah* were critical to Sorabji's potential membership in the legal profession.

By this time, Sorabji had also investigated the admission process for the bar in India, and had discovered that she was entitled, as a graduate of Bombay University, to write the university's LLB examinations in November; the admission rules stated that the LLB degree would automatically entitle her to become an advocate in the High Courts in India.[98] In addition to continuing some legal work, therefore, Sorabji began to study for the LLB examinations at Bombay. At the same time, however, she seems to have been aware that the process might not be entirely smooth, and she grasped at every possible opportunity to achieve her goal. For example, in another letter to Lady Hobhouse in August 1894, Sorabji enclosed a 'hypothetical' question for Lord Hobhouse, who was then a member of the Judicial Committee of the Privy Council. Explaining that she had been retained by a woman client whose appeal would be heard by the Privy Council, Sorabji asked rather coyly whether 'those nice kind Law Lords [would] let me tell them all about it myself – & never mind that I grew no wig. *Not* I expect – but it does not hurt anyone to ask the question. They looked so nice and informal sitting around their Council Table....'[99] In justifying her need to take the case to the Privy Council, Sorabji once again emphasised the difficulties experienced by women clients, because their male counsel often refused to 'lift his very small

97 BL F165/16: letter to Lady Hobhouse, 18 April 1894. The reference to cigar-smoking may be to Eliza Orme, who was known to have smoked a cigar with George Gissing, when they met at his publisher's office in 1894. See also Chapter 3, and BL F165/16: letter to Lady Hobhouse, 16 October 1898.
98 BL F165/16: letters to Lady Hobhouse, 20 June 1897 and 19 August 1897.
99 BL F165/16: letter to Lady Hobhouse, 9 August 1894. Lord Hobhouse was then a member of the Judicial Committee of the Privy Council: see above, n 60.

finger in their behalf much less his valuable voice – without heavy "gilding."'[100] Lord Hobhouse must have discouraged Sorabji in relation to an appearance in the Privy Council, because she wrote to thank him for his advice in September 1894, saying 'It *is* sad that even those kind old Law Lords will not smuggle me "within the pale."'[101] However, Sorabji did not give up easily. Frankly acknowledging that recognition by the Privy Council would put her 'years forward' in her work in India, she explained to Lady Hobhouse in January 1895 that she believed 'in doing all things where great matters are at stake.' Thus, Sorabji revealed that she had decided after all to take the appeal case for her client and to make 'a spontaneous request in proper form to the Privy Council' to plead the case herself, arguing that '*doing something* where it can hurt nobody, & *might* benefit somebody, is better than *doing nothing because* there is a likelihood of failure.'[102] In spite of her resolve, however, her case did not proceed as expected, so that Sorabji's plans to gain formal recognition at the bar by appearing in the Privy Council were eventually thwarted.[103]

At the same time, Sorabji was pursuing other applications in India, including a request for an appointment as a commissioner for taking oaths of *purdah* ladies, although she acknowledged that she fully expected that Chief Justice Sargent would reject this application, once again because she was a woman.[104] Yet, by November 1894, Sorabji was beginning to experience some success. She had been given permission to plead in the courts of the Political Agent,[105] and the Baroda government had also given her a *sanad* to plead in the District Court there.[106] Moreover, Sorabji was clearly beginning to enjoy her court appearances. In December 1894, she wrote to Lady Hobhouse:

> Did I tell you that pleading a case was not so very extraordinary an experience after all. It was simply talking to a rather sleepy old judge, across [the counsel] Table – with all one's soul in one's work, & no thought of aught else.... The judge was rather [cynical] at first, & the Court was packed with Vakils, ready I

[100] BL F165/16: letter to Lady Hobhouse, 9 August 1894.

[101] BL F165/16: letter to Lady Hobhouse, 19 September 1894. In this letter, Sorabji identified how women clients were 'too poor to pay heavy Costs and Counsel's fees, & it is for the sake of these one wants to be able to plead....'

[102] BL F165/16: letter to Lady Hobhouse, 4 January 1895; Sorabji acknowledged the invitation to stay with the Hobhouses, and thanked Whately for his help: BL F165/19: letter to Whately, 18 January 1895.

[103] See BL F165/16: letters to Lady Hobhouse, 14 April 1895 and 2 May 1896.

[104] BL F165/16: letter to Lady Hobhouse, 9 August 1894.

[105] Sorabji was probably referring to the Political Agent in the Kathiawar State: see BL F165/16: letter to Lady Hobhouse, 2 November 1894. In *India Calling*, above, n 3 at 65–6, she noted that she was enrolled in the Agencies at Indore (Central India) and Rajkot (Kathiawar).

[106] BL F165/16: letter to Lady Hobhouse, 2 November 1894. As Sorabji noted, 'I knew you would be glad to hear this: and you have *a right* to hear it – seeing it is all owing to you that these widows can be helped at all....'

believe to sneer on any provocation, but everyone was very courteous – and *I have come to the conclusion that work is never intrinsically of any gender, particularly – it is the way in which it is done which classifies it – what think you?*[107]

As her comment suggested, Sorabji still believed that gender was irrelevant to her plans to do legal work in India.

Although it seems that Sorabji's legal work continued to increase throughout 1895, it is possible that she was not experiencing financial success. Perhaps for this reason, she left the firm in Bombay and moved back to her family home in Poona; since her father had died in August 1894, it is also possible that she wanted to be closer to her mother and sisters, who remained involved in education work there.[108] As she reported to Lady Hobhouse, she began to work with a Maratha criminal defence lawyer, Mr Gadgil,[109] and in February 1896, she appeared for the first time in a court in Poona, defending an old woman charged with assisting in making away with stolen property. Sorabji revealed that she had feared opposition to her representation but that 'the Judge accepted [her] as a matter of course.' As she noted, this was 'a great step forward,' especially because the courts in Poona were much stricter than those in the native states where she had previously been appearing.[110] By this time, she was also convinced that pleading involved 'nothing formidable – one forgets to be nervous – indeed one has so completely to identify one's self with the Client, that there is no time or room for a thought for one's self.'[111] By March 1896, Sorabji announced to Lady Hobhouse that she had established her own office in Poona, and was technically designated a 'legal practitioner.'[112] However, her diary entries in early 1896 suggest that she was still continuing to work with Gadgil and that, on his recommendation, she had sought leave to plead in the criminal courts. As a result, Sorabji met with Judge Crowe, the District and Sessions judge, noting in her diary, 'He is decent. Will refer my request re pleading in his courts to the High Court. Advises me to write it – which I come home and do instantly – basing my application on the *Criminal Procedure Code* section 4,' the provision permitting an accused to have 'any person' (defined as male or

107 BL F165/16: letter to Lady Hobhouse, 6 December 1894 (emphasis added). See also BL F165/19: letter to Whately, 18 January 1895.

108 From April 1895, Sorabji's address in her correspondence was her family home, Langrana House, in Poona. See BL F165/56: diary for 1895.

109 Sorabji's diary entries for 1896 often referred to Gadgil: on 4 February, Sorabji and Gadgil 'work[ed] together;' and on 26 February, 'Gadgil says he has cases for me, but I must get Plunket's leave to plead': see BL F165/57: entries for 3 February and 26 February 1896.

110 See BL F165/16: letter to Lady Hobhouse, 13 February 1896. See also BL F165/16: letters to Lady Hobhouse, 10 January 1896 and 18 June 1896.

111 BL F165/16: letter to Lady Hobhouse, 27 February 1896.

112 BL F165/16: letter to Lady Hobhouse, 13 March 1896. See also C Sorabji, *India Calling*, above, n 3 at 97–9.

female) for the defence.[113] Thus, with the permission of the court, Sorabji was retained for the defence in a murder case in July 1896, the case which made her the first woman to plead in a British court in the Empire.

Yet, in spite of the significance of Sorabji's court appearance for the history of women lawyers, it is difficult to determine precisely what happened in this case in Poona in 1896. Sorabji herself described the case at some length in *India Calling*, noting the mendacity of the Indian witnesses and their propensity to accept bribes, and her adversary's sudden decision, when he was faced with a woman opponent, to dress up in English patent leather shoes instead of his usual turned up, red leather Maratha shoes. In her account, she also described the vulnerability of her woman client, charged with murdering her husband, and Sorabji's careful cross-examination of witnesses to reveal flaws in their evidence, particularly in relation to the climatic effects of a monsoon on the night of the murder. Sorabji's account emphasised the judge's excellent charge to the jury and her own agony as she waited for the jury's verdict; and then, when the jury returned a 'not guilty,' how she wanted to hug 'the dear old Foreman!' Thus, the story in *India Calling* clearly identified this case as a significant achievement, not just for her client – but also for her.[114]

However, it appears that the colourful description in *India Calling* was not an accurate description of the murder case in which she appeared for the defence in July 1896. In fact, in a letter to Lady Hobhouse, written shortly after her appearance in a murder case in July, she described her recent appearance in the Sessions Court on behalf of *four* persons accused of murder, a case that was substantially different from the one described in *India Calling*. In her detailed description of the case in the letter to Lady Hobhouse, Sorabji explained that the murder charge arose out of an altercation in which one man had beaten another so severely that the victim had died. Then, the perpetrator had drowned himself, making it impossible to convict him in relation to his violent act. According to Sorabji's letter, 'the Police and the relations of the murdered man [then] ... accused the friends and relations' of the perpetrator. Referring to the witnesses for the prosecution, Sorabji suggested that 'they built up (as you know how they can in India) a most likely story, and strengthened it by three dying declarations....' Although she did not explain her cross-examination in detail, she reported that she made the most of 'some bad and improbable discrepancies.'[115] Interestingly, the description in her letter of the judge's

---

[113] BL F165/57: diary entry for 4 March 1896. See also *Code*, above, n 3; and letters confirming Sorabji's permission to plead as a '*mukhtar*' in the Sessions and Magistrates courts in Poona in BL F165/118: Poona Sessions Court re criminal proceedings, 7 March 1896; City Magistrate, 13 March 1896; and District Magistrate, 25 April 1896.

[114] C Sorabji, *India Calling*, above, n 3 at 59–63. See also BL F165/57: diary entry, 9 July 1896.

[115] See BL F165/16: letter to Lady Hobhouse, 16 July 1896; and C Sorabji, *India Calling*, above, n 3 at 63.

charge to the jury and the return of a 'not guilty' verdict was almost identical to Sorabji's account in *India Calling*. These details also appeared in a diary entry for 3 July 1896, in which Sorabji noted that 'Crowe charges jury *splendidly*: I spend the most awful moments of my life while they are considering. Then they come out, verdict: *not guilty*. Thank God.'[116]

Thus, although there is ample evidence that Sorabji appeared for the defence in a murder case in Poona in July 1896, the precise details of the case are less clear. It is possible that Sorabji's account in *India Calling* represented a 'composite' of several cases in which she was involved in 1896: just a few months before this case, involving a murder charge against four accused in July 1896, she had appeared for the woman charged with assisting with stolen property.[117] Perhaps, Sorabji combined the client from one case with the criminal charge from another, making the story more dramatic for her readers. This possibility is supported by the fact that Sorabji's description of the Maratha pleader's actions, so carefully described in *India Calling*, actually occurred in a case later on in 1896: Sorabji's diary entry for 21 October 1896 included reference to a pleader named Bhore who had removed his Maratha shoes and sent for his patent leather shoes, putting them on 'in the presence of the Assembly' when he discovered that Sorabji was participating in the court proceedings.[118] Thus, Sorabji's account of her first murder case may represent a composite of several of her courtroom experiences in 1896; although it is possible that she was protecting the privacy of her former clients, it is equally likely that Sorabji chose to use her skill as an accomplished story-teller to enliven the drama of her memoirs in *India Calling*. Clearly, her account of the case, which identified for her British readers an innocent woman accused of murder and a scrupulously fair British judge, along with the contrasting characters of an 'uncivilised' Maratha prosecutor and his mendacious witnesses, affirmed the significance of Sorabji's role as a woman lawyer who had fostered British justice in India, particularly for Indian women.[119] In the circumstances, it is possible that Sorabji was consciously recounting the story of her first case in her memoirs in the 1930s to affirm a continuing need for British justice in India in the context of Gandhi's nationalist movement. Yet, notwithstanding the problem of defining the precise details of the case in which Sorabji appeared in July 1896, her accomplishment as the first woman in the Empire to provide represen-

116 BL F165/57: diary entry for 3 July 1896.
117 BL F165/16: letter to Lady Hobhouse, 13 February 1896. In his report of the case, Frank indicated that Sorabji achieved acquittals for 'all her clients,' suggesting that she acted for multiple accused: see L Frank, above, n 82 at 67–8, quoting *Bombay Champion*, 31 July 1896.
118 BL F165/57: diary entry for 21 October 1896.
119 See C Sorabji, *India Calling*, above, n 3 at 65; and BL F165/16: letters to Lady Hobhouse, 16 July 1896 and 23 August 1896. Sorabji expressed the wish to 'grow grey in pleading the cause of justice.'

tation for an accused on a murder charge in a British court seems clearly established.

Moreover, Sorabji's success in this murder case was followed by other achievements in 1896. Judge Crowe continued to permit her to appear in criminal cases in Poona,[120] and in August of that year, she obtained permission to practise in the Court of the Agent to the Governor General and all other courts in Central India.[121] Then, in late November, shortly after her thirtieth birthday, she went to Bombay for the second level of examinations for the LLB degree, and was clearly delighted to announce her success to Lady Hobhouse in early January 1897:

> This is a very scraggy (sic) and telegraphic mail, to carry to you a single piece of intelligence. The final Bachelor of Laws Lists are just out, and I am now a fully fledged *LLB* .... I shall be convoked shortly, & be given a gorgeous scarlet hood. The best of the examination is that it is the regular Bar Examination in India, & *I shall now be admitted to the Courts as of right, & not by courtesy. The question is fought at last I hope for all women.*[122]

As Sorabji explained more fully to Lady Hobhouse a few months later, the LLB examinations at Bombay University constituted the Indian bar examination, thus conferring on her the right to plead in all District and Session courts, as well as on the appellate side of the High Court in Bombay.[123] More importantly, her new status permitted her to participate effectively in civil proceedings relevant to issues of property and succession for women in *purdah*. Indeed, in early 1897, Sorabji travelled again to some of the native states, describing a number of cases involving maintenance petitions for dowager *Thakranis*, and her efforts to overcome the legal problems they experienced as a result of the resumption of their lands by the government.[124]

However, by June 1897, Sorabji was again experiencing frustration and discouragement. As she explained to Lady Hobhouse, she had been

[120] See BL F165/57: diary entry for 20 November 1896: 'Make application re the ... case. Crowe hears me but "sees no reason to interfere."' As Sorabji confirmed, 'criminal cases are as a rule "poor"': BL F165/16: letter to Lady Hobhouse, 3 February 1897.

[121] See BL F165/16: letter to Lady Hobhouse, 23 August 1896; and BL F165/118.

[122] BL F165/16: letter to Lady Hobhouse, 8 January 1897 (emphasis added). Sorabji's diary entries for 1895 and 1896 reveal that she went to Bombay in late November or December in both of these years; it seems that she wrote both the LLB I examinations and the LLB II examinations in 1895, and then went to Bombay again in 1896 to (re)write the LLB II examinations: BL F165/56, entries for 22 November to 27 November; and F165/57, entries for 30 November to 2 December. The diary entry for 20 December 1895 suggests that she may have failed the LLB II examinations in 1895. Sorabji obtained the LLB degree, second division: see BL F165/116, LLB degree 5 April 1897; the *Englishwoman's Review*, above, n 1 at 217–18, (incorrectly) reported that Sorabji attained the LLB degree with first class honours.

[123] BL F165/16: letter to Lady Hobhouse, 5 March 1897.

[124] BL F165/16: letter to Lady Hobhouse, 3 February 1897. According to Sorabji, at the death of a Raja, the government resumed the widow's 'life interest,' providing a money payment compensation.

precluded from submitting an application for formal admission to the bar until after her university convocation, and the 1897 convocation at Bombay University had been postponed until April as a result of plague that year. By then, the courts were not in session because of the hot weather, so that her application was not actually filed until June.[125] She waited for a decision for several weeks, and finally, in August, Sorabji received a letter from the new Chief Justice, who had replaced Sargent, with news that the High Court in Bombay had rejected her application. According to Sorabji, the judges conceded that they would have had no hesitation in admitting Sorabji herself; their concerns related to 'those who are to follow.' Thus, even though they expressed sympathy for Sorabji's wish to provide legal services to women in *purdah*, the judges were prepared to admit her only if they could do so 'without making a precedent.' In her report to Lady Hobhouse, Sorabji criticised the judges' reasoning, noting that the rules of the High Court permitted three groups to be admitted to the rolls: barristers (of the Inns of Court); LLBs of Bombay University; and those who passed the pleaders' (*vakils*) examinations. Sorabji argued that she had obtained the LLB degree from Bombay University, and that the university's degrees were known to be open to women as well as men, so that the High Court should not, belatedly, have introduced a sex barrier to those who obtained the degree qualification. As she put it, 'the High Court knew or ought to have known that the University was so open, and had it so wished, might have made a special rule excluding women LLBs. It has not done this: & for the present, must face the equitable consequences of its own rule.'[126] Yet, even after an interview with the Chief Justice, the court's decision remained unchanged. As Sorabji noted caustically, the Chief Justice had suggested that the court would receive her with pleasure if she were to 'eat [her] dinners at the Inns [of Court in Britain]: ... a thing he deems an impossibility, & is therefore generous about!'[127] As she had lamented a few months earlier, 'it is hard to be the first person to fight a big question, & to have to fight it practically alone too.'[128]

In the midst of this new quandary, Sorabji appealed to Lord Hobhouse for advice once again. As she explained, she was very alone, with 'no one to help me, or fight for me.' Significantly, she said that she had no support from the Parsi community because she was Christian, and thus her '*community* [was] limited to the individuals who [composed her] immediate family.'[129] By 1897, Sorabji may have felt even more alone; her father was

---

[125] BL F165/16: letter to Lady Hobhouse, 20 June 1897.
[126] BL F165/16: letter to Lady Hobhouse, 19 August 1897. Apparently, Lord Hobhouse counselled patience: see BL F165/16: letter to Lady Hobhouse, 12 October 1897.
[127] BL F165/16: letter to Lady Hobhouse, 19 August 1897; and BL F165/118, letter from the Registrar of the High Court at Bombay, 16 July 1897.
[128] BL F165/16: letter to Lady Hobhouse, 20 June 1897.
[129] BL F165/16: letter to Lady Hobhouse, 19 August 1897.

dead, and she was then separated from her mother and sisters as well, having moved to Allahabad to share an office with her barrister brother, Richard. However, she was determinedly hopeful about the move to Allahabad, believing that it offered greater opportunities than 'any other part of India' for legal work on behalf of women in *purdah*. As she noted in a letter to Lady Hobhouse, a leader at the bar in Allahabad had already advised her that he had many *purdah* cases: 'wills & deeds unduly influenced; acts of all kinds wrongly presumed to be authorized by *purdah* ladies of property who are at the mercy of men who swear to the registrar that they are their authorized agents ... & such like.'[130] In this context, Sorabji applied for admission to the High Court in Allahabad in March 1897. At first, the court rejected her application, stating that Sorabji did not have the qualifications for admission as either an advocate or *vakil*; in a letter to Lady Hobhouse, Sorabji surmised that the court had rejected her application because women did not practise law in Britain, suggesting that the judges had worried 'how can we go faster than England?' Once again, the problem was the absence of precedent.[131] However, in response to a second request from Sorabji, the court's registrar responded in May 1897, stating that its rules did not permit any 'special cases.' Significantly, however, the registrar added:

> I am ... to point out that you appear to be entitled under the rules of the 18th March 1895 to go up for the *vakils* examination to be held in December next....'[132]

Not surprisingly, Sorabji was initially disconsolate to receive this response to her application. In her report to Lady Hobhouse, she said 'You can imagine my disappointment. *Another* examination, & after all it might not bring me the privileges which every fifth rate Babu, who has had no training beyond a school one, can claim.'[133]

For Sorabji, the requirement to pass the *vakil* examination meant another two years, and although she was confident of her legal knowledge, the *vakil* qualification in Allahabad required her to pass an examination in the Urdu language as well. She again sought advice from Lord and Lady Hobhouse: was it preferable to return to Poona, where she would still not

---

[130] BL F165/16: letter to Lady Hobhouse, 20 June 1897; this letter was written from Allahabad. Richard had moved to Allahabad in March 1897, and she then joined him because there was an abundance of *purdah* cases at Allahabad.

[131] BL F165/16: letter to Lady Hobhouse, 20 June 1897. Sorabji applied to the Allahabad High Court on 29 March 1897, and her application was rejected on 14 April 1897; she then submitted a further application on 27 April 1897, noting her special circumstances: see BL F165/118.

[132] BL F165/118: letter from the Registrar of the Allahabad High Court, 10 May 1897.

[133] BL F165/16: letter to Lady Hobhouse, 20 June 1897. See also C Sorabji, 'Babuisms' (1901) 124 *Temple Bar* 376 at 377–8.

be able to practise by right, or remain in Allahabad and work outside the courts, assisting her brother until she could obtain the *vakil* qualification? Her financial situation was likely to remain precarious in either case, since clients preferred to be advised by someone who could also plead on their behalf; even in relation to *Purdahnashins*, it would be difficult to become known to potential clients without access to the courts. As she poignantly explained, 'I cannot afford to risk an experiment, being dependent solely on any income which I may make for myself.'[134] At the same time, she continued to be enthusiastic about legal work, suggesting 'there *is* a need for the kind of work for which I have been preparing myself – all I want is *leave to do it*.'[135] Indeed, as she complained, 'What aggravates me is that the Judges own the necessity of my legal existence, and yet will not help me to justify it.'[136]

In due course, Sorabji received Lord Hobhouse's advice to submit to the court's decision, and she then began to study, once again. In December 1897, she successfully passed the *vakil* examinations. Although there were no preparatory classes for students, and the ten papers of three hours each were 'very stiff,' she reported that she was one of only thirteen candidates, out of a field of sixty, who had passed. As she explained, however, she could not be enrolled formally for a year, until she had received the Urdu certificate.[137] In the meantime, however, she was gratified to be able to continue to work on *purdah* cases, many of which would not be ready for pleading until the following year when she expected to be fully qualified. Eventually, in December 1898, she also passed the Urdu test, declaring that she was 'so happy & so tired, & I feel so emancipated! I don't think any success has given me more pleasure, possibly because none has been so great a *gamble*; unless they invent new [barriers], the very last is *taken*.'[138] At the same time, Sorabji was pleased about the publication of her article on women's legal status in India in *The Nineteenth Century* in November 1898; she had augmented her 1893 speech in London with examples from her legal work in the native states to demonstrate the need for legal advisors for women in *purdah*.[139] Sorabji was particularly gratified when an experienced Indian administrator declared that 'no need could have been better stated; & that no suggestions for meeting it could be sounder.'[140] Finally, it

---

134 BL F165/16: letter to Lady Hobhouse, 20 June 1897. See also BL F165/16: letter to Lady Hobhouse, 21 July 1898, confirming her interest in doing 'journalistic work.'
135 BL F165/16: letter to Lady Hobhouse, 4 July 1897.
136 BL F165/16: letter to Lady Hobhouse, 19 August 1897.
137 BL F165/16: letter to Lady Hobhouse, 20 January 1898. See also BL F165/20: letters to Mrs Darling, 20 January 1898 and 30 January 1898.
138 BL F165/16: letter to Lady Hobhouse, 22 December 1898.
139 C Sorabji, 'The Legal Status of Women in India,' n 7; Sorabji confirmed that this article was an 'enlargement of the one I read long ago at Mrs Haweis' on the law': BL F165/16: letter to Lady Hobhouse, 12 October 1897.
140 BL F165/16: letters to Lady Hobhouse, 8 December 1898 and 22 December 1898.

seemed, Sorabji had reason for optimism about her prospects in the legal profession in India.

However, a few months before Sorabji's application for admission as a *vakil* of the High Court in Allahabad could be processed, a new Chief Justice, Arthur Strachey, was appointed to the court. Sorabji described him as 'charming personally,' but as she also noted, Strachey had 'a deeply rooted prejudice on the subject of women lawyers, or women anything unusual.'[141] Thus, she breathed a sigh of relief that she had completed her examinations prior to his arrival, and that she had the assurance of the court's 1897 letter, stating in writing that she would be eligible for admission if she passed the *vakil* examinations. She was also comforted when other judges on the Allahabad High Court indicated that the matter of her eligibility for admission had been completely settled prior to Chief Justice Strachey's arrival.[142] At the same time, Sorabji continued to provide reassurance to Lady Hobhouse about her plans for legal practice, suggesting that she realised that 'folk who don't know me, think I mean to be a kind of Miss Orme, & put in train ugly divorce proceedings – than which nothing of course is wider than the mark....'[143] Clearly, Sorabji wanted to reassure her friends, as well as the court at Allahabad, that *her* goals for legal practice were entirely reasonable.

Later that year, she finally received her Urdu certificate and immediately submitted her request for admission to the Allahabad High Court. Weeks passed without any response from the court. Perhaps to relieve her own fears, Sorabji forwarded a detailed account of her situation to Lady Hobhouse in March 1899, once again requesting Lord Hobhouse's advice. In doing so, Sorabji suggested that she could claim that the High Court had made a promise to her, evidenced by the letter suggesting that she was eligible to take the *vakil* examinations, and that she had relied on it to her detriment, wasting two years in obtaining qualifications which were otherwise useless to her. Her frustration was clearly evident:

> All I seek is honest work & the chance of helping my own sex, and it seems incredible that it should be so difficult in the getting, especially in this country where there are no old conservative bodies who are trammelled by long-estab-

---

[141] BL F165/16: letter to Lady Hobhouse, 30 June 1898. Strachey graduated from Trinity Hall, Cambridge, was called to the bar in 1883, and practised at the Allahabad High Court. He became a Public Prosecutor in the NWP and was then appointed a puisne judge of the Bombay High Court in 1895. He became Chief Justice of the Allahabad High Court in 1899 at the age of forty one, and died two years later: CE Buckland, above, n 67 at 406.

[142] BL F165/16: letter to Lady Hobhouse, 30 June 1898. Sorabji reported that her friend on the High Court, Justice H F Blair, had explained to Chief Justice Strachey that 'the question was settled before he came & he cannot touch it.'

[143] See BL F165/16: letter to Lady Hobhouse, 16 October 1898. The reference is probably to Eliza Orme's assistance to the novelist, George Gissing, in obtaining a legal separation from his second wife; Orme so recommended in early 1898: see J Halperin, *Gissing: A Life in Books* (Oxford, Oxford University Press, 1987) at 267–72, see above, pp 150–52.

lished rules & customs, & can't easily be liberal-minded, even if they would....
Where then is the rub? When too, the need for women workers is also acknowledged – Pure *cussedness*, I fear.[144]

A month later in April 1899, Sorabji's worst fears were confirmed when
the court voted to reject her application. In a letter to Lady Hobhouse, she
described herself as 'stunned & bruised & hurt' by the decision, because it
represented so clearly 'faith not kept with an individual.' As her words
revealed, Sorabji clearly distinguished her case from decisions which
refused to admit women to the bar as a matter of principle. Relying on the
letter from the Registrar of the High Court in May 1897, Sorabji claimed
that she had acted on a promise that she would be admitted if she passed
the *vakil* examinations, and that the Court's decision to reject her application in the end represented a fundamental betrayal of her trust as an
individual:

> I have no quarrel with the HC or with any HC because on general grounds it
> objects to women or because though its rules do not exclude them *nomine*, it
> still refuses them admittance – that is, and would be regrettable – one would
> rant at the prejudice, but understand it, be lenient to it – forgive it. Mine is a
> far, different case....[145]

In explaining the adverse decision to Lady Hobhouse, Sorabji acknowledged that one of the five judges, as well as the new Chief Justice, had
always been opposed to women lawyers; however, she knew that the other
four judges had all initially favoured her admission. Yet, when the matter
came up for consideration by the court, Sorabji understood that the only
Indian judge, a Bengali, had 'ratted' and voted with the Chief Justice and
the judge who was opposed to women in law. As a result, there were three
votes in favour and three against her admission, and so the Chief Justice
had cast a deciding vote: *against* Sorabji's application. Sorabji met with the
Chief Justice, but found him 'obdurate.' In the context of this formal
rejection of her application after so much hard work, she revealed the
depth of her personal anguish in a request for Lord Hobhouse's advice
about appealing to the Privy Council:

> The thing *must* be fought out for if let alone, it damns the whole question for-
> ever. It leaves it in a *far worse* position than had I never girt up my loins &
> faced those two tests.... Of the personal side of the question I *daren't* speak. You
> will understand what it must mean to me.... And the fact that we all thought the
> matter fought & done with makes it the harder: Every day since the HC sent me
> what I thought its ultimatum in '97, I've felt 'Tis one day nearer,' & the cruel

---

[144] BL F165/16: letter to Lady Hobhouse, 24 March 1899.
[145] BL F165/16: letter to Lady Hobhouse, 13 April 1899.

dashing of it all at first felt too dreadful to realize. I am realizing it now – *alas*! – and my one thought is – I must not be a *coward*. I must face & do the 'nextye thyngs'... – only, all the *rebound* seems sapped out of me. Ah! 'tis hard of fate. I have paid the penalty to the uttermost farthing & shirked nothing.... If all fails, I must give up the legal idea, & seek other work, but at present I feel as if that would break my heart....[146]

In the face of this profound setback, Sorabji described herself as 'on a perpetual see-saw of hope & depression.' She initially expressed dismay when a report of her rejected application was published in an Indian news-paper, especially because it was followed by 'garbled versions & undesirable reflections in papers of every degree of reliability.' As she explained, she was advised to write to the paper herself, and she did so, even though she claimed that it felt 'like holding up the broken stump of a right hand that a street public might peer.'[147] However, her report of the court's actions also produced sympathetic publicity about her situation, and some newspapers criticised the decision of the Allahabad High Court for missing the oppor-tunity to respond more imaginatively to an application for admission to the bar submitted by a woman:

The *Pioneer*, in discussion of the probable reason for the refusal [of Sorabj's application] says: 'For one thing, until the Inns of Court at home sanction the admission of lady barristers, it would seem odd that any Indian Court, presided over by an English barrister should lead the way. Miss Sorabji, moreover, had been refused in Bombay, and yet her admission by the Allahabad Court would have permitted her to practise in all the subordinate courts throughout the Bom-bay Presidency. Finally, Allahabad is the junior High Court in India, and no doubt felt a certain diffidence about rushing in where its elders have hitherto feared to tread.' The excuse for the failure to do an act of justice simply because others had refused to do it is a lame one at the very best.... The plea that Allahabad is the junior court of India goes for nothing, as that court had thrown away a splendid opportunity of showing an independent youthfulness of old fogeydom, and preferred the flowing tide of progress instead....[148]

In addition to public support, moreover, Sorabji was pleased to find that the Allahabad bar was not opposing her admission as a *vakil*. Perhaps as a result of her reputation in the native states, she also received an offer from the Maharajah of Rajputana to organise a petition from the Princes of India to the government, but Sorabji explained to Lady Hobhouse that she had declined as it seemed 'too much like an advertisement, & I am not "Colman's Mustard."' In the same letter, she explained that she was con-

---

[146] BL F165/16: letter to Lady Hobhouse, 13 April 1899.
[147] BL F165/16: letter to Lady Hobhouse, 3 May 1899.
[148] 'Our Lady Lawyer,' *Telegraph and Deccan Herald*: BL F165/16; and letters to Lady Hobhouse, 3 May 1899 and 6 July 1899.

sidering asking 'someone of authority in England,' perhaps Sir William Markby, to write a letter to the papers to support her.[149] She had also been expressly advised to write to Mrs Fawcett about her case.[150] As well, she remained interested in the possibility of an appeal to a higher court, although she later reluctantly agreed with the advice of Lord Hobhouse that the court's discretion on admission matters would effectively preclude appellate review.[151] At the same time, in spite of its publicity value, a question in the British Parliament resulted in Sorabji expressing annoyance because it had been posed 'in the very wrongest way,' failing to reflect the court's explicit promise to *her* and her *special* entitlement to admission.[152]

For several months, Sorabji continued to seek reconsideration of the decision of the Allahabad High Court. In doing so, however, she attempted to avoid criticism of her assertiveness, making frequent references to the fact that she enjoyed the enthusiastic support of the three judges who had voted in favour of her application for admission as a *vakil*, and that they approved of her action.[153] Yet, in spite of considerable support, there was no reconsideration of the High Court's decision. In the circumstances, Sorabji's future in 1899 looked increasingly precarious, even bleak. As she explained to Lady Hobhouse, although she had made enough money in Bombay and Poona to 'keep her going,' her fees had often been 'docked by the middle man' on whom she was reliant for work, a situation which resulted from her lack of recognition by the courts; thus, a return to Bombay or Poona appeared unpromising. She had also decided to decline an offer of work from a barrister at Lucknow because she had no income of her own to set up a house separate from her brother. Moreover, even her chamber work was becoming tenuous because, without being on the rolls, she was concerned about being classified as a tout, 'a class much despised & rightly, for many malpractices.'[154]

Thus, perhaps reluctantly, Sorabji began to look for other work. She initiated inquiries about an appointment as a Revenue Agent, but received a negative response in September 1899.[155] Moreover, even though she had been recognised three years earlier in Poona as a 'lady barrister' pursuant to the *Criminal Procedure Code*, Sorabji's opportunities to undertake criminal cases were suddenly foreclosed when the Magistrates Court in

---

[149] BL F165/16: letter to Lady Hobhouse, 3 May 1899.

[150] BL F165/16: letter to Lady Hobhouse, 6 July 1899.

[151] BL F165/16: letter to Lord Hobhouse, 1 June 1899. According to S Gooptu, above, n 1 at 113–14, an appeal to the Privy Council was unsuccessful; however, it seems that there was no formal appeal.

[152] BL F165/16: letter to Lady Hobhouse, 6 July 1899. After learning that the Parliamentary question was asked by H Roberts, a man unknown to Sorabji, she said 'Save me from my (would-be) friends!'

[153] BL F165/16: letter to Lady Hobhouse, 20 July 1899.

[154] BL F165/16: letters to Lady Hobhouse, 3 May 1899 and 6 July 1899.

[155] BL F165/118: letter to Sorabji, 26 September 1899; as she was not qualified as a pleader and had not passed the examinations for a Revenue Agent, she was not eligible for appointment.

Allahabad decided that it could not act 'in a way that would be contradictory of the High Court;' since the High Court had concluded that
Sorabji was not eligible to be a *vakil*, the magistrates concluded that they
were no longer authorised to exercise discretion to permit her to plead in
criminal law cases.[156] Thus, in spite of her achievement only three years
earlier in Poona, Sorabji concluded that 'absolutely every door is shut to
me.'[157] The depth of her discouragement was evident in a letter to her old
friend Henry Whately at the firm of Lee and Pemberton in London, asking
whether the firm would offer her work and promising that she would
'*slave* heart & soul' for them. Reiterating her query a few weeks later, she
posed the question bluntly:

> Have you room for me at the office? And, could you make use of me? Perhaps
> the Inns would give me the title, denied by the HC.... At any rate, I want, for
> the present, only to keep myself going – & let my brain simmer in your pecu-
> liarly desirable intellectual atmosphere – in the hope of *waiting*.... I think you
> know my personal circumstances, & that I cannot afford to wait on opportu-
> nity forever.... I expect 'tis a case of Moses & the promised land. I must be
> content to have pointed the way – others will enter into possession.... Perhaps *if*
> you had no room in the office itself, you might know of someone who wants a
> Secretary.[158]

Obviously concerned, Whately contacted Lord Hobhouse, who responded
that he thought that Sorabji should give up her efforts to gain admission to
the High Court, and 'return to the more humble but safer and more
promising course in which she started.'[159]

In fact, Sorabji had never abandoned her commitment to provide legal
services to women living in *purdah*. Moreover, as she explained in a letter
to Whately, she was doing her best 'not to relinquish [her] plans till absolutely *everything* fails,'[160] although Sorabji was clearly struggling to find a
way to implement her plan effectively. As she stated pointedly in a letter to
Lord Hobhouse in June 1899, the problem was *how* to achieve her goal of
providing legal services to women living in *purdah*: if admission to plead in
the courts was foreclosed, an alternative was a governmental appointment:

> Would Government create a position [of] Adviser to women & Infant Wards in
> Bengal, Oudh & the NWP? That it would be the very opening which I want is
> undeniable: that it would meet a great need in the country – is also I think
> beyond contention. Perhaps it would be the very best way of getting to work.

---

[156] BL F165/118: letters to Sorabji, 4 July 1899 and 5 July 1899. See also BL F165/19: letter to
Whately, 22 June 1899.
[157] BL F165/16: letter to Lady Hobhouse, 20 July 1899.
[158] BL F165/19: letters to Whately, 25 April 1899 and 4 May 1899.
[159] BL F165/19: letter from Hobhouse to Whately, 18 May 1899.
[160] BL F165/19: letter to Whately, 4 May 1899.

But how is it to be accomplished? Help me to answer that, please, dear Lord Hobhouse.[161]

With other options for legal work no longer available, Sorabji began to pursue the possibility of a governmental appointment as a special legal advisor to the Court of Wards, the administrative agency responsible for ensuring the well-being of widows, and minor children, in northern India. Yet, in the context of the bureaucracy of imperial administration in India, Sorabji feared that such an appointment would not be created without difficulty. Indeed, her initial inquiries suggested that the Court of Wards did not 'feel itself powerful enough to *create* a post ... and the *executive* [branch was] always *timid* about acting.'[162] Thus, in addition to requesting advice about such an appointment from Lord Hobhouse, Sorabji herself continued to pursue her goal. She eagerly accepted an offer from another British friend for financial assistance to enable her to go to Simla to submit her petition in person to the government, and to lobby for the creation of a special position of adviser to women in *purdah*.[163] However, recognising that the success of a petition would probably depend on wider public support, she continued to request help from Lady Hobhouse, urging 'If you know the Curzons [Viceroy of India], or anyone who knows them, it would be kind of you to ask them to be good to me.'[164] Perhaps in response to such requests, Lady Hobhouse requested that 'the urgent need' of female lawyers for India be reported at the meeting of the International Council of Women, which took place in London in July 1899:

[Lady Hobhouse] did not think anyone knew how isolated the women of India were at present. They were debarred from speaking in the courts, and she did not see how they could have justice done them unless there were female lawyers who could come and see them in their homes. The International Council could do no better work for the women of India than to advance the appointment of women lawyers.[165]

Sorabji also attempted to obtain professional support for her plan in India, travelling to speak at a meeting of the Punjab Law Society in September 1899, and recording that the members were 'kind and sympathetic,' although they firmly recommended that her plan be implemented in Bengal or the NWP, but not in Punjab.[166]

161 BL F165/16: letter to Lord Hobhouse, 1 June 1899.
162 BL F165/16: letter to Lady Hobhouse, 3 May 1899.
163 BL F165/16: letter to Lady Hobhouse, 1 June 1899.
164 BL F165/16: letter to Lady Hobhouse, 10 August 1899.
165 *International Council of Women: Report of Transactions of the Second Quinquennial Meeting, London, July 1899* (London, T Fisher Unwin, 1900) at 132. Lady Hobhouse's views were included in the national report on India presented by Flora Annie Steel.
166 BL F165/16: letter to Lady Hobhouse, 5 October 1899. The Punjab Law Society reconsidered Sorabji's plans at a meeting in May 1903: see *Punjab Law Society Journal*, BL F165/120.

As her situation deteriorated financially in 1899, Sorabji faced an increasingly urgent need to obtain paid work. As her letters revealed, she was considering the prospect of giving up legal work altogether to take a position as an inspectress of schools, an option which she described as putting on 'the *green goggles*!' Although she lamented that she could 'weep at the thought,' she also recognised that she must find paying work by the end of the year.[167] However, it seems that Lady Hobhouse again provided a reprieve with a gift of further financial assistance, as Sorabji wrote to her in November 1899 to thank her profusely for her generosity, and made plans to press her case for a government appointment with officials in Calcutta at Christmas.[168] In the meantime, she kept busy assisting nurses as a member of the local Dufferin Committee, reporting that she was 'studying home remedies with a vengeance!' In November 1899, Sorabji also reported meeting Sara Jeanette Duncan, the Canadian journalist and author who had arrived at Allahabad with her husband; and Sorabji carefully noted Duncan's success in using her experiences in India in her writing.[169] In addition to these other activities, however, Sorabji continued to take on legal advice work for women in *purdah*, even though it paid little or nothing, and she began to publish accounts of her work to demonstrate the urgent need for legal services among Indian women. For example, the *Nineteenth Century* published her sensational story about rescuing an imprisoned *rani* in 1901;[170] it not only provided financial support but also confirmed Sorabji's unwavering faith in British justice. As she had confidently explained when she set out on her admittedly dangerous rescue mission, she was confident that 'no one dare touch me as I come from British India.'[171]

However, by early 1900, Sorabji had received a discouraging response to her lobbying efforts in Calcutta. Although she was relieved to learn that the Chief Justice there had realised that she was not a 'shrieking sister,'[172] he had offered no practical assistance at all. Moreover, her efforts to engage the bishop's assistance to speak to Lord Curzon and her own interviews

---

[167] BL F165/16: letters to Lady Hobhouse, 15 August 1899 and 5 October 1899. See also BL F165/20: letters to Lady Darling, 27 July 1899, 3 August 1899, 7 August 1899 and 15 August 1899.

[168] BL F165/16: letter to Lady Hobhouse, 21 November 1899; Sorabji sounded relieved that with Lady Hobhouse's 'kind benefaction,' she would not have to wear the 'green goggles.'

[169] BL F165/16: letter to Lady Hobhouse, 27 November 1899. See also M Fowler, *Redney: A Life of Sara Jeannette Duncan* (Toronto, Anansi, 1983).

[170] C Sorabji, 'Concerning an Imprisoned Rani' (1901) 50 *Nineteenth Century* 623. This story was retold in *India Calling*, above, n 3 at 105–15; and see BL F165/16: letters to Lady Hobhouse, 15 August 1899 and 5 October 1899.

[171] BL F165/20: letters to Lady Darling, 15 August 1899 and 24 October 1899. Sorabji assured Lady Darling that she understood that her task was dangerous and had 'left last words.'

[172] 'Shrieking sister' was a derogatory term for suffragists, apparently coined by Mrs Lynn Linton; in return, Sarah Grand, an English novelist, characterised the opponents of women's suffrage as 'the bawling brotherhood': see S Coney, *Standing in the Sunshine: A History of New Zealand Women since They Won the Vote* (Auckland, Viking Press, 1993) at 27.

with other British officials had resulted in no concrete help.[173] By March 1900, completely discouraged about obtaining legal work, she once again decided to put on the 'green goggles,' although when she later discovered that all the Inspectress posts had already been filled, she did not sound entirely disconsolate.[174] By this time, she reported that she had a number of writing projects underway, including a legal monograph, and was grateful to have received permission to use the High Court library at Allahabad for her research.[175] She also reported intermittently about ongoing discussions concerning a challenge to the High Court's decision. In July 1900, for example, Sorabji acknowledged receiving a kind letter from Louis Frank, the Belgian barrister who had been supportive of the admission of women lawyers in Europe. In his letter, Frank described his efforts to assist Jeanne Chauvin to be admitted to the bar in Paris and he generously offered his assistance to Sorabji as well. By this time, Sorabji had decided that it was time to 'let others fight the question' and thus, she had promised to forward details of her case to him.[176] At the same time, she declared to Lady Hobhouse that she was no longer 'worrying about the rolls.... The "forty years" must end some time – for others certainly, if not for me.'[177]

For the remainder of 1900, Sorabji continued 'to advise when opportunity' arose although, as she acknowledged, many of her cases continued to be 'in the credit account with Heaven list' in terms of financial compensation. She also 'scribble[d] when inspired' and kept house for her brother, who was prospering.[178] In February 1901, however, she wrote to Lady Hobhouse and, after expressing sadness about the death of Queen Victoria, mentioned that she might be visiting Britain again.[179] Although it is difficult to know precisely why Sorabji returned to Britain in 1901, it is possible that she hoped that her personal presence would better promote her plans for a governmental appointment to advise women in *purdah*. She may also have wanted to be in Britain to look for opportunities for publishing her articles and short stories. As well, there is some evidence that her health had broken down and that her living arrangements with her brother may have become unsuitable.[180] In any event, it is clear that Sorabji did not have a substantial legal practice in Allahabad to detain her.

---

173 BL F165/17: letter to Lady Hobhouse, 4 January 1900.
174 BL F165/17: letters to Lady Hobhouse, 21 March 1900 and 12 April 1900.
175 BL F165/17: letters to Lady Hobhouse, 17 July 1900 and 6 December 1900.
176 BL F165/17: letter to Lady Hobhouse, 17 July 1900. Sorabji noted that she had received the letter 'some time ago' and had not yet acknowledged it because she 'was not quite sure how far one might court public and strange advocacy.' See also L Frank, above, n 82.
177 BL F165/17: letter to Lady Hobhouse, 14 September 1900.
178 BL F165/17: letter to Lady Hobhouse, 6 December 1900. Sorabji acknowledged that she had hated housekeeping at first, but that she was now keeping the house 'quite nicely;' she then said ''tis a pity I shall never marry for I should be quite a treasure to any man.....'
179 BL F165/17: letter to Lady Hobhouse, 13 February 1901.
180 In *India Calling*, above, n 3 at 117, Sorabji explained that she experienced a breakdown in her health and was ordered by her doctors to leave India; in a letter to HF Blair, her friend

Lord and Lady Hobhouse must have supported her plans because, by May 1901, she was once again in Britain and staying with them. She visited other friends as well, while finalising proofs for her first collection of short stories, *Love and Life Behind the Purdah*; it appeared in late November 1901, with an introductory comment from Lord Hobhouse about the need for legal advice for women living in *purdah* in India.[181] By the time Sorabji's book appeared, Lord Hobhouse had leased a flat for her in London for some months so that she could continue her lobbying for a governmental appointment.[182] In addition, Lord Hobhouse had recommended that Sorabji be permitted to use the library at Lincoln's Inn for her legal research on *Purdahnashins*.[183] Sorabji's efforts culminated in the publication of her detailed letter to *The Times* on 26 September 1902, outlining the legal problems of women living in *purdah* and her proposal for meeting their needs.[184] Sorabji's prodigious talent for organising effective support was clearly evident in the letters she received from a number of friends.[185] In addition, her proposal received public support: for example, the *Englishwoman's Review* reported in detail on the contents of Sorabji's letter to *The Times*, describing the problems of enforcing rights of property, succession and maintenance for Indian women, and reinforcing Sorabji's recommendation for reforms which fully accorded with traditions in India. Quoting Sorabji, the review asked:

who was a judge at Allahabad, she explained that she was receiving treatment for rheumatic gout: BL F165/21: letter to HF Blair, 17 October 1901. In letters to Blair, Sorabji also noted the breakdown in her relationship with her brother, which may also have contributed to her decision to leave Allahabad: see BL F165/21: letters of 13 June 1901 and 12 December 1901.

181 BL F165/21: letter to HF Blair, 21 May 1901. Sorabji's letters to Blair suggest a warm friendship. Lord Hobhouse had initially refused her invitation to write an introduction, saying that her outlook was too gloomy and that her tales presented 'a picture of life that was quite untrue;' his published comments avoided views about Sorabji's stories, but asserted a need for legal advice for *Purdahnashins* in India: see BL F165/17: letter from Lord Hobhouse, 26 September 1901.

182 BL F165/21: letter to HF Blair, 3 October 1901. Lord Hobhouse apparently leased the flat for his daughter Emily, who was involved in supporting the Boers in South Africa; Sorabji and her sister Alice were permitted to live there until Emily's return: letter to HF Blair, 15 November 1901.

183 BL F165/17: letter from Lord Hobhouse, November 1902. Lord Hobhouse reassured the Benchers that Sorabji was well-accustomed to working in a male environment, and that her request constituted a 'special order for special indulgence under highly peculiar circumstances.' Sorabji's use of the library at Lincoln's Inn was reported at the International Congress of Women in Toronto: see E Spencer Mussey, 'The Woman Attorney and Counsellor' in *Report of the International Congress of Women, held in Toronto 24th – 30th June 1909*, vol II (Toronto, Geo Parker & Sons, 1910) 332 at 333.

184 'Purdahnishins in India' *The Times*, 26 September 1902 at 6. Sorabji's letter was described as making 'a very strong case for her clients': see 'The Seclusion of Indian Women' *The Queen*, 11 October 1902.

185 Sorabji's letter to *The Times* appended letters of support from Justice Ameer Ali of the High Court of Calcutta, Justices Knox and Blair of the High Court of Allahabad, and Sir William Markby: see 'The Need for Lady Lawyers in India' (1902) 33 *Englishwoman's Review* 234 at 237; and BL F165/119: letters from Markby, 15 February 1902 and 31 August 1902.

Cannot some way of help be found? Something which will not offend the prejudices and customs of the people, and yet be sufficiently intelligent and interpretive of the need? Is it not possible to give the widowed Purdahnashin access to a 'man of business' of her own sex, with whom she can speak face to face? She might be attached to the Court of Wards Department of Government and work under authority.[186]

Moreover, as Sorabji had also pointed out, Oxford and Cambridge were producing women capable of 'good, cool-headed, non-hysterical work,' who would be well able to provide the necessary 'tact and sympathy as well as legal knowledge and business capacity' required to do this work.[187] Further support for Sorabji's plan also appeared in the *Juridical Review*, which commended an announcement by the Secretary of State in the House of Commons that the Government was considering a proposal to provide women as legal advisors to *Purdahnashins*.[188]

Sorabji herself also continued to lobby for such an appointment. In an article about *Purdahnashins* published in early 1903, she provided an overview of the history of legal principles relating to deeds and contracts signed by women living in *purdah*. However, after concluding that the cases had fully recognised the vulnerability of these women, Sorabji noted the absence of measures to ensure their protection *in practice*. Quoting Justice Blair of the Allahabad High Court, she alleged that 'there seems to exist between [women living in *purdah*] and the fountain of justice an almost insuperable bar.'[189] As her article then explained, she recommended that the government appoint a woman trained in law to do this work under the auspices of the Court of Wards:

Ask of her a particularly good legal education, theoretical and practical, let her be a nominee of the Government so that she might be a picked person in every way, and make her work under the direct control of the officer of the district. You would thus have given her the authority and protection which she needs for the difficult work of protecting those less fortunate than herself from unknown dangers and unconscious dishonesties.[190]

Later in 1903, at the end of a two-year sojourn in Britain, Sorabji returned to India, relatively confident that an appointment to the Court of

[186] *Englishwoman's Review*, above, n 185 at 236, quoting Sorabji's letter to *The Times*.

[187] *Englishwoman's Review*, above, n 185 at 237, quoting Sorabji's letter to *The Times*. Sorabji confronted the British government's unwillingness to interfere in private family matters and in customary practices, suggesting that the plan be limited to widows and minors, without their 'natural male protectors.'

[188] JP Coldstream, 'Women and the Law in India' (1903) *Juridical Review* 185. See also BL F165/119: 'Miss Cornelia Sorabjee's Scheme for Legal Aid to Purdahnishin Women' (undated) *The Indian Ladies' Magazine* 251; and K Shavaksha, 'The Purdahnashin Question' (1903) *The Indian Review* 217

[189] 'Safeguards for Purdahnishins,' n 5 at 70–73.

[190] 'Safeguards for Purdahnishins,' n 5 at 77.

Wards would ensue. While still en route to India by ship, Sorabji learned news of the unsuccessful outcome of Bertha Cave's application to Gray's Inn; indeed, she reported to Lady Hobhouse that she was 'beset by Editors and Reporters of every newspaper' who wanted to interview her about Miss Cave. Sorabji was somewhat critical of Cave, who had launched her application after just a few months of study, provoking Sorabji to worry that 'the question [would be] put back very appreciably' as a result.[191] In a later letter, she also mentioned Ivy Williams, noting briefly that she wanted to contact her to suggest that 'we should combine about anything we do.'[192] A few weeks later, Sorabji expressed more detailed concerns about these 'unripe' applications for women's admission to the legal profession. Her sense of a need for strategy was clearly evident as she lamented:

> How annoying it is to hear of the progress of refusals about women & the Bar! I wish they had not put the question to such unripe test. It bespeaks neither *prudence* nor *tact*: & the possession of either of these gifts seems to be an absolute necessity for the working of any new or forward movement....[193]

In addition to obvious concerns about how the decision in Cave's case might undermine all her recent efforts to achieve a governmental appointment to provide legal services in India, Sorabji may have felt little sympathy for Bertha Cave and Ivy Williams. After all, by 1904, Sorabji had been pursuing *her* goal for fifteen years. By that time, she was nearly thirty-eight years old, and she was still struggling to achieve economic independence in the practice of law.

However, in May 1904, Sorabji finally announced the good news to Lord and Lady Hobhouse that she had received an offer of appointment to the Court of Wards from the Government of Bengal. She was ecstatic: finally, 'the bitterness of the waiting time [was] over.' Ever diplomatic, Sorabji expressed the hope to Lady Hobhouse that the newspapers would not revive the information about her rejected application for admission to the Allahabad High Court, confiding that 'I may *some time* re-ask the privilege, backed by the Government, & I should like it then to be remembered that I did not take advantage of any opportunity for crowing!'[194] Thus, in 1904, Sorabji was formally appointed Lady Assistant to the Court of Wards for Bengal, Bihar and Orissa, and Assam. In this position, she intervened on behalf of the British government pursuant to the Court of Wards legislation, investigating property, succession and maintenance

---

191 BL F165/17: letter to Lady Hobhouse, 29 December 1903. As Sorabji stated, 'she has my sympathy – together with my righteous annoyance!'
192 BL F165/17: letter to Lady Hobhouse, 1 February 1904.
193 BL F165/17: letter to Lady Hobhouse, 23 February 1904.
194 BL F165/17: letters to Lady Hobhouse, 7 April 1904 and 10 May 1904. Sorabji decided to leave the details of the appointment to the government, a decision that later created problems with her pension entitlement: see BL F165/121.

disputes involving widows and minor children.[195] Her detailed annual reports of her work on the estates under her jurisdiction illustrate the extent and variety of her interventions and the necessity of travelling long distances from her office in Calcutta to visit wards on their estates. For example, in her report for 1916, she confirmed that she had dealt with 110 estates, representing 276 women, as well as 139 boys and 95 girls, in 510 *zenanas*. In that year, she had travelled more than 20,000 miles by rail, road and water.[196]

Sorabji's work required a breadth of legal knowledge, as well as tact and judgment, in providing legal advice and other assistance to wards of estates under governmental protection and control. For example, Sorabji was involved for several years in providing advice about the Janbazar Estate in Bengal, and there is a record of her legal opinion in March 1907, quoting extensively from legal authorities, in relation to the mother's position as guardian of minors pursuant to Hindu law.[197] Similarly, in relation to the Narhan Estate in Bihar and Orissa, Sorabji was involved in advising about rights to succession, and in providing legal advice about *stridhan* and estate property.[198] However, as her reports revealed, she also needed practical skills in her dealings with the wards. In her report about another estate in Bihar and Orissa, for example, she noted succinctly 'Quarrel between late Proprietor's two widows. Matter negotiated. Peace made.'[199] Similarly, in a report about the Kumar Ward's Estate in Assam, Sorabji indicated '... serious circumstances [made] it advisable to take immediate charge of the persons of the minor girls of this Estate. Control obtained.... Monthly bills checked, tradesmen's disputes settled, leases negotiated and other business done for minors of this Estate....'[200] In addition to her annual reports, Sorabji submitted a lengthy report to the Board of Revenue in 1914, summarising the scope of her work. In this report, she explained how she was responsible for implementing governmental policies in relation to both legal and business affairs on the subject estates, for persuading minor wards to be educated 'without offending any rules of religion or any custom or practice of orthodoxy,' and for supervising the health of wards in accordance with traditional customs. As she

195 Sorabji identified the legislation in *India Calling*, above, n 3 at 118: *Court of Wards Act*, Bengal, Bihar and Orissa 1879; Bombay 1905; Madras 1902; and United Provinces 1912. In a report on her activities for 1914–15, Sorabji divided her work into five categories: inspection tours and visits on request to estates; legal work; the education, health, domestic comfort and contentment of the wards; correspondence and routine office work; and the special work necessitated by the War: see BL F165/131.

196 BL F165/132. Sorabji's appointment initially permitted her to take on private work in her own time, but from 1909, Sorabji worked full time in her governmental position: see BL F165/121.

197 BL F165/135: Bengal (Janbazar Estate), 5 March 1907.

198 BL F165/135: Bihar and Orissa (Narhan Estate), March 1905 and September 1912.

199 BL F165/135: Bihar and Orissa (Ratan Estate), July 1905.

200 BL F165/135: Assam (Kumar Ward Estate), October to December 1917.

explained, she was also responsible for ensuring the wards' loyalty to the government of British India, and for creating trust in relation to British justice by being ready:

> ... with knowledge and professional skill and tact and cheerfulness, and hope, for whatever situation, and at a time when her own nerves are tried with the arduousness of District touring or her spirits at ebb from the difficulties of official relationships.... To be at peace with the entourage of a Rajbari and yet untouched by its intrigues – and to hold no work outside her duties and no hour of time her own.... All these things and many more are included in the position of trust to which the Government appoints the Lady Assistant to the Court of Wards.[201]

As the volume of work steadily increased, Sorabji's regular letters to her friend, Elena Rathbone, revealed that she was actively lobbying for an assistant, a woman lawyer who was either Indian or British. However, in spite of repeated requests, no additional appointments were made, and on Sorabji's retirement in 1922, the position of Lady Assistant to the Court of Wards became permanently vacant. Although no official explanation was provided, societal changes may have rendered such a position no longer necessary. It is also possible that Sorabji was irreplaceable.[202]

CORNELIA SORABJI: 'NO PEER AMONG THE WOMEN OF INDIA'[203]

> The dear old Master [Benjamin Jowett] used to tell me that my duty in life was as far as possible to interpret the East to the West. But this is [an] almost impossible task. The East is so conglomerate and the West – as a nation so insular – and I seem to stand midway between the two: my birth allotting me to one hemisphere but my education and instincts and friendships allotting me to the other.[204]

[201] BL F165/53: letter from the Lady Assistant to the Court of Wards to the Secretary of the Board of Revenue, Bengal, 14 October 1914.

[202] See BL F165/121. See also BL F165/53: letters to Elena Rathbone, 11 June 1913 and 9 February 1915. Elena Rathbone (1878–1964) was a supporter of District Nursing, and was appointed in 1917 to the council of the Queen's Institute for District Nursing, serving from 1919 to 1952 as honorary secretary; she was also a pioneer in the registration of midwives. In 1913, Elena Rathbone married Bruce Richmond, later Lord Richmond, Editor of the *Times Literary Supplement* from 1915: http://sca.lib.liv.ac.uk/collections/rathbone (accessed 14 June 2002). Elena Rathbone was appointed Sorabji's literary executor pursuant to her will; C Lokugé, above, n 3 at 247, mis-identified Rathbone as Eleanor Rathbone (1872–1946), MP for the Combined English Universities: see Johanna Alberti, *Eleanor Rathbone* (London, Sage Public- ations, 1996).

[203] *Manchester Guardian Weekly*, above, n 10. See also *New York Times*, 8 July 1954. Sorabji was awarded the Kaisar-i-Hind gold medal in 1909, with the bar of the first class in 1922: BL F165/160.

[204] BL F165/20: letter to Mrs A Darling, 17 October 1897.

In this letter to a friend in 1897, written a few years after she had completed her studies at Oxford and returned to India, Cornelia Sorabji revealed her sense of 'mission' to interpret India and its culture to the British. Describing her commitment to both countries, another friend poetically suggested that she had 'warmed her hands at two fires, without being scorched.'[205] Thus, particularly in *India Calling*, Sorabji described her work in India, explaining her mission to bring British justice to her women clients there. Her stories were colourful and entertaining, and not infrequently sensational, including descriptions of travelling by elephant, and of her narrow escapes from natural disasters like floods and cholera, as well as from nefarious attempts on her life.[206] Although many of the 'cases' described in *India Calling* were also discussed in her official reports and in her letters and diaries, the accounts in *India Calling* were frequently enlivened by additional facts, and some reports were combined, perhaps to make them more dramatic as story-telling. Certainly, neither the heartache and personal anguish which Sorabji experienced in her repeated attempts to enter the legal profession, nor her ongoing administrative problems as Lady Assistant, were emphasised in *India Calling*. Instead, Sorabji described her successful efforts to enforce the legal rights of Indian widows and minor children who might otherwise have fallen prey to treachery or misfortune. In doing so, her sense of mission and professional acumen were clearly revealed, by contrast with the traditional simplicity and even ignorance of her clients, the women living in *purdah*.[207] As a result, Burton concluded that Sorabji's accounts 'pathologized the world of the *purdahnashin*,' while demonstrating that Sorabji was aligned with 'the modern, secular, and male colonial/legal establishment.'[208]

Although Burton's assessment seems apt for much of Sorabji's published writing, Sorabji's relationship to the legal profession in India was more ambiguous: although she may have been 'aligned' with the male colonial and legal establishment, she was never fully accepted as part of it. Her gender excluded her from membership in the profession, even as she steadfastly refused to accept a gendered identity. Thus, at the time of the rejection of her application for admission as a *vakil* in Allahabad in May 1899, Sorabji off-handedly complained, 'What a bother one is a woman!'[209] and continued to press for women who could be 'men of business' to advise the *Purdahnashins*.[210] At the same time, it seems clear that Sorabji's entitlement to work as a legal practitioner in India depended

---

[205] In *India Calling*, above, n 3 at ix, Sorabji identified this as a comment of Sir Mountstuart Grant Duff.

[206] See *India Calling*, above, n 3 at 84 and 228–30.

[207] As Sorabji explained in *India Calling*, above, n 3 at 120, the Lady Assistant to the Court of Wards was the 'liaison officer' between the *zenana* and the government.

[208] A Burton, above, n 5 at 145 and 149.

[209] BL F165/16: letter to Lady Hobhouse, 3 May 1899.

[210] See 'The Law of Women's Property in India,' n 82; and R Blackshaw, above, n 47.

for more than two decades on the need to have a *woman* lawyer to advise *women* clients in northern India. No other option for legal practice was available to Sorabji, either in India or in Britain, until after 1919 when the British Parliament enacted amending legislation which enabled women to become barristers and solicitors.[211] As a result, Sorabji needed her women clients as much as they needed her, as she created a niche for her legal work which 'supplemented,' but did not 'supplant,' the work of male lawyers.[212] Thus, the needs of 'innocent' *Purdahnashins* for her legal services were intricately tied to *her* need for professional work in law.

In addition, as Burton and others have argued, however, Sorabji's political temperament, which contributed to her descriptions of 'primaeval' Muslim and Hindu women in India,[213] was fundamentally conservative; as Lokugé noted, she participated enthusiastically in upper-class life in Britain and in the social life of judges and British administrators in India.[214] Indeed, there are some indications that Lord and Lady Hobhouse, who were staunch liberals, made efforts to restrain Sorabji's more conservative and imperial views, particularly in relation to the Boer War;[215] and her imperialism was clearly evident in her manipulative treatment of a woman terrorist in Calcutta in 1907.[216] When she returned to Calcutta to practise at the bar in the 1920s, she continued to provide advice and representation to *Purdahnashins* and began to organise social services for women. However, these plans became sidetracked by her association with Katherine Mayo's *Mother India*, published in 1927. As Mrinalini Sinha argued, Sorabji's reformist efforts on behalf of Indian women had not previously involved an attack on Indian, especially Hindu, culture; however, her assistance with Mayo's project meant that Sorabji became associated, not just with Mayo's imperialist (and anti-nationalist) views but also with her indictment of Indian culture.[217] As Burton suggested, moreover, Sorabji's descriptions of the *Purdahnashins* in *India Calling* may have been influ-

---

211 *Sex Disqualification Removal Act*, 1919, 9&10 Geo 5, c 71.

212 See 'The Law of Women's Property in India,' above, n 82 at 10.

213 See A Burton, above, n 5; and BL F165/16: letter to Lady Hobhouse, 20 June 1897.

214 C Lokugé, above, n 3 at *xviii–xix*, noted that Sorabji assimilated 'with the elitist British society of Bombay and later, in Calcutta, she [socialised] with the Viceroy and the administrative hierarchy.' Sorabji herself expressed concern that 'fate will some day hold [me]... *An Advanced Woman* ...': see BL F165/16: letter to Lady Hobhouse, 18 April 1894.

215 In a letter to Lady Hobhouse in 1900, Sorabji mentioned news of the Boer War, declaring that 'one feels an imperialist's pride in Lord Roberts.' In a subsequent letter, she thanked Lady Hobhouse for the cutting about 'the other side' of the war question: see BL F165/17: letters to Lady Hobhouse, 21 March 1900 and 10 May 1900; and F165/21: letter to HF Blair, 15 November 1901.

216 C Sorabji, 'A Bengali Woman Revolutionary,' above, n 8; the event occurred in relation to the partition of Bengal in 1907.

217 K Mayo, *Mother India* (New York, Harcourt, Brace and Company, 1927); and see M Sinha, 'Reading *Mother India*: Empire, Nation and the Female Voice' (1994) 6:2 *Journal of Women's History* 6 at 16–20. See also BL F165/161; 'The Old and the New in India' (29 September 1927) 32 *The Near East and India* 402; and S Gooptu, above, n 1 at 230.

enced by her anti-nationalist politics in the 1930s. Certainly, there is evidence of a stream of letters to the editors, public presentations, and published articles, all of which supported continuing British involvement in India and challenged the nationalist movement.[218] Indeed, Sorabji's interview with Gandhi in London in September 1931 reveals her critical assessment of his political goals, particularly the ambiguity of his demands for 'complete independence' for India, at the same time as he championed India's 'partnership with Britain.'[219] Her conclusion, that Gandhi was 'a man exploited by others – by the extremists, by his immediate domestic entourage, and by his admirers outside India' clearly marked her as an opponent of both Gandhi and the nationalist movement.[220]

At the same time, an assessment of Sorabji requires an understanding of the challenges which she faced as she tried to create a legal career and to achieve economic independence. For example, after her retirement as Lady Assistant to the Court of Wards, she was formally admitted to the bar in Britain in 1923, but her decision to return to practise at the bar in Calcutta may have been necessitated, at least in part, by an inadequate pension.[221] Then, after moving permanently to Britain, she published *India Calling* and several other books in the 1930s, perhaps again needing the income from royalties to augment her pension; it is possible that this necessity may have influenced the 'imperial' tone she adopted for British readers of *India Calling*.[222] Even in her work for the Citizens Advice Bureau in 1939, at the outbreak of World War II, she described her efforts to do useful legal work for 'troubled old women' – at a time when she was seventy-three years old.[223] As her nephew, Richard's son, explained, although five of his Indian aunts had retired to Britain, travelling about in wartime London, 'with darkened street lights and reduced traffic' in their brilliant coloured *saris*, it was Cornelia who was 'the most formidable;'[224] and his memories of her during the bombing of London confirm this assessment. As Cornelia had reported, in a letter written in May 1941, she had attended Sunday

218 Sorabji addressed the Ladies' Imperial Association on 'India at the Crossroads' on 21 October 1932; and the Royal Empire Society on 24 October 1932: see *The Times*, 22 and 25 October 1932. She also regularly published letters to the Editor of *The Times*; for example, see 'American Views on India' 3 June 1932; 'Terrorism in Bengal' 8 September 1933; 'Women's Franchise' 8 June 1934; 'Child Marriage in India' 6 August 1936; and 'India and the Atlantic Charter' 8 November 1941. See also 'Salute to Loyal India: Answering the Congress Grievances,' above, n 8.

219 C Sorabji, 'Gandhi Interrogated,' above, n 8 at 454.

220 C Sorabji, 'Gandhi Interrogated,' above, n 8 at 457. Sorabji's presentation to the Foreign Policy Association in November 1930, above, n 8 at 27, emphasised the British gift to India of self-government; she firmly declared her support for 'self-government within the Empire.'

221 Although the situation is unclear, this conclusion is reinforced by the details of her pension in 1922, in an amount of about £400 per annum: see BL F165/52: letter from Whately to Richmond, 5 June 1945.

222 Sorabji published a number of books in the 1930s: see above, n 16.

223 BL F165/51: letter to Elena Rathbone, 2 October 1939.

224 R Sorabji, 'Afterword' in C Lokugé, above, n 3 at 213–14.

service at St Dunstan's as usual, even though 'the dear old Padre had been up all night with his boy scouts helping to put out fires.'[225] In Richard's memories, however, he described how Sorabji regularly worshipped in the Temple church in the neighbouring Inn, and 'when it was bombed flat by enemy bombs, she turned up as usual and [*she*] insisted on the priest conducting a service ... among the steaming ruins.'[226]

'Formidable' is an apt characterisation for Sorabji, who continued to take on all the challenges presented during her life, even as she was striving to avoid becoming an advanced woman. Whether she was making repeated efforts to gain entry to the Indian legal profession in the 1890s, or living bravely, old and almost blind, in London during the Blitz,[227] her spirit was modern even though her values remained traditional. Underneath her efforts to disguise her ambition and desire for independence, it is clear how much joy she experienced in doing work that allowed her the freedom of travel and adventure. As she explained in a letter to Lady Hobhouse in 1904, when she had travelled to Darjeeling and had just received word that she was to be appointed Lady Assistant to the Court of Wards, she was thrilled that 'always, always, there are the glorious snows to companion me. I long for the wonder & beauty of them to become a part of my life, somehow.'[228] As a woman who chose to study law thirty years before she was entitled to formal recognition in the profession, and years before other women became entitled to enter the legal professions in India,[229] Sorabji was determined to achieve economic independence and to live her life fully.

Yet, in the end, Burton argued against rehabilitating Sorabji as an

225 BL F165/51: letter to Elena Rathbone, 11 May 1941. Sorabji also reported that Gray's Inn was 'practically demolished as an Inn;' and that thirty-three enemy planes had been shot down.

226 R Sorabji, 'Afterword' in C Lokugé, above, n 3 at 214 (emphasis added).

227 In a letter to Elena Rathbone, Sorabji described her efforts to attend a doctor's appointment (she was becoming increasingly blind): 'The Strand & Fleet Street closed, time bomb in front of St Dunstan's, awful crater near St Clements Danes & up Norfolk St – other gaps near Kingsway & where not – equal obstructions in Holborn. The only way I [could] get to [the doctor's office] was by walking – turned off into by-ways every little while – & it was not till I got [through] Leicester Sq to [Oxford] St that I found a taxi.... Poor London....': BL F165/51: letter to Elena Rathbone, 18 April 1941. Sorabji underwent an optical operation in June 1941; and an eye operation again in May 1943: see *The Times*, 28 June 1941; 5 May 1943; and 21 May 1943.

228 BL F165/17: letter to Lady Hobhouse, 31 May 1904.

229 Sorabji requested information in 1934 from Indian High Courts about the admission of women to the legal profession; the responses indicated that most women were admitted to the legal profession in India only after 1919: see BL F165/169. Mithan Tata Lam was the first Indian woman called to the bar in England in 1923; she practised at the Bombay High Court: see M Tata, 'Women and the Law' in EC Gedge and M Choksi (eds), *Women in Modern India* (Bombay, D B Taraporewala Sons & Co, 1929) at 124. According to JJ Paul, above, n 11 at 160, the Bengal High Court refused the admission of Regina Guha as a pleader in 1916, and the Patna High Court similarly refused an application from SB Hazra; but 'a breakthrough occurred when the Allahabad High Court ignored the verdict of the Calcutta High Court and admitted Sorabji as a vakil on 24 August 1921.'

'unsung feminist heroine,' recognising that Sorabji would have abhorred such a characterisation as she had no time for 'women's rights women' of her day.[230] Indeed, her exclusion from the (male) legal profession and her consistent efforts to distinguish herself from less 'civilised' Indian women, even as she devoted her career to their interests, resulted in highly complex roles for Sorabji as the interpreter of the East to the West; and in the formation of her identity in terms of race and religion, as well as class and gender.[231] In this context, her obituary notice in *The Times*, identifying her as an 'Indian feminist' at her death in 1954 appears unconvincing. More ambiguously, the *Manchester Guardian Weekly* declared that Sorabji 'had no peer among the women of India,' emphasising that, although she was a *woman*, she was nonetheless without a *woman* peer in all of India.[232] In spite of a lifetime of ignoring it, gender remained a defining issue of Cornelia Sorabji's legal career.

---

[230] A Burton, above, n 17 at 114.

[231] Amartya Sen described the 'spectacular uniqueness of [Sorabji's] chosen combination of identities': A Sen, 'Other People: Beyond Identity' (18 December 2000) 223:25 *New Republic* 23.

[232] *The Times* and *Manchester Guardian Weekly*, above, n 10. Sorabji's will (dated 19 March 1936) bequeathed her personal belongings to her sister, Alice Pennell, and a small legacy to a god-daughter, with the residue in trust for her niece and nephew, Richard's children. A codicil appointed Whately (junior) her executor. Sorabji nominated Elena Rathbone to act as her literary executor. Sorabji's estate was valued at 3163 pounds, 4 shillings and 7 pence at her death on 6 July 1954: see probate documents, 7 October 1954.

6

European Connections: Women in Law and the Role of Louis Frank

---

LA FEMME-AVOCAT AND EUROPEAN WOMEN LAWYERS

La question de la femme-avocat est une face du grand et complexe problème de l'affranchissement du sexe féminin. Non seulement nous souhaitons que toutes les carrières intellectuelles et libérales, y compris le barreau, soient rendues accessibles aux femmes, mais notre désir est de voir disparaître enfin les incapacités injustifiables qui frappent encore les femmes....[1]

Louis Frank, a thirty-four-year-old Belgian barrister, published these ideas about women lawyers in his treatise, *La Femme-Avocat*, in 1898. *La Femme-Avocat* provided a comprehensive review of women and the legal professions in the late nineteenth century, clearly demonstrating Frank's enthusiasm for women's rights and his skilful advocacy in support of legal reforms to achieve equality for women. His treatise included a sociological analysis of women's roles, as well as a detailed history of women's legal status pursuant to principles of civil law (including ancient Greek and Roman law), customary law prior to the French Revolution, and the state's recognition in 1791 that everyone, *sans distinction*, was entitled to practise the profession of their choosing. In addition, Frank presented arguments supporting women's eligibility for admission to the bar, specifically suggesting that provisions of the *Code Civil*, which did not expressly exclude women from the practice of law, should be interpreted as including them; as he asked rhetorically, '*Où donc est le texte légal interdisant à la femme le droit de postuler? On le chercherait en vain. Il n'existe pas.*'[2]

However, *La Femme-Avocat* was not merely an academic treatise on the

---

[1] L Frank, *La Femme-Avocat: Exposé Historique et Critique de la Question* (Paris, V Giard et E Brière, 1898) at ii [hereafter *La Femme-Avocat* 1898]. See also a shorter version, published in 1888: *La Femme-Avocat: Exposé Historique et Critique de la Question* (Bruxelles, Ferdinand Larcier; and Bologne, Nicolas Zanichelli, 1888) [hereafter *La Femme-Avocat* 1888].

[2] L Frank, *La Femme-Avocat* 1898, above, n 1 at 59; see also 1–59 and Frank's discussion of the Chevalière Eon de Beaumont, a woman born in 1728, who was received by the French Parliament as an advocate.

subject of women's access to the bar. As its title page revealed, the treatise was published *en cause de Mlle Chauvin*, and it included a record of the arguments presented to a Paris court in November 1897 in support of Jeanne Chauvin's application to take the oath to become an *avocat*, the first woman to challenge the bar's male exclusivity in France. Indeed, Frank arranged for *La Femme-Avocat* to be submitted for publication just a few weeks before the presentation of Chauvin's application to the court.[3] Pointing to the success of women lawyers in the United States, as well as the admission of Clara Brett Martin in Ontario and Ethel Benjamin in New Zealand a few months earlier, Frank suggested that the steady progress of *fin de siècle* ideas about justice and equality clearly favoured the admission of women as *avocats* in France; in addition, he argued that a positive decision from the Parisian court would confirm the wisdom and justice of the French judiciary throughout Europe.[4]

As a report in the *Illustrated London News* in November 1897 recorded, Chauvin's application to take the oath to become an *avocat* was controversial; indeed, it had 'thrown every individual connected with the Paris Palace of Justice, from the Judges to the Ushers, into a state of great emotion' because, although she was not the only woman who had successfully attended law school in France, Chauvin was the first to claim the right to take the oath, a necessary step in becoming entitled to practise in the Paris courts.[5] As the press report also noted, Chauvin's application was particularly supported by the distinguished Belgian barrister, Louis Frank, who had 'written a learned treatise proving her absolute right to practise [law];' at the same time, opponents of her application, referred to as 'Anti-Chauvinists,' were '[hinting] darkly at the probable influence to be exercised by the Chauvin Portias of the future....'[6] As it turned out, the Anti-Chauvinists were successful, and Chauvin's application was rejected by the court.[7] However, with the help of sympathetic legislators, amending

---

[3] See 'Introduction,' *La Femme-Avocat* 1898, above, n 1, signed by Frank and dated 15 October 1897. Chauvin's claim was presented to the court in Paris on 24 November 1897: see E Charrier, *L'Évolution Intellectuelle Féminine* (Paris, Éditions Albert Mechelinck, 1931) at 336.

[4] Frank argued that all civilizations were evolving to provide women with equality and justice: L Frank, *La Femme-Avocat* 1898, above, n 1 at xvi; and at 68 (Canada), 69 (New Zealand), and 126 (USA).

[5] *Illustrated London News*, 13 November 1897, at 696. See also SL Kimble, 'Justice Redressed: Women, Citizenship, and the Social Uses of the Law in Modern France, 1890–1939' (PhD thesis, University of Iowa, 2002).

[6] *Illustrated London News*, above, n 5. This usage of the word 'chauvinism' may have reflected ideas of uncritical support for Chauvin's cause, an intended pun on the origins of the word: 'chauvinism' was first applied in the 1860s to the excessive patriotism of one of Napoleon's soldiers, Nicholas Chauvin: see T McArthur (ed), *The Oxford Companion to the English Language* (Oxford, Oxford University Press, 1992) at 209. No connection between Nicholas and Jeanne Chauvin has been identified.

[7] According to E Charrier, above, n 3 at 337, the court concluded that Chauvin's request required legislative action. See also *Chauvin v Procureur Géneral*, Cour d'appel de Paris (1er Chambre) GP 2, 1897, 600.

legislation was enacted in France on 1 December 1900, and Chauvin was then permitted to take the oath to become an *avocat* in Paris on 19 December 1900.[8] Chauvin's experience in Paris was cited in Annie Macdonald Langstaff's case in Québec in 1915–1916; significantly, however, Langstaff's claim was denied in part because Chauvin's case had confirmed the need for legislative, and not judicial, intervention.[9] All the same, women in France were among the first in Europe to become eligible for admission to the bar, and they achieved this goal nearly two decades before the enactment of similar amending legislation in Britain and in some other European jurisdictions after World War I.[10]

Frank's treatise provided detailed information about the progress of women's claims for admission to the bar in different parts of the world at the end of the nineteenth century. For example, his treatise identified Marya Sandoyal, the first woman to obtain a doctorate in law in Latin America, who was practising law in Mexico; and Almeda E Hitchcock, who had graduated from the University of Michigan and then been admitted to the bar in her native Hawaii. He also noted two women lawyers in Santiago, Chile: Léodice Lebrun and Mathilde Thrup; and he identified *Mlle* Tel Sono, a Japanese woman who had studied law in Tokyo.[11] Significantly, he also noted the appearance of Cornelia Sorabji in a British court in Poona in 1896.[12] As the treatise revealed, Frank's interest in these comparative developments had resulted in extensive correspondence with women's rights partisans in many different jurisdictions, including male and female suffrage activists, editors of women's journals, and women lawyers. Fortunately, much of this late nineteenth-century correspondence has been preserved in Frank's archival papers; indeed, Frank's collection of photographs of women lawyers in the late 1890s is remarkably similar to the sketches that appeared with the report in the

[8] *Loi ayant pour objet de permettre aux femmes munies des diplômes de licencié en droit de prêter le serment d'avocat et d'exercer cette profession*: Dalloz, 1900-4-81, cited in E Charrier, above, n 3 at 344. Although not the first woman to take the oath in France, Chauvin was the first woman to register as an *avocat*, having completed her training, in 1905: see E Charrier, at 345; and A Boigeol, 'French Women Lawyers (*Avocates*) and the "Women's Cause" in the First Half of the Twentieth Century' (2003) 10:2 *International Journal of the Legal Profession* 193.

[9] In both the initial hearing and in the *Cour d'Appel*, the Québec judges referred briefly to the *Chauvin* case in France: see *Langstaff v Bar of Québec* (1915) 47 Rapports Judiciaires de Québec 131 at 142; and (1916) 25 Rapports Judiciares de Québec 11 at 17 and 20. See also Justice Lavergne, dissenting, at 14; and 'Les Femmes et le Barreau,' *Le Franc-Parleur*, 23 December 1916.

[10] See JC Albisetti, 'Portia Ante Portas: Women and the Legal Profession in Europe, ca 1870–1925' (2000) 33 *Journal of Social History* 825. See also CA Corcos, 'Lawyers for Marianne: The Nature of Discourse of the Entry of French Women into the Legal Profession, 1894–1926' (1996) 12 *Georgia State University Law Review* 435, citing L Frank, above, n 1 and F Corcos: see *Les Avocates* (Paris, Éditions Montaigne, 1931).

[11] L Frank, *La Femme-Avocat* 1898, above, n 1 at 125–6; see also M Griffith, 'A Japanese Lady Lawyer and Reformer in England' (1893) 10 *Great Thoughts* 91.

[12] L Frank, *La Femme-Avocat* 1898, above, n 1 at 67–8, citing the *Bombay Champion*, 31 July 1896. Frank incorrectly stated that Sorabji was Hindu and that she had completed a *stage* at Lincoln's Inn.

Illustrated London News in 1897, suggesting that Frank was an important source for this article about Chauvin's case in Paris.[13]

However, Frank's treatise was particularly significant for its review of the status of women lawyers in European jurisdictions in the late 1890s. For example, Frank examined the Swiss court's rejection of an application for admission to the bar presented by Emilie Kempin-Spyri in Zurich in 1887.[14] Interestingly, Kempin-Spyri's pursuit of legal work took her to New York in 1888, where she was involved in law teaching for a few years; after returning to Switzerland, she taught Roman Law at the university in Zurich from 1892 to 1895, and then moved to Germany where she opened an office providing advice on English and American law.[15] However, as James Albisetti noted, Kempin-Sypri was 'buffeted by personal and professional difficulties, as well as conflicts with leading German feminists' and she entered a mental hospital in September 1897, where she died of cancer in 1901.[16] In one of her last letters to Frank in August 1896, she confirmed that she was not taking part in an international women's meeting in Berlin because she did not agree with recent developments in the feminist movement.[17] Indeed, as Gisela Shaw suggested, Kempin-Spyri was increasingly shunned by more radical feminists; her need to earn a living for her family and the '*habitus* of the profession she had made such sacrifices to join' worked together to compromise Kempin-Spyri's ability to pursue her feminist goals.[18] As Frank reported, moreover, it was Lina Graf, who graduated with a doctorate in law from Bern in 1895, who became the first woman to practise law in Switzerland in July 1896.[19]

Frank also reported on the status of women lawyers in Germany. As in

[13] Bibliothèque Royale, Bruxelles, *Papiers Frank* [hereafter *Papiers Frank*]. The photos in *Papiers Frank* #7791 (file 1) include almost all the women lawyers profiled in the *Illustrated London News*, above, n 5.

[14] G Shaw claimed that Kempin-Spyri was the 'first woman in Europe to be awarded a doctorate in law': see G Shaw, 'Conflicting Agendas: The First Female Jurists in Germany' (2003) 10 *International Journal of the Legal Profession* 177 at 179. However, Olgiati noted that Marisa Pellegrina Amoretti obtained a doctorate in law at the University of Pavia in Italy in 1777: see V Olgiati, 'Professional Body and Gender Difference in Court: The Case of the First (Failed) Woman Lawyer in Modern Italy' in U Schultz and G Shaw (eds), *Women in the World's Legal Professions* (Oxford, Hart Publishing, 2003) 419 at 423.

[15] L Frank, *La Femme-Avocat* 1898, above, n 1 at 108–15; and G Shaw, above, n 14 at 180–81. See also Virginia G Drachman, *Women Lawyers and the Origins of Professional Identity in America: The Letters of the Equity Club, 1887 to 1890* (Ann Arbor, University of Michigan Press, 1993) at 281–3.

[16] JC Albisetti, above, n 10 at 832.

[17] *Papiers Frank*, above, n 13 at #6031 (file 5): letter from Kempin-Spyri, 27 August 1896. See also letters, 13 August 1888; 3 July 1894; and 19 November 1896.

[18] G Shaw, above, n 14 at 185; Shaw noted especially the critical publication by M Stritt, 'Die Frauenfrage auf dem evangelisch-sozialen Kongress' (1897) 3 *Die Frauenbewegung* 133–6.

[19] L Frank, *La Femme-Avocat* 1898, above, n 1 at 114–15, noting a minor change in the rules; and *Papiers Frank*, above, n 13 at #6031 (file 5): letter from L Lugeon, Geneva, 7 October 1896, confirming that 'Mlle LG ... peut exercer la profession dans son canton d'origine.'

Austria and Hungary, women in Germany were precluded from becoming lawyers because they were excluded from university courses which were prerequisites for law studies; however, by the late 1890s, Frank reported that two German women had succeeded in obtaining doctorates in law at Zurich: Anna Mackenroth and Anita Augspurg. In a letter to Frank, Augspurg reported that Mackenroth had obtained her doctorate in law at Zurich in 1894, and had then taken Swiss citizenship in order to be able to practice there; Augspurg indicated that she had obtained her doctorate in 1897, having studied partly at Zurich and partly in Berlin, and that she was hoping to practise.[20] However, as Shaw noted, Augspurg's family was financially secure so that she did not have to engage in formal legal practice; instead she pursued her interest in issues of inequality and oppression, and was particularly active in the campaign to reform the Civil Code. Indeed, after the women's movement's efforts to change the Code in Germany were defeated in 1896, Augspurg published an analysis of the reform process, urging continuation of the struggle.[21] Similarly, in a report about the Woman's Congress in Brussels in August 1897, a British participant noted that Augspurg had presented a 'brilliant though rather academic appeal' on the question of civil rights for women.[22] According to Shaw, Augspurg continued to follow her curiosity, 'using her considerable legal skills outside the structured framework of an organized profession' until the 1930s, when she and her longtime partner, Lida Gustava Heymann, were forced to flee to Switzerland by the Nazis; both died in exile in 1943.[23]

In addition to his examination of Kempin-Spyri and Augspurg, Frank carefully documented a number of other jurisdictions, including England, Spain, Cuba, Portugal, Greece and Iceland, where university courses were open to women, but where they were not yet eligible for admission to the bar.[24] He also reported that two young women were on the point of completing their law studies in Holland, and that the President of Advocates in Amsterdam had indicated that they would likely be admitted as *avocats* because there appeared to be nothing in law to prevent them.[25] As Albisetti noted, Elisabeth van Dorp successfully earned the first law degree in Holland in 1899; and Adolphine Kok graduated in law four

---

[20] L Frank, *La Femme-Avocat* 1898, above, n 1 at 64–5; see also *Papiers Frank*, above, n 13 at #7791–3: letter from Augspurg, 30 September 1897; #7791–6, letter from Mackenroth, 8 December 1898; and G Shaw, above, n 14 at 181–2.

[21] G Shaw, above, n 14 at 186–7.

[22] DB Montefiore, 'Women's Congress in Brussels,' *Daily Chronicle*, August 1897, in *Papiers Frank*, above, n 13 at #7782.

[23] G Shaw, above, n 14 at 182.

[24] L Frank, *La Femme-Avocat* 1898, above, n 1 at 66, 99 and 123.

[25] L Frank, *La Femme-Avocat* 1898, above, n 1 at 84–5; see also *Papiers Frank*, above, n 13 at #6031 (file 5): letters from A Philips, Advocaat, Amsterdam, 13 August 1888 and 29 August 1888. See also #7793–3: statistics on women in Dutch university law programmes, showing two women students in 1896–97.

years later and was accepted as a member of the bar in Rotterdam.[26] In addition, Frank reported that women were already practising law in three Scandinavian countries. In Sweden, university law degrees became open to women in 1895, and legislation in 1897 permitted women to act in the courts; Elsa Eschelsson earned a doctorate at Upsala in 1898 and then embarked on a university teaching career.[27] Women also began to appear in courts in Finland in 1895, and Marie Katrine Doll earned a law degree in Norway in 1890; however, contrary to Frank's treatise, it seems that the practice of law was not formally opened to women there until 1904.[28] As Frank correctly noted, however, women were not entitled to practise law in Denmark. As early as 1888, a Danish court had rejected Nanna Berg's application to appear in a court in Copenhagen; the court interpreted the relevant statutory language to exclude women applicants for admission to the bar, and the Supreme Court of Denmark confirmed the decision in October 1888. Although not included in Frank's treatise, a letter from Berg's counsel in 1896 indicated that Berg had abandoned law to become 'the happy wife of a manager of [a high school] and the mother of two sons.'[29] Frank's treatise did, however, report on plans to permit women to practise law in Russia, although it appears that it was not until 1917 that legislation opened the bar to them.[30] Frank also claimed that Sarmisa Bilcescu, who was the first woman to graduate with a *docteur en droit* in Paris in 1890, had been admitted to practise in her native Romania in June 1891. Although Albisetti argued that Bilcescu's registration was abortive, official documents in Frank's correspondence files, including a formal letter from the office of the *Bâtonnier* and a formal list of the names of advocates, suggest that Bilcescu was indeed admitted to the bar in Romania in June 1891.[31]

In addition to these wide-ranging reports about the status of women lawyers in jurisdictions in Europe and elsewhere, Frank's treatise is particularly useful for its detailed description of two early cases concerning applications for admission to the bar: Lydia Poët's application in Italy[32]

---

26 JC Albisetti, above, n 10 at 837.

27 L Frank, *La Femme-Avocat* 1898, above, n 1 at 100–105. See also JC Albisetti, above, n 10 at 837, who reported that Eschelsson committed suicide in 1911, 'apparently frustrated by her failure to gain promotion.'

28 L Frank, *La Femme-Avocat* 1898, above, n 1 at 105–8; JC Albisetti, above, n 10 at 837.

29 L Frank, *La Femme-Avocat* 1898, above, n 1 at 97–9; JC Albisetti, above, n 10 at 837; and *Papiers Frank*, above, n 13 at #6031 (file 5): letter from Svend Hogsbro, 29 July 1896.

30 L Frank, *La Femme-Avocat* 1898, above, n 1 at 115; and JC Albisetti, above, n 10 at 834.

31 JC Albisetti, above, n 10 at 838; but see *La Femme-Avocat* 1898, above, n 1 at 120–23, and *Papiers Frank*, above, n 13 at #6031 (file 5): letter from CJ Poleysz, December 1896, enclosing '*l'arret du Conseil qui a admis*' Bilcescu, and '*Tabloul Advocatilor Judetului Ilfov, Pentru Anul 1892*', showing '*D Sarmisa Bilcescu ... inscris la 26 juin 1891*.'

32 L Frank, *La Femme-Avocat* 1898, above, n 1 at 85. According to the *Illustrated London News*, above, n 5, Poët joined her brother, a 'well-known Italian barrister, and though she does not appear in court, she is known to be one of the great authorities on penal law.' See also VG Drachman, above, n 15 at 44.

and Marie Popelin's application in Belgium.[33] Both these applications had been submitted in the 1880s, a decade before Chauvin's application was about to be launched in Paris. Significantly, Frank had already published accounts of these earlier applications, and he had personally participated in the presentation of arguments in support of Popelin, with whom he had studied law in Brussels.[34] Thus, his 1898 treatise evidenced Frank's continuing support for women's equality, particularly in relation to access to the legal professions. Indeed, he was later described by the Belgian press as having thrown himself '*de coeur et d'âme*' into law reform work, particularly in relation to women's rights:

> *Ce tout jeune homme rêvait à sa façon une vie brûlante d'activité utile et peut-être aussi glorieuse.... Louis Frank écrivait des brochures de vulgarisation, portait des articles aux journaux, essayait de convaincre à sa cause les uns et les autres. Son activité était presque de la fièvre. Il était partout, parlant à tout le monde....*[35]

This chapter focuses on the claims presented by Lydia Poët in Italy, Marie Popelin in Belgium, and Jeanne Chauvin in France, and on the role of Louis Frank in supporting their aspirations for admission to legal professions in Europe. Frank's involvement connects these three aspiring women lawyers: although Chauvin was clearly aware of the earlier applications submitted by Poët and Popelin, there is no evidence that she ever met them; by contrast, Frank corresponded with all three women and met both Popelin and Chauvin in person. Since all three cases confronted arguments based on provisions of the civil codes,[36] they also provide interesting comparisons with women's claims for admission to the bar in common law jurisdictions. For example, in the civil law context, where university legal education was generally a prerequisite to admission to the bar, courts were required to address the precise relationship between

---

[33] L Frank, *La Femme-Avocat* 1898, above, n 1 at 70; see also VG Drachman, above, n 15 at 193–9 and at 281.

[34] See L Frank, *De L'Exercice de la Profession d'Avocat en Italie: Exposé Sommaire des Règles* (Bruxelles, J B Moens & Fils, 1887) at 59; and *La Femme-Avocat* 1888, above, n 1 at *Avant-Propos*. For details of the relationship between Frank and Popelin, see *La Femme-Avocat* 1898, above, n 1 at 71.

[35] H Chainaye, 'A propos du vote du sénat français: L'initiateur du féminisme en Belgique,' *Messager de Bruxelles*, 21 June 1910, quoted in F De Bueger-Van Lierde, 'Louis Frank, Pionnier du Mouvement Féministe Belge' (1973) IV:3–4 *Revue Belge d'Histoire Contemporaine* 377 at 377–8. De Bueger-Van Lierde concluded that the views in *Messager de Bruxelles* were somewhat extreme ('*outranciers*'), although they captured Frank's personality and his support for women's equality.

[36] See L Frank, *La Femme-Avocat* 1898, above, n 1 at 70–80 (Popelin); at 85–97 (Poët); and at 183–299 (Chauvin). See also B Durand, 'Maîtres Popelin, Chauvin et Le Vigoureux, Pionnières du Barreau' in B Durand and L Mayali (eds), *Excerptiones Iuris: Studies in Honor of André Gouron* (Berkeley, Robbins Collection Publications, University of California, 2000) at 163.

women's access to the universities and their eligibility to become *avocats*.[37] In addition, the re-establishment of the bar after its demise during the French Revolution, and the adoption of the Napoleonic Code in 1804 and the decree about the professions in 1810, resulted in a professional context that was rather different from the situation in common law jurisdictions; moreover, although there were some distinctions, it seems that provisions of the *Code* were substantially similar in Belgium and France, and that the French *Code* continued to exert an important influence in Italy in the late nineteenth century.[38] In this way, an exploration of Frank's support for the applications presented by Poët, Popelin and Chauvin for admission as *avocats* provides an opportunity to examine the experiences of women who sought to become lawyers in European civil law jurisdictions at the end of the nineteenth century.

LYDIA POËT, MARIE POPELIN AND JEANNE CHAUVIN: LOUIS FRANK'S SUPPORT FOR WOMEN IN LAW

Les femmes qui dans un siècle d'ici seront avocats célèbres, professeurs distingués, magistrats ou ministres, vous devront une bien grande reconnaisance; je suis très heureuse que le hassard va en Providence! m'ait fait naître pour être votre contemporaine et vous connaître....[39]

This comment about the significance of Frank's support for aspiring women lawyers appeared in a letter from Chauvin in August 1896, in the midst of their joint preparations to submit her application to take the oath to become an *avocat* in Paris. Her enthusiastic appreciation of his efforts is clearly evident; indeed, her comment suggests that Frank is deserving of more recognition for his supportive work on behalf of women lawyers in the late nineteenth century. Yet, it seems that women who have become the famous lawyers, distinguished professors, judges and politicians, as described by Chauvin, are generally unaware of his role in challenging

---

[37] Candidates for admission as *avocats* were required to obtain the *licencié en droit*; Popelin and Chauvin both completed these qualifications, and then a further qualification, the *docteur en droit*. They argued that availability of university studies to women and men required that they also be equally entitled to become *avocats*: see E Charrier, above, n 3 at 336; and JC Albisetti, above, n 10 at 838.

[38] See L Karpik, *French Lawyers: A Study in Collective Action, 1274 to 1994* (Oxford, Clarendon Press, 1999); JH Crabb, *The Constitution of Belgium and the Belgian Civil Code* (Littleton, CO, Fred B Rothman & Co, 1982); and A Mazzacane, 'A Jurist for United Italy: The Training and Culture of Neapolitan Lawyers in the Nineteenth Century' in M Malatesta (ed), *Society and the Professions in Italy 1860–1914* (New York and Cambridge, UK, Cambridge University Press, 1995, translated by Adrian Belton) 80. See also M Burrage and R Torstendahl (eds), *Professions in Theory and History: Rethinking the Study of the Professions* (London, Sage Publications, 1990); and RL Abel and PSC Lewis (eds), *Lawyers in Society: The Civil Law World*, vol II (Berkeley, University of California Press, 1988).

[39] *Papiers Frank*, above, n 13 at #7791–3: letter from Chauvin, 27 August 1896.

women's exclusion from the bar in a number of different European jurisdictions. Thus, while it is necessary to acknowledge the possibility of an
excess of enthusiasm in Chauvin's comment, Frank's role in fostering
acceptance of the *femme-avocat* in Europe provides an opportunity to
examine how male lawyers supported women's efforts to gain admission
to the legal professions.

Louis Frank was born in Brussels in 1864, about three decades after the
popular uprising in 1830 that resulted in the creation of an independent
Belgian state. After centuries of occupation by foreign powers, including
France under Napoleon, the Congress of Vienna in 1815 established a new
country, uniting the territories of Belgium and Holland under a Dutch
king. On 25 August 1830, however, apparently following a revolutionary
aria in a performance at the Brussels Opera House, crowds revolted
against the Dutch king, and he departed a few days later; on 4 October
1830, the provisional government declared Belgium independent.[40] Frank's
maternal grandparents were French, and it is possible that they had settled
in the Belgian territory when it was annexed by France after the
Revolution;[41] many of these French settlers apparently remained in
Belgium after Napoleon's defeat. According to John Crabb, French ideas
of 'the rights of man' had been warmly received in the Belgian territory:
'the romantic liberalism set in motion by the French Revolution had found
enthusiastic reception' there, and thus many French settlers in Belgium
continued to embrace French culture and ideas after the establishment of
an independent Belgian state.[42]

In addition, there is evidence that Frank's family was originally Jewish;
indeed, it is possible that his French grandparents were among the first
Jews to be 'emancipated' in Europe when Jews were granted French
citizenship after the Revolution. As Paula Hyman suggested, the decision
to grant citizenship to Jews after the French Revolution reflected the
impact of Enlightenment theories about 'the common humanity of (at
least) male members of society.'[43] At the same time, some scholars have
noted that French citizenship encouraged the Jewish community to

---

[40] See L van der Essen, *A Short History of Belgium* (Chicago, University of Chicago Press,
1915) at 149–54; and H Pirenne, *Histoire de Belgique* (Bruxelles, Maurice Lamertin, Librarie-
Éditeur, 1948), tome VII (de la Révolution de 1830 à la Guerre de 1914) at 2–36. JH Crabb,
above, n 38 at 13, noted that Belgian independence, its territorial boundaries, and its permanent
neutrality were settled by the London Conference in 1831; see also F de Bueger-Van Lierde,
above, n 35 at 378.

[41] 'Biographical Note' in *Papiers Frank*, above, n 13 at #7787, stating that Frank was 'Belge de
grands-parents maternels français.' See also JH Crabb, above, n 38 at 10–12; and L van der
Essen, above, n 40 at 141–4.

[42] JH Crabb, above, n 38 at 12.

[43] PE Hyman, *The Jews of Modern France* (Berkeley, University of California Press, 1998) at
17–18. See also PE Hyman, 'French Jewish Historiography since 1870' in F Malino and
B Wasserstein (eds), *The Jews in Modern France* (Hanover and London, University Press of New
England for Brandeis University Press, 1985) at 328.

embrace not just emancipation but also assimilation:[44] as Michael Marrus argued, 'emancipation was ... linked with assimilation; the Jews were freed and, as a part of their freedom, were in some sense obliged to become French.'[45] This heritage, reflecting the idealism of European ideas of the Enlightenment, seems to have been embraced by Frank; indeed, a friend of his late father wrote to Frank in 1888 to commend him for following his father's commitment to liberal Judaism.[46] At the same time, Frank's passionate support for equality and his progressive views about legal and social reforms evidenced an abiding commitment to the inclusion of women, as well as men, within Belgian/French intellectual culture at the end of the nineteenth century.

Frank's father was a stockbroker and his parents were comfortably middle class. However, his family circumstances changed when his father died suddenly at a relatively young age; at the time, Frank was just sixteen years old, and his mother apparently experienced some ongoing difficulty in maintaining the family's economic status, a situation which appeared to create financial challenges for Frank later on.[47] From the outset, however, Frank was an outstanding student, and he eventually graduated in philosophy and law from the *Université Libre de Bruxelles* in 1886, with grades of distinction and high distinction. The following year, he presented a thesis at the University of Bologna on the topic of illegitimate children, for which he received the degree of *docteur en droit* (*laurea in Giurisprudenza con lode*).[48] At the same time, he completed research for his first major publication, *De L'Exercice de la Profession d'Avocat en Italie*, an early study of the role and organisation of the bar in Italy.[49] Frank's publication was timely; as Vittorio Olgiati explained, 'a completely new cultural, political and institutional scenario emerged just after the *Risorgimento* ... [and the unification of Italy] in 1861.'[50] Two statutes were enacted in the 1870s, which affected the role and organisation of the legal profession in Italy: the *Professions Act* of 1874, which imposed a university law

[44] PE Hyman, above, n 43 (*The Jews of Modern France*) at 18.

[45] Michael Marrus, *The Politics of Assimilation: The French Jewish Community at the Time of the Dreyfus Affair* (Oxford, Clarendon Press, 1971) at 87.

[46] *Papiers Frank*, above, n 13 at #7791–3, letter from E Aristotle, 7 June 1888; the writer thanked Frank for his article about *La Bienfaisance Israelite à Bruxelles*.

[47] 'Biographical Note' in *Papiers Frank*, above, n 13 at #7787, describing Frank's father as an *agent de change* in Brussels; after his death, his wife, *[une] femme inexperimentée et de caractère faible*, wasted the family wealth (*gaspilla toute*). See also F De Bueger-Van Lierde, above, n 35 at 378. Frank later dedicated a treatise to his mother, Mme Eugénie Frank-Armand: see Frank, *L'Éducation Domestique des Jeunes Filles ou La Formation des Mères* (Paris, Librairie Larousse, 1904).

[48] F De Bueger-Van Lierde, above, n 35 at 378–9; and *Papiers Frank*, above, n 13 at #7787.

[49] See above, n 34. See also *Papiers Frank*, above, n 13 at #7791–5, describing *Le College Jacobs* at Bologna and its connection with students from Brussels.

[50] V Olgiati, above, n 14 at 423–4. See also V Olgiati and V Pocar, 'The Italian Legal Profession: An Institutional Dilemma' in RL Abel and PSC Lewis (eds), above, n 38 at 336; and Andrea Cammelli, 'Universities and Professions' in M Malatesta (ed), above, n 38 at 27.

degree as a prerequisite for access to the legal profession, and the *Public Education Act* of 1876, which expressly allowed women to study law at university.[51] Frank's treatise on the newly organised Italian legal profession, published in Brussels in 1887, described the significance of these post-unification reforms in Italy, and enthusiastically pointed to the bar's responsibility for maintaining the honour, dignity and culture of the profession. In commending this legislative initiative, Frank argued that Italy had recognised the importance of the bar for the administration of justice, including the provision of representation for the poor; his treatise clearly reflected Frank's idealism about European *avocats* and his interest in legal reform.[52]

Yet, Frank's treatise on the Italian legal profession was significant for another reason. In the final section of the treatise, Frank focused on the issue of women lawyers, and the application presented by an aspiring woman *avocat*, Lydia Poët, for admission to the bar in Turin in the early 1880s.[53] As Olgiati noted, the two statutes enacted in Italy in the 1870s had different purposes; however, taken together, they appeared to permit women to attend university law programmes, and thus to acquire a university degree, the essential qualification for admission to the legal profession.[54] Indeed, Lydia Poët obtained a law degree from the University of Turin in 1881 and then completed a two-year apprenticeship in a lawyer's office, which included regular attendance at court proceedings. On completion of these requirements in 1883, Poët applied for admission as an *avocato* to the Council of the *Ordine* of Barristers of Turin, and the Council approved her admission, although not unanimously.[55] However, pursuant to the 1874 statute regulating the legal profession, the *Pubblico Ministero* requested the Attorney General to appeal the decision. Thus, in November 1883, the *Ordine's* decision was reviewed and eventually repealed by the Court of Appeals, and a further appeal to the *Cour de Cassation* at Turin was dismissed in April 1884. As Frank reported in his later treatise in 1898, the Italian courts decided that the functions of an

---

[51] V Olgiati, above, n 14 at 424.

[52] L Frank, above, n 34 at *Avant-Propos*; and at 21: 'De La Défense Gratuite.'

[53] L Frank, above, n 34 at 59–64. See also JC Albisetti, above, n 10 at 829, describing Poët as an 'elusive' pioneer woman lawyer, citing S de Sio, *La Donna e l'Avvocatura: Studio Giuridico-Sociale* (Rome, Tip Della Nuova Roma, 1884); and M Raichich, 'Liceo, Università, Professioni: Un Percorso Difficile' in S Soldani (ed), *L'Educazione delle Donne: Scuole e Modelli di Vita Femminile nell'Italia dell'Ottocento* (Milan, Fernando Santoni de sio Angeli, 1989).

[54] See above, n 14 at 425: The *Public Education Act* was intended to encourage and democratise access to education; while the *Professions Act* was intended to preclude legal titles for (unqualified) members of the nobility.

[55] V Olgiati, above, n 14 at 426–7, reported that the Council experienced heated debate prior to voting in favour of Poët's admission on 9 August 1883; 'two eminent members of the professional Governing Body, who were also members of Parliament, offered their resignation' to register their dissent.

avocat were more than professional; they constituted a 'public office,' foreclosed to women.[56]

Probably in response to an inquiry from Frank, Poët provided a detailed description of her experiences in a letter to him more than a decade later in January 1897.[57] Although her family had lived in Italy for many years, she explained that the Poëts were originally French, having emigrated to Italy after the revocation of the Edict of Nantes; Poët's family was Protestant, and she identified her older brother as the first Protestant lawyer to obtain his degree at an Italian university. Poët herself initially obtained a diploma as a teacher, and then spent two years in Switzerland, learning English and German; at some point, however, she decided that she wanted more education, and expressed her wish to attend university. Apparently, her family was supportive of her ambition, and she began to learn Latin and Greek in preparation for her university courses. Poët successfully obtained her law degree in June 1881; she was the second woman student in any programme at the University of Turin, and her memories of her life as a law student reveal a subtle balance between social constraints and the joy of her university studies. For example, although she was already the only woman among 180 male students in the first year class, male students in other classes and in other faculties regularly attended her lectures for several weeks at the beginning of her course, apparently out of curiosity to see her; as a result, she was surrounded by even larger numbers of male students. However, she reported that the novelty of her role gradually diminished, and that she greatly enjoyed her time in the lecture halls and porticos of the lovely old university. All the same, Poët never permitted her co-students to accompany her outside the university and she attempted to restrict her conversations with them to matters about the courses; as she explained in her 1897 letter, it was not really possible twenty years earlier in Italy for two sisters to go into town to do errands unless they were accompanied by their mother, or at least by a servant. Thus, Poët wanted to be very careful, and she was pleased to find that she had gained the respect of her colleagues as a result of her discretion.

After completing her law studies at the university, Poët told Frank that she returned to her family home in Pignerol and did two years of practical work with Senator Bertea, a family friend; she appeared regularly in a number of tribunals and reported that she was even asked to sign her name in the book for 'practicants' in the Court of Appeal in Turin. After the decision of the *Cour de Cassation* precluded her admission as an

[56] L Frank, *La Femme-Avocat* 1898, above, n 1 at 85; Frank reported on the arguments presented and, at 89–97, on an exchange in the Chambre des députés in June 1884. See also (1883) XX *La Giurisprudenza* 1076 and (1884) XXI *La Giurisprudenza* 321; V Olgiati, above, n 14 at 427; and JC Albisetti, above, n 10 at 829.

[57] *Papiers Frank*, above, n 13 at #6031 (file 4), letter to Frank, 24 January 1897; there are also two earlier letters from Poët in 1896, all written in French.

avocat in 1884, however, Poët settled down to work in her brother's law office; as she explained, she was really working as an *avocat*, except that she could not sign letters and she could not plead in court. However, she reported that her clients accepted her work and advice with *confiance parfaite*; and both her colleagues and the judges treated her well. Indeed, when her brother went to Vichy for his health each year, she took over the practice completely, and, if necessary, she found a colleague to plead in court on behalf of her clients. In addition to this work, Poët had become quite involved with penal reform issues, and she recounted her enthusiastic attendance at the International Penal Congress in Rome in 1885, where she was an active participant in the proceedings; although she did not attend the Congress in St Petersburg in 1890, she reported that she was again present for the Congress in Paris in 1895.

Moreover, Poët described a gala dinner that was held in her honour in Pignerol after the 1885 Congress; she had received considerable publicity for her work at the Congress and many of the press reports continued to comment on the issue of women lawyers. However, as Poët explained to Frank, the judges did not attend this dinner, perhaps because the occasion appeared to represent a protest against the courts' decisions; nonetheless, they sent her a splendid gift of flowers. Interestingly, a similarly positive report about Poët was circulated to members of the Equity Club in the United States in a letter written in 1887 by Cora Benneson, an American law graduate, after her visit to Italy; as Benneson noted, the decision to reject Poët's application had been criticised by a number of legal scholars.[58] In her letter to Frank a decade after Benneson's visit, Poët appeared relatively content with her legal work in her brother's office, and she expressed satisfaction about her professional relationships with legal colleagues. As Frank noted, the judges had concluded in her case that a statutory amendment, *expressly* declaring that women were capable of discharging all the duties of an *avocat*, was necessary; although it seems that a few other Italian women challenged this view in the early twentieth century, it was not until after World War I that legislation was enacted in Italy, permitting women to take up 'all professions and forms of employment.'[59] By that time, it was too late for Poët.

Frank's analysis of Poët's case in his 1887 publication about the Italian legal profession included only a brief examination of the courts' reasoning, but the issue of women's access to the bar had obviously engaged his interest. Moreover, as he indicated in his discussion of Poët's case, he intended

---

[58] Letter of Cora A Benneson, 12 December 1887, in VG Drachman, above, n 15 at 43–4. See also V Olgiati, above, n 14 at 432.

[59] L Frank, *La Femme-Avocat* 1898, above, n 1 at 89; and V Olgiati, above, n 14 at 427–8. According to Olgiati, there were a number of women applicants rejected by the courts until the 1919 legislation; even this legislation continued to exclude women from the judiciary, the police and the army. See also JC Albisetti, above, n 10 at 829.

to publish a more complete work about women's eligibility for admission to the bar in the future.[60] His intention was realised shortly after his return to Belgium, when Marie Popelin decided to submit an application to take the oath to become an *avocat* in Brussels in 1888. Although Popelin was almost two decades older than Frank, they had been students at the university in Brussels at the same time, and Frank charmingly described attending classes with her, sitting '*à côté d'elle, sur les bancs de la Faculté.*'[61] Born in Schaerbeek on the outskirts of Brussels in 1846, Popelin began to work at the age of eighteen as a teacher in a newly established *école moyenne*, and eventually was appointed director of a similar school at Laeken, just north of Brussels, in 1882. However, her appointment to the Laeken position was rescinded, apparently because it did not comply with all the administrative requirements; in this situation, at the age of thirty-seven, Popelin decided to abandon her teaching career, and enrolled as a law student at the university in Brussels.[62] She graduated with distinction in 1888, two years after Frank, and immediately announced her intention to take the oath to become an *avocat* before the Court of Appeals, a plan which excited great controversy in the Belgian press as *L'affaire Popelin*.[63] It was in this context that Frank first published his short treatise in 1888, titled *La Femme-Avocat*, which provided historical background on the legal principles concerning women's eligibility to become *avocats*, and in which he systematically confronted the arguments of Popelin's opponents. Idealistically appealing to equity and legal progress, Frank suggested that a favourable decision from the court, permitting Popelin to take the oath as an *avocat*, would confirm the wisdom and justice of the Belgian judiciary throughout Europe.[64]

Popelin's application was based on Belgian legislation enacted in 1876; according to Frank, this legislation permitted women to attend university courses and to receive degrees.[65] Popelin may have been inspired by her

60 L Frank, above, n 34 at 64.

61 L Frank, *La Femme-Avocat* 1888, above, n 1 at *Avant-Propos*; the book was described as having a *rigueur scientifique, ordonnance logique de l'exposé, style clair et incisif*: see F Van Lierde, 'La "Ligue Belge du Droit des Femmes," 1892–1897' (Mémoire presenté en vue de l'obtention du grade de licencié en Philosophie et Lettres, L'Université Catholique de Louvain, 1971) at 41.

62 F De Bueger-Van Lierde, 'A L'Origine du Mouvement Féministe en Belgique: "L'Affaire Popelin"' (1972) 50 *Revue Belge de Philologie et d'Histoire* 1128.

63 F De Bueger-Van Lierde, above, n 62 at 1129. See also F Van Lierde, above, n 61 at 35–65.

64 L Frank, *La Femme-Avocat* 1888, above, n 1 at *Avant-Propos* and at 94; and F Van Lierde, above, n 61 at 51. Frank reported that Popelin came from a distinguished Belgian family; her brother had charge of the second Belgian expedition to east Africa where he died at Karema at age 30.

65 L Frank, 'University Opportunities for Women' (1894) *Educational Review* 471 at 475–6. Earlier, Frank had reported that 156 women were registered as students in Belgian universities between 1882–83 and 1888–8; three English women obtained medical diplomas in 1888, the year that Popelin obtained the first law degree awarded to a woman: see L Frank, 'La Loi sur L'Enseignement Supérieur et L'Admission des Femmes dans les Facultés Belges' (1889) LXIII *Revue de Belgique* 289 at 291–3.

sister, who had earlier obtained a university diploma in pharmacy and had then become the first woman admitted to the Royal Society of Pharmacy in Belgium; in addition, according to Albisetti, women's access to Belgian universities was encouraged by the absence of any requirement for a classical secondary diploma.[66] In this context, Popelin succeeded in her law studies, hoping that women's access to university legal education would lead to its logical result: recognition that she was eligible to become an *avocat*. Her aspiration was undoubtedly fuelled by supporters like Frank, who pointed out that nothing in the Belgian Civil Code expressly excluded women from the practice of law: first, the Belgian Code, based on the Napoleonic Code of 1804 and adopted in the Belgian territory during the period of French rule over Belgium, contained no such express provisions; and second, there were no such provisions in the decree of 1810 concerning the organisation of the legal profession, which also applied in Belgium.[67] Moreover, these provisions remained unchanged following the establishment of the Belgian state, pursuant to the constitution adopted after the uprising of 1830; indeed, as one scholar argued, 'Belgian law [continued to have] a particularly close resemblance to French law.'[68] In such a context, proponents like Frank argued that nothing in either of these Codes precluded women from taking the oath as *avocats*.

In addition to supporting Popelin's application with such arguments in his 1888 treatise, Frank personally participated in the presentation of Popelin's claim to the Court of Appeals. He appeared, as a *jeune stagiaire*, on behalf of Popelin, along with Jules Guillery, a distinguished member of the Belgian bar, who was both a former *bâtonnier de L'Ordre des Avocats* and a former president of the *Chambre des Représentants*.[69] However, in spite of Guillery's prestige and the legal arguments presented on behalf of Popelin, the Court of Appeals rejected her claim in December 1888; and when she appealed the decision the following year, her appeal was similarly dismissed by the *Cour de Cassation* in November 1889.[70] As Popelin explained in her letter to the Equity Club the following year, the court's reasoning included discussions about Roman law, the customs of the Middle Ages, the decree of 1810 and the Napoleonic Code, 'but no

66 L Frank, *La Femme-Avocat* 1888, above, n 1 at *Avant-Propos*; and JC Albisetti, above, n 10 at 829.

67 L Frank, *La Femme-Avocat* 1888, above, n 1 at 46–54. See also JH Crabb, *The French Civil Code* (Littleton, CO, Rothman & Co; and The Netherlands, Kluwer Law and Taxation Publishers, 1995) rev edn at xx–xv. For arguments opposing Popelin's claim, see F Van Lierde, above, n 61 at 53–5 and 60–63.

68 JH Crabb, above, n 38 at 3.

69 F De Bueger-Van Lierde, above, n 62 at 1133; and Frank, *La Femme-Avocat* 1888, above, n 1 at *Avant-Propos*. See also F Van Lierde, above, n 61 at 52.

70 F Van Lierde, above, n 61 at 35–65; and JC Albisetti, above, n 10 at 830. The *Cour de Cassation* suggested a need for legislative action; although considered by the Belgian Parliament in 1890, the proposed amendment was rejected: see also F De Bueger-Van Lierde, above, n 62 at 1134–5.

one discussed the progress made in ... woman's condition, of her entry [into] most of the liberal careers, and especially of the woman lawyer, and the experience, tried with success in the United States.'[71]

Indeed, the court's reasoning was criticised by a number of legal commentators: for example, it was suggested that arguments based on the '*office viril*' in Roman law and on Napoleon's opinion about the subordinate role of women were far from definitive with respect to Popelin's application; and that taking the oath should have been clearly distinguished from the right to plead.[72] In addition, a lengthy critique by Professor Glasson, a supporter of women's equality rights at the University of Paris, appeared with a report of the court's decision; as Glasson argued, since both the Code and the decree of 1810 were silent on the question of women *avocats*, it was necessary to determine the issue on the basis of general principles of law. Rejecting the idea that women were excluded from participating in professional work that involved a 'public function,' Glasson quoted approvingly another commentator who had argued that:

> ... [L]a profession d'avocat n'est pas un privilege, elle n'est pas fermée; au contraire, elle s'oeuvre devant la vocation de tous ceux qu'aiment le gout de travail, le sentiment delicat de l'honneur et l'amour de l'indépendence.[73]

As Frank later noted in his 1898 treatise, *L'Affaire Popelin* continued for some time after the 1889 decision. For example, at a session of the *Fedération des Avocats Belges* in 1891, a motion about the issue of women lawyers was equally supported and rejected. In October 1893, a commission investigating reforms to the bar recommended (by three votes to two) the admission of women lawyers; but the *Conseil de l'Ordre* refused to accept the recommendation (by eight votes to four).[74] By 1901, however, there was a strong majority vote in favour of women lawyers at a meeting of the *Fedération*; and there was increasing support for amending legislation introduced in 1912 and again in 1920, but neither proposal achieved success. Indeed, it was not until 1922 that legislation was finally enacted to permit women in Belgium to become *avocats*.[75] Perhaps accepting that her goal of becoming an *avocat* was unlikely, Popelin had turned her skills to organisations and projects involving women's equality

71 VG Drachman, above, n 15 at 199: letter from Marie Popelin (dated by Drachman, at 281, as 1890; and translated by Barbara Pajot).

72 MV Jeanvrot, 'Observations' (15 January 1889) *Revue de la Réforme Judiciare et Législative* 64. See also *Papiers Frank*, above, n 13 at #6031 (envelope 5): submission of Jules Guillery and Me Carl Devos to the *Cour de Cassation*.

73 E Glasson, 'Note' (1889) 2 *Jurisprudence Générale: Recueil Périodique et Critique de Jurisprudence, de Législation et de Doctrine* at 36. See also J Signorel, *La Femme-Avocat: Exposé Historique, Juridique et Critique* (Toulouse, Imprimerie Saint-Cyprien, 1894).

74 L Frank, *La Femme-Avocat* 1898, above, n 1 at 83–4.

75 F De Bueger-Van Lierde, above, n 62 at 1136–7; and *Pasinomie*, 5th série, (1922) XIII, no 106, p 65–76. See also JC Albisetti, above, n 10 at 829–30; and E Charrier, above, n 3 at 438.

in law. As President of the Belgian National Council of Women, for example, she participated in the meeting of the International Council in Toronto in 1909; and she also organised an important *Congrès féministe internationale* in Brussels in 1912.[76]

For Frank, the negative outcome of Popelin's case in Belgium seemed to mark a turning point in his career, becoming a catalyst for even greater involvement in women's legal rights; as Françoise De Bueger-Van Lierde noted: '*Devant le refus exprimé par la Cour d'appel, puis la Cour de cassation, il décida de se consacrer au féminisme.*'[77] Significantly, he resigned from a brief period of employment at the Rothschild Bank in Paris, explaining that he found the work uncongenial;[78] returning to Brussels, Frank offered a course in *Droit Pénal* at the university,[79] and he began his lifelong involvement in the international peace movement.[80] In 1891, he also decided to participate in the Rossi constitutional law competition at the Paris Law School. The subject for the *concours* was *De la condition des femmes au point de vue de l'exercice des droits publics et des droits politiques: Étude de législation comparée*.[81] The study which Frank submitted for the competition was well-received and he was awarded the title of *lauréat* of the Paris Law School for his accomplishment. As a review in the *New York Herald* explained, the Rossi prize was divided among three competitors: Moisei Ostrogorski, Léon Giraud and Frank; it appears that Ostrogorski took first prize, but the review nonetheless described Frank's essay as 'probably the most voluminous and comprehensive work ever devoted to the social and political condition of the charming sex.'[82]

Frank's study was published in 1892 as *Essai sur la Condition Politique de la Femme*, an ambitious treatise of more than six hundred pages, to great acclaim; as *L'Étoile Belge* noted, it was '*un beau livre, original, complet,*

76 See M Popelin, 'Laws on Marriage and Divorce in Belgium' in *Report of the International Congress of Women, Toronto: 24–30 June 1909* (Toronto, Geo Parker & Sons, 1910) Vol II, at 248; and Ligue Belge du Droit des Femmes, *Actes du Congrès Féministe Internationale de Bruxelles 1912* (Bruxelles, Imprimerie Scientifique Charles Bulens, 1912).

77 F De Bueger-Van Lierde, above, n 35 at 379.

78 F De Bueger-Van Lierde, above, n 35 at 379; see also *Papiers Frank*, above, n 13 at #7793.

79 See L Frank, *Résumé du Cours de Droit Pénal* (Bruxelles, Gustave Mayolez, 1887).

80 Frank was active in the Belgian section of *La Fédération Internationale de l'Arbitrage et de la Paix* between 1889–1890, and an early partisan of world federation: see H Josephson (ed), *Biographical Dictionary of Modern Peace Leaders* (Westport, CT, Greenwood Press, 1985) at 300. See also Frank's later publications: *Les Belges et La Paix* (Bruxelles, Henri Lamertin, 1905); and *La Paix et le District Fédéral du Monde* (Paris, Librairie Larousse, 1910); these works and an assessment appear in SE Cooper (ed), *Peace Activities in Belgium and the Netherlands* (New York and London, Garland Publishing Inc, 1972).

81 L Frank, *Essai sur la Condition Politique de la Femme: Étude de Sociologie et de Législation* (Paris, Arthur Rousseau, 1892) at *Avant-Propos*.

82 *New York Herald*, 21 February 1892. See also SL Kimble, above, n 5 at 55–8, in relation to Ostrogorski. *Papiers Frank*, above, n 13 at #7782 includes numerous press cuttings, sometimes identifying Frank as Franck.

*plein d'érudition, attrayante, ... comme un petit monument définitif,
l'encyclopédie de la question féminine,'* and the work generated a sensation
in Belgium and elsewhere.[83] Frank's treatise contained two parts: the first
comprehensively reviewed ideas about women's economic and political
emancipation, methodically examining legal arguments and outlining a
detailed programme for reforming the civil codes, while the second
provided the results of Frank's research surveys about the circumstances of
women's lives at the end of the nineteenth century in a large number of
jurisdictions, including France and other European countries, Britain and
the colonies, the United States, parts of Latin America, Hawaii and Japan.
On the basis of his research in all these jurisdictions, Frank argued that an
important evolution toward the goal of sex equality was occurring in all
parts of the world, and he urged that European civil codes be amended to
reflect this emerging commitment to women's equality worldwide.[84]

Clearly, Frank's surveys of all these different jurisdictions resulted in
important contacts for his future comparative work. As he noted at the
outset, he had received assistance from a large number of correspondents
in Europe and elsewhere, including the Prime Minister of Canada, Sir John
A Macdonald, who had assigned one of his assistants to make inquiries
about the suffrage issue in all seven provinces of Canada; Frank also
reported on the failure to enact women's suffrage as part of the federal
electoral bill in Canada in 1885.[85] In a similar fashion, Frank provided
details about several petitions for women's suffrage in the British
Parliament,[86] and he documented the extent to which women's suffrage
had been achieved in some American states.[87] He also examined women's
employment and the role of women as police matrons, as members of
juries, and as lawyers, restating the views about women *avocats* that he
had expressed earlier in 1888 in *La Femme-Avocat*.[88] According to De
Bueger-Van Lierde, Frank's *Essai* received a highly enthusiastic reception;
indeed, the press in Paris was particularly enthusiastic about Frank's
book because it encouraged rights for women without a loss of femininity,
a *féminisme modère*.[89]

Significantly, Frank's treatise warmly embraced the writings of John

[83] *L'Étoile Belge*, 16 February 1892; and F De Bueger-Van Lierde, above, n 35 at 380–81. See also the review by Mary A Greene, *The Woman's Journal*, Boston, 5 November 1892.
[84] L Frank, *Essai*, above, n 81 at 221.
[85] L Frank, *Essai*, above, n 81 at *Avant-Propos* and 380; see also *Papiers Frank*, above, n 13 at #7787.
[86] L Frank, *Essai*, above, n 81 at 343, and Annexe at 353; Frank also noted the letter in *The Nineteenth Century* in 1889, signed by a number of prominent women anti-suffragists, including Beatrice Potter.
[87] L Frank, *Essai*, above, n 81 at 383.
[88] L Frank, *Essai*, above, n 81 at 274; Frank also noted, at 281, the 1891 bill in the Indiana legislature, providing that the jury should be entirely female if the accused was female. See also *La Femme-Avocat* 1888, above, n 1.
[89] F De-Bueger-Van Lierde, above, n 35 at 382–3.

Stuart Mill, even though Mill's ideas were generally rejected by some *redoutables adversaires*, including eminent faculty members at the Paris Law School where the Rossi competition was held.[90] Indeed, it is possible that Frank particularly admired Mill because Mill had not only *written* about women's equality, but had also *worked actively* to achieve this goal. Citing Mill's courage in 1866, when he had persisted in presenting the petition signed by 1500 women to the British Parliament, in spite of laughter from a majority of members of the House of Commons, Frank concluded that *'l'hostilité du Parlement était impuissante à décourager un homme tel que Stuart Mill.'*[91] In this context, Frank may have been inspired by Mill's activism when he used the opportunity created by all the favourable press reports of his *Essai* to join with Popelin and others to establish *La Ligue Belge du Droit des Femmes* in 1892:

> *D'une haute tenue scientifique, frappant par son féminisme modère, it fut pris au sérieux dans la presse. Il permit ainsi à l'opinion publique de reconnaître la valeur intellectuelle de Louis Frank et de réfléchir à la question, si bien qu'elle approuva sans moquerie la création de la Ligue belge du droit des femmes.*[92]

At the outset, Frank played a leading role in *La Ligue*, the 'first feminist organization in Belgium,' assuming responsibility as the organisation's secretary general.[93] At its first assembly in a hall at the *Université Libre* in November 1892, for example, Frank presented a detailed report, outlining the proposed programme and other arrangements for *La Ligue*, and concluding with an expression of hopefulness about reforms and *le triomphe final du féminisme*.[94]

In this context, Frank became energetically involved in a number of writing projects and publications, all designed to encourage reforms concerning the legal and social status of women. In the first half of the 1890s, for example, he published articles and pamphlets about women's higher education,[95] marriage and married women's earnings,[96] women doctors and pharmacists,[97] and suffrage.[98] He also authored an important

[90] L Frank, *Essai*, above, n 81 at 53: see A Duverger, *De la Condition Politique et Civile des Femmes* (Paris, A Marescq, 1872); E Glasson, *Éléments du Droit Français dans ses Rapports avec le Droit Naturel et L'Économie Politique* (Paris, Guillaumin, 1875); and Jalabert, *Cours de Droit Constitutionnel*, Lecture of 27 March 1890.

[91] L Frank, *Essai*, above, n 81 at 345.

[92] F De Bueger-Van Lierde, above, n 35 at 383; see also F Van Lierde, above, n 61 at 66–90.

[93] F De Bueger-Van Lierde, above, n 62 at 1137.

[94] F Van Lierde, above, n 61 at 88.

[95] See L Frank, above, n 65; see also 'Les Femmes et L'Enseignement Supérieur' (February 1893) *Revue Universitaire* 234.

[96] L Frank, 'La Question du Mariage' (June 1890) *Revue du Belgique*; and *L'Épargne de la Femme Mariée* (Bruxelles, A Vromant et Cie, 1892).

[97] L Frank, 'La Femme-Médecin' (March 1893); 'La Femme-Médecin aux Indes' (June 1893); 'La Femme-Médecin en Orient' (June 1895); and 'Les Femmes-Pharmaciens' (October 1894).

[98] L Frank, 'Le Suffrage des Femmes en Nouvelle-Zélande' (November 1893); and 'Le Suffrage des Femmes au Kansas' (November 1894).

and somewhat controversial report about women in public employment in Belgium.[99] Moreover, in addition to analysing the need for reform, Frank's publications frequently included detailed legal proposals for amending the civil codes. His work was also appearing in American journals: for example, his 1888 treatise on women lawyers, which had been written in support of Popelin's claim, had been translated into English by Mary Greene, an American woman lawyer, and published in the *Chicago Law Times* during *L'Affaire Popelin*.[100] Similarly, another article written by Frank, which championed women's access to higher education in Europe, was translated and published in the *Educational Review* in the United States in 1894.[101] He also published a short tribute to Prime Minister Gladstone at the time of the British election in 1892.[102]

In addition to these projects, Frank decided to publicise his reformist ideas to a larger audience by publishing *Le Grand Catéchisme de La Femme* in 1894.[103] Outlining the laws affecting women, the *Catéchisme* was frankly designed to educate the public about women's legal status and to encourage reform in three areas: women's rights in marriage, their right to work in all occupations and professions, and their right to participate in public life. The *Catéchisme* included twenty one 'lessons,' incisively exploring, through questions and answers, women's intelligence and mission, their position in marriage, the situation for women doctors, lawyers and administrators, the legal regulation of women's work, and issues relating to suffrage. Conversational and often humourous in tone, the *Catéchisme* reflected Frank's flamboyant style as well as his earnest commitment to women's legal rights. For example, Frank explained the courts' rejection of the applications submitted by Poët in Italy and Popelin in Belgium, making fun of the Italian court's concerns about what kind of hats women lawyers would wear to court. He also ridiculed the views expressed by the Belgian court, including the conclusion that all women had a 'mission to marry;' pointing to the large numbers of 'excess' single women over the age of twenty-five, Frank argued that they needed to be able to support themselves independently, as women lawyers were already

99 L Frank, *La Femme dans les Emplois Publics: Enquête et Rapport* (Bruxelles, Charles Rozez, 1893). For a review of this publication and its controversy, see F De Bueger-Van Lierde, above, n 35 at 384–8; and F Van Lierde, above, n 61 at 113–14 and at 246–52.

100 Mary A Greene was a member of the Massachusetts bar and the Equity Club: see VG Drachman, above, n 15; the work appeared in four parts in the *Chicago Law Times* in 1889: see vol 3 at 74, 120, 253 and 382.

101 L Frank, 'University Opportunities for Women,' above, n 65.

102 L Frank, *MWE Gladstone et Le Féminisme* (Gand, Imprimerie C Annoot-Braeckman, 1893).

103 L Frank, *Le Grand Catéchisme de la Femme* (Paris, Verviers, 1894). This work was dedicated to 'Miss Mary A Greene, *Avocat au Barreau de Providence: Hommage de Sympathie & d'Amitié*': see n 100. Greene acknowledged that she felt 'much honoured to have it dedicated to [her]': see *Papiers Frank*, above, n 13 at #7791(file 4); it was translated into six languages: see F De Bueger-Van Lierde, above, n 35 at 390.

doing in Chile, Hawaii and the United States.[104] Criticising legal regimes which divided men and women into different categories in relation to their rights, Frank asked rhetorically:

> *Comment donc pourrait-elle être rationnelle, cette prétention téméraire de l'homme, de vouloir diviser en deux l'unité humaine; de créer deux natures, deux âmes, deux cerveaux humains? Cette prétention qui blesse la nature, viole l'équité, offense la raison, parâitre à nos descendants non moins absurde ni moins vaine que la prétention émise jadis par le pape, de partager le monde entre les Espagnols et les Portugais.*[105]

Concluding that feminist demands would ultimately succeed because they were *justes et utiles*, Frank suggested that women would eventually attain legal reforms because '*[C]e que femme veut, Dieu le veut.*'[106]

However, by the time the *Catéchisme* appeared, Frank had been forced to resign from *La Ligue Belge du Droit des Femmes*. Although his research skills and his success in gaining attention in the press were initially useful to the *Ligue*, Frank was apparently unable to separate his activities from those of the organisation; in addition, he wanted to take part in all aspects of the work of *La Ligue* and to draft articles for its bulletin, but he also did not want to abandon any of his own publication projects.[107] There is also evidence that some women members of the *Ligue* thought that he was making too many decisions without consultation; in late 1893, for example, one member had asserted angrily, '*C'est Napoléon Frank qui règne ici.*'[108] Frank's letter of resignation appeared in *L'Indépendence belge*, and he then published a short article, arguing that women would never succeed in attaining their equality goals without the support of men; as he stated pointedly: '*Les dames seules, entre elles, n'engendreront jamais un Stuart Mill.*'[109] As De Bueger-Van Lierde reported, moreover, quarrels had erupted early on between the 'Frankistes' and the 'Popelinistes' about who was the real founder of the organisation; eventually, Popelin was regarded as the founder, while Frank's contribution became almost invisible.[110]

---

[104] L Frank, above, n 103 at 77–9; lesson 14 'La Femme Avocat' at 77.

[105] L Frank, above, n 103 at 9. Frank argued, at 15, that women were subjected to laws that they did not make, required to pay taxes for which they did not vote, and compelled to submit to justice which they did not render.

[106] L Frank, above, n 103 at 120 and 123.

[107] F De Bueger-Van Lierde, above, n 35 at 389. See also F Van Lierde, above, n 61 at 118–19.

[108] Quoted in F Van Lierde, above, n 61 at 117. The comment was made by Isabelle Gatti de Gamond, a leader in the establishment of girls' education, who had actively participated with Popelin and Frank in the establishment of *La Ligue*; in response to her words, Frank responded '*Vous voudriez sans doute que ce soit Catherine Gatti de Gamond,*' perhaps a reference to Catherine the Great of Russia. See also M Boël and C Duchene, *Le Féminisme en Belgique, 1892–1914* (Bruxelles, Éditions du Conseil National des Femmes Belge, 1955) at 31.

[109] F Van Lierde, above, n 61 at 118; see also L Frank, 'Dames Seules,' *L'Indépendence belge*, 7 February 1894.

[110] F Van Lierde, above, n 61 at 82.

Nonetheless, undeterred by his forced resignation from *La Ligue*, Frank continued to write and to participate in conferences about women's legal rights, and he continued to take part in activities organised by *La Ligue*, including its international congress in 1898.[111] Moreover, Frank's ardent support for women's equality continued to be recognised in the press; in May 1894, for example, *Le Petit Bleu* published a charming cartoon of Frank, enrobed in women's skirts, designating him *un Bruxellois par jour*.[112]

And, indeed, Frank continued to involve himself in projects concerning women's equality. In the academic year 1894–1895, Frank presented an extension course at the *Université Libre de Bruxelles*, where he had been named a *docteur spécial en droit public*; entitled *Cours sur La Législation Féministe,* Frank's published lecture notes reveal that his course provided an outline of laws affecting women from a comparative perspective, ranging from ancient times to current legal regimes in different jurisdictions in the world. Not surprisingly, his course also reflected the idea that both men and women had an interest in women's emancipation.[113] In addition, in 1896, Frank established the *Office Féministe Universel*, with the stated goal of creating an international and central depository for all documents concerning women's rights, both for purposes of study and for lobbying; as he explained, the *Office* intended to publish law reform proposals and to study scientifically all the elements of the woman question. Although it appears that the *Office* never existed independently of Frank, it provided a formal base for his reform work for several years.[114] For example, Frank published three pamphlets in 1896, under the auspices of the *Office*, concerning proposed reforms of the civil codes: *Le Témoinage de la Femme* (women's right to give evidence); *L'Épargne de la Femme Mariée* (married women's rights to their own savings); and *Les Salaires de la Famille Ouvrière* (workers' family salaries).[115] For each pamphlet, he provided a succinct historical context and detailed drafts of his proposed legal reforms; all three proposals were reviewed positively in Britain by the *Englishwoman's Review*.[116] In this context, Frank envisaged undertaking similar *travaux préparatoires* in relation to all the other reforms to the Codes that were necessary to foster women's legal equality.

---

[111] See F Van Lierde, above, n 61 at 119, identifying the 1898 congress as the first sign of reconciliation between Frank and Popelin.

[112] *Le Petit Bleu*, Bruxelles, 2 May 1894.

[113] F De Bueger-Van Lierde, above, n 35 at 384; and L Frank, *Cours sur La Législation Féministe: Notions Élémentaires* (Bruxelles, J H Moreau, 1895).

[114] F De Bueger-Van Lierde, above, n 35 at 391. See also L Frank, *Le Témoinage de La Femme: Rapport (Proposition de Loi No 1)* (Bruxelles, Henri Lamertin, 1896) at 56, setting out the goals of the *Office*.

[115] L Frank, above, n 114; L Frank, *L'Épargne de la Femme Mariée: Rapport (Proposition de Loi No 2)* (Bruxelles, Henri Lamertin, 1896); and L Frank, *Les Salaires de la Famille Ouvrière: Rapport (Proposition de Loi No 3)* (Bruxelles, Henri Lamertin, 1896).

[116] *Englishwoman's Review*, 15 October 1896.

Moreover, beyond the reform of existing laws, Frank focused on broader ideas that could effect real equality for women; for example, he collaborated with an actuary and an obstetrician to design a proposal for an insurance system for women workers who were unable to work when they gave birth to children.[117] Thus, apparently undaunted by his forced separation from *La Ligue*, Frank firmly asserted that his primary goal was to continue the struggle for women's rights.[118]

By the mid-1890s, Frank had demonstrated expertise on a wide range of legal issues concerning women's equality, and he had established contact with a number of reformers in other countries. In this same period, Jeanne Chauvin had become actively involved with a reformist organisation established in Paris in 1893 by Jeanne Schmahl;[119] *L'Avant-Courrière* had been created by Schmahl to lobby for two specific changes to the French *Code* to achieve women's equality goals: one proposal was designed to protect the earnings of married women (without the necessity of expensive marriage contracts),[120] and the other was intended to permit women to give evidence (*témoinage*) before notaries and other state officials.[121] Significantly, both these issues were matters about which Frank was also publishing reform proposals in the mid-1890s,[122] and it appears that his first communication with Chauvin related to their mutual interests in these legal reforms; thus, in a letter to Frank in mid-1895, Chauvin thanked him for his help in sending her some information to assist her reform activities with *L'Avant-Courrière*.[123] It was not until the following year that her letters focused on her application to take the oath to become an *avocat* at

---

117 L Frank, L Maingie and Dr Keiffer, *L'Assurance Maternelle* (Bruxelles, Henri Lamartin; and Paris, G Carré et N Naud, 1897). Frank argued that the state required women to leave work at the time of giving birth, thus creating financial difficulties; he proposed extending sick benefits to maternity.

118 See L Frank, *Les Salaires de la Famille Ouvrière*, above, n 115 at *Avant-Propos*.

119 See M Albistur and D Armogathe, *Histoire du Féminisme Français de l'Empire Napoléonien à Nos Jours*, vol 2 (Paris, Éditions des Femmes, 1977) at 520. Jeanne Schmahl (1847–1915) was born in England to an English father and French mother, and came to Paris to study medicine; she wanted to reform the French *Code* to reflect the goals of the *Married Women's Property Acts* in England. She founded *L'Avant-Courrière*, a group of about 200 members which combined 'uncompromising feminism with conservative standards of behaviour': see SC Hause with AR Kenney, *Women's Suffrage and Social Politics in the French Third Republic* (Princeton, Princeton University Press, 1984) at 56–7. See also JW Scott, *Only Paradoxes to Offer: French Feminists and the Rights of Man* (Cambridge, MA, Harvard University Press, 1996); and SC Hause, *Hubertine Auclert: The French Suffragette* (New Haven, Yale University Press, 1987).

120 '*Proposition de Loi sur la Capacité des Femmes Mariées de Disposer du Produit de leur Travail ou de leur Industrie Personnel*' (Paris, L'Avant-Courrière, 1893).

121 '*Proposition de Loi sur la Capacité des Femmes d'Etre Témoin dans les Actes Publics ou Privés*' (Paris, L'Avant-Courrière, 1893).

122 See above, n 115. It seems that Frank may have been aware of Chauvin's work as early as 1893, since a note appeared in the publication of *La Ligue* in Brussels in January 1893: '*Le Mouvement Feministe: Mlle Jeanne Chauvin*': see SL Kimble, above, n 5 at 42.

123 *Papiers Frank*, above, n 13 at #7791–7, letter from Chauvin, 14 May 1895.

the Paris bar.[124] Even though Chauvin had been a student at the University of Paris when Frank participated in the Rossi competition in 1891, it seems that it was not until the mid-1890s that their mutual commitment to reforming the civil codes brought them together.

Chauvin graduated with her *docteur en droit* in 1892; she was then nearly thirty years old, having been born into a bourgeois family in 1862 at Jargeau, near Orléans.[125] The next year, her parents had moved to Proviers, where her father practised as a notary until his early death in 1879; according to Chauvin, her father's death left the family in difficult financial circumstances. At some point, her mother decided to move with her daughter and son to Paris, where Jeanne Chauvin was among the first women in France to take the baccalaureate examinations;[126] she was an excellent student, successfully completing the *licencié ès lettres* in 1890. In 1892, Chauvin graduated with a *docteur en droit*, with a thesis on the topic of women's right to engage in the professions.[127] It seems that both her thesis topic and her role as a woman doctoral student were controversial, as her oral defence was noisily disrupted by large numbers of students who were unable to fit into the small room allocated for the occasion. As a result, Chauvin's defence was postponed; when it was re-scheduled four days later, on 6 July 1892, Chauvin again attracted a crowd.[128] As a correspondent to the *New York Times* reported:

> She is undoubtedly a bright woman, although I failed to catch one word of her discourse, but her reasoning reads well.... She is taken *au serieux*, however, and what a gigantic stride that means only a long resident of Paris can begin to understand. The same public, outside of the students and professionals, flocking to the Neuilly fair at night and delighting in the vexation of the new plaything – the peacock feathers... – this same public, eager for a new sensation, was attracted to the hearing of *Mlle* Chauvin. They even listened; and this was a triumph indeed. She was scarcely at ease amid so much interruption, but her manner remained calm and her expression and constant smile were even supercilious; her judges affected a condescension of manner....[129]

[124] *Papiers Frank*, above, n 13 at #7791-3, letter from Chauvin, 26 July 1896.

[125] 'Jeanne Chauvin' in *Dictionnaire de Biographie Française* (Paris, Librairie Letouzey et Anê, 1959) at 929; and Anne Commire (ed), *Women in World History*, vol 3 (Waterford, CT, Yorkin, 1999) at 661.

[126] SC Hause with AR Kenney, above, n 119 at 24. See also J Burr Margadant, *Madame le Professeur: Women Educators in the Third Republic* (Princeton, Princeton University Press, 1990); and K Offen, 'The Second Sex and the Baccalauréat in Republican France, 1880–1924' (1983) 13 *French Historical Studies* 252.

[127] *Papiers Frank*, above, n 13 at #7791-6 (envelope 1): biographical statement of Jeanne Chauvin (undated). Chauvin graduated with a prize in civil law: see L Frank, *La Femme-Avocat* 1898, above, n 1 at iv and SL Kimble, above, n 5 at 28–9. Chauvin's thesis was *Étude Historique sur les Professions Accessibles aux Femmes: Influence du Sémitisme sur l'Évolution de la Position Économique de la Femme dans la Société* (Paris, A Giard & E Brière, 1892).

[128] SL Kimble, above, n 5 at 32–3. SC Hause with AR Kenney, above, n 119 at 24, also suggested that Chauvin faced a riot that halted the defence of her thesis.

[129] LK, 'At the Dudley Sale' *New York Times*, 24 July 1892, at 5; the report described

In spite of her success in obtaining the *docteur en droit*, however, Chauvin later reported to Frank that she had not dared to present herself at the Paris bar; knowing about the earlier rejection of Popelin in Belgium, Chauvin concluded in the early 1890s that she should look elsewhere for legal work.

Thus, Chauvin began to provide lessons on law in five girls' *lycées* in Paris. A few years later in 1895, she published her *Cours de Droit Professé dans les Lycées de Jeunes Filles de Paris*, described by the Dean of the Faculty of Law of Paris as *une encyclopédie juridique en miniature*.[130] In addition to teaching, Chauvin became actively involved in writing about legal reforms for *L'Avant-Courrière*. Chauvin's pamphlets reveal her ability to explain the issues clearly, and her expert knowledge about precisely how the *Code* could be amended to achieve the proposed reforms. As a report in the *Englishwoman's Review* explained, *L'Avant-Courrière* represented a practical approach to the advancement of women by 'advocating a programme of a very fundamental, but at the same time restricted, scope...: the right to serve as witnesses in public and private transactions, and for married women the right to dispose of the product of their own labour.'[131] In spite of the restricted scope of the proposed amendments, however, it was not until 1897 that women achieved the right to give evidence; moreover, married women were not entitled to their own earnings in France until 1907.[132]

However, by the mid-1890s, Chauvin and Frank were both actively involved in similar reform activities relating to women's legal rights; although it seems that Chauvin had aspirations for a university teaching appointment at the time, her efforts to attain this goal may have been thwarted because she was a woman.[133] In these circumstances, Chauvin seems to have been enthusiastic about presenting an application to take the oath to become an *avocat* in Paris; this plan was clearly consistent with her commitment to advancing women's interests, and it also permitted her to pursue in practice the arguments which she had articulated in her thesis in 1892 about women's access to the professions. Significantly, Chauvin's application to take the oath also presented a new opportunity for Frank to argue in support of a favourable interpretation of the provisions of the Code with respect to the admission of a *femme-avocat*. Indeed, Frank may have hoped that if Chauvin were admitted as an *avocat* pursuant to the

---

Chauvin, stating that 'she is not good-looking, and her face will never be her fortune. She has a big nose, a big mouth, and only sweetly gentle eyes, to make up for the very plain features.'

130 C de Santerre, 'Preface' in J Chauvin, *Cours de Droit Professé dans les Lycées de Jeunes Filles de Paris* (Paris, V Giard & E Brière, 1895) at *vi–vii*.

131 'L'Avant-Courrière' (1893) *Englishwomen's Review* 81.

132 M Albistur and D Armogathe, above, n 119 at 584.

133 See *Papiers Frank*, above, n 13 at #7791–3: letters from Chauvin, 26 July 1896 and 2 August 1896.

Code in France, the issue would have to be reconsidered in Belgium because the two Codes were so similar. In addition, Chauvin's application provided a rationale for a substantial revision and enlargement of Frank's 1888 treatise, *La Femme-Avocat*; Frank appears to have been enthusiastic about a new publication, incorporating the information about the evolution of women's equality that he had obtained from his correspondents in jurisdictions around the world. In this context, the plan for Chauvin to take the oath to become an *avocat* advanced the reform agenda of both Frank and Chauvin.

Certainly, Chauvin's letters to Frank in 1896–1897 reveal her sense of the significance of her case for the goals of women's equality in Europe at the end of the nineteenth century. In July 1896, for example, she described her aspiration to become an *avocat* as part of the feminist struggle: '*Je brûle du désir de me jeter dans la melée, presque certaine d'obtenir de bons résultats*'; at the same time, she expressed her gratitude for Frank's '*sage prudence [et] l'autorité de votre appui et vos excellents conseils.*' She thanked him especially for sending her some propositions of law, and confirmed that she believed him to be '*le seul feministe serieux et travaillant utilement pour le succès de notre cause.*'[134] All the same, it appears that Chauvin was intent on thinking independently about her *cause*. In response to Frank's suggestion that she seek to take the oath a few months later in 1896, for example, Chauvin cautioned that they needed to create broader support before making the application. Thus, even as she stressed that Frank was her *conseil et ... principal défenseur*, she acknowledged that she very much wanted to present her arguments '*s'il y a lieu et selon le circonstances.*'[135] Chauvin's weekly letters to Frank at this point frequently asked him to tell her *ce que j'aurais faire*, and she explained how she had been actively discussing the plan with a few supportive *avocats* and with some of her former professors at the university; she also suggested that it might be prudent to make the application at a time when there was a *bâtonnier* in office who was sympathetic to the issue of women's legal rights. In addition, Chauvin strategically pointed out to Frank that these supporters were important in winning over the press. Yet, in spite of providing this strategic advice, Chauvin modestly characterised her role as merely one aspect of Frank's larger project of reforming the legal status of women: '*J'estime de mon devoir de contribuer même ainsi à côté de vous [au] progrès à la grande cause qui parrait l'unique souci de votre vie.*'[136] In this context, she stated her confidence

134 *Papiers Frank*, above, n 13 at #7791–3: letter from Chauvin, 26 July 1896. Chauvin may be referring to the *Ligue*'s demand for Frank's resignation in 1893.

135 *Papiers Frank*, above, n 13 at #7791–3: letter from Chauvin to Frank, 26 July 1896: Chauvin signed this letter with the usual cordial phrases addressed to her *cher confrère et ami*.

136 *Papiers Frank*, above, n 13 at #7791–3: letters from Chauvin, 8 August 1896 and 27 August 1896.

that Frank's contribution to the cause of women's equality would never be forgotten, particularly by women lawyers, professors and judges in the future.[137]

According to Chauvin's letters, it seems that Frank initially planned to go to Paris in October 1896, and that Chauvin hoped to present her application in November. However, Chauvin's application was not considered until the following year, apparently because Frank became ill in the fall of 1896. In a letter to him at the end of October 1896, Chauvin asked him to slow down and *vivre en bonne santé*, expressing concern that his illness might have occurred as a result of overwork on her case. Encouraging Frank to put his health in order, Chauvin argued that her application could be presented *aujourd'hui ou demain*, and that it was much more important that Frank attend to his health: '*Vous êtes le plus serieux et le plus habile défenseur de la cause féministe, il est de votre premier devoir de vous conserver le plus longtemps possible son savant et sage Directeur....*'[138] By mid-July 1897, however, Chauvin's letters suggest that their preparations were almost complete for submission of her application in October, and she was providing Frank with detailed analyses of provisions of the French Code to assist in honing their legal arguments. Finally, in August 1897, Chauvin wrote to say '*J'ai remis mardi* notre *manuscrit à M Grière*,' the publisher of *La Femme-Avocat* in 1898, and she signed her letter *Jeanne Chauvin, avocat en expectative*.[139]

Chauvin's appearance before the Paris Court of Appeals took place on 24 November 1897. According to Edmée Charrier, Chauvin presented her own case with the assistance of M Guyon, *avoué*, and she offered a *judicieuse défense* to the arguments of the *Procureur Général* who opposed her application.[140] The *Procureur Général* presented three arguments. The first was based on sections 24 and 31 of the law which had re-established the legal profession after the French Revolution; according to the *Procureur Général*, these provisions established the requirements for *avocats*, the licence and the oath, and they were clearly reserved for males only. Thus, he argued that Chauvin was not entitled to take the oath because of her sex. Second, the *Procureur Général* argued that the decree of 1810, which further defined the requirements for an *avocat*, was based on French

---

137 See n 39.
138 *Papiers Frank*, above, n 13 at #7791–3: letter from Chauvin, 31 October 1896. See also letters 20 September 1896 and 26 October 1896.
139 *Papiers Frank*, above, n 13 at #7791–3: letter from Chauvin, 6 August 1897; the letters contain no discussion about authorship, and Chauvin was not named as a co-author of this treatise. See also letters of 9 July 1897, 21 July 1897 and 24 September 1897; in the letter of 21 July, Chauvin reported a meeting with M Plager, bâtonnier for 1897–1898, who indicated his support for women *avocats*.
140 E Charrier, above, n 3 at 336; Charrier's account did not mention Frank's presence. The 'Biographical Note' in *Papiers Frank*, above, n 13 at #7787, recorded that he pleaded for Popelin in Brussels, and for Chauvin in Paris; however, his 'pleadings' in Paris seem to have been restricted to *La Femme-Avocat* 1898, above, n 1.

customary laws, which precluded women from practising law; thus, the decree of 1810 was based on an assumption that *avocats* were to be male only. And finally, the *Procureur Général* submitted that the actual practice of the profession of *avocat* was based on civil rights and the exercise of public duties in the administration of justice, requirements which were implicitly confined to male persons. According to Charrier, Chauvin presented her case, systematically refuting the arguments presented by the *Procureur Général*.[141] Moreover, the *New York Times* enthusiastically reported on her appearance and her advocacy:

> [Chauvin's application] excited considerable interest.... Mlle Chauvin is handsome, tall, well made, and has dark eyes and a fine complexion. She was attired ... in a neat black satin dress, and made an excellent impression. She replied to the Procureur General's objections in a clever speech, arguing that in the absence of an explicit text against women advocates in the French Code, she was entitled to claim admission to the bar. Her manner and diction were faultless, and her address was quite free from declamation.[142]

However, six days later, on 30 November 1897, the court released its decision, refusing Chauvin's claim. The court decided that customary law, which reflected established principles of Roman law, excluded women from the profession of *avocat*, and that the profession of *avocat* constituted an '*office viril;*' the court also indicated that the profession of *avocat*, like the magistrature, was a public office. In the end, however, the court expressed its firm view that the issue of women's eligibility for admission as *avocats* required action on the part of the legislature; it was not a matter for the court to decide:

> ... [Sans] s'arrêter davantage aux affirmations de la demoiselle Chauvin qu'il serait contraire aux moeurs et au progrès de la civilisation moderne de ne point l'admettre au serment d'avocat, la Cour, faisant simplement observer qu'au législateur seul appartient le droit de modifier les lois et d'en édicter de nouvelles, tandis que le pouvoir judiciare n'est appelé qu'à interpréter et à appliquer les lois existantes....[143]

According to Albisetti, the reasoning in Chauvin's case focused narrowly on issues of legal precedent and legislative intent in relation to the Code, issues on which aspiring women lawyers could not succeed.[144]

---

141 E Charrier, above, n 3 at 336–7; and see L Frank, *La Femme-Avocat* 1898, above, n 1 at 191–2 and at 302–3. See also n 7.

142 *New York Times*, 1 December 1897, at 7; the report was dated 30 November and announced the court's rejection of Chauvin's claim on that date, stating that 'the court was packed with people anxious to hear the result.' See also *New York Times*, 2 December 1897, at 6.

143 E Charrier, above, n 3 at 337. See also SL Kimble, above, n 5 at 69–71.

144 JC Albisetti, above, n 10 at 838–44, provided a detailed account of scholarly arguments supporting women lawyers; as he noted, there were fears about overcrowding, and concerns that if women were to gain entry to the legal professions, they would also seek political rights (such as the vote).

More pointedly, Dorothea Wayand concluded that the provisions of the Code had been drafted at a time when the Enlightenment ideas which had fuelled the French Revolution were beginning to wane, and that the provisions reflected Napoleon's personal 'primitive misogynic views.'[145] In such a context, the Code clearly excluded women from becoming *avocats*. Chauvin's case was not appealed, apparently because the *Cour de Cassation* in Belgium had already ruled on this issue in Popelin's case in 1889; and since the legal rules concerning the profession of *avocat* were based on the same provisions of the Codes in the two jurisdictions, legal experts concluded that there was no point in such an appeal.[146] Chauvin seems to have agreed with this course of action. Writing in *La Revue Blanche* in 1897, for example, she suggested that legislative action was necessary to achieve women's goals of equality:

> On s'occupe enfin au Parlement de réformer en faveur des femmes les dispositions de nos lois qui les maintiennent encore dans une sorte d'inégalité au point de vue juridique, et qui sont, selon l'expression de Stuart Mill, une 'dissonance monstrueuse' dans l'harmonie du concert de toutes les libertés et de toutes les égalités, principes des civilisations modernes.[147]

Yet, although her application was unsuccessful, *L'Affaire Chauvin* generated a great deal of publicity in Paris; as Sara Kimble explained, there were cartoons in the newspapers, popular songs about Chauvin, and ongoing debates about women lawyers, all of which demonstrated how Chauvin's case had become a 'lightning rod for mounting social anxieties about rapidly changing gender roles....'[148] As a report in a British journal explained, moreover, arguments about the need for women *avocats* were increasing; indeed, the report indicated that Chauvin was not only confident that women lawyers could succeed, but also 'convinced that numbers of women would prefer to be defended by one of their own sex, even as they prefer to consult a woman doctor in cases of illness.'[149]

In this context, Chauvin and her supporters began the process of seek-

---

145 D Wayand, 'Women in Enlightenment and Revolution and their Position in the First Modern Codes' (1992) 7:2 *Canadian Journal of Law and Society* 93 at 106.

146 E Charrier, above, n 3 at 337–8, citing Dalloz (1900–4–81).

147 J Chauvin, 'Féminisme et Antiféminisme' (1897) *La Revue Blanche* 321 at 325. Her article was a scathing analysis of Proudhon (antifeminist), by contrast with John Stuart Mill (feminist); it also noted that university education was open to women, as were most professions.

148 SL Kimble, above, n 5 at 119; as she argued, at 123, the issue concerned the representation of women in public life, an issue captured in the phrase '*la robe sur robe ne vaut.*' Kimble also noted, at 124, that Chauvin's case occurred shortly after the first performance in Paris of Ibsen's play, *The Doll House*, in 1894.

149 C Quentin, 'Women as Barristers' (1899) 14 *The Humanitarian* 203 at 203–4; Quentin stated that Chauvin was practising, with a considerable clientele, although she was restricted to chamber work.

ing legislative reform. As Charrier documented, an initial proposal was submitted to the Chamber of Deputies in 1898, and adopted on 30 June 1899; after transmission to the Senate in July 1899, it was considered and adopted there on 13 November 1900, taking effect on 1 December 1900.[150] The legislation was championed by a number of socialist and radical politicians, as well as by women's rights organisations, newspapers such as *La Fronde*, and several legal experts.[151] Interestingly, Chauvin's brother, Emile, had been elected to the Chamber of Deputies for the Department of Seine-et-Marne in the election of May 1898; however, Kimble reported that although he supported the bill, he did not participate in the debate nor vote.[152] As soon as the legislation took effect, Olga Balachowsky-Petit, a Russian woman who had studied law in Paris and then married a French *avocat*, took the oath on 6 December; Chauvin was the second woman to do so on 19 December 1900.[153] Describing the occasion when Chauvin finally took the oath to become an *avocat*, Charrier stated pointedly:

> *Mais ce ne fut pas elle qui eut l'honneur de prêter serment la première. Une Russe mariée à un avocat français, qui n'avait fait aucune démarche pour que la loi fût votée, passa devant celle qui luttait avec ténacité depuis plusieurs années afin que les femmes pussent se faire inscrire au barreau.*[154]

Apparently, Frank wrote to congratulate Chauvin, and she responded with warm thanks for his good wishes.[155]

---

[150] See above, n 8. E Charrier, above, n 3 at 338, citing *J Off* 4 December 1900, identified the progress of the amendment: '*Proposition déposée à la Chambre par M Viviani ..., le 21 novembre 1898; Rapport de M Viviani le 2 décembre 1898; Adoption, après discussion, le 30 juin 1899; Transmission au Sénat, le 3 juillet 1899; Rapport de M Tillaye, le 21 juin 1900; Adoption, après discussion, le 13 novembre 1900.*' See also, at 339–45, details of the reports presented in the Chamber and in the Senate.

[151] René Viviani, who introduced the proposed amendment in 1898, was a member of the Paris bar and deputy for the 5th arondissement in Paris; he 'consistently championed the cause of women's rights throughout his career' and was involved in a long relationship with Marguerite Durand, founder of *La Fronde*: see D Bell, D Johnson and P Morris (eds), *Biographical Dictionary of French Political Leaders since 1870* (New York, Simon and Schuster, 1990) at 432.

[152] SL Kimble, above, n 5 at 89–99; and E Charrier, above, n 3 at 338–45. As Kimble noted, at 96–9, the wording of the legislation was restrictive, in that women were not eligible to become judges.

[153] *Dictionnaire de Biographie Française*, above, n 125 at 929.

[154] E Charrier, above, n 3 at 345; Charrier also included the report published in *La Fronde*: see 354–7.

[155] *Papiers Frank*, above, n 13 at #7791–3: letter from Chauvin, 23 September 1900. See also 'Attorneys at Law' *The Woman's Journal*, Boston, 17 February 1900.

THE CONTEXT OF *L'AFFAIRE CHAUVIN*

The case of Jeanne Chauvin is ... a key to understanding a number of issues faced by the [French] Bar at the turn of the century. In addition to anxiety over the demographic expansion in the profession and the sovereignty of the Order with respect to the state, the admission of women raised the question of the rationalization of antiquated rules and ideals related to the 'moral qualities' of the advocate.[156]

As John Savage suggested, Chauvin's case raised a number of complex issues about the role of *avocats* in the Third Republic at the end of the nineteenth century. In addition to describing concerns about overcrowding and ongoing challenges to the monopoly enjoyed by *avocats* in the courts, Savage noted that the *Ordre des Avocats* was increasingly preoccupied about its identity within the republic, an identity which was defined in terms of masculinity. As he suggested, within 'the language of honour and dignity, masculinity worked as a mainly unspoken, but fundamental first principle;' the masculine virtues of the advocate were most evident in his 'singular talent and exclusive function, public speech.'[157] In addition, however, Chauvin's case challenged the independence and authority of the *Ordre* to determine whether applicants for admission met its high standards, and its power to reject candidates who were unsuitable and to discipline *avocats* whose behaviour was unacceptable.[158]

Thus Chauvin's claim not only created the spectre of even more new entrants to an already overcrowded bar, but it also challenged fundamentally the idea of the *avocat* as an '*office viril*;' clearly, after the legislation was enacted in 1900, women *avocats* were authorised to engage in public speech. Interestingly, arguments supporting Chauvin's claim, which pointed to the success of women lawyers in the United States, also raised concerns for the bar in France; as Lucien Karpik argued, French lawyers at the end of the nineteenth century generally rejected the emerging American model in which lawyers were becoming increasingly engaged in economic activities rather than traditional advocacy.[159] More significantly, the enactment of legislation permitting women to become *avocats* firmly set aside the independent authority of the *Ordre* with respect to its decision making about candidates' eligibility for admission. Similarly, Olgiati argued that more was at stake in Poët's case in Italy than the admission of women to

---

[156] J Savage, 'The Problems of Wealth and Virtue: The Paris Bar and the Generation of the *Fin-de-Siècle*' in WW Pue and D Sugarman (eds), *Lawyers and Vampires: Cultural Histories of the Legal Professions* (Oxford, Hart Publishing, 2003) 171 at 202.

[157] J Savage, above, n 156 at 198–9.

[158] J Savage, above, n 156 at 174–6.

[159] L Karpik, 'Technical and Political Knowledge: the Relationship of Lawyers and Other Legal Professions to the Market and the State' in R Torstendahl and M Burrage (eds), *The Formation of Professions: Knowledge, State and Strategy* (London, Sage Publications, 1990) 186 at 189–90.

the bar; as he explained, her case also raised issues about the authority of the *Ordine*, the nature of lawyers' roles as public or private agents, and fundamental issues about gender and citizenship in Italy. In this context, Olgiati concluded that the decisions of the Italian courts established judicial control over the legal profession, a result with significant implications for *avocats* in the long term.[160] In this way, women's claims to become *avocats* were interwoven with other struggles about legal professionalism. As Savage concluded in relation to the Paris Bar, the admission of women as *avocats* 'marked a very public defeat for the Bar's claim to sovereignty and independence, and, for many older lawyers, more evidence of the decline of the gendered ideal of professional honour.'[161]

For Louis Frank, however, *L'Affaire Chauvin* was also interwoven with another important legal case at the end of the nineteenth century: the Dreyfus Affair.[162] Alfred Dreyfus, a Jewish military officer in the French army, had been found guilty of treason in closed court martial proceedings in December 1894. Dreyfus was accused of having passed written information to the Germans; he was swiftly tried and sentenced to military degradation and deportation for life to Devil's Island.[163] However, his family (particularly Alfred's older brother Mathieu and Alfred's wife Lucie), who were convinced of his innocence, eventually arranged for the publication of a pamphlet about the case in November 1896;[164] at the same time, however, anti-Semitic press reports were circulating widely, condemning both Dreyfus and the Jewish community in France.[165] By

160 V Olgiati, above, n 14 at 421 and 429; see also M Malatesta, 'The Italian Professions from a Comparative Perspective' in M Malatesta (ed), above, n 38 at 15.

161 J Savage, above, n 156 at 204.

162 See A Dreyfus, *Cinq Années de ma Vie (1894–1899)* (Paris, Éditions La Découverte, 1994); PE Hyman, above, n 43 at 91–114; M Marrus, above, n 45 at 10–27; M Burns, *Histoire d'une Famille Française: Les Dreyfus* (Paris, Librarie Arthème Fayard, 1994); RF Byrnes, *Antisemitism in Modern France: The Prologue to the Dreyfus Affair* (New York, Howard Fertig, 1969); and S Wilson, *Ideology and Experience: Antisemitism in France at the Time of the Dreyfus Affair* (London and Toronto, Associated University Press, 1982).

163 PE Hyman, above, n 43 at 99–100. A memo (*'bordereau'*) was found by a French cleaning woman in the wastebasket of the German attaché in Paris; it indicated that a French officer was supplying information to the Germans. Although Hyman suggested reasons for suspecting Dreyfus, she also noted that 'anyone familiar with antisemitic tropes cannot fail to recognize that Dreyfus's Jewishness predisposed his colleagues to seeing him as the traitor in their midst.'

164 See PE Hyman, above, n 43 at 102–3; and M Marrus, above, n 45 at 215. Mathieu and Lucie initially campaigned quietly, but in 1896, they obtained assistance from Bernard Lazare, who published *Une Erreur Judiciare: La Vérité sur L'Affaire Dreyfus* in November, at the expense of the Dreyfus family. According to Hyman, at 103, 'The pamphlet ... opened an offensive against the antisemitic interpretation of the case.' At the same time, Picquart, an army officer, had independently assembled some additional evidence, which implicated Major Esterhazy as a German spy.

165 According to PE Hyman, above, n 43 at 96–7, antisemitism had become acceptable by the 1880s. Edouard Drumont published *La France Juive* in 1886, an excoriation of the Jews which was wildly successful; Drumont, a Parisian journalist, blamed Jews for destroying France by introducing factory production, the railroad and the department store, and he blamed the crash of a Catholic bank on its (Jewish) competitors, the Rothschilds. Drumont's newspaper, *Libre Parole*, firmly declared Dreyfus guilty.

1897, a group of intellectuals and politicians, the first Dreyfusards, had emerged, and they began to campaign forcefully for review of the evidence presented in the Dreyfus case, a campaign which threatened to expose serious corruption in the Ministry of War.[166] On 16 November 1897, the week before Chauvin appeared to argue her right to take the oath to become an *avocat*, Mathieu Dreyfus, Alfred's tireless supporter, published an open letter to the Minister of War in *Le Figaro*: the letter accused another officer, Esterhazy, of having written the message for which Dreyfus was convicted of treason.[167] Then, on 13 January 1898, Émile Zola published his famous indictment of French justice, '*J'Accuse*,' in an open letter to the president of France in *L'Aurore*, Georges Clemenceau's newspaper; his letter accused a number of high-ranking officers and the War Office of knowingly convicting an innocent man. Zola was swiftly charged with defamation and his ten-day trial began in early February 1898.[168]

L'Affaire Dreyfus and the Zola trial became catalysts for anti-Semitic riots all over France; in towns with Jewish residents, 'mobs pillaged stores, desecrated synagogues, and attacked rabbis' until the late spring of 1898, when the *gendarmes* finally restored order.[169] Although Chauvin's brother, Emile, was first elected as a Deputy for the Department of Seine-et-Marne in the election in May 1898, it is unclear whether the Chauvin family took a position about Dreyfus. By contrast, there is no doubt that Frank was actively involved; in 1898, he published a short treatise on the science of graphology, comparing samples of writing by Dreyfus and Esterhazy to prove that the memo which condemned Dreyfus to treason was in fact penned by Esterhazy. As Frank noted in *Affaire Dreyfus, Procès en Revision: Le Bordereau est d'Esterhazy*,[170] he had initially assumed, like many people at the time, that Dreyfus was guilty. However, he then described a meeting with a member of the Parisian press in December 1897, whose intemperate language about the case made him reconsider.[171] After researching the subject, he offered an article to *L'Aurore*; according to Frank, he had wished to remain anonymous, but he then received a request to be a witness in Zola's trial.[172] As Michael Burns reported,

---

[166] See PE Hyman, above, n 43 at 104; among the first Dreyfusards were politicians and journalists, including Georges Clemenceau, political editer of *L'Aurore*; many Dreyfusards were not Jewish.

[167] PE Hyman, above, n 43 at 104. See also M Burns, *France and the Dreyfus Affair: A Documentary History* (Boston and New York, Bedford/St Martin's, 1999) at 82–3.

[168] PE Hyman, above, n 43 at 104. Zola's letter was published immediately after Esterhazy was acquitted by a court martial, and Zola accused the army officers of conducting a major cover-up.

[169] Burns, above, n 167 at 106.

[170] (Bruxelles, Henri Lamertin, 1898; and Paris, P V Stock, 1898).

[171] L Frank, above, n 170 at i. According to M Marrus, above, n 45 at 211–14, most Frenchmen, including Jews, initially assumed that Dreyfus was guilty.

[172] L Frank, above, n 170 at i–ii.

Mathieu Dreyfus had hired an independent French graphologist, but he also commissioned handwriting experts from other countries, including Belgium, to 'corroborate the French opinions and confirm the objectivity of the enterprise.'[173] According to Frank, he appeared before the jury in Zola's trial in Paris on 15 February 1898, testifying that '*le bordereau est et ne peut être que d'Esterhazy*'; for Frank, it was a straightforward question of evidence: *une question d'écriture*. However, the court disagreed, characterising Frank's testimony as *les affirmations fantaisistes*, and suggesting that the French court had no need for '*des étrangers pour dégager la vérité dans les affaires de notre pays....*'[174] By contrast with these dismissive comments, there are brief letters to Frank in his archival papers from Mathieu Dreyfus and from Commandant et Madame A Dreyfus, confirming their gratitude for his intervention.[175]

Thus, it appears that Frank was involved in Chauvin's case in the same period that he was writing his treatise on the Dreyfus case and preparing to appear at Zola's trial. In this context, it is interesting that he linked the two cases, arguing that they both demonstrated a need for France to return to the principles of equality espoused by the Revolution:

> *L'affaire Dreyfus – comme l'affaire Chauvin – a prouvé l'esprit étroit, sectaire et dangereux, dont sont animés en France un trop grand nombre d'hommes investis d'une part de la puissance publique. Le mal qui en résulte est grand, non seulement pour la France, mais pour le monde....* [176]

Clearly, Frank's public testimony at Zola's trial marked him as a Dreyfusard. By contrast, according to Karpik, a majority of lawyers in France were in the anti-Dreyfus camp; indeed, a number of provincial bars engaged in public votes in support of the army, but even in Paris, support for Dreyfus was noticeably absent among *avocats*.[177] Thus, in the context of Chauvin's efforts to obtain legislation to enable women to become *avocats* between 1897 and 1900, it is interesting to speculate about whether she was also involved on one side or the other in *L'Affaire Dreyfus*. In this context, Savage concluded that Chauvin revealed her personal anti-Semitism in the sub-title chosen for her 1892 thesis on women's access to the professions: *Influence du Sémitisme sur l'Évolution de la Position Économique de la Femme dans la Société*; he suggested that her disser-

---

173 M Burns, above, n 167 at 78.

174 L Frank, above, n 170 at i-ii.

175 *Papiers Frank*, above, n 13 at #7791–3: letter to Frank from Mathieu Dreyfus, 12 December 1904, saying that he had been worried by the long silence from Frank; the letter suggests an ongoing relationship. The letter from A Dreyfus with warm thanks has an illegible date; it may be 1898 or 1908.

176 L Frank, above, n 170 at iii.

177 L Karpik, above, n 38 at 138–9. According to J Savage, above, n 156 at 171, law students were anti-Dreyfusards, reflecting the 'Law Faculty as a bastion of conservatism and political reaction;' by contrast, students in the Faculty of Letters were more often Dreyfusards.

tation argued that women's subjection was the result of Jewish influences in the Middle Ages.[178] However, as Kimble argued, Chauvin's thesis as a whole revealed her preoccupation with the origin of ideas of inequality, which she located in ancient religions, including Judaism, Christianity and Islam, and her intent to eliminate these ideas as justifications for a social order based on male dominance; according to Kimble, Chauvin was not really interested in systems of religious belief.[179] Indeed, Chauvin's thesis provided a wide-ranging critique of philosophical and religious views, focussing especially on the significance of Greek thought during the Renaissance, which tended to restrict women's participation in professional work and in the public sphere. All the same, the subtitle of her thesis clearly singled out the influence of Jewish thought as a (special) problem for women's equal participation in society. Thus, although Frank's ideas always seem to have been more influenced by liberalism than by religion, it is possible that his highly public identification as a Dreyfusard discouraged continuation of a working relationship with Chauvin.

Indeed, there appears to be no evidence of collaboration between Chauvin and Frank after 1900, although details of their individual activities remain somewhat obscure. It seems that Chauvin was involved in legal practice for some years, but she also continued to teach at several girls' *lycées*. As Kimble noted, she was registered with the legal aid agency of the Paris bar, *L'Assistance Judiciaire*, and she appeared in at least one criminal case in 1921. She was also active in promoting legal reforms concerning paternity, and in drafting provisions to enforce support payments for illegitimate children.[180] Since Chauvin needed to work to provide support for herself and her mother, her choice of activities was probably based, at least in part, on her need for financial security.[181] At the same time, it appears that she continued to be involved with *L'Avant-Courrière*, at least until the organisation succeeded in reforming the law relating to married women's earnings in 1907;[182] it is less clear whether Chauvin continued to participate in the organisation when Schmahl turned to the campaign for suffrage.[183] Yet, as Maria Vérone, another French

178 J Savage, above, n 156 at 201. See also Emile Chauvin, 'Jeanne Chauvin' (1893) 36 *Revue Philosophique de la France et de l'Etranger* 312.
179 SL Kimble, above, n 5 at 36–7.
180 SL Kimble, above, n 5 at 150–1, 161–2 and 177–9.
181 SL Kimble, above, n 5 at 37.
182 See *Dictionnaire de Biographie Française*, above, n 125. See also Commire (ed), above, n 125, noting that Chauvin was 'the first woman to plead a case' in France in 1907; and that she presented an 'aggressive' report about legal reforms at the meeting of the Congress of Feminine Works and Institutions in 1900.
183 SC Hause with AR Kenney, above, n 119 at 56–7 and 112–13. See also JC Albisetti, above, n 10 at 844, comparing the opening of the legal professions in Europe to women and recognition of women's right to vote. See also LA Tilly, 'Women's Collective Action and Feminism in France, 1870–1914' in LA Tilly and C Tilly (eds), *Class Conflict and Collective Action* (London, Sage, 1981) at 207.

femme-avocat, stated at an event to honour the twenty-fifth anniversary of women at the bar, 'Who will ever know the difficulties *Mlle* Jeanne Chauvin had to endure?'[184]

Unfortunately, there is also little information about Poët and Popelin. It seems likely that Poët continued to do legal work in her brother's office; and that Popelin continued to be involved in suffrage and other women's rights activities. Indeed, the proceedings of the *Congrès Féministe International*, which took place in Brussels in April 1912 to celebrate the twentieth anniversary of the founding of *La Ligue Belge du Droit des Femmes*, clearly demonstrated Popelin's prominence among women's rights activists in Belgium; as the proceedings stated, she represented '*l'âme du Congrès*,' and the preface included a five-stanza poem, *À Mademoiselle Marie Popelin*.[185] Frank was identified in the proceedings as a member of the *Comité d'Honneur*, although there was no indication of his role in establishing *La Ligue*.[186] However, his relationship with Popelin appears to have been reestablished, as she nominated him for the Nobel Prize in literature in 1906; the nomination poignantly explained that the feminist movement had taken:

> ... *une forme concrète d'idéalisme pratique sous l'action d'un jeune penseur belge, M Louis Frank, qui a dépense vingt ans de sa vie et sacrifice toute sa jeunesse a l'étude du féminisme, recherchant dans les divers domaines sociaux la solution scientifique de ce problème nouveau et ardu, consacrant son activité tenace et ses efforts ardents à la défense de cette cause renovatrice.*[187]

The nomination was not successful. Moreover, although Frank continued to be busily occupied with a number of other projects, there is some evidence that he never achieved financial security.[188] In addition, he may have suffered some public censure as a result of his response to a dispute with Émile Vandervelde, a member of the *Chambre des Représentants*; Frank asserted that Vandervelde had used the text of Frank's forthcoming publication concerning married women's earnings as the basis for a law reform proposal, introduced by Vandervelde in April 1896. Frank and Vandervelde engaged in a battle of the press and in arbitration proceedings in early 1896; eventually, Frank publicly accused Vandervelde and the drafter of the law reform proposal of plagiarism, and they sued Frank successfully.[189] Ironically, it was Vandervelde who introduced the legis-

---

184 A Boigeol, above, n 8 at 196.
185 Ligue Belge du Droit des Femmes, above, n 76 at *Avant-Propos*.
186 Ligue Belge du Droit des Femmes, above, n 76 at 25.
187 *Papiers Frank*, above, n 13 at #7791–8 (envelope 4).
188 'Biographical Note' in *Papiers Frank*, above, n 13 at #7787; suggesting that Frank was unsuccessful in applications for public appointment because he was Jewish.
189 The details of Frank's allegations were published in Frank, *Cornelius Nepos, ou le Premier Plagiaire Collectiviste* (Bruxelles, L Istace, 1897) at 83. See also F Van Lierde, above, n 61 at 265.

lation in Belgium after World War I, which permitted women to become *avocats*.[190]

However, Frank did not live to see the legislation finally enacted in Belgium; he died suddenly, apparently of a heart attack, in 1917 during the German occupation of Belgium at the age of fifty-three. According to a biographical note in his archival papers, Frank died '*heureux ... la plume à la main comme un soldat, le visage rayonnant* [because he expected that the Allies would win the war].'[191] Popelin had died four years earlier in 1913 at the age of sixty-seven, '*sans avoir pu réaliser son rêve.*'[192] However, both Chauvin and Poët lived to see the enactment of legislation in Italy, Belgium and other European countries, permitting women's access to the legal professions after World War I; Chauvin died in 1926 at the age of sixty-four, while Poët died in 1947.[193] In the end, the connections between Louis Frank and the legal challenges presented by Lydia Poët, Marie Popelin and Jeanne Chauvin to become *avocats* demonstrate how both men and women were involved in challenging women's exclusion from the legal professions in the *fin de siècle* reformist context of Europe. As an observer of one of Chauvin's first court appearances stated, it was 'a new era' at the *Palais de Justice*.[194]

[190] According to JC Albisetti, above, n 10 at 830, Émile Vandervelde was Minister of Justice and a longtime supporter of women *avocats*; however, although he introduced the legislation, he was out of office when the legislation was finally enacted in 1922.

[191] 'Biographical Note' in *Papiers Frank*, above, n 13 at #7787. See also #7791–4, a letter from Le Grand Rabin de Belgique, dated 30/7/1917, expressing sympathy and admiration for Frank's accomplishments.

[192] *Vies de Femmes 1830–1980* (Bruxelles, Banque Bruxelles Lambert, 1980) at 24–25. According to this account, many of the initiatives undertaken by *La Ligue* were due to Franck's (sic) initiative.

[193] *Dictionnaire de Biographie Française*, above, n 125; and Anna Ruggieri, 'Lidia Poët' www.pariopportunita.gov.it (accessed 3 June 2005).

[194] B Durand, above, n 36 at 176.

Conclusion

Reflecting on the First Women Lawyers

———————◆———————

Individuals respond in different ways to differing historical situations, and a study of any particular life can help both to illuminate these situations as well as aid our understanding of the person being studied.[1]

IN MAKING THIS claim about the intersection of historical situations and individual lives, June Purvis was commenting on current challenges in biographical writing about women. As she explained, women's biographers have been increasingly critical of the tendency to '[weave] a seamless narrative, creating coherence and causal connections' that does not reflect either shifting historical contexts or the fragmentary nature of individual experiences.[2] Thus, Purvis argued that it was not appropriate to approach a biographical project using the metaphor of a microscope, 'where the more information you collect about your subject, the closer [you are] to "the truth."'[3] Rather, it was preferable to conceptualise women's lives in terms of a kaleidoscope – an approach that better reflects the always-changing and interconnected patterns in their lives; as Liz Stanley suggested, approaching biography as kaleidoscope means that 'each time you look you see something rather different, composed certainly of the same elements, but in a new configuration.'[4] In reflecting on patterns of gender and legal professionalism in this comparative study of the first women lawyers, I have used this kaleidoscope metaphor as a way of taking account of the complex interrelationships between different historical contexts and women's responses to different circumstances. An understanding

---

[1] J Purvis, *Emmeline Pankhurst: A Biography* (London and New York, Routledge, 2002) at 6.

[2] J Purvis, above, n 1 at 6. See also M Maynard and J Purvis, *Researching Women's Lives from a Feminist Perspective* (London, Taylor & Francis, 1994).

[3] J Purvis, above, n 1 at 7. See also DC Stanton (ed), *The Female Autograph: Theory and Practice of Autobiography from the Tenth to the Twentieth Century* (Chicago and London, University of Chicago Press, 1987).

[4] See J Purvis, 'Biography as Microscope or Kaleidoscope? The Case of "Power" in Hannah Cullwick's Relationship with Arthur Munby' in L Stanley (ed), *The Auto/Biographical I: The Theory and Practice of Feminist Auto-Biography* (Manchester, Manchester University Press, 1992) at 158.

of the complexity of these relationships is critical to theorising about relationships of gender and legal professionalism.

As the stories of the first women lawyers in this comparative study demonstrate, for example, many claims initiated by aspiring women lawyers were unsuccessful in the courts, and vigorously opposed by bar associations and legislators; however, the patterns of gender challenges to the law's male exclusivity varied considerably. Although many judges clearly deferred to legislatures on the question of women's eligibility to practise law, a few of them nonetheless interpreted legal principles to permit women to succeed in their claims for admission to the bar. Significantly, judges who decided that women were eligible to practise law were frequently using the *same* legal principles as those who concluded that the issue of women lawyers was beyond the scope of judicial decision-making; in such a context, both the choices exercised by individual judges and their motivations for adopting different approaches may be relevant to defining relationships between gender and legal professionalism in the late nineteenth century.[5] In assessing differing judicial approaches in the United States, for example, some American scholars identified a pattern of greater resistance to women's claims for admission to the bar in Eastern states, by contrast with the West.[6] Yet, as the historical record demonstrates, the experiences of women lawyers sometimes diverged from this pattern, both in the East and in the West, suggesting that additional factors may need to be considered: for example, the timing of women's claims for admission to the bar, individual judges' familiarity with women lawyers in other states, issues about overcrowding in the profession or about increasing needs for legal expertise, or relationships between claims for women's suffrage and access to professional work.

Moreover, patterns of women's admission to the bar in Canada suggest further divergence from such a dichotomy between East and West in North America: for example, decisions in the western province of British Columbia concluded unanimously that women were *not* entitled to practise law, while one judge in Québec issued a strong dissenting opinion that clearly defined women's eligibility for admission to the bar. Although it is tempting to explain the dissenting opinion in Québec as the result of greater flexibility in civil law, by contrast with common law, such an explanation hardly accords with the unanimity of all the judges who considered claims pursuant to civil law in Italy, Belgium and France in the late nineteenth century. Moreover, even though British courts steadfastly rejected women's claims to gain admission to the bar until legislation was enacted after World War I, a judge in a British court in India exercised discretion to

---

[5] MJ Mossman, 'Feminism and Legal Method: The Difference it Makes' (1986) 3 *Australian Journal of Law and Society* 30.

[6] See M Matsuda, 'The West and the Legal Status of Women: Explanations of Frontier Feminism' (1985) 24 *Journal of the West* 47.

permit a legally-trained woman to provide representation for the defence in a murder case. In this context, clearly-defined patterns in courts' responses to claims presented by aspiring women lawyers at the turn of the twentieth century remain elusive, requiring assessments of both historical situations and individual actions in each case.

Similarly, although bar associations and legislators were frequently opposed to the admission of women lawyers, there were exceptions. In a few cases in the United States and Canada, for example, examining committees and bar associations recommended women's admission to the bar, or at least did not oppose them; similarly, bar associations in Italy and Belgium were closely divided on the issue of women lawyers, confirming that aspiring women lawyers had some support from individual members of legal professions in Europe. And although some legislators in these jurisdictions were opposed to amending the law to permit women to practise law, several states and provinces in North America, as well as the national legislature in France, enacted statutes to enable women to gain admission to the bar in the late nineteenth and early twentieth centuries, apparently with little or no opposition. In New Zealand, moreover, legislators enacted statutory amendments to permit women to practise law in the absence of litigation and *before* there was a qualified applicant. Although it is arguable that this action on the part of a colonial legislature demonstrated a greater commitment to gender equality than was evident in Britain, it is also clear that some members of the British Parliament provided steadfast support for proposals concerning women's access to the professions decades before British legislation was enacted after World War I. Accordingly, it is necessary to take account of variations in the responses of bar associations and legislatures over a period of several decades; although bar associations and legislatures were generally exclusively male institutions at the turn of the twentieth century, their responses to women's admission to the bar were not at all uniform. Moreover, differing patterns in the roles of courts and legislatures in defining women's eligibility to become members of the legal professions in different jurisdictions reveal a spectrum of views about their respective institutional roles in recognising changes in 'a woman's sphere' at the turn of the twentieth century.

In addition to these institutional responses, this comparative study shows that some aspiring women lawyers received substantial support from individual male lawyers, who presented arguments in favour of women's admission to the bar from *within* the professions. Although some supporters, such as John Stuart Mill, were well-known advocates of women's equality, commentaries in law journals often reveal how the issue of women lawyers was highly contested among members of the legal professions in the late nineteenth and early twentieth centuries: some comments demonstrate unwavering opposition to women's claims for admission to the bar, but there were others that evidenced thoughtful and vigorous support. At the same time, situating male lawyers who supported the first women lawyers within their historical contexts and defining their precise motives presents some challenges. For example, while it is clear that Louis Frank was an ardent supporter of women's equality and other progressive causes in Belgium, he was not a practising barrister, and it is unclear how, or to what extent, he was involved in local bar associations; as a result, while his support for women lawyers probably influenced public opinion, his impact on the organised legal professions in Europe may have been less significant.

By contrast, Sam Jacobs, who provided substantial support for women lawyers in Québec, was a respected barrister who was subsequently elected to serve in the Canadian Parliament for two decades; nonetheless, even his status as a member of the legal and political elite did not result in legislation to permit women to become lawyers in Québec until after his death. Moreover, since both Frank and Jacobs were Jewish, there are intriguing questions about whether their own professional experiences in the context of widespread anti-Semitism in the legal professions at the turn of the twentieth century contributed to their passionate commitment to women's equality in law: is it possible that they had a special understanding of professional ideals of equality, or is their Jewish identity just a coincidence? In assessing patterns of support for the first women lawyers, particularly where individual support existed in the face of vigorous opposition from professional organisations and legislatures, questions like these point to the need for further research about the culture of the legal professions at the turn of the twentieth century.

In addition to promoting women's access to the legal professions, moreover, some male lawyers assisted them in their efforts to practise law. For example, it is likely that Eliza Orme's 'independent' conveyancing practice in London was substantially dependent on referrals from barristers who specialised in this work; although she may have more readily obtained clients in relation to other kinds of legal work, her relationship with conveyancing barristers at Lincoln's Inn appears to have been significant in establishing a viable practice. By contrast, with a few exceptions, members of the legal profession in New Zealand seem to have eschewed a collegial relationship with Ethel Benjamin, and she clearly experienced difficulty in obtaining referrals from them. All the same, it is difficult to determine precisely which factors enabled Orme to obtain the profession's assistance, while Benjamin experienced professional rejection: to what extent do their differing experiences reveal nuances in the professional legal cultures of Britain and New Zealand, or was it more a matter of different personalities and circumstances for these first women lawyers? Such questions suggest a need to examine not only the details of women's *formal* admission to the bar, but also the intricacies of professional cultures in which women were engaged in legal work; after all, Britain remained resolutely opposed to women's formal admission as lawyers, while New Zealand appeared to welcome them, but Orme clearly enjoyed a thriving legal practice and it seems that Benjamin did not. Indeed, it seems that the *habitus* of legal practice[7] and the challenge of establishing professional legal relationships may have constituted more formidable barriers for aspiring women lawyers than achieving admission to the bar. In this way, the experiences of the first women lawyers provide crucial data about norms and values within legal cultures as well as revealing the divergence between formal decision-making and the law in practice.

In this context, the metaphor of kaleidoscope provides a way of exploring variations in the historical situations of courts, legislatures, and professional legal organisations, as well as in the roles of individual actors, including male lawyers, who provided support for the first women who challenged male exclusivity in the legal professions. In addition, the kaleidoscope metaphor may offer insights for women's history by encouraging more complex ways of assessing the achievements of these first women in law. For example, if women lawyers are regarded as 'exceptional women,' it is arguable that their lives were so special that their stories are irrelevant to the history of most nineteenth-century women.[8] Yet, an assessment of the historical context in which women first gained admission to the bar suggests that they were part of the large cohort of women who began to enter paid work and the professions in the last decades of the nineteenth century; some of these women chose to pursue economic independence rather than marriage, but others enjoyed no real 'choice' at all – they simply needed to work.[9] In this comparative study, it is clear that some women who aspired to become lawyers did so because they wanted independence, while others sought professional legal status because they had to work for a living; in this way, it is arguable that women lawyers were not so 'exceptional' within the larger historical context of changes in opportunities for women at the turn of the twentieth century.[10]

At the same time, most of the first women lawyers grew up in families

---

[7] See J Margolis, 'Pierre Bourdieu: *Habitus* and the Logic of Practice' in Richard Shusterman (ed), *Bourdieu: A Critical Reader* (Oxford, Blackwell Publishers Ltd, 1999) 64. See also P Bourdieu, *Outline of a Theory of Practice*, trans R Nice (Cambridge, Cambridge University Press, 1977).

[8] G Lerner, *The Majority Finds its Past: Placing Women in History* (New York, Oxford University Press, 1979) at 145. See also J Parr and M Rosenfeld (eds), *Gender and History in Canada* (Toronto, Copp Clark Ltd, 1996).

[9] See O Hufton, *The Prospect Before Her: A History of Women in Western Europe 1500–1800* (New York, Alfred A Knopf, 1996) 62; M Vicinus, *Independent Women: Work and Community for Single Women 1850–1920* (London, Virago, 1985); and Lee Holcombe, *Victorian Ladies at Work: Middle-Class Working Women in England and Wales 1850–1914* (Hamden, CT, Archon Books, 1973).

[10] See C Hall, *et al*, 'Introduction' in C Hall, K McClelland and J Rendall (eds), *Defining the Victorian Nation: Class, Race, Gender and the British Reform Act of 1867* (Cambridge, Cambridge University Press, 2000).

that enjoyed middle-class status, or at least aspired to middle-class values, families in which women's education was encouraged; and their family circumstances may have fostered women's aspirations to engage in professional, rather than merely paid, work. Arguably, their entry to the professions provided opportunities for independence and adventure, circumstances that were not available to other working women, who were so often engaged in dreary and ill-paying employment at the turn of the twentieth century. However, even if these circumstances rendered the first women lawyers somewhat exceptional in relation to other women in the nineteenth century, their achievements were seldom regarded as significant by comparison with male lawyers; as Virginia Drachman poignantly concluded, the achievements of the first women who became legal professionals were generally 'modest, not monumental.'[11] Even so, by recognising that so many of these first women lawyers were often the *only* women who were attempting to practise law in their respective jurisdictions in the late nineteenth and early twentieth centuries, comparisons between their achievements and those of male professionals seem inappropriate: in such a context, the presence of a woman lawyer, *by itself*, must have rendered her 'exceptional'.[12] Thus, just as in a kaleidoscope, shifting perspectives about the first women lawyers and their gendered patterns of legal work suggest rather different assessments of their significance.

In assessing the strategies adopted by a number of nineteenth-century women professionals in the United States, Glazer and Slater identified four approaches: superperformance, subordination, innovation and separatism.[13] Although these strategies were evident, to greater or lesser degrees, in the lives of early women professionals in their study, Glazer and Slater's research did not include women lawyers, and their four strategies may be less useful in analysing the lives of women in law. For example, although there is evidence that some of the first women lawyers aspired to superperformance, and several of them were highly successful in university law programmes, they were generally unsuccessful in achieving superperformance in practice, particularly by comparison with contemporary male lawyers. In addition, most of the first women who gained admission to the bar worked as sole practitioners; few of them adopted strategies of subordination by working as assistants in the offices of male lawyers, a strategy more often adopted by women whose claims to become lawyers were thwarted. Even for those whose careers might be characterised as subordinate, a strategy of innovation appears more persuasive in explain-

11 VG Drachman, *Sisters in Law: Women Lawyers in Modern American History* (Cambridge, Mass, Harvard University Press, 1998) at 8. See also R Chused, 'Book Review' (1999) 85:4 *Journal of American History* 1621; and N Basch, 'Review' (1999) 104 *American Historical Review* 935.

12 See G Jonçich Clifford (ed), *Lone Voyagers: Academic Women in Coeducational Universities 1870–1937* (New York, Feminist Press, 1989).

13 P Migdal Glazer and M Slater, *Unequal Colleagues: The Entrance of Women into Professions, 1890–1940* (New Brunswick and London, Rutgers University Press, 1987).

ing how they engaged in legal work; that is, women lawyers very often *created* their own opportunities for legal work, evading or overcoming barriers presented by formal legal rules and professional cultures. Most significantly, by contrast with the separate women's hospitals established by nineteenth-century women doctors, separatism was almost never a strategy for the first women lawyers; even though they may have experienced separatism *within* the culture of the legal professions, women were required to practise law alongside male lawyers. This conclusion, that the strategies adopted by other early women professionals were less evident among women lawyers, lends support to Drachman's assertion that women who aspired to enter the legal professions faced obstacles that were *unique* for nineteenth-century women professionals.[14] In this way, although women lawyers may have encountered constraints that were similar to those faced by other women professionals, women lawyers had to confront the law which *defined* their claims as illegal, and the legal professions which *reinforced* their culture as a 'gentlemen's profession.' In addition, these constraints may have curtailed, perhaps in subtle ways, the extent of women lawyers' ongoing involvement in reformist activities of the women's movements: is it significant, for example, that women like Popelin in Belgium and Bradwell in the United States, who did not succeed in gaining admission to the bar, were among the most energetically engaged in reform activities promoting women's rights?

Moreover, although ideas about gender and professionalism were highly contested at the turn of the twentieth century, the challenges presented by the first women lawyers were framed within the rhetoric of women's equality. The rhetoric of equality tended to emphasise the opening up of opportunities for women in relation to higher education, paid work and the professions, but it did not encompass more fundamental reforms, including the transformation of relationships between women's work and their family responsibilities. In this context, advocates of women's equality argued for women's admission to the legal professions 'on the same terms as men;' their goal was to overcome women's exclusion from law and the legal professions, and they trusted that professional ideas about merit would ensure equality of opportunities for women in law. Clearly, however, such a concept of equality did not fundamentally challenge traditional ideas about either gender or professionalism. Interestingly, aspiring women lawyers were often linked in the popular press to Portia, Shakespeare's character in *The Merchant of Venice*.[15] Yet, although Portia provided an

---

14 VG Drachman, above, n 11 at 2 (emphasis added).
15 See CA Corcos, 'Portia and Her Partners in Popular Culture: A Bibliography' (1998) 22 *Legal Studies Forum* 269; C Menkel-Meadow, 'Portia in a Different Voice: Speculations on a Women's Lawyering Process' (1985) 1 *Berkeley Women's Law Journal* 39; and C Menkel-Meadow, 'Portia *Redux*: Another Look at Gender, Feminism, and Legal Ethics' in S Parker and C Sampford (eds), *Legal Ethics and Legal Practice: Contemporary Issues* (Oxford, Clarendon Press, 1995).

excellent model of effective advocacy in the trial scene in Shakespeare's play, all her accomplishments occurred while she was disguised as a man. Dressed as a young legal scholar, Portia was accepted in the Venetian court as a voice of authority; even Shylock praised her as a 'Daniel come to judgment.' Yet, as literary scholars have argued, Portia understood that her authority was absolutely dependent on her disguise: 'as a woman she could never have exercised her intellectual gifts in the Venetian court.'[16] In this way, references to the first women lawyers as 'Portias' appeared to acknowledge women's potential for effective advocacy, but they simultaneously confirmed a male model of legal professionalism. In this way, participation in public life arguably required that the first women lawyers disguise their gender in their professional identities.

This conclusion raises important questions about our contemporary assessments of these nineteenth-century women professionals. For example, Gerda Lerner recommended caution about simply assessing women's contributions to already-defined historical movements, that is 'fit[ting] women's past into empty spaces of historical scholarship,' and about seeing women as victims of oppression within a male-defined conceptual framework.[17] Similarly, Iacovetta and Valverde concluded that accounts of women's lives must move beyond stories of *male* oppression and *female* resistance to confront contradictions and ambiguities in the lives of both men and women.[18] Such comments define important challenges: for example, in attempting to connect the history of women lawyers to the history of professionalism, how can we ensure that the experiences of the first women lawyers are not simply 'fitted into' existing theories about the professionalisation of legal work and legal education, rather than providing an opportunity to (re)assess connections between gender and professionalisation in law? Indeed, in assessing how the first women lawyers constructed their lives at the boundaries between women's traditional sphere and a 'gentleman's profession' in the late nineteenth century, we need to explore what it *meant* to be a woman in law, and the extent to which *fitting into* professional culture was a matter of choice for any of them.[19] If law was the most exclusively male of all nineteenth-century

[16] S Oldrieve, 'Marginalized Voices in *The Merchant of Venice*' (1993) 5 *Cardozo Studies in Law and Literature* 87, at 100. See also J Hankey, 'Victorian Portias: Shakespeare's Borderline Heroine' (1994) 45 *Shakespeare Quarterly* 426.

[17] See G Lerner, above, n 8 at 145–9. See also Beverly Boutilier and Alison Prentice (eds), *Creating Historical Memory: English-Canadian Women and the Work of History* (Vancouver, UBC Press, 1997); and K Offen, R Roach Pierson and J Rendall (eds), *Writing Women's History: International Perspectives* (Bloomington, Indiana University Press, 1991).

[18] F Iacovetta and M Valverde (eds), *Gender Conflicts: New Essays in Women's History* (Toronto, University of Toronto Press, 1992) at xvii. See also JW Scott, 'Women's History' in Peter Burke (ed), *New Perspectives on Historical Writing*, 2nd edn (Pennsylvania, Pennsylvania State University Press, 2001) 43.

[19] See LK Kerber, 'Separate Spheres, Female Worlds, Woman's Place: The Rhetoric of Women's History' (1988) 75:1 *Journal of American History* 9.

professions, as Drachman asserted,[20] the experiences of the first women lawyers provide important evidence about women's strategies for confronting, or evading, the power of male exclusivity.[21] Moreover, since they were not always successful in achieving their goals as practitioners, their experiences in seeking admission to the legal professions and the nature of their opportunities to engage in legal work reveal how gendered legal boundaries sometimes shifted to accommodate women's admission to the bar, but how they were reconfigured to limit women's full participation in professional life. Moreover, the fact that a number of the first women lawyers from Canada, New Zealand and India moved to Britain, leaving behind their countries of origin and even their entitlement to practise law, suggests that the importance of their professional legal qualifications somehow diminished later in relation to other aspects of their lives.

Yet, although gender may have defined the 'limits of the possible' for the first women lawyers,[22] all of these women tended to be individuals who confidently embraced new kinds of opportunities. Indeed, a number of them actively participated in the presentation of legal arguments to courts in their own admission cases, notwithstanding their legal exclusion, and many of them remained resolutely hopeful about the future of women in law. In spite of their individual abilities, however, several of the first women lawyers faced problems in obtaining legal work that was financially rewarding, and a number of them lived precariously on the margins of the profession. Moreover, their responses to professional challenges in law varied significantly according to their individual circumstances.[23] And, of course, gender was never the *only* factor that influenced opportunities and choices for the first women lawyers: racial, ethnic and class differences also shaped women's experiences in the legal professions in the late nineteenth and early twentieth centuries. As Joy Parr argued, historical relationships between gender and other aspects of women's identities are always 'forged in particular spatial and temporal settings... [that are] changeable rather than fixed;' in this way, 'class and gender identities are a matter of history, not universals but specificities....'[24] Thus, any exploration of the relationships of gender and professionalism in the lives of the first women lawyers must recognise how their identities were socially

---

[20] VG Drachman, above, n 11 at 2.

[21] See K Barry, 'The New Historical Syntheses: Women's Biography' (1990) 1:3 *Journal of Women's History* 75.

[22] See PM Glazer and M Slater, above, n 13 at 14.

[23] C Sanger, 'Curriculum Vitae (Feminae): Biography and Early American Women Lawyers' (1994) 46 *Stanford Law Review* 1245.

[24] J Parr, *The Gender of Breadwinners: Women, Men, and Change in Two Industrial Towns 1880–1950* (Toronto, University of Toronto Press, 1990) at 9–11. See also N Zemon Davis, 'Women's History as Women's Education' in N Zemon Davis and J Wallach Scott (eds), *Women's History as Women's Education* (Northampton, MA, Smith College Archives, 1985) at 16; and JK Conway, SC Bourque, and JW Scott (eds), *Learning About Women: Gender, Politics and Power* (Ann Arbor, University of Michigan Press, 1989).

constructed in differing historical contexts, and how their meanings changed in different times and places.[25]

Nonetheless, while their individual lives reveal the significance of factors that affected the opportunities available to the first women lawyers, there are some patterns in their experiences. Some of them devoted their lives to careers in law and related public activities, some did not marry, and some tended to conform to dominant social and political views within their professional milieu; others were more audacious, although they did not always continue to engage in legal work: some married, while others remained single; and some became actively involved in activities of the women's movement while others resolutely pursued a legal career no different from other (male) lawyers. In addition, there were women who *never* succeeded in gaining admission to the legal professions, although some of them were nonetheless engaged in legal work. In the end, their stories reveal their individual opportunities and choices, but they also define patterns in the relationship of gender and legal professionalism.

In reflecting on the histories of women's lives, Ruth Roach Pierson argued that any account of a woman's life is always constructed within a gendered historical context, so that the stories we tell to explain ourselves to others are shaped 'not only by narrative devices and conventions of storytelling but also by cultural notions of believability and hegemonic explanatory theories, of which we, as storytellers, may or may not be aware.'[26] Thus, in a context in which women were entitled to enjoy success in the public sphere 'only if fame was bestowed upon them, *not if they seized and relished it themselves*,'[27] even women lawyers' personal accounts of their experiences may have been constructed, either consciously or unconsciously, to explain or to justify their ambition. In an assessment of late sixteenth- and early seventeenth-century Italian court records, for example, Elizabeth Cohen posed questions about 'the relationship between ... the text and the individual creator, the culture, and the historical circumstances that may have shaped it.' Focussing on notarial records of the oral testimonies of witnesses involved in disputes, Cohen suggested that while the law defined the overall context for these texts 'by defining the subject-matter, the rhetoric, and the genre,'[28] men

[25] See B Boutilier and A Prentice, above, n 17 at 7.

[26] R Roach Pierson, 'Experience, Difference, Dominance and Voice in the Writing of Canadian Women's History' in Offen, *et al* (eds), above, n 17 at 94. See also C Steedman, *Landscape for a Good Woman: A Story of Two Lives* (New Brunswick, NJ, Rutgers University Press, 1987).

[27] See C Sanger, above, n 23 at 1257. See also C Steedman, *Past Tenses: Essays on Writing, Autobiography and History* (London, Rivers Oram Press, 1992).

[28] ES Cohen, 'Court Testimony from the Past: Self and Culture in the Making of Text' in M Kadar (ed), *Essays on Life Writing: From Genre to Critical Practice* (Toronto, University of Toronto Press, 1992) 84 at 89. See also HM Buss and M Kadar (eds), *Working in Women's Archives: Researching Women's Private Literature and Archival Documents* (Waterloo, Ontario, Wilfrid Laurier Press, 2001); J Sangster, 'Telling our Stories: Feminist Debates and

and women who provided their testimonies presented images of themselves that reflected 'what society prescribed as desirable and plausible for a person of their gender, age, rank, and familial position.'[29] Thus, when aspiring women lawyers presented their claims to courts and legislatures, and when they explained their experiences as women legal practitioners to newspapers, and *even to each other*, they undoubtedly realised that their ambitions and circumstances would be subjected to scrutiny; as a result, their assertions may well have conformed to 'what society prescribed as desirable' for women who wished to become lawyers at the turn of the twentieth century: recall, for example, Sorabji's strenuous efforts to distance herself from being labelled an 'advanced woman' like Orme![30] In this way, it may appear that the first women lawyers were not often 'rebel women,'[31] but it is necessary to explore their stories within the constraints of gender and legal professionalism to understand the choices available to them and their responses to different kinds of opportunities. As Berenice Fisher argued, we must engage in a

> radical social analysis that shows the objective constraints under which individual women have achieved what they have achieved, as well as how these women have been able to cope with, test, or challenge those constraints.[32]

In this context, there are also challenging questions about whether the first women lawyers were 'feminists.' In the United States, for example, Babcock argued that a close examination of the lives of the first women lawyers revealed 'a self-conscious feminist in virtually every early woman lawyer.'[33] While acknowledging that the issue was debatable, she concluded that 'feminism ennobled their efforts [at the same time that] being female subjected them to discrimination.'[34] In making these assertions, however, it seems that Babcock was using modern conceptions of 'feminism,' since the word would not have been understood at all by most nineteenth-century women lawyers in the United States. As Karen Offen

the Use of Oral History' (1994) 3 *Women's History Review* 5; and A Burton, *Dwelling in the Archive: Women Writing House, Home, and History in Late Colonial India* (Oxford, Oxford University Press, 2003).

29 See E Cohen, above, n 28 at 89–90.

30 See British Library Mss F165/16: letter from Sorabji to Lady Hobhouse, 18 April 1894.

31 J Eldridge Miller, *Rebel Women: Feminism, Modernism and the Edwardian Novel* (London, Virago Press, 1994).

32 B Fisher, 'The Models Among Us: Social Authority and Political Activism' (1981) 7 *Feminist Studies* 100, at 111. See also CG Heilbrun, *Women's Lives: The View from the Threshold* (Toronto, University of Toronto Press, 1999); HM Buss, *Mapping Our Selves: Canadian Women's Biography in English* (Montréal and Kingston, McGill-Queen's University Press, 1993); and J Rendall, 'Uneven Developments: Women's History, Feminist History and Gender History in Great Britain' in Offen, *et al* (eds), above, n 17 at 45.

33 BA Babcock, 'Book Review: Feminist Lawyers' (1998) 50 *Stanford Law Review* 1689 at 1699: review of VG Drachman, above, n 11.

34 See BA Babcock, above, n 33.

explained, the word 'féminisme' began to be used widely for the first time in France only in the 1890s; as a synonym for women's emancipation, it had gained currency there after the first self-proclaimed 'feminist' congress was held in Paris in 1892.[35] However, as Offen and other scholars have noted, the word 'feminism' was not generally known in English until at least a decade later.[36] As a result, questions about whether nineteenth-century women lawyers were 'feminists,' at least as a matter of linguistic terminology, technically apply only to women in France and among other French-speaking reformers in Europe in the 1890s. Moreover, the meaning of the word was complicated from the beginning by the fact that 'féminisme' embraced a number of different ideas in the late nineteenth and early twentieth centuries, as it does in the contemporary world, and that different kinds of feminisms were promoted within nineteenth-century women's movements.[37] As a result, scholarly assessments of the historical contributions of nineteenth century women, including the first women lawyers, must grapple with connections between the nineteenth-century historical context and our more contemporary perspectives.

In such a context, whether the first women lawyers were 'feminists' is a difficult analytical question; it cannot be addressed without a meaningful attempt to understand the context in which they lived their lives as late nineteenth- and early twentieth-century women lawyers.[38] Yet, efforts to understand their historical situation are difficult, and not only because the archives do not include all the information necessary to an assessment of their lives. In examining the historical situation for the first women lawyers, we also see their lives in the light of our own experiences as women in law: 'the self that researches has an autobiography, marked by the signification of gender, sexuality, ethnicity, class, etc,... [factors] which have effects on the form and outcomes of research.'[39] Particularly for women lawyers who were among the tiny minority who entered the legal professions in the late 1960s and early 1970s, the experiences of nineteenth-century women lawyers often seem quite contemporary; by

---

35 K Offen, 'Defining Feminism: A Comparative Historical Approach' (1988) 14:1 *Signs* 119 at 126–7. According to Offen, the first self-proclaimed 'feminist' in France was the women's suffrage advocate Hubertine Auclert, who used the term in 1882 in her publication *La Citoyenne*, and in her open letter to Susan B Anthony, 27 February 1888, responding to Anthony's invitation to attend the 1888 Congress of Women in Washington DC.

36 See K Offen, above, n 35. See also N Cott, *The Grounding of Modern Feminism* (New Haven and London, Yale University Press, 1987) at 233–4.

37 See K Offen, above, n 35 at 128–31. See also 'Comment and Reply' to Offen, by EC Dubois and NF Cott in (1989) 15:1 *Signs* 195; NES Griffiths, *Penelope's Web: Some Perceptions of Women in European and Canadian Society* (Toronto, Oxford University Press, 1976); and H Silius, 'Making Sense of Gender in the Study of the Legal Professions' 38 (2003) 10 *International Journal of the Legal Professions* 135.

38 See CM Coates and C Morgan, *Heroines and History: Representations of Madeleine de Verchères and Laura Secord* (Toronto, University of Toronto Press, 2002).

39 F Cownie, *Legal Academics: Culture and Identities* (Oxford and Portland, OR, Hart Publishing, 2004) at 21–2. See also J Purvis, above, n 1 at 6.

contrast, significant changes in the demography of the legal professions at the end of the twentieth century have altered women's status as a numerical minority. All the same, because some issues about the intersection of gender and professionalism in law remain unresolved, the stories of the first women lawyers, and their efforts to challenge male exclusivity in the law and the legal professions, remain profoundly significant for contemporary women lawyers.

This study of the lives of some of the first women lawyers reveals how their stories took place at the intersection of new ideas about women's roles and about legal professionalism at the end of the nineteenth and the beginning of the twentieth centuries. Originally excluded altogether from the legal profession, some women succeeded in gaining admission to the bar, while claims by others were rejected. Although there were some patterns in the arguments used by courts and legislatures in responding to women's claims for admission to the bar, their legal claims also need to be understood in relation to fluctuating historical situations and the exigencies of individual circumstances. As Gillian Sutherland argued in her study of women's access to higher education in the nineteenth century, 'description is probably at present the nearest we can get to explanation,'[40] a conclusion that suggests a need to examine individual histories of women lawyers and the historical contexts in which they sought to join the legal professions. In exploring the stories of some of the first women lawyers, this study identifies some of the ways in which contested ideas about gender and about legal professionalism worked to encourage or constrain women's admission to the bar and their opportunities to engage in legal work. In doing so, the study also explores the experiences of nineteenth-century women lawyers, experiences that arguably remain relevant to contemporary issues about gender and professionalism in the twenty-first century.

---

[40] G Sutherland, 'The Movement for the Higher Education of Women: Its Social and Intellectual Context in England, c 1840–80' in P J Waller (ed), *Politics and Social Change in Modern Britain: Essays Presented to A F Thompson* (Sussex, The Harvester Press Limited; and New York, St Martin's Press, 1987) 91 at 110.

Bibliography

ARCHIVAL SOURCES

Bibliothèque Royale, Brussels (Section des Manuscrits, Papiers Frank).
British Library, London (Oriental and India Office, papers of Cornelia Sorabji).
Lincoln's Inn, London.
Principal Probate Registry, London.
Law Society of Upper Canada, Toronto (*Crossing the Bar: A Century of Women's Experience 'Upon the Rough and Troubled Seas of Legal Practice' in Ontario*).
Provincial Archives of Ontario, Toronto (Osgoode Society for Legal History oral history files).
University Archives: Dalhousie University, Halifax; Faculty of Law, McGill University, Montréal; University of British Columbia, Vancouver.

BOOKS AND ARTICLES IN BOOKS

Adams, Pauline, *Somerville for Women: An Oxford College 1879–1993* (Oxford, Oxford University Press, 1996).

Abel, Richard L, 'United States: The Contradictions of Professionalism' in Richard Abel and Philip SC Lewis (eds), *Lawyers in Society: the Common Law World*, vol I (Berkeley, University of California Press, 1988).

——, 'Comparative Sociology of Legal Professions' in Richard L Abel and Philip S C Lewis (eds), *Lawyers in Society: Comparative Theories*, vol III (Berkeley, University of California Press, 1989).

——, *American Lawyers* (New York, Oxford University Press, 1989).

Abel, Richard L and Philip SC Lewis (eds), *Lawyers in Society: The Civil Law World*, vol II (Berkeley, University of California Press, 1988).

Abel-Smith, Brian and Robert Stevens (with Rosalind Brooke), *Lawyers and the Courts: A Sociological Study of the English Legal System 1750–1965* (London, Heinemann, 1967).

Abbott, Andrew, *The System of Professions: An Essay on the Division of Expert Labor* (Chicago, University of Chicago Press, 1988).

Alberti, Johanna, *Eleanor Rathbone* (London, Sage Publications, 1996).

Albistur, Maïte and Daniel Armogathe, *Histoire du Féminisme Français de L'Empire Napoléonien à Nos Jours*, (Paris, Éditions des Femmes, 1977).

Anderson, J Stuart, *Lawyers and the Making of English Land Law 1832–1940* (Oxford, Clarendon Press, 1992).

Ash, Ranjana Sidhanta, 'Two Early-Twentieth-Century Women Writers: Cornelia Sorabji and Sarojini Naidu' in Arvind Krishna Mehrotra (ed), *A History of Indian Literature in English* (New York, Columbia University Press, 2003).

Auerbach, Jerold S, *Unequal Justice: Lawyers and Social Change in Modern America* (New York, Oxford University Press, 1976).

Babcock, Barbara Allen, 'Reconstructing the Person: The Case of Clara Shortridge Foltz' in Susan Groag Bell and Marilyn Yalom (eds), *Revealing Lives: Autobiography, Biography and Gender* (Albany, State University of New York Press, 1990).

Bacchi, Carol Lee, *Liberation Deferred? The Ideas of the English-Canadian Suffragists, 1877–1918* (Toronto, University of Toronto Press, 1983).

——, 'Divided Allegiances: The Response of Farm Women and Labour Women to Suffrage' in Linda Kealey (ed), *A Not Unreasonable Claim: Women and Reform in Canada 1880s–1920s* (Toronto, The Women's Press, 1979).

Backhouse, Constance, 'Lawyering: Clara Brett Martin, Canada's First Woman Lawyer' in Constance Backhouse (ed), *Petticoats and Prejudice: Women and Law in Nineteenth-Century Canada* (Toronto, The Osgoode Society, 1991).

Bacik, Ivana, Cathryn Costello and Eileen Drew, *Gender InJustice: Feminising the Legal Professions?* (Dublin, Trinity College Dublin Law School, 2003).

Baker, G Blaine, 'Legal Education in Upper Canada, 1785–1889: The Law Society as Educator' in David H Flaherty (ed), *Essays in the History of Canadian Law*, vol II (Toronto, The Osgoode Society and University of Toronto Press, 1983).

Banks, Margaret A, 'Evolution of the Ontario Courts 1788–1981' in David H Flaherty (ed), *Essays in the History of Canadian Law*, vol II (Toronto, The Osgoode Society and University of Toronto Press, 1983).

Banks, Olive, *Faces of Feminism: A Study of Feminism as a Social Movement* (New York, St Martin's Press, 1981).

Bannerji, Himani, 'Attired in Virtue: The Discourse on Shame (*lajja*) and Clothing of the *Bhadramahila* in Colonial Bengal' in Bharati Ray (ed), *From the Seams of History: Essays on Indian Women* (Delhi, Oxford University Press, 1997).

Barry, Kathleen, *Susan B Anthony: A Biography of a Singular Feminist* (New York, Ballantine Books, 1988).

Bartley, Paula, *Emmeline Pankhurst* (London and New York, Routledge, 2002).

Basch, Norma, *In the Eyes of the Law: Women, Marriage and Property in Nineteenth-Century New York* (Ithaca, Cornell University Press, 1982).

Bashevkin, Sylvia, 'Independence versus Partisanship: Dilemmas in the Political History of Women in English Canada' in Veronica Strong-Boag and Anita Clair Fellman (eds), *Rethinking Canada: The Promise of Women's History* (Toronto, Copp Clark Pitman Ltd, 1986).

Bell, David, Douglas Johnson and Peter Morris (eds), *Biographical Dictionary of French Political Leaders since 1870* (New York, Simon and Schuster, 1990).

Bell, David G, *Legal Education in New Brunswick: A History* (Fredericton, University of New Brunswick, 1992).

——, 'William Henry Tuck' *Dictionary of Canadian Biography*, vol 14 (Toronto, University of Toronto Press).

Berry, Dawn B, *The 50 Most Influential Women in American Law* (Los Angeles, Lowell House, 1996).

Bird, Florence *et al*, *Royal Commission on the Status of Women in Canada* (Ottawa, Information Canada, 1970).

Birks, Michael, *Gentlemen of the Law* (London, Stevens & Sons Limited, 1960).

Bittenbender, Ada M, 'Women in Law' in Annie Nathan Meyer (ed), *Woman's Work in America* (New York, Henry Holt and Company, 1891).

Bledstein, Burton J, *The Culture of Professionalism: The Middle Class and the*

Development of Higher Education in America (New York, WW Norton & Company, Inc, 1976).

Bloomfield, Elizabeth, 'Lawyers as Members of Urban Business Elites in Southern Ontario, 1860 to 1920' in Carol Wilton (ed), *Beyond the Law: Lawyers and Business in Canada 1830 to 1930* (Toronto, The Osgoode Society, 1990).

Boehmer, Elleke (ed), *Empire Writing: An Anthology of Colonial Literature 1870–1918* (Oxford, Oxford University Press, 1998).

Boël, Marthe and Christiane Duchene, *Le Féminisme en Belgique, 1892–1914* (Bruxelles, Éditions du Conseil National des Femmes Belge, 1955).

Bolt, Christine, *The Women's Movements in the United States and Britain from the 1790s to the 1920s* (Amherst, University of Massachusetts Press, 1993).

Borthwick, Meredith, *The Changing Role of Women in Bengal 1849–1905* (Princeton, NJ, Princeton University Press, 1984).

Bourdieu, Pierre, *Outline of a Theory of Practice*, trans Richard Nice (Cambridge, Cambridge University Press, 1977).

Boutilier, Beverly and Alison Prentice (eds), *Creating Historical Memory: English-Canadian Women and the Work of History* (Vancouver, UBC Press, 1997).

Brandon, Ruth, *The New Women & the Old Men: Love, Sex and the Woman Question* (London, Flamingo, 1991).

Brierley, John EC, 'Historical Aspects of Law Teaching in Québec' in Roy J Matas and Deborah J McCawley (eds), *Legal Education in Canada* (Montréal, Federation of Law Societies of Canada, 1987).

Brittain, Vera, *Lady into Woman: A History of Women from Victoria to Elizabeth II* (London, Andrew Dakers Limited, 1953).

——, *The Women at Oxford: A Fragment of History* (London, George Harrap & Co Ltd, 1960).

Brockman, Joan, 'Exclusionary Tactics: The History of Women and Visible Minorities in the Legal Profession in British Columbia' in Hamar Foster and John PS McLaren (eds), *Essays in the History of Canadian Law: Vol VI, British Columbia and the Yukon* (Toronto, The Osgoode Society, 1995) 508.

——, *Gender in the Legal Profession: Fitting in or Breaking the Mould* (Vancouver, University of British Columbia Press, 2001).

Buckland, Charles E, *Dictionary of Indian Biography* (New York, Greenwood Press, 1969).

Burns, Michael, *Histoire d'une Famille Française: Les Dreyfus* (Paris, Librarie Arthème Fayard, 1994).

——, *France and the Dreyfus Affair: A Documentary History* (Boston and New York, Bedford/St Martin's, 1999).

Burrage M, K Jarausch and H Siegrist, 'An Actor-Based Framework for the Study of the Professions' in Michael Burrage and Rolf Torstendahl (eds), *Professions in Theory and History: Rethinking the Study of the Professions* (London, Sage Publications, 1990).

Burt, Sandra, Lorraine Code and Lindsay Dorney (eds), *Changing Patterns: Women in Canada* (Toronto, McClelland and Stewart, 1988).

Burton, Antoinette, *Burdens of History: British Feminists, Indian Women, and Imperial Culture, 1865–1915* (Chapel Hill & London, University of North Carolina Press, 1994).

——, *At the Heart of the Empire: Indians and the Colonial Encounter in Late-Victorian Britain* (Berkeley, University of California Press, 1998).

——, *Dwelling in the Archive: Women Writing House, Home, and History in late Colonial India* (Oxford, Oxford University Press, 2003).

Buss, Helen M, *Mapping Our Selves: Canadian Women's Biography in English* (Montréal and Kingston, McGill-Queen's University Press, 1993).

Buss, Helen M and Marlene Kadar (eds), *Working in Women's Archives: Researching Women's Private Literature and Archival Documents* (Waterloo, Ontario, Wilfrid Laurier Press, 2001).

Byrnes, Robert F, *Antisemitism in Modern France: The Prologue to the Dreyfus Affair* (New York, Howard Fertig, 1969).

Cammelli, Andrea, 'Universities and Professions' in Maria Malatesta (ed), *Society and the Professions in Italy 1860–1914*, trans Adrian Belton (New York and Cambridge, UK, Cambridge University Press, 1995).

Canadian Bar Association, *Touchstones for Change: Equality, Diversity and Accountability – the Report on Gender Equality in the Legal Profession* (Ottawa, Canadian Bar Association, 1993).

Castle, Barbara, *Sylvia and Christabel Pankhurst* (London, Penguin Books, 1987).

Catran, Ken, *Hanlon: A Casebook* (Auckland, BCNZ Enterprises, 1985).

Chandra, Sudhir, *Enslaved Daughters: Colonialism, Law and Women's Rights* (Delhi, Oxford University Press, 1998).

Chapman, Mrs EF, *Sketches of Some Distinguished Indian Women* (London, WH Allen & Co Ltd, 1891).

Charrier, Edmée, *L'Évolution Intellectuelle Féminine* (Paris, Éditions Albert Mechelinck, 1931).

Chatterjee, Partha A, 'The Nationalist Resolution of the Women's Question' in Kumkum Sangari and Sudesh Vaid (eds), *Recasting Women: Essays in Indian Colonial History* (New Brunswick, NJ, Rutgers University Press, 1990).

Chester, Ronald, *Unequal Access: Women Lawyers in a Changing America* (MA, Bergin & Garvey Publishers, Inc, 1985).

Cleverdon, Catherine, *The Woman Suffrage Movement in Canada* (Toronto, University of Toronto Press, 1950).

Clifford, Geraldine Jonçich (ed), *Lone Voyagers: Academic Women in Coeducational Universities 1870–1937* (New York, Feminist Press, 1989).

Coates, Colin M and Cecilia Morgan, *Heroines and History: Representations of Madeleine de Verchères and Laura Secord* (Toronto, University of Toronto Press, 2002).

Cohen, Elizabeth S, 'Court Testimony from the Past: Self and Culture in the Making of Text' in Marlene Kadar (ed), *Essays on Life Writing: From Genre to Critical Practice* (Toronto, University of Toronto Press, 1992).

Collie, Michael, *George Gissing: A Biography* (Hamden, CT, Archon Books, 1977).

Commire, Anne (ed), *Women in World History*, vol 3 (Waterford, CT, Yorkin, 1999).

Coney, Sandra, *Standing in the Sunshine: A History of New Zealand Women Since They Won the Vote* (Auckland, Viking, 1993).

Conway, Jill K, Susan C Bourque and Joan W Scott (eds), *Learning About Women: Gender, Politics and Power* (Ann Arbor, University of Michigan Press, 1989).

Cook, Ramsay, *The Regenerators: Social Criticism in Late Victorian English Canada* (Toronto, University of Toronto Press, 1985).

Cook, Ramsay and Wendy Mitchinson (eds), *The Proper Sphere: Woman's Place in Canadian Society* (Toronto, Oxford University Press, 1976).

Cooke, Robin (ed), *Portrait of a Profession: The Centennial Book of the New Zealand Law Society* (Wellington, AH and AW Reed, 1969).

Cooper, Sandi E (ed), *Peace Activities in Belgium and the Netherlands* (New York and London, Garland Publishing Inc, 1972).

Cott, Nancy F, 'Women as Law Clerks: Catharine G Waugh' in Donna C Stanton (ed), *The Female Autograph* (New York, New York Literary Forum, 1984).

——, *The Grounding of Modern Feminism* (New Haven and London, Yale University Press, 1987).

——, *Public Vows: A History of Marriage and the Nation* (Cambridge, MA, Harvard University Press, 2000).

Cownie, Fiona, *Legal Academics: Culture and Identities* (Oxford and Portland, OR, Hart Publishing, 2004).

Crabb, John H, *The Constitution of Belgium and the Belgian Civil Code* (Littleton, Colorado, Fred B Rothman & Co, 1982).

——, *The French Civil Code* (Littleton, Colorado, Rothman & Co; and The Netherlands, Kluwer Law and Taxation Publishers, 1995) rev edn.

Crawford, Elizabeth, *The Women's Suffrage Movement: A Reference Guide (1866–1928)* (London, University College London Press, 1999).

Cross, D Suzanne, 'The Neglected Majority: The Changing Role of Women in 19th-Century Montréal' in Susan Mann Trofimenkoff and Alison Prentice (eds), *The Neglected Majority: Essays in Canadian Women's History* vol 1 (Toronto, McClelland and Stewart, 1977).

Cullen, Michael J, *Lawfully Occupied: The Centennial History of the Otago District Law Society* (Dunedin, Otago District Law Society, 1979).

Davenport, Neil, *The United Kingdom Patent System: A Brief History with Bibliography* (Hampshire, UK, Kenneth Mason, 1979).

Davies, Gwendolyn, 'The Literary New Woman and Social Activism in Maritime Literature, 1880–1920' in Janet Guildford and Suzanne Morton (eds), *Separate Spheres: Women's Worlds in the 19th-Century Maritimes* (Fredericton, Acadiensis Press, 1994).

Davis, Natalie Zemon, 'Women's History as Women's Education' in Natalie Zemon Davis and Joan Wallach Scott (eds), *Women's History as Women's Education* (Northampton, MA, Smith College Archives, 1985).

de Santerre, Colmet, 'Preface' in Jeanne Chauvin, *Cours de Droit Professé dans les Lycées de Jeunes Filles de Paris* (Paris, V Giard & E Brière, 1895).

Dicey, AV, *Letters to a Friend on Votes for Women* (London, John Murray, 1909).

Dictionary of National Biography 1901–1911 (London, Oxford University Press).

Dictionnaire de Biographie Française (Paris, Librairie Letouzey et Anê, 1959).

Drachman, Virginia G, *Hospital with a Heart: Women Doctors and the Paradox of Separatism at the New England Hospital, 1862–1969* (Ithaca, Cornell University Press, 1984).

——, *Women Lawyers and the Origins of Professional Identity in America: The Letters of the Equity Club, 1887 to 1890* (Ann Arbor, University of Michigan Press, 1993).

——, *Sisters in Law: Women Lawyers in Modern American History* (Cambridge, MA, Harvard University Press, 1998).

Dranoff, Linda Silver, *Women in Canadian Law* (Toronto, Fitzhenry and Whiteside, 1977).

Dreyfus, Alfred, *Cinq Années de ma Vie (1894–1899)* (Paris, Éditions La Découverte, 1994).

Duman, Daniel, *The English and Colonial Bars in the Nineteenth Century* (London & Canberra, Croom Helm, 1983).

Dumont, Micheline *et al*, *Québec Women: A History* (Toronto, The Women's Press, 1987).

Durand, Bernard, 'Maîtres Popelin, Chauvin et Le Vigoureux, Pionnières du Barreau' in Bernard Durand and Laurent Mayali (eds), *Excerptiones Iuris: Studies in Honor of André Gouron* (Berkeley, Robbins Collection Publications, University of California, 2000).

Duverger, Alexandre JV, *De la Condition Politique et Civile des Femmes* (Paris, A Marescq, 1872).

Epstein, Cynthia Fuchs, *Women in Law* (New York, Basic Books, 1981) and 2nd edn (Chicago, University of Illinois Press, 1993).

——, *Deceptive Distinctions: Sex, Gender and the Social Order* (New Haven and New York, Yale University Press and Russell Sage Foundation, 1988).

Errington, Jane, 'Pioneers and Suffragists' in Sandra Burt, Lorraine Code and Lindsay Dorney (eds), *Changing Patterns: Women in Canada* (Toronto, McClelland and Stewart, 1988).

Figler, Bernard QC, *Sam Jacobs, Member of Parliament* (Ottawa, private pub, 1959).

Findling, John E, *Chicago's Great World Fairs* (Manchester and New York, Manchester University Press, 1994).

Fitzpatrick, Peter, *The Mythology of Modern Law* (London and New York, Routledge, 1992).

Flexner Report, *Medical Education in the United States and Canada* (1910).

Flexner, Eleanor, *Century of Struggle: The Woman's Rights Movement in the United States* (Cambridge, MA, Belknap Press of Harvard University Press, 1959).

Foster, John, *Men at the Bar* (London, Reever and Turner, 1885).

Fowler, Marian, *Redney: A Life of Sara Jeannette Duncan* (Toronto, Anansi, 1983).

——, *Below the Peacock Fan: First Ladies of the Raj* (Toronto, Penguin Books, 1987).

Frank, Louis, *De L'Exercice de la Profession d'Avocat en Italie: Exposé Sommaire des Règles* (Bruxelles, J B Moens & Fils, 1887).

——, *Résumé du Cours de Droit Pénal* (Bruxelles, Gustave Mayolez, 1887).

——, *La Femme-Avocat: Exposé Historique et Critique de la Question* (Bruxelles, Ferdinand Larcier; and Bologne, Nicolas Zanichelli, 1888).

——, *Essai sur la Condition Politique de la Femme: Étude de Sociologie et de Législation* (Paris, Arthur Rousseau, 1892).

——, *L'Épargne de la Femme Mariée* (Bruxelles, A Vromant et Cie, 1892).

——, *La Femme dans les Emplois Publics: Enquête et Rapport* (Bruxelles, Charles Rozez, 1893).

——, *M W E Gladstone et Le Féminisme* (Gand, Imprimerie C Annoot-Braeckman, 1893).

——, *Le Grand Catéchisme de la Femme* (Paris, Verviers, 1894).

——, *Cours sur La Législation Féministe: Notions Élémentaires* (Bruxelles, J H Moreau, 1895).

——, *Le Témoinage de La Femme: Rapport (Proposition de Loi No. 1)* (Bruxelles, Henri Lamertin, 1896)

——, *L'Épargne de la Femme Mariée: Rapport (Proposition de Loi No 2)* (Bruxelles, Henri Lamertin, 1896).

——, *Les Salaires de la Famille Ouvrière: Rapport (Proposition de Loi No 3)* (Bruxelles, Henri Lamertin, 1896).

——, *Cornelius Nepos, ou le Premier Plagiaire Collectiviste* (Bruxelles, L Istace, 1897).

——, *La Femme-Avocat: Exposé Historique et Critique de la Question* (Paris, V Giard et E Brière, 1898).

——, *Affaire Dreyfus, Procès en Revision: Le Bordereau est d'Esterhazy* (Bruxelles, Henri Lamertin, 1898; and Paris, PV Stock, 1898).

——, *L'Éducation Domestique des Jeunes Filles ou La Formation des Mères* (Paris, Librairie Larousse, 1904).

——, *Les Belges et La Paix* (Bruxelles, Henri Lamertin, 1905).

——, *La Paix et Le District Fédéral du Monde* (Paris, Librairie Larousse, 1910).

Frank, Louis, Louis Maingie and Dr Keiffer, *L'Assurance Maternelle* (Bruxelles, Henri Lamartin; and Paris, G Carré et N Naud, 1897).

Fredman, Sandra, *Women and the Law* (Oxford, Clarendon Press, 1997).

Freidson, Eliot, *Professional Powers: A Study of the Institutionalization of Knowledge* (Chicago and London, University of Chicago Press, 1986).

——, *Professionalism: The Third Logic* (Chicago, University of Chicago Press, 2001).

French, Doris, *Ishbel and the Empire: A Biography of Lady Aberdeen* (Toronto and Oxford, Dundurn Press, 1988).

Friedman, Jane M, *America's First Woman Lawyer: The Biography of Myra Bradwell* (Buffalo, Prometheus Books, 1993).

Gall, Susan B and Caroline Zilboorg, (eds), *Women's Firsts* (Detroit, Gaile Research, 1997).

Gallaway, Iain, 'Otago' in Robin Cooke (ed), *Portrait of a Profession: The Centennial Book of the New Zealand Law Society* (Wellington, AH and AW Reed, 1969).

Gallichan, Gilles, *Les Québécoises et le Barreau: L'Histoire d'une Difficile Conquête, 1914–1941* (Québec, Septentrion, 1999).

Gandevia, Firdaus, 'Cornelia Sorabji Recalled' in Nawaz B Mody (ed), *The Parsis in Western India: 1818 to 1920* (Bombay, Allied Publishers Ltd, 1998).

Gardner, WJ, *Colonial Cap and Gown* (Christchurch, University of Canterbury, 1979).

Garner, John, *The Franchise and Politics in British North America 1755–1867* (Toronto, University of Toronto Press, 1969).

Garza, Hedda, *Barred from the Bar: A History of Women in the Legal Profession* (New York, Franklin Watts, 1996).

Gatfield, Gill, *Without Prejudice: Women in the Law* (Wellington, Brooker's, 1996).

Geison, Gerald L (ed), *Professions and Professional Ideologies in America* (Chapel Hill and London, University of North Carolina Press, 1983).

Gibson, Dale and Lee Gibson, *Substantial Justice: Law and Lawyers in Manitoba 1670–1970* (Winnipeg, Peguis Publishers, 1972).

Gibson, Lee 'A Brief History of the Law Society of Manitoba' in Cameron Harvey (ed), *The Law Society of Manitoba 1877–1987* (Winnipeg, Peguis Publishers, 1977).

Gidney, RD and WPJ Millar, *Professional Gentlemen: The Professions in Nineteenth-Century Ontario* (Toronto, University of Toronto Press, 1994).

Gillett, Margaret, *We Walked Very Warily: A History of Women at McGill* (Montréal, Eden Press Women's Publications, 1981).

——, *Dear Grace: A Romance of History* (Montréal, Eden Press, 1986).

Girard, Philip, 'The Roots of a Professional Renaissance: Lawyers in Nova Scotia 1850–1910' in Dale Gibson and W Wesley Pue (eds), *Glimpses of Canadian Legal History* (Winnipeg, Legal Research Institute, 1991).

Glasson, Ernest-Desiré, *Éléments du Droit Français dans ses Rapports avec le Droit Naturel et L'Économie Politique* (Paris, Guillaumin, 1875).

Glazer, Penina Migdal and Miriam Slater, *Unequal Colleagues: The Entrance of Women into the Professions, 1890–1940* (New Brunswick and London, Rutgers University Press, 1987).

Gleadle, Kathryn, *The Early Feminists: Radical Unitarians and the Emergence of the Women's Rights Movement, 1831–51* (New York, St Martin's Press, 1995).

Goldman, Lazarus M, *History of the Jews in New Zealand* (Wellington, AH and AW Reed, 1958).

Gordon, Peter and David Doughan, *Dictionary of British Women's Organizations 1825–1960* (London, Woburn Press, 2001).

Gordon, Robert W, 'Legal Thought and Legal Practice in the Age of American Enterprise 1870–1920' in Gerald L Geison(ed), *Professions and Professional Ideologies in America* (Chapel Hill and London, University of North Carolina Press, 1983).

Gorham, Deborah, 'Flora MacDonald Denison: Canadian Feminist' in Linda Kealey (ed), *A Not Unreasonable Claim: Women and Reform in Canada 1880s–1920s* (Toronto, The Women's Press, 1979).

Gray, Charlotte, *Mrs King: The Life and Times of Isabel Mackenzie King* (Toronto, Viking, 1997).

Griffith, Elisabeth, *In Her Own Right: The Life of Elizabeth Cady Stanton* (New York, Oxford University Press, 1984).

Griffiths, Naomi ES, *Penelope's Web: Some Perceptions of Women in European and Canadian Society* (Toronto, Oxford University Press, 1976).

Grimshaw, Patricia, *Women's Suffrage in New Zealand* (Auckland, Auckland University Press, 1972).

Grossberg, Michael, 'Institutionalizing Masculinity: The Law as a Masculine Profession' in Mark C Carnes and Clyde Griffen (eds), *Meanings for Manhood: Constructions of Masculinity in Victorian America* (Chicago and London, University of Chicago Press, 1990).

Gwyn, Sandra, *The Private Capital: Ambition and Love in the Age of Macdonald and Laurier* (Toronto, McClelland and Stewart Limited, 1984).

Hacker, Carlotta, *The Indomitable Lady Doctors* (Toronto, Clarke Irwin, 1982).

Hagan, John and Fiona Kay, *Gender in Practice: A Study of Lawyers' Lives* (Oxford, Oxford University Press, 1995).

Hall, Catherine, Keith McClelland and Jane Rendall, *Defining the Victorian Nation: Class, Race, Gender and the British Reform Act of 1867* (Cambridge, Cambridge University Press, 2000).

Halliday, Terence C and Lucien Karpik, 'Politics Matter: A Comparative Theory of Lawyers in the Making of Political Liberalism' in Terence C Halliday and Lucien Karpik (eds), *Lawyers and the Rise of Western Political Liberalism* (Oxford, Clarendon Press, 1997).

Halpenny, Francess G, 'Expectations of Biography' in R B Fleming (ed), *Boswell's Children: The Art of the Biographer* (Toronto, Dundurn Press, 1992).

Halperin, John, *Gissing: A Life in Books* (Oxford, Oxford University Press, 1987).

Hamilton, James Cleland, *Osgoode Hall: Reminiscences of the Bench and Bar* (Toronto, Carswell Co Ltd, 1904).

Harrington, Mona, *Women Lawyers: Rewriting the Rules* (New York, Plume Books, 1995).

Harris, Barbara J, *Beyond Her Sphere: Women and the Professions in American History* (Westport, CT, Greenwood Press, 1978).

Harris, Jose, *Private Lives, Public Spirit: A Social History of Britain, 1870–1914* (Oxford, Oxford University Press, 1993).

Harrison, Brian, *Separate Spheres: The Opposition to Women's Suffrage in Britain* (London, Croom Helm, 1978).

Haskell, Thomas L, 'Power to the Experts: A Review of Burton Bledstein's *Culture of Professionalism*' in Thomas L Haskell (ed), *Objectivity is not Neutrality: Explanatory Schemes in History* (Baltimore and London, John Hopkins University Press, 1998).

Hause, Steven C, *Hubertine Auclert: The French Suffragette* (New Haven, Yale University Press, 1987).

Hause, Steven C with Anne R Kenney, *Women's Suffrage and Social Politics in the French Third Republic* (Princeton, Princeton University Press, 1984).

Heilbrun, Carolyn G, *Writing a Woman's Life* (New York, Ballantyne Books, 1988).

——, *Women's Lives: The View from the Threshold* (Toronto, University of Toronto Press, 1999).

Hirsch, Pam, *Barbara Leigh Smith Bodichon 1827–1891: Feminist, Artist and Rebel* (London, Pimlico, 1999).

Hoff, Joan, *Law, Gender, and Injustice: A Legal History of US Women* (New York, University Press, 1991).

Holcombe, Lee, *Victorian Ladies at Work: Middle-Class Working Women in England and Wales 1850–1914* (Hamden, CT, Archon Books, 1973).

——, *Wives and Property: Reform of the Married Women's Property Law in Nineteenth-Century England* (Toronto, University of Toronto Press, 1983).

Holroyd, Michael, *Bernard Shaw, The Search for Love 1856–1898, vol I* (London, Chatto & Windus, 1988).

Holton, Sandra Stanley, *Feminism and Democracy: Women's Suffrage and Reform Politics in Britain, 1900–1918* (Cambridge, Cambridge University Press, 1986).

Honsberger, John D, 'Raymond and Honsberger: A Small Firm that Stayed Small,

1889–1989' in Carol Wilton (ed), *Inside the Law: Canadian Law Firms in Historical Perspective* (Toronto, The Osgoode Society, 1996).

Hufton, Olwen, *The Prospect Before Her: A History of Women in Western Europe 1500–1800* (New York, Alfred A Knopf, 1996).

Hurst, James Willard, *The Growth of American Law: The Law Makers* (Boston, Little Brown and Company, 1950).

Hyman, Paula E, 'French Jewish Historiography since 1870' in Frances Malino and Bernard Wasserstein (eds), *The Jews in Modern France* (Hanover and London, University Press of New England for Brandeis University Press, 1985).

——, *The Jews of Modern France* (Berkeley, University of California Press, 1998).

Iacovetta, Franca and Mariana Valverde (eds), *Gender Conflicts: New Essays in Women's History* (Toronto, University of Toronto Press, 1992).

Innes, C Lyn, *A History of Black and Asian Writing in Britain, 1700–2000* (Cambridge, Cambridge University Press, 2002).

International Council of Women, *Report of Transactions of the Second Quinquennial Meeting, London, July 1899* (London, T Fisher Unwin, 1900).

——, *Report of the International Congress of Women* (Toronto, Geo Parker & Sons, 1910) 2 vols.

Jacobi, Mary Putnam, 'Woman in Medicine' in Annie Nathan Meyer (ed), *Woman's Work in America* (New York, Henry Holt and Company, 1891).

Jayawardena, Kumari, *Feminism and Nationalism in the Third World* (London, Zed Books Ltd, 1986).

Josephson, Harold (ed), *Biographical Dictionary of Modern Peace Leaders* (Westport, CT, Greenwood Press, 1985).

Kanner, Barbara, 'The Women of England in a Century of Social Change, 1815–1914: A Select Bibliography' in Martha Vicinus (ed), *Suffer and Be Still: Women in the Victorian Age* (Bloomington & London, Indiana University Press, 1973).

Karpik, Lucien, *French Lawyers: A Study in Collective Action, 1274 to 1994* (Oxford, Clarendon Press, 1999).

——, 'Technical and Political Knowledge: the Relationship of Lawyers and Other Legal Professions to the Market and the State' in Rolf Torstendahl and Michael Burrage (eds), *The Formation of Professions: Knowledge, State and Strategy* (London, Sage Publications, 1990).

Kealey, Linda (ed), *A Not Unreasonable Claim: Women and Reform in Canada 1880s–1920s* (Toronto, The Women's Press, 1979).

Kessler, Deirdre, *A Century on Spring Street: Wanda Lefurgey Wyatt of Summerside, Prince Edward Island, 1895–1998* (Charlottetown, PEI, Indigo Press, 1999).

'Key Facts about Canadian Common-Law Schools' 2003–2004 in *LSAT Registration and Information Book (Canadian)* (Newtown, PA, Law School Admission Council, Inc, 2003).

Kinnear, Mary, *In Subordination: Professional Women, 1870–1970* (Montréal and Kingston, McGill-Queen's University Press, 1995).

Kirk, Harry, *Portrait of a Profession: A History of the Solicitor's Profession, 1100 to the Present Day* (London, Oyez Publishing, 1976).

Knowles, Valerie, *First Person: A Biography of Cairine Wilson, Canada's First Woman Senator* (Toronto and Oxford, Dundurn Press, 1988).

Kraditor, Aileen, *The Ideas of the Woman Suffrage Movement 1890–1920* (New York, Columbia University Press, 1967).

Kugler, Israel, *From Ladies to Women: The Organized Struggle for Woman's Rights in the Reconstruction Era* (Westport, CT, Greenwood Press, 1987).

Lacey, Candida Ann (ed), *Barbara Leigh Smith Bodichon and the Langham Place Group* (New York and London, Routledge & Kegan Paul, 1987).

Lang, Elsie M, *British Women in the Twentieth Century* (London, T Werner Laurie Ltd, 1929).

Langstaff, Annie Macdonald, *French-English, English-French Law Dictionary* (Montréal, Wilson and Lafleur, Limited, 1937).

LaPierre, Jo, 'The Academic Life of Canadian Coeds, 1880–1900' in Ruby Heap and Alison Prentice (eds), *Gender and Education in Ontario: An Historical Reader* (Toronto, Canadian Scholars' Press, 1991).

Larson, Magali Sarfatti, *The Rise of Professionalism: A Sociological Analysis* (Berkeley, University of California Press, 1977).

Lentz, Bernard and David Laband, *Sex Discrimination in the Legal Profession* (Westport, CT, Quorum Books, 1995).

Lerner, Gerda, 'The Lady and the Mill Girl: Changes in the Status of Women in the Age of Jackson, 1800–1840' in Nancy F Cott and Elizabeth H Pleck (eds), *A Heritage of Her Own: Toward a New Social History of American Women* (New York, Simon and Schuster, 1979).

——, *The Majority Finds its Past: Placing Women in History* (New York, Oxford University Press, 1979).

Liddington, Jill and Jill Norris, *One Hand Tied Behind Us: The Rise of the Women's Suffrage Movement* (London, Virago, 1984).

Ligue Belge du Droit des Femmes, *Actes du Congrès Féministe Internationale de Bruxelles 1912* (Bruxelles, Imprimerie Scientifique Charles Bulens, 1912).

London, Jack R, 'The Admissions and Education Committee: A Perspective on Legal Education and Admission to Practice in the Province of Manitoba – Past, Present and Future' in Cameron Harvey (ed), *The Law Society of Manitoba 1877–1987* (Winnipeg, Peguis Publishers, 1977).

Luhrmann, Tanya M, *The Good Parsi: The Fate of a Colonial Elite in a Postcolonial Society* (Cambridge, MA, Harvard University Press, 1996).

MacDonald, Cheryl, *Adelaide Hoodless: Domestic Crusader* (Toronto and Reading, Dundurn Press, 1986).

MacGill, Elsie G, *My Mother, the Judge* (Toronto, Ryerson Press, 1955).

MacKenzie, Norman (ed), *The Letters of Sidney and Beatrice Webb: Apprenticeships 1873–1892, vol I* (Cambridge, Cambridge University Press, 1978).

MacKenzie, Norman and Jeanne (eds), *The Diary of Beatrice Webb 1892–1905: 'All the Good Things of Life'* vol 2 (London, Virago, 1983).

MacMillan, Margaret, *Women of the Raj* (London, Thames and Hudson, 1988).

MacMurchy, Marjory, 'Women's Organizations, 1916' reproduced in Ramsay Cook and Wendy Mitchinson (eds), *The Proper Sphere: Woman's Place in Canadian Society* (Toronto, Oxford University Press, 1976).

Malatesta, Maria, 'The Italian Professions from a Comparative Perspective' in Maria Malatesta (ed), *Society and the Professions in Italy 1860–1914*, trans Adrian Belton (New York and Cambridge, UK, Cambridge University Press, 1995).

Mani, Lata, 'Contentious Traditions: The Debate on *Sati* in Colonial India' in Kumkum Sangari and Sudesh Vaid (eds), *Recasting Women: Essays in Indian Colonial History* (New Brunswick, NJ, Rutgers University Press, 1990).

Margadant, Jo Burr, *Madame le Professeur: Women Educators in the Third Republic* (Princeton, Princeton University Press, 1990).

Margolis, Joseph, 'Pierre Bourdieu: *Habitus* and the Logic of Practice' in Richard Shusterman (ed), *Bourdieu: A Critical Reader* (Oxford, Blackwell Publishers Ltd, 1999).

Marrus, Michael, *The Politics of Assimilation: The French Jewish Community at the Time of the Dreyfus Affair* (Oxford, Clarendon Press, 1971).

Matsuda, Mari J (ed), *Called from Within: Early Women Lawyers of Hawai'i* (Honolulu, University of Hawaii Press, 1992).

Matteisen, Paul F, Arthur C Young, and Pierre Coustillas (eds), *The Collected Letters of George Gissing* (Athens, Ohio University Press, 1995–1997).

Maynard, Mary and June Purvis, *Researching Women's Lives from a Feminist Perspective* (London, Taylor & Francis, 1994).

Mayo, Katherine, *Mother India* (New York, Harcourt, Brace and Company, 1927).

Mazzacane, Aldo, 'A Jurist for United Italy: The Training and Culture of Neapolitan Lawyers in the Nineteenth Century' in Maria Malatesta (ed), *Society and the Professions in Italy 1860–1914*, trans Adrian Belton (New York and Cambridge, UK, Cambridge University Press, 1995).

McArthur, Tom (ed), *The Oxford Companion to the English Language* (Oxford, Oxford University Press, 1992).

McCann, Larry, 'The 1890s: Fragmentation and the New Social Order' in ER Forbes and DA Muise (eds), *The Atlantic Provinces in Confederation* (Toronto and Fredericton, University of Toronto Press and Acadiensis Press, 1993).

McClean, Sylvie, *A Woman of Influence: Evlyn Fenwick Farris* (Victoria, Sono Nis Press, 1997).

McGlynn, Clare, *The Woman Lawyer: Making the Difference* (London, Butterworths, 1998).

McLaren, John PS, 'The History of Legal Education in Common Law Canada' in Roy J Matas and Deborah J McCawley (eds), *Legal Education in Canada* (Montréal, Federation of Law Societies of Canada, 1987).

McNamee, Gwen Hoerr, 'Alta May Hulett' in Gwen Hoerr McNamee (ed), *Bar None: 125 Years of Women Lawyers in Illinois* (Chicago, Chicago Bar Association Alliance for Women, 1998).

McWilliams-Tullberg, Rita, 'Women and Degrees at Cambridge University 1862–1897' in Martha Vicinus (ed), *A Widening Sphere: Changing Roles of Victorian Women* (Bloomington & London, Indiana University Press, 1977).

Menkel-Meadow, Carrie, 'Feminization of the Legal Profession: The Comparative Sociology of Women Lawyers' in Richard Abel and Philip Lewis (eds), *Lawyers in Society: Comparative Perspectives*, vol III (Berkeley, University of California Press, 1989).

——, 'Portia *Redux*: Another Look at Gender, Feminism, and Legal Ethics' in Stephen Parker and Charles Sampford (eds), *Legal Ethics and Legal Practice: Contemporary Issues* (Oxford, Clarendon Press, 1995).

Miller, Jane Eldridge, *Rebel Women: Feminism, Modernism and the Edwardian Novel* (London, Virago Press, 1994).

Mitchinson, Wendy, 'The WCTU: "For God, Home and Native Land": A Study in Nineteenth-Century Feminism' in Linda Kealey (ed), *A Not Unreasonable Claim: Women and Reform in Canada 1880s–1920s* (Toronto, The Women's Press, 1979).

——, 'The Medical Treatment of Women' in Sandra Burt, Lorraine Code and Lindsay Dorney (eds), *Changing Patterns: Women in Canada* (Toronto, McClelland and Stewart, 1988).

Morello, Karen B, *The Invisible Bar: The Woman Lawyer in America 1638 to the Present* (New York, Random House, 1986).

Morgan, David, *Suffragists and Liberals: The Politics of Woman Suffrage in England* (Oxford, Basil Blackwell, 1975).

Morris, James, *Farewell the Trumpets: An Imperial Retreat* (London, Penguin Books, 1979).

——, *Heaven's Command: An Imperial Progress* (Harmondsworth, Penguin Books, 1979).

Mossman, Mary Jane, 'The Paradox of Feminist Engagement with Law' in Nancy Mandell (ed), *Feminist Issues: Race, Class and Sexuality*, 2nd edn (Scarborough, Prentice Hall Allyn and Bacon Canada, 1998).

Mussey, Ellen Spencer, 'The Woman Attorney and Counsellor' in National Council of Women of Canada (ed), *Report of the International Congress of Women, Toronto: 24–30 June 1909*, vol 2 (Toronto, Geo Parker & Sons, 1910).

Nicholls, CS, (ed), *Dictionary of National Biography – Missing Persons* (Oxford, Oxford University Press, 1993).

Nicholls, Roberta, *The Women's Parliament: The National Council of the Women of New Zealand 1896–1920* (Wellington, Victoria University Press, 1996).

O'Donovan-Polten, Sheelagh, *The Scales of Success* (Toronto, University of Toronto Press, 2001).

Offer, Avner, *Property and Politics, 1870–1914* (Cambridge and New York, Cambridge University Press, 1981).

Olgiati, Vittorio, 'Professional Body and Gender Difference in Court: The Case of the First (Failed) Woman Lawyer in Modern Italy' in Ulrike Schultz and Gisela Shaw (eds), *Women in the World's Legal Professions* (Oxford, Hart Publishing, 2003).

Olgiati, Vittorio and Valerio Pocar, 'The Italian Legal Profession: An Institutional Dilemma' in Richard L Abel and Philip S C Lewis (eds), *Lawyers in Society: The Civil Law World*, vol II (Berkeley, University of California Press, 1988).

O'Neill, William L, *Everyone Was Brave: A History of Feminism in America* (Chicago, Quadrangle Books, 1971).

Orme, Eliza, *Howrah Sessions, November 1894, The Trial of Shama Charan Pal: An Illustration of Village Life in Bengal* (with an Introduction by Miss Orme, LLB) (London, Lawrence and Bullen, 1897).

——, *Lady Fry of Darlington* (London, Hodder and Stoughton, 1898).

Parashar, Archana, *Women and Family Law Reform in India: Uniform Civil Code and Gender Equality* (New Delhi, Sage Publications, 1992).

Parr, Joy, *The Gender of Breadwinners: Women, Men, and Change in Two Industrial Towns 1880–1950* (Toronto, University of Toronto Press, 1990).

Parr, Joy and Mark Rosenfeld (eds), *Gender and History in Canada* (Toronto, Copp Clark Ltd, 1996).

Paul, John, *The Legal Profession in Colonial South India* (Bombay, Oxford University Press, 1991).

Pethick, Lawrence FW (ed), *The Trial of the Suffragette Leaders* (London, St Clements Press, 1909).

Phillips, Roderick, *Divorce in New Zealand* (Auckland, Oxford University Press, 1981).

Pierson, Ruth Roach, 'Experience, Difference, Dominance and Voice in the Writing of Canadian Women's History' in Karen Offen, Ruth Roach Pierson and Jane Rendall (eds), *Writing Women's History: International Perspectives* (Bloomington, Indiana University Press, 1991).

Pilarczyk, Ian C, '*A Noble Roster*': *One Hundred and Fifty Years of Law at McGill* (Montréal, McGill University Faculty of Law, 1999).

Pirenne, Henri, *Histoire de Belgique*, tome VII (de la Révolution de 1830 à la Guerre de 1914) (Bruxelles, Maurice Lamertin, Librarie-Éditeur, 1948).

Popelin, Marie, 'Laws on Marriage and Divorce in Belgium' in *Report of the International Congress of Women, Toronto: 24–30 June 1909*, vol 2 (Toronto, Geo Parker & Sons, 1910).

Prentice, Alison, 'The Feminization of Teaching' in Susan Mann Trofimenkoff and Alison Prentice (eds), *The Neglected Majority: Essays in Canadian Women's History*, vol 1 (Toronto, McClelland and Stewart, 1977).

Pue, W Wesley, *Law School: The Story of Legal Education in British Columbia* (Vancouver, Faculty of Law of the University of British Columbia, 1995).

——, 'Cultural Projects and Structural Transformation in the Canadian Legal Profession' in W Wesley Pue and David Sugarman (eds), *Lawyers and Vampires: Cultural Histories of Legal Professions* (Oxford and Portland, OR, Hart Publishing, 2003).

Purich, Donald, *Our Land: Native Rights in Canada* (Toronto, James Lorimer & Company, 1986)

Purvis, June, *Emmeline Pankhurst: A Biography* (London and New York, Routledge, 2002).

——, 'Biography as Microscope or Kaleidoscope? The Case of "Power" in Hannah Cullwick's Relationship with Arthur Munby' in Liz Stanley (ed), *The Auto/Biographical I: The Theory and Practice of Feminist Auto-Biography* (Manchester, Manchester University Press, 1992).

Radice, Lisanne, *Beatrice and Sidney Webb: Fabian Socialists* (New York, St Martin's Press, 1984).

Raichich, Marino, 'Liceo, Università, Professioni: Un Percorso Difficile' in Simonetta Soldani (ed), *L'Educazione delle Donne: Scuole e Modelli di Vita Femminile nell Italia dell'Ottocento* (Milan, Fernando Santoni de sio Angeli, 1989).

Rankin, Pauline, 'The Politicization of Ontario Farm Women' in Linda Kealey and Joan Sangster (eds), *Beyond the Vote: Canadian Women and Politics* (Toronto, University of Toronto Press, 1989).

Razack, Sherene, *Canadian Feminism and the Law: The Women's Legal Education and Action Fund and the Pursuit of Equality* (Toronto, Second Story Press, 1991).

Reader, William J, *Professional Men: The Rise of the Professional Classes in Nineteenth-Century England* (London, Weidenfeld and Nicolson, 1966).

Redmond, Mary, 'The Emergence of Women in the Solicitors' Profession in Ireland' in Eamonn G Hall and Daire Hogan (eds), *The Law Society of Ireland, 1852–2002: Portrait of a Profession* (Dublin, Four Courts Press, 2002).

Rendall, Jane, *The Origins of Modern Feminism: Women in Britain, France and the United States 1780–1860* (Chicago, Lyceum Books, 1985).

——, 'Uneven Developments: Women's History, Feminist History and Gender History in Great Britain' in Karen Offen, Ruth Roach Pierson and Jane Rendall (eds), *Writing Women's History: International Perspectives* (Bloomington, Indiana University Press, 1991).

——, 'Who was Lily Maxwell? Women's Suffrage and Manchester Politics 1866–1867' in June Purvis and Sandra Stanley Holton (eds), *Votes for Women* (London and New York, Routledge, 2000).

——, 'The Citizenship of Women and the Reform Act of 1867' in Catherine Hall, Keith McClelland and Jane Rendall (eds), *Defining the Victorian Nation: Class, Race, Gender and the British Reform Act of 1867* (Cambridge, Cambridge University Press, 2000).

Rhode, Deborah, *Justice and Gender: Sex Discrimination and the Law* (Cambridge, MA, Harvard University Press, 1989).

Roberts, Wayne '"Rocking the Cradle for the World": The New Woman and Maternal Feminism, Toronto 1877–1914' in Linda Kealey (ed), *A Not Unreasonable Claim: Women and Reform in Canada 1880s–1920s* (Toronto, The Women's Press, 1979).

Rotundo, E Anthony, *American Manhood: Transformations in Masculinity from the Revolution to the Modern Era* (New York, Basic Books, 1993).

Rover, Constance, *Women's Suffrage and Party Politics in Britain 1866–1914* (London, Routledge & Kegal Paul, 1967).

Royal Commission on Labour, *The Employment of Women: Reports by Miss Eliza Orme et al (Lady Assistant Commissioners) on the Conditions of Work in Various Industries in England, Wales, Scotland and Ireland* (London, HMSO, 1893).

Rupp, Leila J, *Worlds of Women: The Making of an International Women's Movement* (Princeton, Princeton University Press, 1997).

Sachs, Albie and Joan Hoff Wilson, *Sexism and the Law: A Study of Male Beliefs and Legal Bias in Britain and the United States* (New York, The Free Press, 1978).

Sadlier, Rosemary, 'Mary Ann Shadd' in Rosemary Sadlier (ed), *Leading the Way: Black Women in Canada* (Toronto, Umbrella Press, 1994).

——, *Mary Ann Shadd: Publisher, Editor, Teacher, Lawyer, Suffragette* (Toronto, Umbrella Press, 1995).

Salokar, Rebecca Mae and Mary L Volcansek (eds), *Women in Law: A Biographical Sourcebook* (Westport, CT, Greenwood Press, 1996).

Sarker, Sonita, 'Unruly Subjects: Cornelia Sorabji and Ravinder Randhawa' in Sonita Sarker and Esha Niyogi De (eds), *Trans-Status Subjects: Gender in the Globalization of South and Southeast Asia* (Durham and London, Duke University Press, 2002).

Savage, Candace, *Our Nell: A Scrapbook Biography of Nellie L McClung* (Saskatoon, Western Producer Prairie Books, 1979).

Savage, John, 'The Problems of Wealth and Virtue: The Paris Bar and the Generation of the *Fin-de-Siècle*' in W Wesley Pue and David Sugarman (eds), *Lawyers and Vampires: Cultural Histories of the Legal Professions* (Oxford, Hart Publishing, 2003).

Schreiner, Olive, *Woman and Labour* (Toronto, Henry Frowde, 1911).

Schultz, Ulrike and Gisela Shaw (eds), *Women in the World's Legal Professions* (Oxford, Hart Publishing, 2002).

Scott, Joan Wallach, *Only Paradoxes to Offer: French Feminists and the Rights of Man* (Cambridge, MA, Harvard University Press, 1996).

——, 'American Women Historians, 1884–1984' in Joan Wallach Scott (ed), *Gender and the Politics of History* (New York, Columbia University Press, 1999).

——, 'Women's History' in Peter Burke (ed), *New Perspectives on Historical Writing* (Pennsylvania, Pennsylvania State University Press, 2001).

Scutt, Jocelynne A, *Women and the Law: Commentary and Materials* (Sydney, The Law Book Co Ltd, 1990).

Smith, John Clay, Jr, *Rebels in Law: Voices in the History of Black Women Lawyers* (Ann Arbor, University of Michigan Press, 1998).

Smith, Mary Larratt, *Young Mr Smith in Upper Canada* (Toronto, University of Toronto Press, 1980).

Sommerlad, Hilary and Peter Sanderson, *Gender, Choice and Commitment: Women Solicitors in England and Wales and the Struggle for Equal Status* (Aldershot, Ashgate/Dartmouth, 1998).

Sorabji, Cornelia, *Love and Life Behind the Purdah* (London, Freemantle & Co, 1901).

——, *Sun Babies* (London, John Murray, 1904; and London, Blackie, 1918 and 1926).

——, *Between the Twilights: Being Studies of Indian Women by One of Themselves* (London and New York, Harper and Bros, 1908).

——, *Indian Tales of the Great Ones* (Bombay, Blackie and Son Ltd, 1916).

——, *The Purdahnashin* (Calcutta, Thacker Spink & Co, 1917).

——, *Therefore: An Impression of Sorabji Kharsedji Langrana and his Wife Francina* (London, Oxford University Press, 1924).

——, *Gold Mohur Time: 'To Remember'* (London, De La More Press, 1930).

——, *Susie Sorabji: Christian-Parsee Educationalist of Western India, A Memoir by Her Sister* (London, Oxford University Press, 1932).

——, *India Calling: The Memories of Cornelia Sorabji* (London, Nisbet & Co Ltd, 1934); republished as Chandani Lokugé (ed), *India Calling: The Memories of Cornelia Sorabji, India's First Woman Barrister* (New Delhi, Oxford University Press, 2001).

——, *India Recalled* (London, Nisbet & Co Ltd, 1936); republished as Cornelia Sorabji, *India: Ancient Heritage* (New Delhi, SBW Publishers, 1992).

—— (ed), *Queen Mary's Book for India* (London, George G Harrap & Co, 1943).

Spiller, Peter, Jeremy Finn, and Richard Boast, *A New Zealand Legal History* (Wellington, Brooker's, 1995).

Stanton, Donna C (ed), *The Female Autograph: Theory and Practice of Autobiography from the Tenth to the Twentieth Century* (Chicago and London, University of Chicago Press, 1987).

Stanton, Elizabeth Cady, *Eighty Years and More, 1815–1897* (New York, Schocken Books, 1971).

Stager, David (with Harry W Arthurs), *Lawyers in Canada* (Toronto, University of Toronto Press, 1990).

Steedman, Carolyn, *Landscape for a Good Woman: A Story of Two Lives* (New Brunswick, NJ, Rutgers University Press, 1987).

——, *Past Tenses: Essays on Writing, Autobiography and History* (London, Rivers Oram Press, 1992).

Stern, Madeleine B, 'Belva Ann Lockwood' in Madeleine B Stern, *We the Women: Career Firsts of Nineteenth-Century America* (Lincoln and London, University of Nebraska Press, 1962).

Stevens, Robert, *Law School: Legal Education in America from the 1850s to the 1980s* (Chapel Hill and London, University of North Carolina Press, 1983).

Stricker, Frank, 'Cookbooks and Law Books: The Hidden History of Career Women in Twentieth-Century America' in Nancy F Cott and Elizabeth H Pleck (eds), *A Heritage of Her Own: Toward a New Social History of American Women* (New York, Simon and Schuster, 1979).

Strong-Boag, Veronica, '"Setting the Stage": National Organization and the Women's Movement in the Late 19th-Century' in Susan Mann Trofimenkoff and Alison Prentice (eds), *The Neglected Majority: Essays in Canadian Women's History*, vol 1 (Toronto, McClelland and Stewart, 1977).

—— (ed), *Elizabeth Smith: A Woman with a Purpose, the Diaries of Elizabeth Smith 1872–1884* (Toronto, University of Toronto Press, 1980).

——, '"Ever a Crusader": Nellie McClung, First-Wave Feminist' in Veronica Strong-Boag and Anita Clair Fellman (eds), *Rethinking Canada: The Promise of Women's History* (Toronto, Copp Clark Pitman Ltd, 1986).

——, 'Canada's Women Doctors: Feminism Constrained' in Linda Kealey (ed), *A Not Unreasonable Claim: Women and Reform in Canada 1880s–1920s* (Toronto, The Women's Press, 1979).

Sugarman, David, 'A Hatred of Disorder: Legal Science, Liberalism and Imperialism' in Peter Fitzpatrick (ed), *Dangerous Supplements: Resistance and Renewal in Jurisprudence* (London, Pluto Press, 1991).

Suleri, Sara, *The Rhetoric of English India* (Chicago and London, University of Chicago Press, 1992).

Sutherland, Gillian, 'The Movement for the Higher Education of Women: Its Social and Intellectual Context in England, c 1840–80' in P J Waller (ed), *Politics and Social Change in Modern Britain* (Sussex, The Harvester Press; and New York, St Martin's Press, 1987).

Tata, Mithan, 'Women and the Law' in Evelyn C Gedge and Mithan Choksi (eds), *Women in Modern India* (Bombay, D B Taraporewala Sons & Co, 1929).

Tharu, Susie and K Lalitha, *Women Writing in India 600 BC to the Present, vol 1* (New York, The Feminist Press, 1991).

Thornton, Margaret, *Dissonance and Distrust: Women in the Legal Profession* (Melbourne, Oxford University Press, 1996).

Tilly, Louise A, 'Women's Collective Action and Feminism in France, 1870–1914' in Louise A Tilly and Charles Tilly (eds), *Class Conflict and Collective Action* (London, Sage, 1981).

Tilly, Louise A and Joan W Scott, *Women, Work, and Family* (New York, Holt, Rinehart and Winston, 1978).

Trofimenkoff, Susan Mann, 'Feminism, Nationalism, and the Clerical Defensive' in

Veronica Strong-Boag and Anita Clair Fellman (eds), *Rethinking Canada: The Promise of Women's History* (Toronto, Copp Clark Pitman Ltd, 1986).

Tulchinsky, Gerald, *Taking Root: The Origins of the Canadian Jewish Community* (Toronto, Lester Publishing Ltd, 1992).

——, *Branching Out: The Transformation of the Canadian Jewish Community* (Toronto, Stoddard, 1998).

Uglow, Jennifer, *Dictionary of Women's Biography* (London, MacMillan, 1998).

van der Essen, Léon, *A Short History of Belgium* (Chicago, University of Chicago Press, 1915).

Vicinus, Martha (ed), *A Widening Sphere: Changing Roles of Victorian Women* (Bloomington & London, Indiana University Press, 1977).

——, *Independent Women: Work and Community for Single Women 1850–1920* (London, Virago, 1985).

Vickers, Jill McCalla, 'Feminist Approaches to Women and Politics' in Linda Kealey and Joan Sangster (eds), *Beyond the Vote: Canadian Women and Politics* (Toronto, University of Toronto Press, 1989).

Vies de Femmes 1830–1980 (Bruxelles, Banque Bruxelles Lambert, 1980).

Viswanathan, Gauri, *Masks of Conquest: Literary Study and British Rule in India* (New York, Columbia University Press, 1989).

Wagner-Martin, Linda, *Telling Women's Lives: The New Biography* (New Brunswick, NJ, Rutgers University Press, 1994).

Watts, Alfred QC, *History of the Legal Profession in British Columbia 1869–1984* (Vancouver, The Law Society of BC, 1984).

Weisberg, D Kelly, 'Barred from the Bar: Women and Legal Education in the United States, 1870–1890' in D Kelly Weisberg (ed), *Women and the Law: A Social Historical Perspective*, vol II (Cambridge, MA, Schenkman Publishing Company, Inc, 1982).

Willis, John, *A History of Dalhousie Law School* (Toronto, University of Toronto Press, 1979).

Wilson, Stephen, *Ideology and Experience: Antisemitism in France at the Time of the Dreyfus Affair* (London and Toronto, Associated University Press, 1982).

Wilton, Carol (ed), *Inside the Law: Canadian Law Firms in Historical Perspective* (Toronto, The Osgoode Society, 1996).

Witz, Anne, *Professions and Patriarchy* (London and New York, Routledge, 1992).

Woolf, Virginia, *Three Guineas* (London, Hogarth Press, 1977) (1st pub 1938).

Zimmern, Alice, *The Renaissance of Girls' Education in England: A Record of Fifty Years' Progress* (London, A D Innes & Company, 1898).

——, *Women's Suffrage in Many Lands* (London, Francis & Co, 1909).

ARTICLES IN JOURNALS AND PERIODICALS

'A Pioneer in Law' (15 October 1896) *Englishwoman's Review* (ns) 217.

Abel, Richard L, 'Comparative Sociology of Legal Professions: An Exploratory Essay' (1985) 1 *American Bar Foundation Research Journal* 5.

Albisetti, James C, 'Portia Ante Portas: Women and the Legal Profession in Europe, ca 1870–1925' (2000) 33 *Journal of Social History* 825.

Appleby, Mary, 'The Entry of Women into the Profession of Law and Their Hopes' *Obiter Dicta* (Toronto, 17 January 1934).

'Attorneys at Law' *The Woman's Journal*, Boston, 17 February 1900.

Axford, Phyllis, 'Portias of the Province' *Saturday Night*, 28 February 1948.

Babcock, Barbara Allen, 'Clara Shortridge Foltz: Constitution-Maker' (1990–91) 66 *Indiana Law Journal* 849.

——, 'Book Review: Feminist Lawyers' (1998) 50 *Stanford Law Review* 1689.

Backhouse, Constance, 'Clara Brett Martin: Canadian Heroine or Not?' (1992) 5:2 *Canadian Journal of Women and the Law* 263.

——, '"To Open the Way for Others of my Sex": Clara Brett Martin's Career as Canada's First Woman Lawyer' (1985) 1 *Canadian Journal of Women and the Law* 1.

Barry, Kathleen 'The New Historical Syntheses: Women's Biography' (1990) 1:3 *Journal of Women's History* 75.

Basch, Norma, 'Review' (1999) 104 *American Historical Review* 935.

'Be a Queen but not Lawyer' *Gazette* (Montréal, 27 February 1915).

Bell, Edward, 'Admission of Women' (1912) 56 *Solicitors Journal and Weekly Reports* 814.

Benjamin, Ethel, 'Women and the Study and Practice of the Law' (13 September 1897) *Press* 5.

——, 'Interview with Kate Sheppard' (August 1897) 26:3 *White Ribbon* 1–2.

Betcherman, Lita-Rose, 'Clara Brett Martin's Anti-Semitism' (1992) 5:2 *Canadian Journal of Women and the Law* 280.

'Between You and Me' *Saturday Night* (8 January 1898).

Bilson, Beth, '"Prudence Rather than Valor": Legal Education in Saskatchewan 1908–23' (1998) 61 *Saskatchewan Law Review* 341.

Blackshaw, Randall, 'A Parsee Portia: Miss Cornelia Sorabji, Oxford Graduate, Lawyer and Author Too' (1903) 43 *Critic and Good Literature* 432.

Boigeol, Anne, 'French Women Lawyers (*Avocates*) and the "Women's Cause" in the First Half of the Twentieth Century' (2003) 10:2 *International Journal of the Legal Profession* 193.

Brockman, Joan and Dorothy E Chunn, '"A New Order of Things": Women's Entry Into the Legal Profession in British Columbia' (2002) 60:3 *The Advocate* 385.

Brown, Carol, 'New Zealand's First Woman Lawyer' (6 August 1985) *Critic* 12.

Brumberg, Joan Jacobs and Nancy Tomes, 'Women in the Professions: A Research Agenda for American Historians' (1982) 10:2 *Reviews in American History* 275.

Brunet, Elise, 'The 19th-Century Case against Women Becoming Lawyers' *Ontario Lawyers Gazette* (March/April 1998).

——, 'The Law Office at the Turn of the Century' *Ontario Lawyers Gazette*, (May/June 1999).

Bucknall, Brian D, Thomas CH Baldwin and J David Lakin, 'Pedants, Practitioners and Prophets: Legal Education at Osgoode Hall to 1957' (1968) 6 *Osgoode Hall Law Journal* 137.

Burrage, Michael, 'From a Gentlemen's to a Public Profession: Status and Politics in the History of English Solicitors' (1996) 3:1 & 2 *International Journal of the Legal Profession* 45.

Burton, Antoinette, 'The White Woman's Burden: British Feminists and the Indian Woman, 1865–1915' (1990) 13:4 *Women's Studies International Forum* 295.

——, '"Stray Thoughts of an Indian Girl" by Cornelia Sorabji, *The Nineteenth Century*, October 1891' (1996) 3:2 *Indian Journal of Gender Studies* 249.

——, 'The *Purdahnashin* in Her Setting: Colonial Modernity and the *Zenana* in Cornelia Sorabji's Memoirs' (2000) 65 *Feminist Review* 145.

Campbell, Ruth, 'That Girl with the Terrible Name' (1975) 49 *Law Institute Journal* 502.

Chauvin, Emile, 'Jeanne Chauvin' (1893) 36 *Revue Philosophique de la France et de l'Étranger* 312

Chauvin, Jeanne, 'Proposition de Loi sur la Capacité des Femmes Mariées de Disposer du Produit de leur Travail ou de leur Industrie Personnel' (1893) *L'Avant-Courrière*.

——, 'Proposition de Loi sur la Capacité des Femmes d'Etre Témoin dans les Actes Publics ou Privés' (1893) *L'Avant-Courrière*.

——, 'Féminisme et Antiféminisme' (1897) *La Revue Blanche* 321.

Chused, Richard, 'Book Review' (1999) 85:4 *Journal of American History* 1621.

Coldstream, John P, 'Women and the Law in India' (1903) *Juridical Review* 185.

Collier, Richard, '"Nutty Professors," "Men in Suits" and "New Entrepreneurs": Corporeality, Subjectivity and Change in the Law School and Legal Practice' (1998) 7 *Social and Legal Studies* 27.

Corcos, Christine Alice, 'Lawyers for Marianne: The Nature of Discourse of the Entry of French Women into the Legal Profession, 1894–1926' (1996) 12 *Georgia State University Law Review* 435.

——, 'Portia and Her Partners in Popular Culture: A Bibliography' (1998) 22 *Legal Studies Forum* 269.

——, 'Portia Goes to Parliament: Women and their Admission to Membership in the English Legal Profession' (1998) 75:2 *Denver University Law Review* 307.

Cossman, Brenda and Marlee Kline, '"And if Not Now, When?": Feminism and Anti-Semitism Beyond Clara Brett Martin' (1992) 5:2 *Canadian Journal of Women and the Law* 298.

Cowper, JS, 'Confidences of a Woman Lawyer' (1912) 39 *The Canadian Magazine* 142.

Coyle, Dorothy F, 'Women in the Legal Profession in Canada' (1952) 38:3 *Women Lawyers Journal* 14.

Crawford, Lindsay, 'Current Events' *The Canadian Magazine* (November 1914) 85.

De Bueger-Van Lierde, Françoise, 'L'Origine du Mouvement Féministe en Belgique: L'Affaire Popelin' (1972) 50:4 *Revue Belge de Philologie et d'Histoire* 1128.

——, 'Louis Frank, Pionnier du Mouvement Féministe Belge' (1973) IV:3–4 *Revue Belge d'Histoire Contemporaine* 377.

de Villiers, Melius, 'Women and the Legal Profession' (1918) 35 *South African Law Journal* 289.

Dilke, Emilia FS, 'Women and the Royal Commission' (October 1891) *Fortnightly Review* 535.

Drage, Geoffrey, 'Mrs Sidney Webb's Attack on the Labour Commission' (September 1894) 36 *The Nineteenth Century* 452.

Dranoff, Linda Silver, 'Women as Lawyers in Toronto' (1972) 10 *Osgoode Hall Law Journal* 177.

Dubois, Carol and Nancy F Cott, '"Comment and Reply" to Karen Offen' (1989) *Signs* 195.

Duman, Daniel, 'Pathway to Professionalism: The English Bar in the Eighteenth and Nineteenth Centuries' (1980) 13 *Journal of Legal History* 615.

'Eliza Orme, Senior Lady Assistant Commissioner, Report on the Condition of Women in the Chain, Nail and Bolt Making Industries in the Black Country' (April 1893) 24 *Englishwoman's Review* 73.

Ewan, Elizabeth, 'Scottish Portias: Women in the Courts of Mediaeval Scottish Towns' (1992) 3 *Journal of the Canadian Historical Association* 27 (new ser).

Fisher, Berenice, 'The Models Among Us: Social Authority and Political Activism' (1981) 7 *Feminist Studies* 100.

Flos Greig, Grata, 'The Law as a Profession for Women' (1909) 6 *Commonwealth Law Review* 145.

'Flotsam and Jetsam' (1896) 32 *Canada Law Journal* 84.

Foley, Caroline A, 'Review of the *Royal Commission on Labour: The Employment of Women*' (1894) 4 *The Economic Journal* 185.

Foltz, Clara, 'Public Defenders' (12 August 1893) 25 *Chicago Legal News* 431.

Foster, James C, 'Antigones at the Bar: Women Lawyers as Reluctant Adversaries' (1986) 10:3 *Legal Studies Forum*.

Frank, Louis, 'Les Femmes et L'Enseignement Supérieur' (1893) *Revue Universitaire* 234.

——, 'University Opportunities for Women' (1894) *Educational Review* 471.

——, 'La Loi sur L'Enseignement Supérieur et L'Admission des Femmes dans les Facultés Belges' (1894) LXIII *Revue de Belgique* 289.

——, 'La Question du Mariage' (June 1890) *Revue du Belgique*.

——, 'La Femme-Médecin' (March 1893); 'La Femme-Médecin aux Indes' (June 1893); 'La Femme-Médecin en Orient' (June 1895); and 'Les Femmes-Pharmaciens' (October 1894).

——, 'Le Suffrage des Femmes en Nouvelle-Zélande' (November 1893); and 'Le Suffrage des Femmes au Kansas' (November 1894).

Gale, George, 'Myra Bradwell: The First Woman Lawyer' (1953) 39 *ABA Journal* 180.

Gilliam, Nancy T, 'A Professional Pioneer: Myra Bradwell's Fight to Practice Law' (1987) 5 *Law and History Review* 105.

Gisborne, Henry Paterson Solicitor, 'The Admission of Women to the Legal Profession' (March 1917) *International Law Notes* 46.

Glasson, Ernest-Desiré, 'Note' (1889) 2 *Jurisprudence Générale: Recueil Périodique et Critique de Jurisprudence, de Législation et de Doctrine* 36.

Greene, Mary A, 'A Woman Lawyer' (1891) 14 *Chautauquan* 218.

——, *The Woman's Journal* (5 November 1892).

——, 'Married Women's Property Acts in the United States and Needed Reforms' (12 August 1893) 25 *Chicago Legal News* 433.

——, 'Mrs Lelia Robinson Sawtelle – First Woman Lawyer of Massachusetts' (April 1918) 7:7 *Women Lawyers Journal* 51.

Griffith, M, 'A Japanese Lady Lawyer and Reformer in England' (1893) 10 *Great Thoughts* 91.

Hall, Margaret, 'Women as Lawyers' (1901) 1 *New Liberal Review* 222.

Hankey, Julie, 'Victorian Portias: Shakespeare's Borderline Heroine' (1994) 45 *Shakespeare Quarterly* 426.

Harvey, Cameron, 'Women in Law in Canada' (1970–71) 4 *Manitoba Law Journal* 9.

Haselmayer, Louis A, 'Belle A Mansfield' (1969) 55 *Women Lawyers Journal* 46.

Howsam, Leslie, 'Sound-Minded Women: Eliza Orme and the Study and Practice of Law in Late-Victorian England' (1989) 15:1 *Atlantis* 44.

Hull, Kathleen and Robert Nelson, 'Gender Inequality in Law: Problems of Structure and Agency in Recent Studies of Gender in Anglo-American Legal Professions' (1998) 23 *Law and Social Inquiry* 681.

Jeanvrot, M Victor, 'Observations' (15 January 1889) *Revue de la Réforme Judiciare et Législative* 64.

Johns, Walter H, 'History of the Faculty of Law' (1980) 25 *Anniversary Edition Alberta Law Review* 1.

Kanter, Rosabeth Moss, 'Reflections on Women and the Legal Profession: A Sociological Perspective' (1978) 1 *Harvard Women's Law Journal* 1

Kasirer, Nicholas, 'Apostolat Juridique: Teaching Everyday Law in the Life of Marie Lacoste Gérin-Lajoie (1867–1945)' (1992) 30 *Osgoode Hall Law Journal* 427.

Kercher, Bruce, 'A Convict Conservative: George Crossley and the English Legal Tradition' (1999) 16:1 *Law in Context* 24.

Kerber, Linda K, 'Separate Spheres, Female Worlds, Woman's Place: The Rhetoric of Women's History' (1988) 75:1 *Journal of American History* 9.

Kernaghan, Lois K, 'The Madonna of the Law' *Hearsay* (Dalhousie Law School, Fall 1991) 26.

King, Richard, 'The Admission of Women to the Legal Profession' (2 December 1916) *Law Journal*.

Kirk, Linda J, 'Portia's Place: Australia's First Women Lawyers' (1995) 1 *Australian Journal of Law and History* 75.

——, 'Sisters Down Under: Women Lawyers in Australia' (1995–96) 12 *Georgia State University Law Review* 491.

'Lady Law Students' (January 1904) *Englishwoman's Review* 49.

Langstaff, Annie Macdonald, 'Rights: Civil Status of Women' (November 1933) 1:1 *Woman's Circle* 2.

——, 'Rights: Civil Status of Women' (February 1934) 1:2 *Woman's Circle* 5.

'L'Avant-Courrière' (1893) *Englishwomen's Review* 81.

Lee, RW, 'Legal Education: A Symposium' (1919) 39 *Canadian Law Times* 138.

'The Legal Lady' *Maclean's Magazine* (1949).

'Les Femmes et le Barreau' *Le Franc-Parleur*, 23 December 1916.

Lockwood, Belva A, 'An International Arbitration Court and a Congress of Nations' (26 August 1893) 25 *Chicago Legal News* 447.

——, 'The Congress of Law Reform' (1893) 3 *American Journal of Politics* 321.

MacKay, IA, 'The Education of a Lawyer' (1940–42) *Alberta Law Quarterly* 103.

Martin, Robert, 'The Meteoric Rise and Precipitous Fall of Clara Brett Martin' *Inroads Issue* 4 at 182.

Matsuda, Mari, 'The West and the Legal Status of Women: Explanations of Frontier Feminism' (1985) 24 *Journal of the West* 47.

Mayhew, Judith, 'Woman at Law' (1992) *New Zealand Law Journal* 85.

Mazer, Brian M, 'An Analysis of Gender in Admission to the Canadian Common Law Schools from 1985–86 to 1994–95' (1997) 20 *Dalhousie Law Journal* 135.

McInnis, H, 'For and About Women' *The Dalhousie Gazette* (7 April 1882).

McPaul, Bek, 'A Woman Pioneer' (1948) 22 *Australian Law Journal* 1.

Menkel-Meadow, Carrie, 'Portia in a Different Voice: Speculations on a Women's Lawyering Process' (1985) 1 *Berkeley Women's Law Journal* 39.

——, 'The Comparative Sociology of Women Lawyers: The "Feminization" of the Legal Profession' (1987) 24 *Osgoode Hall Law Journal* 897.

——, 'Exploring a Research Agenda of the Feminization of the Legal Profession: Theories of Gender and Social Change' (1989) 14 *Law and Social Inquiry* 289.

——, 'Portia *Redux:* Another Look at Gender, Feminism, and Legal Ethics' (1994) 2 *Virginia Journal of Social Policy and Law* 75.

Minow, Martha, '"Forming Underneath Everything that Grows": Toward a History of Family Law' [1985] *Wisconsin Law Review* 819.

Monk, Elizabeth C, 'Memorandum' reproduced in Cameron Harvey, 'Women in Law in Canada' (1970–71) 4 *Manitoba Law Journal* 9.

Morgan, Cecilia, ' "An Embarrassingly and Severely Masculine Atmosphere": Women, Gender and the Legal Profession at Osgoode Hall, 1920s–1960s' (1996) 11:2 *Canadian Journal of Women and the Law* 19.

Morrow, WG, 'An Historical Examination of Alberta's Legal System – The First Seventy-Five Years' (1981) 29:2 *Alberta Law Review* 148.

Mossman, Mary Jane, '"Otherness" and the Law School: A Comment on Teaching Gender Equality' (1985) 1 *Canadian Journal of Women and the Law* 213.

——, 'Feminism and Legal Method: The Difference it Makes' (1986) 3 *Australian Journal of Law and Society* 30.

——, 'Portia's Progress: Women as Lawyers – Reflections on Past and Future' (1988) 8 *Windsor Yearbook of Access to Justice* 252 at 266.

Mullins, Christine, 'Mabel Penery French' (1986) 44:5 *The Advocate* 676.

'The Need for Lady Lawyers in India' (1902) 33 *Englishwoman's Review* 234.

Norgren, Jill, 'Before it was Merely Difficult: Belva Lockwood's Life in Law and Politics' (1999) 23 *Journal of Supreme Court History* 16

Observer, 'The Labour Commission' (1894) 23 *The National Review* 201.

Offen, Karen, 'The Second Sex and the Baccalauréat in Republican France, 1880–1924' (1983) 13:2 *French Historical Studies* 252.

——, 'Defining Feminism: A Comparative Historical Approach' (1988) 14:1 *Signs* 119.

'The Old and the New in India' (29 September 1927) 32 *The Near East and India* 402.

Oldrieve, Susan, 'Marginalized Voices in *The Merchant of Venice*' (1993) 5 *Cardozo Studies in Law and Literature* 87.

Orme, Eliza, 'University Degrees for Women' (May 1874) *The Examiner* 508.

——, 'University Degrees for Women' (July 1874) *The Examiner* 707.

——, 'Sound-Minded Women' (August 1874) *The Examiner* 820.

——, 'Women's Work in Creation: A Reply' (1886–87) 9 *Longman's Magazine* 149.

——, 'A Commonplace Correction' (1892) 1 *Welsh Review* 467.

——, 'The Legal Status of Women in England' 25 *Chicago Legal News* 431; and (1897) 48 *Albany Law Journal* 145.

——, 'How Poor Ladies Live: A Reply' (April 1897) *The Nineteenth Century* 613.

——, 'Our Female Criminals' (1898) 69 (ns 63) *Fortnightly Review* 790.

Pearlman, Lynne, 'Through Jewish Lesbian Eyes: Rethinking Clara Brett Martin' (1992) 5:2 *Canadian Journal of Women and the Law* 317.

Pearson, Rose and Albie Sachs, 'Barristers and Gentlemen: A Critical Look at Sexism in the Legal Profession' (1980) 43 *Modern Law Review* 400.

Petersson, Sandra, 'Ruby Clements and Early Women of the Alberta Bar' (1997) 9 *Canadian Journal of Women and the Law* 365.

Pettus, Isabella Mary, 'The Legal Education of Women' (1900) 38 *Journal of Social Science* 234.

Prest, Wilfrid, '"One Hawkins, A Female Sollicitor": Women Lawyers in Augustan England' (1994) 57:4 *The Huntington Library Quarterly* 353.

Price, LL, 'The Report of the Labour Commission' (1894) 4 *The Economic Journal* 444.

Pue, W Wesley, 'Rebels at the Bar: English Barristers and the County Courts in the 1850s' (1987) 16 *Anglo-American Law Review* 303.

——, 'In Pursuit of Better Myth: Lawyers' Histories and Histories of Lawyers' (1995) 33:4 *Alberta Law Review* 730.

——, 'Common Law Legal Education in Canada's Age of Light, Soap and Water' (1996) 23 *Manitoba Law Journal* 654.

Quentin, Charles, 'Women as Barristers' (1899) 14 *The Humanitarian* 203.

Ramusack, Barbara, 'Cultural Missionaries, Maternal Imperialists, Feminist Allies: British Women Activists in India, 1865–1945' (1990) 13:4 *Women's Studies International Forum* 309.

Resnik, Judith, 'Ambivalence: The Resiliency of Legal Culture in the United States' (1993) 45 *Stanford Law Review* 1525.

Riddell, William R, 'Women as Practitioners of Law' (1918) 18 *Journal of the Society of Comparative Legislation* 200.

Robinson, Lelia J, 'Women Lawyers in the United States' (1890) 2 *The Green Bag* 10.

Rogers, William P, 'Is Law a Field for Women's Work?' (1901) 24 *American Bar Association Reports* 548.

Roth, Theresa, 'Clara Brett Martin – Canada's Pioneer Woman Lawyer' (1984) 18 *The Law Society Gazette* 323.

Sanger, Carol, 'Curriculum Vitae (Feminae): Biography and Early American Women Lawyers' (1994) 46 *Stanford Law Review* 1245.

Sangster, Joan, 'Telling our Stories: Feminist Debates and the Use of Oral History' (1994) 3 *Women's History Review* 5.

'The Seclusion of Indian Women' (11 October 1902) *The Queen*.

Sen, Amartya, 'Other People: Beyond Identity' (18 December 2000) 223:25 *New Republic* 23.

Shavaksha, Khursheedbai, 'The Purdahnashin Question' (1903) *The Indian Review* 217.

Shaw, Gisela, 'Conflicting Agendas: The First Female Jurists in Germany' (2003) 10:2 *International Journal of the Legal Profession* 177.

Sibenik, Peter M, 'Doorkeepers: Legal Education in the Territories and Alberta, 1885–1928' (1990) 13 *Dalhousie Law Journal* 419.

Sinha, Mrinalini, 'Reading *Mother India*: Empire, Nation and the Female Voice' (1994) 6:2 *Journal of Women's History* 6.

Smart, Carol, 'Feminism and Law: Some Problems of Analysis and Strategy' (1986) 14 *International Journal of the Sociology of Law*.

Sangster, Joan, 'Telling our Stories: Feminist Debates and the Use of Oral History' (1994) 3:1 *Women's History Review* 5.

Silius, Harriet, 'Making Sense of Gender in the Study of the Legal Professions' (2003) 10:2 *International Journal of the Legal Profession* 135.

Sommerlad, Hilary, 'The Myth of Feminisation: Women and Cultural Change in the Legal Profession' (1994) 1 *International Journal of the Legal Profession* 31.

Sorabji, Cornelia, 'Legal Status of Women in India' (12 August 1893) 25 *Chicago Legal News* 434.

——, 'Stray Thoughts of an Indian Girl' (Oct 1891) *The Nineteenth Century* 638.

——, 'The Parsees' (Oct 1893) *The Nineteenth Century* 605.

——, 'The Legal Status of Women in India' (Nov 1898) *The Nineteenth Century* 854.

——, 'Babuisms' (1901) 124 *Temple Bar* 376.

——, 'Concerning an Imprisoned Rani' (1901) 50 *The Nineteenth Century* 623.

——, 'English and Indian: A Study' (1902) *The Monthly Review* 133.

——, 'Safeguards for Purdahnishins' (Jan 1903) *Imperial and Asiatic Review* 69.

——, 'Benjamin Jowett – Master of Balliol College: Some Reflections' (1903) 54 *Nineteenth Century and After, A Monthly Review* 297.

——, 'Portraits of Some Indian Women' (March 1905) *The Nineteenth Century* 481.

——, 'Comments' in *India: Discussed by Dr Haridas T Muzumdar, Miss Cornelia Sorabji, C F Andrews and C F Strickland* (New York, Foreign Policy Association, 1930).

——, 'Prospice: The New India' (Feb 1931) *The Nineteenth Century* 176.

——, 'Gandhi Interrogated: An Interview' (April 1932) *Atlantic Monthly* 133.

——, 'India: The Sympathy which Debilitates' (2 July 1932) *The Saturday Review* 6; and (9 July 1932) 35.

——, 'Temple-Entry and Untouchability' (June 1933) *The Nineteenth Century* 689.

——, 'A Bengali Woman Revolutionary' (Nov 1933) *The Nineteenth Century* 604.

——, 'An Indian Looks at the New Proposals' (Jan 1935) *The National Review* 63.

——, 'Where Stands India?' (26 Jan 1939) 52 *Great Britain and the East* 102.

——, 'Stocktaking in India' (April 1939) *Asiatic Review* 218.

——, 'Salute to Loyal India! Answering the Congress Grievances' (2 Nov 1940) 55 *Great Britain and the East* 387.

——, 'Congress Party in India' (9 Jan 1941) *Great Britain and the East* 36.

——, 'The Situation in India' *The Spectator* (4 Sept 1942) 216, and (18 Sept 1942) 264.

——, 'Majority Community in India' (3 Oct 1942) *Great Britain and the East* 21.

'The Story of the Century' (March 1999) *American Lawyer*.

Strickland, Martha, 'Woman and the Forum' (1891) 3 *The Green Bag* 240.

Stritt, Maria, 'Die Frauenfrage auf dem evangelisch-sozialen Kongress' (1897) 3 *Die Frauenbewegung*.

Thornton, Margaret, 'Feminist Jurisprudence: Illusion or Reality' (1986) 3 *Australian Journal of Law and Society* 5.

——, 'Feminism and the Contradictions of Law Reform' (1991) 19 *International Journal of the Sociology of Law* 453.

Walker, H Newton, 'Women and the Bar' (June 1919) *The Englishwoman* 129.

Wayand, Dorothea, 'Women in Enlightenment and Revolution and their Position in the First Modern Codes' (1992) 7:2 *Canadian Journal of Law and Society* 93.

Webb, Beatrice, 'The Failure of the Labour Commission' (July 1894) 36 *The Nineteenth Century* 2.

Weisberg, D Kelly, 'Barred from the Bar: Women and Legal Education in the United States 1870–1890' (1977) 28 *Journal of Legal Education* 485.

Whitten, Charlotte, 'Is the Canadian Woman a Flop in Politics?' (26 January 1946) *Saturday Night*.

Williams, Frances Fenwick, *Beck's Weekly* (20 February 1915).

Wilson, Bertha, 'Will Women Judges Really Make a Difference?' (1990) 28 *Osgoode Hall Law Journal* 507.

Wilton, Peter, 'Inappropriate for Women...' *Law Now* (November 1992) 23.

'Women and the Bar' (12 December 1903) *The Law Journal* 620.

'Women as Lawyers' (November 1875) 6 *Englishwoman's Review* 510.

'Women as Lawyers' (1879) 23 *Lippincott's Magazine of Popular Literature and Science* 386.

'Women Barristers' (1896) 32 *Canada Law Journal* 84.

'Women in the Law Reform Congress' (2 September 1893) 95 *The Law Times* 402.

'Women Lawyers' (1896) 83 *Leslie's Illustrated Weekly* 363.

'Women Lawyers at the Isabella Club House' (26 August 1893) 25 *Chicago Legal News* 447.

'Women's Rights' (Nov 1869) 5 *Canada Law Journal* 307.

'The Year "That's Awa"' (December 1875) 6 *Englishwoman's Review* 533.

York, Lois K, 'Mabel Penery French (1881–1955): A Life Re-created' (1993) 42 *University of New Brunswick Law Journal* 3.

THESES AND DISSERTATIONS

Bannerjee, S, 'Imperial Diasporas and the Politics of Nation-Space: Indian Identities and Metropolitan Englishness (1855–1935)' (University of California, PhD thesis, 2001).

Brown, Carol, 'Ethel Benjamin: New Zealand's First Woman Lawyer' (Dunedin, University of Otago, BA Hons thesis, 1985).

Chauvin, Jeanne, *Etude Historique sur les Professions Accessibles aux Femmes: Influence du Sémitisme sur l'Évolution de la Position Économique de la Femme dans la Société* (Paris, A Giard & E Brière, 1892).

Cole, Curtis, '"A Learned and Honorable Body": The Professionalization of the Ontario Bar, 1867–1929' (University of Western Ontario, PhD thesis, 1987).

Gooptu, Suparna, 'Cornelia Sorabji 1866–1954: A Woman's Biography' (University of Oxford, D Phil thesis, 1997).

Kimble, Sara Lynn, 'Justice Redressed: Women, Citizenship, and the Social Uses of the Law in Modern France, 1890–1939' (University of Iowa, PhD thesis, 2002).

Thorpe, Wendy, 'Lady Aberdeen and the National Council of Women' (Queen's University, MA thesis, 1973).

Van Lierde, Françoise, 'La Ligue Belge du Droit des Femmes, 1892–1897' (Mémoire presenté en vue de l'obtention du grade de licencié en Philosophie et Lettres, L'Université Catholique de Louvain, 1971).

Vasudevan, Shoba, 'Spatial Subjectivities: Gender in Indian Narratives, 1900–1940' (Austin, University of Texas, PhD thesis, 1997).

SELECTED OTHER SOURCES

Baines, Beverley, 'Women and the Law: Course Materials' (Kingston, Queen's University Faculty of Law, 1974).

CLE Programme, 'Women in Law: Old Dilemmas, New Dilemmas' (Toronto, Law Society of Upper Canada, 13 May 1986).

Cole, Curtis, *A History of Osgoode Hall Law School 1889–1989* (unpublished MS).

Fisher, Kathy, 'Sounding Down the Years: Roma Stewart Goodwin Blackburn's Journey in Law' (unpublished MS).

Justice M Rothman: Interview, Montréal, November 2000.

Lien-Li, Tie, *Life in Three Countries: China, Jamaica and England* (unpublished MS).

Ryan, HR Stuart, 'A Pilgrim's Progress: Clara Brett Martin's Campaign for Admission to the Bar of Ontario' (unpublished MS).

Women's Legal History/Biography Project, Stanford University.

Index

LaVergne, TN USA
24 September 2010

198352LV00002B/5/P